Linn's

More Who's Who on U.S. Stamps

By Richard Louis Thomas

Published by *Linn's Stamp News*, the largest and most informative stamp newspaper in the world. *Linn's* is owned by Amos Press, 911 Vandemark Road, Sidney, Ohio 45365. Amos Press also publishes *Scott Stamp Monthly* and the Scott line of catalogs.

Library of Congress Cataloging-in-Publication Data

Thomas, Richard Louis.
    Linn's more who's who on U.S. stamps / Richard Louis Thomas.
        p. cm.
    Updated ed. of: Linn's who's who on U.S. stamps. c1991.
    Includes index.
    Summary: Presents capsule biographies of 258 individuals who have been
portrayed or had their works depicted on United States postage stamps.
    ISBN 0-940403-50-1 (paperback) : $14.95. -- ISBN 0-940403-51-X
(hardcover) : $30.00
    1. Biography. 2. United States--Biography. 3. Postage-stamps-United
States. [1. Biography. 2. Postage stamps.] I. Thomas, Richard Louis. Linn's
who's who on U.S. stamps. II. Linn's stamp news. III. Title. IV. Title: More
who's who on U.S. stamps. V. Title: Linn's more who's who on U.S. stamps.
VI. Title: Linn's more who's who on United States stamps.
CT104. T438 1992
920 . 073--dc20
(B)

                                    92-36043
                                        CIP
                                        AC

Preface

When I wrote biographical sketches of people on stamps, it was but an extension of a topical collection of people on stamps. I did not include stamps that showed multiples of people of four or more, nor did I consider people who had acted as models. "People on stamps" to me meant people who had contributed something that formulated our history in one way or another, or contributed to the arts in an appreciable manner, or changed the course of events. From my collection, *Linn's Stamp News* selected one biographical sketch at a time and published it in the weekly stamp newspaper. In 1991, *Linn's* selected some 413 and published them in *Who's Who on U.S. Stamps.*

Almost at once, critics began to complain that it did not include all the people on stamps. So true. Therefore, I am adding 257 more but, sorry, still not all. Now I realize that if a stamp collector, or anyone for that matter, looks at a stamp and it brings up the question "Who?" no matter in what context, and if that "who" is at all notable, then I will include him or her in a sketch.

Of course all the people portrayed on stamps issued since Volume 1 are included in *More Who's Who on U.S. Stamps.* To satisfy this deficiency as well as my own curiosity, I began to look at all U.S. stamps for all the people.

The first shock was the stamps depicting people attending the Declaration of Independence, July 4, 1776 (Scott 120, 130, 1687 and 1694a). Of the 56 signers and the people who did not sign but were in attendance at the formulation of the Declaration, only 47 were depicted on these stamps. I made a biographical sketch of those identified on the stamp. Since this is a who's who on stamps, I sketched only those shown on the Declaration of Independence stamp and omitted the signers not shown. Incidentally, 50 of the 56 signatories, including John Hancock, affixed their names on August 2, 1776, to the document adopted on July 4, and toasted the event with Madeira wine, which was probably smuggled in on one of Hancock's ships.

I also made a biographical sketch of all the people on the Signers of the U.S. Constitution stamp (Scott 798). In the painting hanging in the U.S. Capitol by Howard Chandler Christy titled *Scene at the Signing of the Constitution of the United States*, each person is identifiable. But this scene is not identical to the one on the stamp. Therefore, except for identifying Benjamin Franklin and George Washington, just who is who on the stamp? I cannot determine with any accuracy. Therefore, I included all the signatories and assigned them to this stamp, but I did not locate them on the stamp individually. This book includes all the signatories except those who had appeared previously on other stamps that had already been featured in *Who's Who on U.S. Stamps.*

Likewise with the people who signed the Mayflower Compact (Scott 550) and the landing of the Pilgrims (Scott 549 and 1420). Again I wrote biographical sketches of all I could find references to. Alas, I was not able to identify who is who on the stamp, but I know they are somewhere in the picture.

More Who's Who on U.S. Stamps

Of the people at the surrender of Burgoyne (Scott 644 and 1728) and the surrender of Cornwallis (Scott 1686), I identified those who were identifiable and sketched all those who are notable persons of history. Likewise of those present at *Washington Taking Oath of Office in New York in 1789*, several have already been covered in Volume 1, and I selected two more.

Of the people on the Columbus stamps (Scott 118, 231, 234, 239, 242) who are identifiable, I wrote what I thought might be interesting and pertinent of what information I could find and believe.

Of the artists, if the name was on the stamp, such as the traditional Christmas stamps, the Universal Postal Union series, and special issues honoring individual artists, I wrote about them. If the name was not on the stamp but the painting or sculpture on the stamp was easily recognized as being that of a particular artist who is notable, I wrote about them: Norman Rockwell, Thomas Hart Benton, Myron, the Borglums, for example.

As one pages through the latest Scott *Specialized Catalogue of United States Stamps*, often the artist is noted in the caption. These I certainly included. By artists I am including painters, sculptors, and some selected lithographers and photographers. The same for architects. I did not include the artists who are not notable in my list, even though they were lucky enough to have their work chosen to grace the face of a U.S. stamp. I did not include persons who designed a stamp or painted a picture to be used on a stamp even though they are artists of considerable note (Robert T. McCall, the Calles and several others).

If the stamp is issued honoring a certain person, but that person is not pictured nor his name shown, but the catalog lists his or her name in the caption — Liberty Hyde Bailey, John Ringling as examples — I included them.

I took the liberty to write about people who are in the scene but not seen, such as the five astronauts hidden only by their space suits and Lindbergh in his plane *The Spirit of St. Louis*, although his name appears on the stamp. I had intended to include the other astronauts in space capsules and ships, but I decided that only if the human form is discernible would I do so.

Some famous names appear on stamps naming objects or events for them — Verrazano, Graf Zeppelin, San Xavier, Stutz and Stanley, for example. Since it brings up the question "Who?" I took that as an excuse to write a biographical sketch on them since volumes have been written on them. Yet I omitted Pierce, Cord, Packard and Duesenberg (Scott 2382-2385). That's where my discretion comes into play. I included Otis of elevator fame.

What it boils down to is that I am using my stamp collection as a guide to selecting persons to read about their place in history and as an excuse to write a biographical sketch. Obviously not everyone is included. The ones selected are "potted," as one critic stated, because they are on one page, like a plant in a pot, and they are "breezy" in style, as another critic said. Breezy meaning "delightful in the telling but serious in its basic intent." That's what stamp collecting is all about, and so I write in no other way. Since bonsai are delightful little potted plants, I would like to call these studies "bonsai-biographies," and like bonsai plants some grow and some don't.

Preface

Of the bonsai-biographies in this collection, I hope you will enjoy them and that they will stimulate you to read the available complete biographies and history books that tell about the exciting events in our history created by the people depicted on our stamps. When Margaret Truman Daniel wrote about her father in *Harry S. Truman* (William Morrow & Company, Inc. New York, 1973) she said: "But my father spent most of his time reading books that Mamma Truman (his mother) carefully selected for him. His favorite was a red-backed four-volume set of biographies by Charles Francis Horne, *Great Men and Famous Women*. These were the books that made him fall in love with history. To this day he still insists that reading biographies is the best way to learn history. He is also a firm believer in what some cynical historians have called the great man theory (Carlyle). Dad sums it up more positively. 'Men make history. History does not make the man.' "

Richard Louis Thomas

Acknowledgments

My grateful thanks to *Linn's Stamp News* for finding space in the weekly stamp publication for my articles concerning people on stamps. *Linn's* published some of the topical articles, then gathered the rest of my submissions into *Who's Who on U.S. Stamps*, a book of 413 biographies. That only showed that many people who were on stamps had been left out. To remedy the deficiency, I wrote a biographical sketch for an additional 257 people. The final result is this book, *More Who's Who on U.S. Stamps*.

But to create this book took the monumental task of the *Linn's* editorial staff, and one person especially, Donna O'Keefe, senior editor and ancillary products manager. For her to shrink my articles to page size, to correct errors in spelling, to put into chronological sense and create an interesting and readable page was nothing short of Brobdingnagian! Each article had to be subjected to critical plastic surgery, and one or two required multiple transplants. Thanks to Miss O'Keefe, it was done.

The creation of the articles that form this book would not have come about had it not been for the input of several people whom I must recognize. They are:

Barth Healy of *The New York Times*, for his valuable critique and personal correspondence, with constructive suggestions and useful input, not only about who is who on stamps but where they are located in the picture. As much as possible, I tried to satisfy this requirement in the second book. His remarks in *The Philatelic Communicator*, the journal of the American Philatelic Society's Writer's Unit No. 30, showed that he gave me (a fellow member) prime time that reiterated his earlier criticisms.

William G. Tyrrell, for a fine unsolicited detailed study of *Linn's Who's Who on U.S. Stamps*, pointing out certain glaring omissions and commissions that hopefully someday will be corrected. Tyrrell's correspondence was the burr in my saddlecloth that spurred the *More Who's Who on U.S. Stamps*, and nearly everyone on a U.S. stamp to date is included.

Jacob Kisner who corrected my glaring error in the Saroyan biographical sketch as it appeared in *Linn's* (September 2, 1991). Thanks to Mr. Kisner's kind letter the error has been corrected in this book.

George Griffenhagen, whose review in the *Topical Time* was most generous in spite of my inadequate topical index that he quickly noted as well as the "nearly every person" statement. His views and remarks prodded me to make it "every person" (with a few prudent exceptions), and the inadequate topical index will certainly be repaired at the next printing.

Nicholas Shestople was almost too generous in his review of the first book in *The American Philatelist*. His remarks encouraged me to work more diligently on the biographical sketches of the second book, which is an answer to the deficiencies of the first book. Though Shestople said I left out one person

(Thomas Grosvenor), on second glance the count would look more like 257, all of whom are in this second book.

Richard M. Cochran, who suggested I trace Lieutenant Grosvenor through the National Geographic Society. His remark that they are an "Old American Family" prompted me to get in touch with the Pomfret Historical Society.

Mary Jo Page, secretary of the Pomfret Historical Society, for supplying me with the very essential information on Lieutenant Thomas Grosvenor. Without her help that article would still be wanting, except for those persons who very thoughtfully supplied the same data later.

John M. Hotchner for his "Twenty Secrets of High Productivity" and personal communication of which I proudly took every word to heart.

William P. Wergin, whose exchange of ideas have been most helpful and encouraging.

Allison W. Cusick who cleared up a statement that I made on Cole Porter, which seemed too good to be true, and it was too good to be true. Porter did not join the French Foreign Legion as Porter said and that has oft been reported. The book Cusick recommended, *Cole Porter, A Biography*, by Charles Schwartz (Dial Press, 1977), put me straight on that matter.

Al Gerstenberger, for suggesting how to use articles in *Linn's Who's Who on U.S. Stamps* as a guide to making a specific collection of precancels. He used precanceled stamps of the definitive 14¢ Hollow Horn Bear issue as an example.

Robert T. McCall, space stamp artist, and the late Ron Evans, astronaut, who generously filled me in on space stamp trivia.

Bob Frederick who spent a good bit of his newspaper's column telling of *Linn's Who's Who on U.S. Stamps* in kind and descriptive words. John A. Dell, for useful and interesting correspondence. J. Walter Allen for his correspondence and interest. Michael W. Scott whose interest in my work and whose correspondence has been heartwarming and inspiring. John Rose for suggestions concerning Helen Keller's connection with Swedenborgianism.

I am repeatedly grateful to Joseph H. Boatwright, for considerable correspondence and many useful and intelligent suggestions. Helen Holloway, former secretary for Robert A. Millikan, who made an important date correction and has since sent much useful correspondence. Donald B. Stevens, for sending me many useful brochures, newspaper clippings and photographs of places pertaining to people on stamps as well as delightful personal communications. Ronnell B. Townsend, for swapping useful ideas. Joseph and Betty Taussig Jr., for their humorous and thoughtful communications. John G. Peebles for his confidence in my work. Robert Barron for his several and detailed contributions of the persons on stamps of whom he had intimate knowledge. Jon Wallach, whose inquiry goaded me on to completion. Rudy M. Gross whose wise suggestions have been useful and whose correspondence has been a delight. Jim Holmes for incorporating my articles in his creative art displaying stamps of famous people. Jim Watson, whose repeated jovial encouragement and sensible suggestions have settled some questionable points. To the members of our Westminster Village Stamp Club, Arthur Streng, George Hooper, Gordon Nielson, and Paul Christenson, who kept me humble. My thanks.

Last, and by no means least, my wife, Virginia Thomas, who gave me more support, more suggestive criticism, and more proofreading than anyone, except perhaps Donna O'Keefe.

I don't doubt that among my cluttered papers and somewhere in my cluttered mind someone whom I should have acknowledged has been overlooked. For those, I'll thank them personally when they surface.

Richard Louis Thomas

William A. 'Bud' Abbott

Scott 2566
Born: October 2, 1895, Asbury Park, New Jersey
Died: April 24, 1974, Woodlawn Hills, California

From 1931 to 1957, the comedy team of Abbott and Costello delighted the audiences of vaudeville, stage, radio, motion pictures and finally television. Abbott was the know-it-all, fast-talking straight man whose function it was to take the punch lines from his sidekick, comedian Lou Costello. Costello was the immature tubby, pudgy, chunky gracioso — the child-like buffoon — who asked all the questions. This comedy formula proved to be one of the most popular of all the many show-business attractions. From it came the famous baseball skit, "Who's on First?" now inscribed on a plaque in the National Baseball Hall of Fame in Cooperstown, New York.

Before he teamed up with Costello, Bud Abbott worked as a seaman. He found his way into the theater business as the manager of a traveling burlesque show and cashier in a Brooklyn theater.

Beginning in 1931, and for the next eight years, Abbott and Costello toured the vaudeville circuit. By 1938, they appeared at Loew's State in New York City and on the Kate Smith radio show. The following year they starred in their own Broadway review billed *Streets in Paris*. The next year they were in Hollywood making their first motion picture, *One Night in the Tropics*.

If money measures success, Abbott and Costello were ranked in the top 10 for the next 10 years. All tallied, the pair made 35 films from 1941 to 1956, including such hits as *Buck Privates, In the Navy, Rio Rita, Lost in a Harem, Jack and the Bean Stock,* and *Abbott and Costello in Hollywood*. Their last film was *Dance with Me Henry* in 1956. It would be a monumental feat of show biz research to tally all the Abbott and Costello vaudeville, stage, radio and movie comediettas. Many of their film skits were reproduced later on television. The famous "Who's on First?" dialogue alone was repeated several thousand times.

Abbott and Costello dissolved their partnership in good friendship in 1957. Two years later Costello died. Abbott continued to appear occasionally on stage and television, but it was not the same without his faithful buffoon. He faded into retirement.

Abbott appears with his partner, Lou Costello, in the Comedians by Hirschfeld booklet of five different stamps issued in 1991.

Samuel Adams

Scott 1691
Born: September 27, 1722, Boston, Massachusetts
Died: October 2, 1803, Boston, Massachusetts

Samuel Adams, "man of the revolution," was the son of Samuel Adams, a well-to-do businessman, and Mary Fifield Adams. Young Samuel entered Harvard College at the age of 14. He studied John Loche's *Of Civil Government*. He held firm to Loche's principles of man's natural rights of life, liberty and property and that taxation could not be imposed without the consent of the people. He graduated in 1740, and earned a masters degree in 1743. He married Elizabeth Checkley in 1749, with whom he had two children. She died in 1757, and a few years later he married Betsy Wells.

When the Stamp Act was imposed in 1765, Adams inspired the rioting that ensued. He was elected to the Massachusetts House of Representatives and led the radical patriots.

In 1766 came the Townshend Act, establishing import duties. Adams fired protests that may have sparked the Boston Massacre on March 5, 1770. The duties were withdrawn by Parliament, except on tea. Adams signaled the dumping of tea off a ship into the harbor, which came to be known as the Boston Tea Party. The response from the British was the Intolerable Acts of 1774. The Massachusetts state capital was temporarily moved to Salem. Here, behind locked doors, Adams maneuvered the election of representatives for the First Continental Congress. He was one of those elected. He, with John Hancock, avoided arrest by British troops at Concord and returned to Philadelphia in May 1775. Both men signed the Declaration of Independence.

Adams sat in Congress until 1781, then took his seat in the state Senate. He was not elected to Congress in 1788. He vacillated on the ratification of the Constitution but finally supported it. He was elected lieutenant governor with Hancock. Adams was elected governor and served until 1797, when he retired.

On the 1976 Declaration of Independence stamps, of the men seated before the men standing, Adams is second from the left.

Adolphus II, Elector of Mainz

Scott 1014

Adolphus II was the elector of Mainz in 1452 when Johannes Gutenberg was attempting to gain recognition as the inventor of printing from movable type. Gutenberg accomplished this feat by printing a Bible. Johann Fust provided financial support.

The electors, Kurfuersten, were a body of German princes with whom rested the election of the German king. This procedure began in the 13th century and ended in the 19th century. The electors determined the German kingship, or "king of the Romans," who invariably became the Holy Roman emperor.

By the end of the 14th century, the seven electors were recognized as a corporate body that formed the first house of the Imperial Diet. As such, they became politically influential. At times, they sought to dictate terms to the kings they elected.

Mainz became the seat of an archbishop in the 8th century and a free city in 1118. The archbishops were imperial electors, and Mainz flourished as a center of trade and culture.

The archbishopric of Mainz dated from 747 and became a powerful state during the Middle Ages, retaining some of its importance until the end of the empire in 1806. Its archbishop was president of the electoral college, archchancellor of the empire and primate of Germany.

When Gutenberg presented the product of his printing press to Adolphus II, he was facing considerable power.

In 1462, a serious rivalry arose between two contesting archbishops. The citizens who espoused the losing cause were deprived of their privileges. Many of the inhabitants were driven into exile. Gutenberg was among those who were exiled. When he returned in 1465, the archbishop, Adolphus II, restored Gutenberg's good standing, gave him a pension and a tax exemption.

Adolphus II is seen seated on the left on the Gutenberg Bible stamp of 1952. He is shown examining the vellum of print being presented to him by Gutenberg and Fust.

Josef Albers

Scott 1833
Born: March 19, 1888, Bottrop, Westphalia, Germany
Died: March 25, 1976, New Haven, Connecticut

Josef Albers was considered by his contemporaries as the Prince of Op Art, though he himself identified with no particular school of geometric abstraction. He concentrated on problems of perception.

In Germany, he was a school teacher for 10 years. He studied at the Royal Art Academy in Berlin from 1913 to 1915, and the School of Applied Arts in Essen from 1916 to 1919. He was influenced by the works of Paul Cezanne and the new art of Cubism. Albers created a series of linoleum cuts called *Sandpit*.

He studied at the Weimar Bauhaus. At the Bauhaus, he was invited in 1922 to reorganize the glass workshop. His glass pieces became increasingly more geometric, causing a change in the emphasis at the Bauhaus favoring engineering and constructivist aesthetics. He was appointed to the faculty of the Bauhaus. This lasted until the Nazi takeover in 1933. In his last two years at the Bauhaus, he began to investigate problems in the Step series, a complicated system in which the principal image consists of steplike shapes that could not be read according to the rules of linear perspective.

Albers fled Germany in 1933. He came to the United States and continued his work at the North Carolina Black Mountain College from 1933 to 1949. He served as chairman of art at Yale University from 1950 to 1960. Throughout his career in the United States, he used various media, such as zinc lithographs, woodcuts, engravings and linocuts, producing such works as *Graphic Tectonics*, *Structural Constellations*, *Top Center*, and *Homage to the Square* series.

In Albers' most important book, *The Interaction of Color* (1963), he indicated that color was not subordinate to form in his work but rather the chief medium of pictorial language. He expanded his work to murals. An example is the large bronze-and-glass piece in the Time-Life Building, New York City.

His *Homage to the Square: Glow* is shown on the "Learning never ends" stamp of the 1980 Education issue.

4

John Alden

Scott 549
Born: 1599, in or near Southampton, England
Died: September 12, 1687, Duxbury, Massachusetts

John Alden lived to nearly 88 years of age. He died at Duxbury, a small village he helped found on the north end of Plymouth Bay. He was the last survivor of the signers of the Mayflower Compact. Tradition has it that Alden was the first of the Pilgrims on the *Mayflower* to step foot on the large stepping stone known as Plymouth Rock. Of the 41 male passengers who are listed as heads of the families, Alden does head the list alphabetically.

Alden was a wine-cask maker in Southampton, when he signed on for the voyage to America with the group of religious dissenters known as Separatists. English law dating to 1543 required that a cooper be aboard any ship carrying beer to make good the loss of barrel-stock. Alden was only 21 when he sailed from Plymouth, England, September 16, 1620, on the *Mayflower*.

The 103 passengers arrived in what is now Provincetown on November 21. That same day they compiled and signed the Mayflower Compact, thus organizing themselves into a self-governing community. Not having a charter, they promised to obey the rules they made. They did not set foot on their new home until December 26, when they established the community of Plymouth.

By 1627, Alden was one of the bondsmen responsible for assuming the colonial debt. He moved to Duxbury. Later, he acquired land at Bridgwater. He and Myles Standish were neighbors. In 1634, Alden served as an agent for the colony at the trading post on the Kennebec River. He also was on the local committee for raising a force against the Indians. He served as deputy of Duxbury. He was on the local council of war and was the treasurer from 1656 to 1658. He was assistant to the governor, and served in that post from 1650 to 1686. He also was deputy-governor.

In 1621, he married Priscilla Mullens, the daughter of William Mullens. Both William and Priscilla Mullens came over on the *Mayflower* with him. John and Priscilla Alden had 11 children. Alden was buried in South Duxbury near Standish, who died 30 years earlier.

Alden is shown on the 1920 2¢ Pilgrim Tercentenary stamp.

Edwin Eugene Aldrin Jr.

Scott 2419
Born: January 20, 1930, Montclair, New Jersey

Edwin "Buzz" Aldrin's father, Edwin Eugene Aldrin Sr., was an Army Air Corps pilot and aide to General Billy Mitchell in the Philippines in 1920. His mother, Marion Moon, was the daughter of a Methodist Army chaplain.

The Aldrin's only son, Edwin Eugene Aldrin Jr., called "Buzz," was a 1951 graduate of the U.S. Military Academy. He later became an Air Force colonel and a scientist. In the Korean War, "Buzz" Aldrin flew 66 combat missions, winning the Distinguished Flying Cross and the Air Medal. At the Massachusetts Institute of Technology, he earned his doctorate of science degree in astronautics. He was chosen as an astronaut in 1963.

Aldrin earned his astronaut's wings in *Gemini XII,* November 11, 1966, making 63 orbits of Earth. The *Gemini* spacecraft was twice as large as the *Mercury* capsule and accommodated two astronauts. In *Gemini XII*, Aldrin was accompanied by James Arthur Lovell Jr. Extravehicular activities (EVA), called space walks, provided information for later walks on the moon.

The opportunity to walk on the moon came on July 16 when *Apollo 11* took Neil A. Armstrong, Michael Collins and Aldrin to the moon. The lunar capsule *Eagle* separated from the command module *Columbia* and settled on the moon's surface. Armstrong set foot on the moon first, and Aldrin followed.

Aldrin had difficulty coping with the post-*Apollo 11* feat as a new-found celebrity. He found his assignment as commander of the Aerospace Research Pilots School at Edwards Air Force Base, California, was something he was not trained for. He checked into the military hospital in San Antonio for treatment of mental illness and alcoholism. He recovered. Today he lectures about both.

Aldrin retired from the Air Force and wrote *Return to Earth.* He established his own firm, Research & Engineering in Los Angeles. In 1989, he wrote another book, *Men From Earth,* detailing his *Apollo 11* adventure.

Aldrin is one of the two astronauts pictured on the Moon Landing 20th Anniversary $2.40 stamp issued July 20, 1989.

Horatio Alger

Scott 2010
Born: January 13, 1832, Revere, Massachusetts
Died: July 18, 1899, Natick, Massachusetts

Horatio Alger's father wanted him to become a Unitarian minister like himself. He sent Horatio to Harvard and to the Harvard Divinity school. Horatio studied diligently and graduated in 1860. His friends called him "Holy Horatio." Young Alger received an unexpected windfall of money that he used to pay for a trip to Paris, where he stayed for a year, living a bohemian life much in contrast with his Puritan upbringing and education. When he returned to the United States, he did not serve in the Union Army because of ill health.

Alger was ordained in 1864 and served as minister of the Unitarian Church in Brewster, Massachusetts. Two years later he resigned. He wanted to write.

Alger move to New York City in 1866. He became associated with the Newsboys' Lodging House. Some of the waifs who lived in the home became his "ragged Dicks" and "tattered Toms" in the stories that made him famous in later years. He wrote 135 books. *Fame and Fortune, Struggling Upwards* and *Strive and Succeed* are examples in which the hero exemplifies to the young readers that they too could become a millionaire or president if they worked hard and, above all, were honest. These heroes were a delight to Alger's readers because they were capable of living virtuous lives despite poor surroundings.

Alger's simple literary quality was directed toward the young reader. He published a novel, *Helen Ford*, but it was the popular *Gan'ther Baldwin's Thanksgiving, with Other Ballads and Poems* that introduced the "Luck and Pluck," "Ragged Dick" and "Tattered Tom" series that attained wide success.

In 1895, he moved to Peekskill, New York. He went again to Paris, where he became romantically involved, but this affair did not materialize into marriage. Alger suffered a nervous breakdown. He returned to the United States and moved in with his sister in Natick, Massachusetts.

Horatio Alger was honored on a 1982 stamp for American authors.

Isaac Allerton

Scott 550
Born: circa 1586, London?, England
Died: February 1659, New Haven, Connecticut

Isaac Allerton was one of the most important members during the Leiden period and during the first 10 years at Plymouth. He was a tailor in London and moved to Leiden in 1608 before another group of Separatists from Scrooby, South Yorkshire, arrived. He joined them. He married Mary Norris, a Scrooby member, in 1611 and became a citizen of Leiden in 1614.

The Separatists decided to move to America. Allerton was one of the principal persons to complete the necessary arrangements and to buy and outfit the *Speedwell*. The *Speedwell* proved unseaworthy. Allerton, his wife and three children transferred to the *Mayflower*. They arrived at Cape Cod in November, near the site of Provincetown. On December 26, they stepped foot on Plymouth.

When William Bradford was elected governor upon the death of John Carver in 1621, Allerton was the only assistant of the colony. He held that position for the next three years. In the harsh winter of 1621, Allerton's wife died. A few years later he married Fear Brewster, the daughter of the colony's spiritual leader, Elder William Brewster.

In 1625, the colony learned that their support had ceased. Allerton made several trips to England and, by 1626, received some repayments. At the same time, he arranged for more Pilgims to come over from Leiden in 1629. He interested other English merchants to invest in the Plymouth colony, and in 1630, he was instrumental in obtaining a patent giving the Pilgims a title to their lands and property, thus securing their future.

Allerton's successes caused him to become overly ambitious. He raised more support with loans, acquired a ship, bought supplies and managed to double the colony's indebtedness, which the colony rejected. In 1631, the colony renounced Allerton as their agent. He seems to have left the colony, even though his wife and children remained in Plymouth. He went to Marblehead. In 1644, he moved to New Haven, where he died. His daughter Mary, one of his three girls who sailed with him in 1620, died in Plymouth in 1699 and was the last surviving passenger of the *Mayflower*.

Allerton is depicted on the 1920 5¢ Pilgrim Tercentenary stamp.

Antonello

Antonello, National Gallery

Scott 2514
Born: circa 1430, Messina, Sicily, Italy
Died: February 1479, Venice? or Messina?, Italy

Antonello was the son of a marble worker. By 1456, Antonello had his own studio. Sometime prior to 1460, he was in the Netherlands, where he learned from the methods acquired by the followers of Jan van Eyck (1385-1441). Van Eyck's paintings are remarkable for realism with faithful detail, brilliance of color and subtle effects of light made possible by his perfection of a fluid oil medium and varnish. With this secret knowledge, Antonello returned to Messina in 1460 and spent the next five years at home painting.

He traveled to Rome to study the Flemishlike works of Piero Della Francesca. He was in Messina in 1473 and 1474, when he completed the *Polyptych of St. Gregory, A Young Man, Ecce Homo* and *The Annunciation. A Young Man* is considered his greatest work now in existence. It is in the Dahlem Museum, Berlin. *Ecce Homo* is in the Metropolitan Museum, New York.

In 1475 and 1476, he went to Venice, where he painted for the Council of Ten. While in Venice, he produced a *Crucifixion*, now in the Musee Royal des Beaux-Arts, Antwerp, and the *Altarpiece of St. Cassiano*, now in the Kunsthistorisches Museum, Vienna. Also of note is his *Portrait of a Man* or *Il Condottoiere* that now hangs in the Louvre, Paris.

He was in Milan to paint portraits for the Duke of Milan, Galeazzo Maria Sforza. Here the story of his life takes two paths. According to an earlier, but not too reliable account by biographer Giorgio Vasari, in his *Lives of the Painters, Sculptors, and Architects* (1550), Antonello returned to Messina in September 1476 and worked at his home studio until he died sometime between February 14 and 25, 1479. A much later account of Antonello's life, by Venturi in an article in Thieme-Becker, *Kunstlerlexikon*, 1907, traces him to Venice and says he died in February 1479 while working for the Council of Ten.

Antonello, in his mastery of the oil painting and techniques of the Flemish masters, was one of the most important painters of southern Italy of the Renaissance period during the first half of the 15th century.

His *Madonna and Child* is shown on the 1990 traditional Christmas stamp.

Antoniazzo

Scott 2578
Born: 1460, Viterbo? Italy
Died: 1508, Rome, Italy

The year dates of Antoniazzo Romano's birth and death have been substantiated by historians. It is possible that he was from Viterbo (since his initial preparation was similar to that of Lorenzo da Viterbo) and that he spent the most productive time of his life in Rome. That he painted in Rome along with other masters of the High Renaissance is known.

Antoniazzo was influenced by Melozzo, Ghirlandajo and Raphael. In Rome, Antoniazzo's works are in the Pantheon, Church of St. Maria Sopra Minerva and Vatican museums. One of his greatest influences was Melozzo da Forli, who studied under Piero Della Francesca, one of the early masters of the Umbrian school. Della Francesca taught Melozzo the principles of perspective. These principles became a consuming interest for Antoniazzo. He developed the use of foreshortening, used to create striking effects in decorating cupolas with which contemporary Renaissance architects crowned their buildings.

In Rome, various painters felt the impact of Melozzo's art, including Antoniazzo. Originally oriented toward Gozzoli, Antoniazzo assimilated Florentine and even Umbrian influences, but later became a faithful follower of Melozzo's style. He recaptured Melozzo's scope in frescoes in the Church of St. Giovanni Evangelista in Tivoli. This style can also be seen in his *St. Illuminata with Saints Vincenzo and Nicoa da Tolentaino*, Montefalco (near Foligno), Umbria, in the Church of St. Francesco, and in his *The Virgin with Pope Leo IX*, now in the Dublin National Gallery of Ireland.

He recaptured Melozzo's scope in his frescoes in the Church of St. Giovani Evangelista in Tivoli. Later, because of his excessive abundant production, his work became less monumental. This is evident in his frescoes in the apse of the Church of St. Croce in Gerusalemme, Rome. Among his many panels is the one depicting the *Madonna and Saints with Members of the Rota* in the Vatican museums. Antoniazzo's *Madonna* is as fine as any of the masters of the High Renaissance. It follows the trend originated by Della Francesca and Melozzo.

Antoniazzo's *Madonna* appears on the 1991 traditional Christmas stamp.

10

John Armstrong

Scott 644
Born: November 25, 1758, Carlisle, Pennsylvania
Died: April 1, 1843, Red Hook, New York

John Armstrong was the son of Major General John and Rebecca Lyon Armstrong. Young Armstrong was in college at Princeton, New Jersey, when the Revolutionary War broke out. He left college to join Generals Mercer and Gates and participated in the Saratoga campaign. He was present at the surrender of Burgoyne. While the Army was camped at Newburgh, New York, in 1783, Armstrong composed the notorious and anonymous "Newburgh Letters" to Congress, asking for payment due. The letter threatened that the Army would take matters into its own hands if Congress did not act.

After the war, Armstrong returned to Pennsylvania as secretary of the Supreme Executive Council of the State. In 1784, he was placed in command of the militia sent to the Wyoming Valley on the Susquehanna to restore order between the settlers from Connecticut and Pennsylvania land speculators' agents. Armstrong wrongly sided with the agents.

He was made state adjutant-general. In 1787, he was elected a delegate to Congress. He married Alida Livingston, a sister of Robert R. Livingston of New York. They moved to Red Hook, New York, and farmed. Armstrong became absorbed into the Livingston family that was aligned with the Clinton clan politically. This landed Armstrong a seat in the U.S. Senate in 1800.

Armstrong became minister to France in 1804. He resided in France from 1804 to 1810. As a diplomat dealing with Napoleon, he ensnarled matters. He must bear part of the responsibility for the resulting War of 1812.

In the presidential race, Armstrong favored Madison over De Witt Clinton. Madison commissioned him a brigadier-general in command of New York City. In January 1813, Madison nominated him for secretary of war. Armstrong took charge of the War Department on February 8. He promoted to generals Andrew Jackson, Jacob Brown and Winfield Scott, but he made a series of mistakes and failures. The campaign on Lake Ontario was a disaster, and the autumn campaign against Montreal was a failure. On September 3, 1814, he mailed his resignation to Madison, thus putting an end to his political career.

Of the men standing on General Gates' left, Armstrong is the eighth man from the left on the 1927 Surrender of Burgoyne at Saratoga stamp.

Neil Alden Armstrong

Scott C76
Born: August 5, 1930, Wapakoneta, Ohio

Aviation interested Neil Armstrong even when he was a small boy. By the time he was 16, he had his pilot's license. Armstrong left Purdue University to join the U.S. Navy. He flew combat missions in the Korean War. After the war, he returned to Purdue and completed his degree in aeronautics in 1955. He went to work with the National Aeronautics and Space Administration (NASA) as a research pilot. In 1962, he was selected to become an astronaut.

On March 16, 1966, his first venture into space almost ended in disaster when, after six and one-half orbits, his two-man spacecraft, *Gemini 8*, went out of control. Armstrong and fellow astronaut David Scott had to maneuver the spacecraft down for an emergency landing 600 miles east of Okinawa.

Three years later, Armstrong, along with astronauts Colonel Edwin E. Aldrin Jr. and Lieutenant Colonel Michael Collins, ventured into space to make the first landing on the moon in *Apollo 11*. The mission took place July 16-24, 1969, in a nearly flawless trip. The *Saturn 5* rocketed into space from Launch Complex 39 at Cape Kennedy with its manned *Apollo* payload. At 115 miles above Earth, *Apollo 1* entered into a temporary parking orbit, then reignited its S-4B stage and entered its translunar path at a speed of nearly 24,300 miles per hour. The service module and the linking command module were turned about so as to dock with the lunar module. Then the four connections that joined the lunar module *Eagle* to its adapter and the S-4B stage were separated from the command module *Columbia* using spring thrusters and explosive bolts.

Aldrin reported to Earth that "The view is out of this world." Collins circled the moon in the *Columbia* while Armstrong and Aldrin set down in the detached lunar module on the moon below. Armstrong was the first to leave the lunar module. His first words were, "That's one small step for man, one giant leap for mankind." The date was July 20, 1969. The two astronauts collected mineral samples from the surface of the moon before blasting off to rejoin the *Columbia* for the return leg of the historic journey.

Armstrong is depicted in his space suit in a painting, *First Man on the Moon* by Paul Calle. This painting was the basis of the 1969 10¢ Moon Landing airmail stamp. Armstrong is seen at the bottom of the ladder setting foot on the moon's surface beside one foot of the lunar module *Eagle*.

Liberty Hyde Bailey

Scott 1100
Born: March 15, 1858, South Haven, Michigan
Died: December 25, 1954, Ithaca, New York

The allegory *Bountiful Earth* portrays horticulture and botany to honor Liberty Hyde Bailey. He was the son of a farmer. He graduated from the Michigan State Agricultural College in 1882. He did graduate study under the tutelage of the renowned Dr. Asa Gray, physician turned botanist, at Harvard University. Bailey returned to Michigan State Agricultural College as professor of horticulture and, in 1885, organized the nation's first department of horticulture and landscape gardening. He spent the next three years at Michigan before going to Cornell in 1888. He organized the New York State College of Agriculture at Cornell and introduced extension courses in horticulture to farmers. He was named dean of the College of Agriculture at Cornell in 1903.

Bailey retired in 1913 to devote his time to writing and collecting plants. He established the Liberty Hyde Bailey Hortorium in 1920, at Cornell, which houses his entire library and botanical collection. The Bailey Hortorium is devoted to studying and classification and identification of cultivated plants. Among Bailey's writings was his *Manual of Cultivated Plants* (revised in 1949), which is a basic work in horticulture.

Many standard reference works in horticulture were authored by Bailey, including *Cyclopedia of American Horticulture* (revised 1935), *Standard Cyclopedia of Horticulture* (revised 1935), *Cyclopedia of American Agriculture* (1907-09), *Hortus* (1930) and *Hortus Second* (1941).

In 1908, he was appointed by President Theodore Roosevelt as chairman of the Commission of Country Life. In 1926, he was president of the American Association for the Advancement of Science. He was the first president of the American Society of Horticultural Science.

In 1958, a stamp for gardening and horticulture was issued to honor garden clubs of American and in connection with the centenary of Bailey's birth.

13

Josiah Bartlett

JULY 4, 1776

Scott 1691
Born: November 21, 1729, Amesbury, Massachussets
Died: May 19, 1795, Kingston, New Hampshire

Josiah Bartlett was a physician in Kingston, Rockingham County, New Hampshire. Early in his practice he was confronted with an inflamed throat epidemic (probably streptococcal), the fever of which was life threatening. He knew of the effects of the bark of the cinchona tree called "Peruvian bark," since it had been used by natives of the Andes region for years because it contained quinine and quinidine. The quinine relieved the feverish symptoms of malaria, and the quinidine relieved cardiac irregularity. Bartlett made effective use of this natural antipyretic drug in the epidemic of 1754.

John Wentworth, the royal governor at the time, gave him important appointments, which also enhanced his station. In 1775, when Bartlett sided with the patriots of the Colonial cause, Wentworth cut him off.

Bartlett was selected as a delegate to the Continental Congress. The delegates of the farthest north colony, New Hampshire, were called first; thus, the honor fell to Bartlett to cast the first vote for the Declaration of Independence. He later signed the document on July 4, 1775. The honor of being the first delegate to vote for the Articles of Confederation also fell to him.

In 1779, he received the appointment as chief justice of the New Hampshire court of common pleas. In 1788, he was appointed chief justice of the Supreme Court of New Hampshire. The same year, as an active member of the state convention, he supported the ratification of the federal Constitution.

In 1790, Bartlett was elected chief executive of New Hampshire. When the state constitution was newly amended in 1792, he was elected governor. He was the last state president (1790-92) and the first state governor (1792-94).

He was registered as being a Democratic-Republican. He held the office of governor for nearly two years. He retired in 1794, months before his death.

Of the men seated behind the men standing in the first stamp of the four se-tenant series of July 4, 1975, Josiah Bartlett is the third from the left.

14

Richard Bassett

Scott 798
Born: April 2, 1745, Bohemia Ferry, Cecil County, Maryland
Died: September 15, 1815, Bohemia Manor, Maryland

Although Richard Bassett was a Marylander, he spent most of his life in Delaware. Cecil County, in the northeast corner of Maryland, is just a few miles from Wilmington, a growing industrial and shipping center.

In 1777, when the naval battles were fought on the Delaware River along the docks of New Castle, it prompted the Delaware Assembly to flee to safety in Dover, where the capital remained. Bassett spent much time in Dover. His father was a tavern owner in Bohemia Ferry, Maryland. Bassett did not follow his father's profession but instead chose politics.

When the Revolutionary War broke out, he captained a troop of Dover light horse cavalry. He served in both houses of the legislature and as a member of the state constitutional convention.

In 1787, he was one of the representatives from Delaware at the Constitutional Convention and signed the Constitution. When it came time for Delaware to ratify the Constitution, he, along with John Dickinson and Gunning Bedford Jr., was one of the most ardent supporters from Delaware. On December 7, 1787, Delaware became the first state to ratify the Constitution.

Bassett was one of the first U.S. senators from Delaware, serving from 1789 to 1793, when Delaware adopted the Second State Constitution and changed its name to "State of Delaware." In 1793, he was appointed chief justice of the Court of Common Pleas and held this post until 1799. Bassett followed Governor Bedford (1796-97) and Daniel Rogers (acting 1797-99) as governor and served from 1799 to 1801 as a Federalist.

In 1801, President John Adams appointed Bassett judge of the U.S. Circuit Court. He was a fervent Methodist and an adherent of the Colonial itinerant Methodist minister Francis Asbury who, along with Thomas Coke, was the first bishop of the Methodist Episcopal Church in the United States. Asbury came to the Colonies in 1771 and was a close friend of Bassett. Bassett served his church and his country in a superior capacity and with honesty and efficiency.

He is depicted in the painting *Adoption of the Constitution* on the Constitution Sesquicentennial issue of September 17, 1937.

Gunning Bedford

Scott 798
Born: 1747, Philadelphia, Pennsylvania
Died: March 30, 1812, Wilmington, Delaware

The name Gunning caused confusion at the time of Gunning Bedford's life and for historians and biographers afterward. He signed his name followed by "Jun." or "Jr." for junior. His father's name was also Gunning. His mother was Susanna Jocquett Bedford. His cousin, Gunning Bedford (1742-97), revolutionary soldier and politician, identified himself as "Colonel" or "Governor" Bedford. The cousins held high offices in Delaware and in the nation at the same time, which added to the confusion. Dr. Gunning S. Bedford (1806-70), a nephew of Gunning Jr., added to the confusion. Dr. Bedford was a renowned physician and obstetrician, who moved to New York City in 1836. He founded the University Medical College in 1840 and the first free obstetrical clinic.

In Philadelphia, Gunning Bedford Jr. studied law with Joseph Read and was admitted to the bar. He had studied at Princeton and graduated in the class of 1771 along with James Madison. Soon after he finished his law studies, he married Jane Bellareau Parker. The couple moved to Dover, Delaware, and then to Wilmington. Years later they settled on a farm called "Lombardy" on the Brandywine Creek near Wilmington. Family records indicate that Bedford served as an aide to General Washington in the War for Independence.

He was a member of the Delaware legislature and the state council. In 1785-86, he was a delegate to the Continental Congress and was one of the Delaware representatives at the Annapolis Convention in 1786 and at the Federal Convention in 1787. He signed the U.S. Constitution as "Gunning Bedford Jun." He was an opponent of a strong central government and championed the rights of the states. In December 1787, he attended the Delaware Convention that ratified the Constitution.

He served as attorney general of Delaware from 1784 to 1789. In 1789, Washington appointed him judge for the Delaware district, the office he held until his death. He was a presidential elector in 1789 and again in 1793. He was president of the board of trustees of Wilmington Academy and continued in this post when it became Wilmington College.

Gunning Bedford is depicted in the painting *Adoption of the Constitution* on the Constitution Sesquicentennial issue of September 17, 1937.

Giovanni Bellini

Scott 2710
Born: circa 1430, Venice, Italy
Died: November 1516, Venice, Italy

Giovanni Bellini was the son of the painter Jacopo Bellini. Giovanni Bellini's earliest work was not recognized until perhaps 1456. He worked as an assistant in his father's studio in Venice until he was 30. In 1465, he painted in the studio with his brother-in-law Andrea Montegna, who married Jacopo's daugher Niccolosia in 1453. Bellini and Montegna each painted the same picture, *Agony in the Garden*. Bellini's work is lyrical and spacious; Montegna's work is stiff and flat. The comparison is seen especially in the treatment of the landscapes. Both works are in London's National Gallery.

A few years later Bellini began using oil paint instead of tempora. Oil was especially good for him since it accentuated the warmth and the treatment of light and harmonies of color that were so characteristic of his paintings and of which he was most masterful.

Over the many years he executed numerous paintings that today grace the halls and walls of many of the major galleries and collections throughout the world. His *Allegory of Purgatory* in the Uffizi, Florence, is an example, as well as *Agony in the Garden* in London's National Gallery. *Portrait of Coleoni, Booth Madonna, Feast of the Gods* and *Portrait of a Youth* are in the National Gallery, Washington, D.C.

Bellini had many students including such Venetian greats as Titian, Giorgione and Tintoretto. He painted altarpieces, many featuring the Madonna and Child, landscapes, portraits and large allegorical and mythological pictures. Most had religious themes.

On February 26, 1483, Giovanni was appointed painter to the Republic of Venice and thereby exempted from all obligations to the guild of painters.

Bellini was buried in the Church of SS. Giovanni e Paolo. His death date is noted as November 29, 1516, in Marino Sanudo's diary.

One of Bellini's many Madonna and Child renditions was chosen for the traditional Christmas stamp of 1992.

Jack Benny (Benjamin Kubelsky)

Scott 2564
Born: February 14, 1894, Chicago, Illinois
Died: December 26, 1974, Beverly Hills, California

When Jack Benny was 8 years old, his father, a Russian Jewish immigrant, gave him a violin. Benny became an accomplished violinist, but in his comedy acts, he purposely played poorly a portion of *Love in Bloom*.

Benny took a serious approach to comedy. Though his relaxed posture gave him the appearance of being a successful businessman, he was first of all a funny man. It was this dignity, or his miserliness, that was challenged in his acts. With precise timing, he would address his coadjutors by their first name, "Now, Dennis!" whether it was Don Wilson, Rochester (Eddie Anderson), Dennis Day or Mary Livingstone. He pedantically reprimanded them. His cast carried the punch lines, leaving Benny to bear the brunt of the jokes. When asked his age, he would indignantly respond that he was "39."

In 1927, Benny married Sadie Marks, who became his Mary Livingstone. In real life, Benny was a generous man, giving willingly of his time, talents and fortunes. On stage, he played the calculating tightwad. When he was a small boy, his father moved his family to Waukegan, Illinois, and opened a shop. In his comedy routines, Benny claimed Waukegan as his birthplace.

Benny left school after the ninth grade and began making vaudeville appearances. An assignment on a road show under the auspices of the Navy in World War I further developed his comedy routine and technique. In 1926, he appeared on Broadway in *The Great Temptation*. He went to Hollywood, where he played in his own National Broadcasting Company (NBC) radio show. This followed his appearance in 1932 on the Ed Sullivan radio show.

His radio programs were so successful that in 1948 he reached an agreement with the Columbia Broadcasting System (CBS). He went into television in 1955. From 1960 to 1965, he had his own television show.

He retired in 1965 but continued to perform in nightclubs, in television programs and in programs to benefit charitable organizations. Of the movies he made, the most memorable are *Hollywood Review of 1929*, *Artists and Models*, *Buck Benny Rides Again*, *Charley's Aunt* and *The Horn Blows at Midnight*.

Benny is depicted on a stamp in the 1991 booklet series of famous comedians by the cartoonist Albert Hirshfeld.

Thomas Hart Benton

Missouri 1821-1971 United States 8c

Scott 1426
Born: April 15, 1889, Neosho, Missouri
Died: January 19, 1975, Kansas City, Missouri

Thomas Benton was the son of Congressman Maecenas E. Benton and grandnephew of Senator Thomas Hart Benton, whose name he bears. He painted seriously in the 1930s. Painters of his style were known as "regionalists," for they depicted stories and scenes of their own home environs, its history and its folklore.

Benton's paintings were done in colorful and earthy canvasses or as murals. They were scenes of action, such as the painting *Independence and the Opening of the West,* which hangs in the Harry S Truman Library in Independence, Missouri. It depicts a Pawnee facing a hunter-trapper and a group of settlers. In this painting, the Pawnee Indian is shown offering a calumet (peace pipe) to the white men carrying deadly firearms.

Benton studied at the Art Institute of Chicago for a year, 1906 to 1907, and in Paris from 1908 to 1911, which included a spell at the Academie Julian. When he returned to the United States, he made New York City his home.

In 1916, he showed his painting *Figure Organization No. 3* in the Forum exhibition. From 1926 to 1935, he taught and painted at the Art Students League in New York City. He received commissions to paint murals. His scenes can be seen in the New School for Social Research, New York; the Whitney Museum of American Art, New York; the Missouri Statehouse, Jefferson City; and the Harry S Truman Library, Independence. One of his most notable works is the mural of the history of Indiana in the auditorium at Indiana University in Bloomington.

In World War I, he served in the Navy as an architectural draftsman. This caused him to return to realism. He made trips to the prairie states to paint subjects of those areas depicting its history. *Louisiana Rice Fields* in 1928 and *Homestead* in 1934 are examples. *Wreck of the Old 97,* shows a family in a horse-drawn wagon meeting a train at a railroad crossing.

After 1935, Benton lived in Kansas City, Missouri, and tells about his life and work in his book *An Artist in America.*

Benton's work is shown on the Missouri Sesquicentennial issue of 1971.

Edgar Bergen (Edgar Bergren)

Scott 2563
Born: February 16, 1903, Chicago, Illinois
Died: September 30, 1978, Las Vegas, Nevada

Edgar Bergen discovered, during grade school, that he could throw his voice as a ventriloquist. He sought professional guidance and caught on to the tricks rapidly. In high school, he was entertaining professionally with his $35 wooden dummy, Charlie McCarthy, the mouthy manikin that supposedly resembled a pugnatious little freckle-faced Irish newsboy. During summer vacations, Bergen toured with the Chautauqua circuits. In 1924, his performances helped pay for his premedical studies at Northwestern University.

He joined vaudeville in 1926. He toured America and Europe for the next 10 years. He was discovered by Hollywood and was featured in numerous short comedy skits. Rudy Vallee invited him for a radio appearance on his Fleischmann Hour. This opened the way for Bergen's own hour radio show sponsored by the Chase and Sandborn Coffee Company. McCarthy's nasty, disrespectful personality won him, and Bergen, a first-place radio rating for three years running.

Bergen was a debonair gentleman, treating his famous guest artists with the most proper decorum. His little wooden sidekick, perched on Bergen's right knee, would embarrass him and shame him with derogatory remarks. When the guest was W.C. Fields, it was a verbal free-for-all between Fields and McCarthy. Bergen was the helpless moderator. This feud was long-running and, in 1939, led to the motion picture *You Can't Cheat an Honest Man.*

In 1938, the film *A Letter of Introduction,* starring Bergen and McCarthy, won a special Academy Award, an Oscar carved out of wood. Several films were produced in the 1940s featuring the Bergen-McCarthy duo. The last, in 1947, was a Walt Disney feature, *Fun and Fancy Free.*

Bergen introduced two other minor characters, the stuffy-nosed, laughing lumpkin Mortimer Snerd and the unrestrainable old maid Effie Klinker. He hosted a television show, "Do You Trust Your Wife?" for a short time. On September 21, 1978, he announced that he would retire October 11. He died September 30. Charlie McCarthy now sits silently in the Smithsonian.

Bergen appears with McCarthy in the 1991 stamp booklet featuring comedian caricatures by Hirschfeld.

John Blair

Scott 798
Born: 1732, Williamsburg, Virginia
Died: August 31, 1800, Williamsburg, Virginia

John Blair was educated at the College of William and Mary and Middle Temple in London. In 1766, he was elected to the Virginia House of Burgesses and represented the College of William and Mary from 1766 to 1770. He became clerk of the governor's council and held this post until 1775. He was a supporter of the cause for independence. He backed the non-importation movements against the British. In 1776, he helped draft the constitution for the commonwealth of Virginia and was elected to the Privy Council.

Blair began his career as a judge in 1778, when he was elected to the general court. Two years later he was elevated to the High Court of Chancery. He also sat as a judge of the Court of Appeals. On the Court of the Chancery, in the case of Commonwealth versus Caton, he held with the majority that the court could declare legislative acts unconstitutional. This was a landmark decision in lawmaking and legal checks and balances.

In 1787, he was a member of the Constitutional Convention. He signed the U.S. Constitution as a delegate from Virginia. He sided with the nationalists against the states' rights supporters in the Virginia delegation.

George Washington was elected president of the new United States in 1789, and Blair was among the first justices of the Supreme Court he appointed. Blair sat on the court with Chief Justices John Jay of New York, from 1789 to 1795, and John Rutledge of South Carolina in 1795. It was a period of little judicial activity. Blair retired in 1796, when Oliver Ellsworth of Connecticut became chief justice.

Blair held to the letter of the Constitution with regards to his judicial duties. In all the positions he held, from the House of Burgesses to the Supreme Court of the new United States, he brought broad learning, professional competence, and an eminent Virginia family name. He was the same age as George Washington, and they were close friends. Blair returned to Williamsburg in 1796 and spent the last four years of his life in quiet retirement.

Blair is one of the persons depicted on the Constitution Sesquicentennial stamp issued on September 17, 1937.

William Blount

Scott 798
Born: March 26, 1749, Bertie County, North Carolina
Died: March 21, 1800, Knoxville, Tennessee

Willam Blount had an excessive desire for wealth and gain. His activities in government earned him the distinction of being the first U.S. senator to be expelled from office. Nevertheless, his ambitions helped ultimately to found the state of Tennessee. President George Washington appointed Blount governor of the Tennessee Territory (1790-96) and superintendent of Indian affairs.

Agitation in favor of statehood continued to grow in Tennessee. When a head count in 1795 revealed that the population had passed the required 60,000, a constitutional convention assembled in Knoxville, the capital. The convention completed the drafting of the state's first constitution and, without waiting for congressional approval, provided for the immediate organization of the state government. In the election in March 1796, members of the General Assembly were chosen, and John Sevier was selected as governor. On June 1, Tennessee became the 16th state.

Blount had moved west from North Carolina to Tennessee because he was unable to win a seat in the U.S. Senate from North Carolina. He had served in the Revolutionary War. He was a delegate to the Continental Congress in 1787 and signed his name to the U.S. Constitution. He was a member of the North Carolina Legislature.

When Tennessee became a state, he was elected to the U.S. Senate. It was discovered that while he was governor of the Territory, he had been involved in illegal real-estate speculations. He had joined an ill-fated conspiracy to attack Spanish possessions in order to recoup his losses. In 1797, the House of Representatives voted to expel him. Nevertheless his popularity in Tennessee was so high that he was re-elected to the Senate. In 1799, the charges were dropped on the grounds that U.S. senators were not subject to impeachment.

In 1794, the University of Tennessee in Knoxville was chartered as Blount College, one of the first colleges west of the Blue Ridge Mountains.

Blount died in 1800. He is depicted in the painting *Adoption of the Constitution* on the Constitution Sesquicentennial stamp issued in 1937.

John Gutzon de la Mothe Borglum

Scott 1011
Born: March 25, 1871, Bear Lake, Idaho Territory
Died: March 6, 1941, Chicago, Illinois

Gutzon Borglum and his brother Solon Hannibal Borglum were the sons of Danish immigrants. At age 12, Gutzon left home and went to San Francisco. He worked as an apprentice to a lithographer, then for a fresco painter. He attended St. Mary's College in Xavier, Kansas. At age 19, he journeyed to New York, then went to Paris. In Paris, he attended the Academie Julien and the Ecole des Beaux-Arts. He became a good friend of the famous sculptor Francois Auguste Rodin. Borglum was pronouncedly influenced by Rodin.

In 1893, Borglum returned to New York City. Two year later he went to London, where his work was exhibited at the behest of Queen Victoria. In 1901, he returned to New York City to work mostly in sculpturing. The first piece of American sculpture purchased by the Metropolitan Museum of Art was Borglum's *Mares of Diomedes*. He created numerous sculptures, including the large head of Lincoln in the rotunda of the Capitol, Washington, D.C.

Borglum was commissioned to do a rendition of Robert E. Lee for the Daughters of the Confederacy to be placed on Stone Mountain, Georgia. He instead designed a huge 1,300-foot panoramic relief sculpture to be carved on the face of Stone Mountain. It depicts General Lee, his lieutenants and a procession of 2,000 soldiers. By 1924, the mounted figure of Lee was unveiled. The work stopped because of a disagreement between Borglum and the sponsors. The project was completed by others.

Borglum had his sights on a project on Mount Rushmore in the Black Hills of South Dakota dedicated in 1927. It featured 60-foot heads of George Washington, Thomas Jefferson, Abraham Lincoln, and Theodore Roosevelt. Upon Borglum's death in 1941, it fell to his son, James Lincoln de le Mothe Borglum, to finish the project.

Mount Rushmore is depicted on a 3¢ stamp issued in 1952.

Solon Hannibal Borglum

Scott 973
Born: December 22, 1868, Ogden, Utah
Died: January 31, 1922, Norwalk, Connecticut

Solon Borglum was the fourth child of six sons and three daughters of Danish immigrants to Utah. His father was a woodcarver, who later became a physician and practiced at Fremont, Nebraska. Borglum was the older brother, by three years, of the more famous Gutzon Borglum and uncle of the well-respected sculptor and photographer James Lincoln Borglum.

Solon Borglum's early schooling was at Fremont and Omaha and at Creighton College. At age 16, he was sent to western Nebraska as a cowboy on his father's 6,000-acre ranch, where he learned the form and movements of horses. His brother Gutzon, returning from Paris, saw Solon's drawings and urged him to take up art. Solon worked with his brother and moved to Santa Ana, California. One day a week he worked in his studio. The rest of the week he hobnobbed with the local Indians in the Sierra Madre Mountains. He made enough money to study at the Art Academy in Cincinnati and to study live horses at the United States Mail stables.

He studied under Louis F. Ribisso from 1895 to 1897 in the Cincinnati art school and in Paris under Emmanuel Fremiet, whose influence turned Borglum to sculpting figures of animals. He spent six months studying under Denys Puech at l'Academie Julien. His work progressed and was well received.

On December 10, 1898, he married Emma Vignal in Paris. The next summer the couple lived with the Sioux Indians on the Cow Creek Reservation located in central South Dakota. Borglum's sculptures centered around Indians, cowboys, horses and cattle. Other works of note were Soldiers and Sailors Monument, Danbury, Connecticut, and the Hurley Monument, Topeka, Kansas. He could also carve in marble and in wood. Five colossal portrait busts of generals of the Civil War by Borglum are in the Vicksburg National Park.

During World War I, he was too old to serve as a soldier, so he served as secretary to the Young Men's Christian Association. For his services, he was honored with the Croix de Guerre for courage under fire.

Borglum died in 1922, a few days after an operation for acute appendicitis at the relatively young age of 54.

His *Rough Riders* statue in Prescott, Arizona, is shown on a 1948 stamp.

Sandro Botticelli

Scott 2399
Born: 1445, Florence, Italy
Died: May 17, 1510, Florence, Italy

Sandro Botticelli was a Florentine Renaissance painter much favored by the Medici family. He painted large paintings featuring mythological subjects, such as *The Birth of Venus* (1778-86), depicting a nude female standing in a seashell, the first nude goddess in a major painting since the time of the Romans. He also provided a complete set of 19 small drawings to illustrate Dante's *Divine Comedy* printed by Lorenzo della Magna in 1481. In 1492-95, he again created drawings of Dante's work, about 100 in all. Through his brother Simone di Mariano, who shared his home at the Via Nuova, he became acquainted with the religious reformer and martyr, the Dominican friar Girolamo Savonarola. This may have influenced his painting in his later years.

Botticelli was born in a house in the Via Nuova, Borg' Ognissanti. His given name was Alessandro di Mariano dei Filipepi. His father was a tanner. His oldest brother, Giovanni, a prosperous broker, was called "Il Botticello," which means "the little barrel." For reasons unknown, Alessandro took this name and shortened his first name to Sandro.

A frail youth, he had a penchant for painting. When he was about 15, his father apprenticed him to Fra Filippo Lippi. He began painting as a livelihood in the 1470s, during the rule of Lorenzo il Magnifico (1449-92) of the House of Medici in Florence. Lorenzo had an earnest love both for letters and art. Under this pleasant tyrant, Florence prospered. Botticelli was busy satisfying the painting wants of these wealthy patrons, especially the Medicis.

During 1481-82, Botticelli served a commission at the Vatican, along with other artists, to decorate Sixtus IV's chapel. In Florence from 1482 to 1492, he painted most of his great altarpieces, such as the one now in the Uffizi with its circle of dancing angels around the Virgin in the sky. This was finished in 1490.

Botticelli produced little in his last 10 years. He died in 1510 and was buried in the Oraccio, the Borg' Ognissanti garden burial ground. The Madonna and Child by Botticelli was chosen for the 1988 Christmas stamp.

Henry Bouquet

Scott 1123
Born: 1719, Switzerland
Died: September 2, 1765, Pensacola, Florida

At age 17, Henry Bouquet became a professional soldier. He served in the military forces of Victor Amadeus II of the House of Savoy, king of Sardinia, and of William IV, prince of Orange. He transferred to the British Army, serving in the Royal American Regiment of Foot consisting of men from the Colonies during the French and Indian War (1754-60). The American segment of this Seven Years' War, pitting Britain against France, terminated in the Treaty of Paris, making Britain the pre-eminent Colonial power.

Bouquet was involved in disputes concerning the quartering of troops in Philadelphia and Charleston, which he handled with professional skill. He was placed second in command to General John Forbes on the expedition to capture Fort Duquesne (renamed Fort Pitt and later called Pittsbourgh by Forbes). Forbes had a force of 6,500, which included Bouquet's battalion of the Royal American Regiment of Foot, Richard Montgomery's Black Watch Hylanders, and 5,000 troops raised from Maryland, Pennsylvania, North Carolina and Virginia that included a detachment under the command of Colonel George Washington. The victory at Duquesne won the western frontier from France.

As Forbes' chief of staff, Bouquet issued the Proclamation Line of 1763, prohibiting English movement west of the Appalachian Mountains.

Bouquet was in command of troops during Chief Pontiac's rebellion, the so-called "Pontiac's War" that gained allegiance of tribes as far south as the lower Mississippi River. Pontiac was opposed to the Treaty of Paris. Bouquet was marching west from Carlisle, Pennsylvania, with a relief force of 460 men. Within 30 miles of Fort Pitt, at Edge Hill, a force of Indians fell upon his advance guard. Fighting lasted through the afternoon of August 5, 1763. The next morning the Indians stormed the hill, but Bouquet had two companies concealed that quickly pushed the Indians back into the forest. Bouquet camped at Bushy Run and thus gave his battle that name. Four days later he marched into Fort Pitt. He was awarded a military command of the southern Colonies, but in two years he died of a fever at Pensacola, Florida.

He is seen raising his hat in salute to Forbes, who is on the litter, on the 1958 Fort Duquesne stamp. Bouquet is just left of Washington, who is in the center.

William Bradford

Scott 550
Born: March 1590, Austerfield, Yorkshire, England
Died: May 9, 1657, Plymouth, Massachusetts

William Bradford was the son of William and Alice Bradford. His father was a farmer, who died before William was a year and a half old. His mother died before he had reached the age of 8. He was brought up by his grandparents and uncles. He became involved with the Separatist when he was about 16. These dissenters were persecuted by officers of the crown. To escape, Bradford went to Amsterdam with the Scrooby group in 1607. When the group found Leiden, Holland, more hospitable, Bradford moved to that city in 1609, along with John Robinson and his followers. In 1617, he became interested in moving to America with members of Robinson's congregation.

In the fall of 1620, he sailed on the *Mayflower* with 102 passengers. He left with his wife, Dorothy, but his son John remained behind. It took the *Mayflower* six weeks to cross the Atlantic to Cape Cod, where they anchored for a month, exploring the land for a suitable site to establish living quarters. Bradford's wife drowned while the ship was anchored.

In preparation for their future, 41 of the men, including Bradford, composed the Mayflower Compact of "just and equal laws, ordinances, acts ... unto which we promise all due submission and obedience . . ." The men were required to sign it before they were permitted to go ashore. Within four months, half of the company, including the first elected governor, John Carver, were dead from the severe winter and illness. Bradford was elected governor in April and was re-elected every year for 30 years, except five when he was an assistant.

He worked diligently to keep peace within the colony itself and with the surrounding Indians. He and Edward Winslow made peace with Chief Massasoit that lasted as long as both he and Massasoit lived.

In 1650, Bradford completed a *History of Plymouth Plantation*. In 1623, Bradford married Alice Southworth, the widow of one of his Leiden friends. Chief Massasoit stood by as one of their honored wedding guests.

Bradford was a signer of the Mayflower Compact depicted on the 5¢ stamp of the Pilgrim Tercentenary issue of December 21, 1920.

Matthew B. Brady

Scott 179
Born: 1823, Warren County, New York
Died: Janaury 15, 1896, New York, New York

To represent a likeness of a person, place or thing before photography, it was necessary for an artist to paint a picture, carve a statue or make a scratching in rock as accurately as possible.

Until photography was invented, an exact likeness was not possible. It took an artist days, weeks and months to render a likeness that today takes a cameraman a few minutes to snap and develop.

Matthew Brady was one of the most famous photographers of the 19th century. He established a portrait studio in New York City as early as 1842 using the daguerreotype to create his portraits.

By 1859, he had a branch studio in Washington, D.C. Before this time, he exhibited his pictures annually from 1844 to 1878 in the American Institute competition, receiving a silver medal each year. He received the first gold medal ever awarded for a daguerrotype in 1849. In 1850, he held an exhibition called the "Gallery of Illustrious Americans."

In 1855, photography was well developed, and Brady converted his studio to the new techniques. He photographed every U.S. president, from John Quincy Adams through William McKinley, except William Henry Harrison, who died only one month after he took office.

When the Civil War came along, Brady decided to tell the complete story of the war with photographs. He hired a staff of photographers to cover the battles and events. He personally went into the battlefields and photographed scenes of the war. His pictures have formed the basis for illustrations in many history books.

At first, the government refused to buy his photographs. The enthusiasm of his work in the Civil War and the Panic of 1873 left Brady in poor financial straits from which he never recovered.

The daguerreotype *Zachary Taylor, Hero of the Mexican War*, attributed to Matthew B. Brady, was used for a 5¢ stamp issued June 1875.

David Brearly

Scott 798
Born: June 11, 1745, Spring Grove (near Trenton), New Jersey
Died: August 16, 1790, Trenton, New Jersey

David Brearly's pre-American forebears lived in Yorkshire, England. Ancestor John B. Brearly emigrated to America in 1680 and settled near Trenton, New Jersey. David was the son of David and Mary Clark Brearly, who lived at Spring Grove, now Groveville, a village on Crosswicks Creek.

Young David studied law and set up law practice in nearby Allentown, a village 10 miles southwest of the heart of Trenton. About 1767, at age 22, he married Elizabeth Mullen of Trenton. She died. On April 17, 1783, he married Elizabeth Higbee.

Brearly was so vociferous as a Whig at the beginning of the Revolutionary movement that he was jailed for treason. The citizens were on his side, and a large group mobbed the jail and freed him. On November 28, 1776, he was appointed a lieutenant colonel of the 4th New Jersey militia. A month later, January 1, 1777, he was assigned to the 1st New Jersey militia. He served until August 4, 1779, when he resigned. He continued to serve after the war as a colonel in the militia. Though he was an officer and assigned to a unit, his military career was inconspicuous.

He was a member of the New Jersey Constitutional Convention. On June 10, 1779, he was elected chief justice of the Supreme Court of New Jersey. The most important case that came before him was the case of Holmes versus Walton. His decision, rendered in 1780, represented an early expression of the principle of judicial power over unconstitutional legislation.

Brearly was a delegate to the Federal Convention of 1787. On September 17, with the other members of the convention from New Jersey, he affixed his signature to the U.S. Constitution.

Brearly was a presidential elector and was U.S. district judge from 1789 until his death at age 45. He was active in the Masonic lodge and was the vice president of the New Jersey Society of the Cincinnati. At the Episcopal General Convention in 1786, he was a delegate and helped compile its prayer book.

David Brearly and the other signers of the U.S. Constitution are memorialized on the sesquicentennial stamp issued September 7, 1937.

William Brewster

Scott 550
Born: January 1567, South Yorkshire? England
Died: April 10, 1644, Plymouth, Massachusetts

In 1571, when he was 4 years old, William Brewster moved to Scrooby Manor, South Yorkshire, with his parents. It is likely that he was born nearby. In 1575, his father was appointed bailiff of Scrooby Manor, one of the exempt estates of the Archbishop of York. In 1588, Queen Elizabeth appointed the elder Brewster master of the post-house at Scrooby.

William Brewster entered Peterhouse College, Cambridge, in December 1580. It was here that he was indoctrinated into the ideology of separatism. In 1583, without finishing his education at Cambridge, he entered the house of William Davison, secretary to Queen Elizabeth, as a retainer. He accompanied Davison on missions to Scotland and the Netherlands. Davison was retired because of his close connection in the execution of Mary Stuart on February 8, 1587, but Brewster remained in his service until 1589, when he returned to assist his ailing father. He served for his father until the elder Brewster's death in 1590. He assumed the positions his father had held in Scrooby.

In 1591, William Brewster married. With his wife Mary, he had six children. They separated from the Church of England in 1606, and Brewster served as one of the principal members of the Separatists. In 1607, John Robinson joined them. In 1608, the group went to Amsterdam, then in 1609 to Leiden, Holland. The same year Robinson was ordained as the minister and Brewster as the the ruling elder of the congregation. Robinson was instrumental in getting the group together for sailing to America, but he stayed behind.

Brewster sailed on the *Mayflower* with two of his sons and as guardian of two other boys. In Plymouth, he was the spiritual leader, but not the minister. He held services of prayer and praise, but was not allowed to preach, baptize or celebrate the communion. Nevertheless he remained the true leader of the Plymouth church. Brewster was second only to Governor William Bradford. In 1627, he became one of the undertakers who assumed the colony's debt.

Brewster is one of the signers of the Mayflower Compact depicted on the 5¢ stamp of the Pilgrim Tercentenary issue of December 21, 1920.

Fanny Brice

Scott 2565
Born: October 29, 1891, New York, New York
Died: May 29, 1951, Los Angeles, California

Fanny Brice had a natural clown face. Her impish eyes and her large, smiling mouth with a pouting lower lip gave her a teasing, puckish look that she exploited in her act as the misbehaving, stubborn Baby Snooks. Baby Snooks sat on the floor dressed in white frills and, as any baby would do, squalled and fussed until she was pacified with a lollipop. Baby Snooks was a brat.

Brice's parents were Jewish immigrants to New York City. Her father was a barkeeper on the Lower East Side. Early in her career, Fanny changed her name from Fannie Borach to Fanny Brice, which became her stage name. She started her career at the Keeney Theater in Brooklyn when she was 13. At an amateur contest, she won first place singing a song titled *When You Know You're Not Forgotten by the Girl You Can't Forget*. At age 16, Brice auditioned for a part as a dancer in the chorus line in *Talk of New York*, produced by George M. Cohan and Sam Harris. She didn't get the job.

When she was 19, Brice was spotted by Florenz Ziegfeld, who went to a performance at a third-rate burlesque house in Brooklyn where Brice was a singer. Ziegfeld signed her up for his *Follies*. She starred in more performances at the *Follies* than any other artist. Her real fame came when she sang *My Man*. This heart-throbbing, French torch song became her trademark. At the *Follies*, Brice performed with such greats as W.C. Fields, Will Rogers and Eddy Cantor. She also starred in *Music Box Review* in 1924 and *Crazy Quilt* in 1930.

She appeared in one play, David Belasco's *Fanny*, and a few movies. She also played the Baby Snooks role at the *Follies*, more or less for friends. It was her standard persona on her radio show from 1936 until her death in 1951.

Brice's two marriages ended in divorce. The first marriage was to Nicholas Arnstein, a shady Broadway gambler and speculator, with whom she had two children. The second was to Billy Rose, the stage producer of *Crazy Quilt*.

In 1939, Brice's remarkable career was the subject of the movie *Rose of Washington Square*, and her life story was told in the 1964 Broadway musical *Funny Girl*. In 1968, it was made into a movie starring Barbara Streisand.

Brice was honored philatelically in 1991 on one of five 29¢ commemoratives in the Comedians by Hirschfeld booklet.

John Brooks

Surrender at Saratoga 1777 by Trumbull

US Bicentennial 13 cents

Scott 1728
Born: May 1, 1752, Medford, Massachusetts
Died: March 1, 1825, Medford, Massachusetts

John Brooks' parents, Caleb and Ruth Albee Brooks, were farmers. Young Brooks studied with Dr. Simon Tufts, the local physician, from 1766 to 1773. He was awarded a medical degree from Dr. Tufts' college. Brooks practiced medicine in Reading, Massachusetts. He met and married Lucy Smith.

During his boyhood, he was much impressed by soldiers. He joined the Minute Men and captained the company from Reading. He answered the call to Concord on April 19, 1775, and took his company into the fight at Meriam's Corners. His company then pursued the Red Coats as they retreated. For this, Massachusetts awarded him the rank of major. Brooks was in the fight at Bunker Hill. On January 1, 1776, he was appointed a major in the Continental Army. He took part in the battles of Long Island and White Plains.

When he was with the 8th Massachusetts line regiment, he was promoted to lieutenant colonel. His unit was instrumental in taking Breyman's fort on Bemis' Heights on October 7, 1777. He served General Washington on Baron Friedrich von Steuben's staff. He was one of three to present to Congress compaints from discontented officers who served at Newburgh in the winter of 1782-83. The results were discouraging. Brooks was accused of stirring up insurrection. Nevertheless, he received an honorable discharge on June 12, 1783, and returned to take over Dr. Tufts' medical practice at Medford.

Brooks was appointed major general over the militia of Middlesex in 1786. When Daniel Shays rebelled, Brooks marched to Worcester. In 1791, Washington appointed him federal marshal for the Massachusetts district and made him a brigadier-general in 1792. President Adams nominated him major general in the provisional army during the French troubles.

Brooks was a member of the Massachusetts ratifying convention. He was twice elected to the House and was state senator for Middlesex County. In 1816, he was elected governor of Massachusetts. He was re-elected six times.

Brooks is the third person from the right in Trumbull's painting *Surrender at Saratoga* on the stamp issued October 7, 1977.

Jacob Broom

Scott 798
Born: 1752, Wilmington, Delaware
Died: April 10, 1810, Philadelphia, Pennsylvania

Jacob Broom was a man of many talents. His birthplace and home was Delaware. His father was a blacksmith and farmer. Jacob was the eldest son. He followed in his father's footsteps in farming. He also was a mathematician and put his knowledge to work as a surveyor. However, he made his living in shipping and real estate. He was a talented map maker. During the Battle of Brandywine, his detailed maps were of considerable value. This was his only record of military service.

He represented his state in political matters. He was assistant burgess of Wilmington from 1776 to 1785. He served as chief burgess four times. He also served as borough assessor and justice of the peace for New Castle County.

Broom sat in the Delaware state legislature from 1784 to 1786 and again in 1788. He was chosen as a delegate to the Annapolis Convention, although he did not attend. In 1787, he was one of the Delaware representatives to the Constitutional Convention. He signed the U.S. Constitution. From 1784 to 1788, he served in the Delaware state legislature.

Following the Constitutional Convention, Broom returned to Wilmington. His home was located near the Brandywine River. He served the city in various capacities, both in politics and business. He was Wilmington's first postmaster.

Jacob Broom saw the necessity of producing cotton goods in America by modern methods with machines. He established the first cotton mill in the Brandywine region in 1795. He was successful in his business and was a levelheaded man in his dealings with government. He chaired the board of directors of Wilmington's Delaware Bank.

Broom also served on the board of trustees of the College of Wilmington. He died at age 58 while in Philadelphia on business. He was buried at Christ Church Burial Ground in Philadelphia.

Broom is depicted in the painting *Adoption of the Constitution* on the Constitution Sesquicentennial issue of September 17, 1937.

Charles Bulfinch

Bulfinch 1763-1844 Boston State House

Architecture USA 15c

Scott 1781
Born: August 8, 1763, Boston, Massachusetts
Died: April 4, 1844, Boston, Massachusetts

Charles Bulfinch was the son of Thomas Bulfinch, a Boston physician, and Susan Apthorp. Charles was educated in the Boston Latin school and Harvard, graduating in 1781. He spent the next several years in Europe, where he studied architectural works recommended to him by Thomas Jefferson.

He settled in Boston in 1787 as Boston's first professional architect. In 1788, he married Hanna Apthorp, with whom he had 11 children. One son was Stephen Greenleaf Bulfinch, a prominent Unitarian clergyman. Another was Thomas Bulfinch, an author of classical history and mythology, the author of *Bulfinch's Mythology* in three works of mythological and legendary lore.

One of Charles Bulfinch's first commissions was the Massachusetts State House. This building on Beacon Hill served Oliver Wendell Holmes as "the hub of the universe." Completed in 1800, it was the most conspicuous public building in the United States (the nation's Capitol was not completed until 1830). The Boston Theater is Bulfinch's architectural rendition. In 1788, the old Hossis Street Church was built from his design, as were churches in Taunton and Pittsfield. He is also responsible for the design of the Connecticut State House in Hartford. For Washington's reception in Boston, he designed and erected the triumphal arch.

From 1792, he designed and built several important houses using, for the first time in New England, the circular staircase. At age 27, he was elected to the Board of Selectmen of Boston. He saw to it that Boston had lighted streets and new systems of drainage. He reorganized the police and fire departments and promoted the admission of both sexes to the public schools.

In the depression of 1796, he declared bankruptcy, but he recovered. He was re-elected to the Board of Selectmen as its chairman until December 1817, when President James Monroe selected him to be fourth in line in supervising the building of the nation's Capitol. Hallet, Thornton, and Latrobe preceded him. He also designed the Unitarian church in Washington and the state capitol in Augusta, Maine. He returned to Boston at the age of 67 and retired.

Bulfinch is honored in the 1976 American Architecture issue showing the Boston State House building.

34

Pierce Butler

Scott 798
Born: July 11, 1744, County Carlow, Ireland
Died: February 15, 1822, Philadelphia, Pennsylvania

Pierce Butler was born in Ireland, the third son of Sir Richard Butler, baronet, member of Parliament for County Carlow from 1729 to 1761. His mother's name was Henrietta (Percy) Butler.

Pierce Butler was a major in His Majesty's 29th Regiment. When he met and married, in 1771, Mary Middleton of South Carolina, he made his home in South Carolina. He devoted himself to planting and delved into politics. He resigned his commission with the 29th Regiment in 1773.

In 1779, he held the office of adjutant general of South Carolina and was a representative in the state legislature. In 1784, he was at odds with Christopher Gadsden by opposing the planter-merchant group in state politics and championing the democracy of the back country instead. He wanted to remove the state capital, and wanted property re-evaluation.

Nevertheless, he was elected by the legislature in commissions to establish the boundaries of the state. On March 6, 1787, he was elected to the Congress of the Confederation, and on March 8, to the Federal Convention. He authored the fugitive slave clause, promoted a strong central government and proposed that property be part of the basis for representation. He was one of the signers from South Carolina of the U.S. Constitution on September 17, 1787. He returned to South Carolina in time to defend the Constitution in assembly but did not sit in the ratification convention. Butler was elected to the Senate as a Federalist in 1789 and was re-elected in 1792. He opposed the Jay Treaty.

In 1796, he resigned from the Senate and returned to his home state with the intention of becoming a candidate for governor. But when the time came for nomination, he refused to have his name entered. In 1802, he was elected to fill an unexpired term in the Senate.

Butler denounced the 12th Amendment. He charged that the Republican party was abusing its powers as the Federalists had done. In January 1806, he again resigned his senatorial seat.

He is depicted on the painting *Adoption of the Constitution* on the Constitution Sesquicentennial stamp issued September 17, 1937.

Juan Rodriguez Cabrillo

Scott 2704
Born: between 1500 and 1510, in Portugal
Died: early 1543, San Miguel Island (now California)

In Southern California, the name Cabrillo is well known. After World War II, four major freeways were built leading to the city's suburbs: Mission Valley, Wabash, Montgomery and Cabrillo. A peninsula between the Pacific Ocean and San Diego Bay curves down and out from Old Town San Diego. At its southernmost tip is the Point Loma Lighthouse, adjacent to which is a half-acre site set aside by the U.S. Government in 1913 for the Cabrillo National Monument. Running down the center of this peninsula, alongside Rosecrans National Cemetery through the Fort Rosecrans Military Reservation, is the Cabrillo Memorial Drive. These landmarks are named to honor Juan Rodriguez Cabrillo, an early explorer of the California coast.

Cabrillo was probably born in Portugal. This is conjecture since nothing is recorded of him prior to 1520, when he was in service with Panfilo de Narvaez. He left Narvaez at Vera Cruz to take part in the conquest of Mexico with Hernan Cortez. Afterward, in Guatemala and Honduras, he was associated with Pedro de Alvarado, planning explorations in the Pacific.

In 1541, Alvarado was killed in the Mixton War. Antonio de Mendoza, viceroy of New Spain, assigned two ships to Cabrillo to carry on the Pacific Coast exploration. The following year, 1542, Cabrillo sighted San Diego, then San Pedro Bay at Long Beach, Santa Catalina Island, Santa Monica Bay, Santa Barbara Channel and its islands in the Pacific. He went north to Monterey Bay and on up the coast as far as Point Reyes, just north of San Francisco's Golden Gate. He failed to see the Golden Gate.

Cabrillo and his fleet returned to Santa Barbara Channel islands to spend the winter. Near San Miguel Island, early in 1543, Cabrillo sustained a serious fall. He broke his leg and died from complications. A projection of land 110 miles north of Cabrillo's farthest northern discovery is called Point Cabrillo.

Cabrillo is honored with a 1992 29¢ stamp.

Thomas Carlyle

Scott 1082
Born: December 4, 1795, Ecclefechan, Dumfriesshire, Scotland
Died: February 5, 1881, London, England

Thomas Carlyle was the son of James Carlyle, a mason and farmer, and his second wife, Margaret Aitken. Thomas was the eldest of nine children. He started school at age 5 and entered Annan grammar school at age 10. In 1809, he entered the University of Edinburgh. In 1814, he was the master of mathematics at Annan. He obtained a position at Kirkcaldy under Edward Irving, with whom he became a close friend. When Irving left the school in 1818, Carlyle also resigned. Carlyle studied Goethe extensively. He suffered anxieties and dyspepsia. In 1822, through Irving's recommendation, he became a private tutor. This and some literary work enabled him to help his brother John study medicine and his brother Alexander to acquire a farm.

Irving introduced Carlyle to Jane Baille Welsh. They married on October 17, 1826, and lived in Edinburgh. Later they moved to the farm at Craigenputt on Alexander Carlyle's farm. Thomas quietly labored through *Sartor Resartus*.

In late 1831, he went to work in London but returned to the farm in 1832. In 1833, the Carlyles went to Edinburgh, and in the summer of 1834, they settled in London, at 5 Cheyne Row, Chelsea, their home the remainder of Carlyle's life. He was eager to write the *French Revolution*. The publication marked the turning point of his career. In 1839 appeared *Chartism*. His next great work was *Life and Letters of Oliver Cromwell*. Carlyle's *History of Frederick the Great* was finished in 1865, the year he received the rectorship of the University of Edinburgh. In 1866, he began his *Reminiscences*.

As he had requested, when he died, he was buried in Ecclefechan instead of in Westminster Abbey. He gave his books to Harvard College.

Carlyle's name and a quotation, "Labor is Life," appears on a scroll in the lower left corner of the Labor Day stamp issued September 3, 1956.

Lodovico Carracci

CHRISTMAS
USA 25
Carracci, National Gallery

Scott 2427
Born: (Baptized) April 21, 1555, Bologna, Italy
Died: November 13, 1619, Bologna, Italy

Lodovico Carracci, with his two cousins Annibale and Agostino Carracci, and the anatomist Anthony de la Tour, opened an academy in Bologna under the name of the Incamminati, about 1586. They worked together until 1600. Their school has been called eclectic since they combined what they learned from Tintoretto and other masters in Venice, Antonio Correggio's works in Parma, and from nature. Their works, combining elegant forms and grotesque ornamentation, helped establish the style known as baroque.

Lodovico Carracci was the son of a butcher in Bologna. Lodovico began his studies under Tintoretto in Venice, and other painters in the cities of northern Italy. He persuaded Agostino, who was studying goldsmithing, and Annibale, who was to be a tailor like his father, to study painting. He sent Agostino to study with Prospero Fontana in Bologna. He later sent both Annibale and Agostino to Parma and Venice to copy the work of Titian, Tintoretto and Correggio. Upon their return, they formed their family studio. The three worked together on many commissioned frescoes.

In the Pinacoteca, Bologna, is Lodovico's *Madonna dei Bargellina,* done about 1588. The *Holy Family with St. Francis,* in the Museo Civico in Cento, a town just north of Bologna on the Reno River, was finished in 1591. His *Transfiguration* in the Pinacoteca shows a change in his technique, following the style of Tintoretto, whose figures appear elongated.

Lodovico abandoned the discipline of following carefully executed and composed drawings and began spontaneous painting, as exemplified in the *Martyrdom of St. Angelus* in the Pinacoteca, finished in 1599.

Agostino died in Parma in 1601. Annibale died in 1609. Lodovico carried on alone at the Bologna studio until his death in 1619 at age 64.

An example of Lodovico's painting, the Madonna and Child from *The Dream of St. Catherine of Alexandria* at the National Gallery of Art in Washington, D.C., is shown on the 1989 traditional Christmas stamp.

Charles Carroll

Scott 1691
Born: September 19, 1737, Annapolis, Maryland
Died: November 14, 1832, Baltimore, Maryland

Because Charles Carroll lived to age 95, and being relatively young, 39, at the time of the Declaration of Independence, he was the last surviving signer of the Declaration. Carroll studied in France at Jesuit schools and in England at the Inner Temple, London. He returned to Maryland in 1765 at age 28. The Stamp Act piqued his interest in politics. He was a firm advocate of the Colonial patriots and gained notice through a newspaper debate with Daniel Dulany, a Loyalist Maryland lawyer.

From 1773 to 1776, Carroll was active in local committees and served on the committees of correspondence and safety. In 1774 and 1776, he attended the first Maryland convention and in 1776, on behalf of the Continental Congress, went with Benjamin Franklin, Samuel Chase and his cousin Bishop John Carroll on a fruitless mission to secure Canadian aid for the Revolution.

In July 1776, Carroll was elected to the Second Continental Congress. He signed the Declaration of Independence on August 2, 1776, though he had not been elected until the day on which that document was adopted.

In 1777, Carroll took an active part in politics and was elected to the Maryland Senate. Later in 1777, he returned to the Continental Congress and served on several committees, especially the Board of War. Although he was urged to serve on the Continental Congress of 1787, he gave his full support to the Maryland Senate instead. In 1789, he was elected to the U.S. Senate. He served in the Senate from 1789 to 1792.

In 1801, he retired to manage his estate. The first stone was laid at Mount Clare, an estate on the outskirts of Baltimore, on July 4, 1828, 52 years following the Declaration of Independence. He was one of the original directors of the Baltimore and Ohio Railroad.

Of the men seated before the men standing in the first stamp of the Declaration of Independence set issued in 1976, Carroll is fifth from the left.

Daniel Carroll

Scott 798
Born: July 22, 1730, Upper Marlboro, Maryland
Died: May 7, 1796, Rock Creek, Forest Glen, Maryland

The name Carroll was an old and distinguished name in the Colonies. Charles Carroll established the line of descendants that included Charles Carroll of Carrollton, signer of the Declaration of Independence, and Kean Carroll of Upper Marlboro. Kean married Eleanor Darnall and with her had two sons, John Carroll and Daniel Carroll. John was appointed a bishop of the Roman Catholic Church and as such went with Samuel Chase, Benjamin Franklin and his cousin Charles Carroll to Canada in a futile effort to obtain support from the Catholic French for the American Revolution.

Daniel went to Flanders for his education in 1742, as did John a few years later. Daniel remained in Flanders for six years. John went on to France, where he entered the Jesuit order at Walten. Daniel returned and married Elizabeth Carroll of Duddington, a first cousin of Charles Carroll of Carrollton. Daniel must have fallen heir to his father's rather considerable estate. About 1781, he is spoken of as "a man of large fortune and influence in his state."

In 1781, he was elected a delegate to the Continental Congress and on March 1 signed the Articles of Confederation. He was the only Catholic to do so. On May 26, 1787, he was appointed a delegate to the Constitutional Convention. He, along with other wealthy property owners, favored a centralized government. Chase had written to advise his countrymen to delay ratification, and Carroll wrote a persuasive and judicious letter to the *Maryland Journal* in answer to Chase. Carroll drafted the First Amendment that spelled out the freedoms of religion, speech, press and the right to assemble.

He was elected senator from Maryland to the First U.S. Congress. He voted to have the District of Columbia located on the banks of the Potomac. His friendship with George Washington resulted in Carroll being one of the commissioners to survey these limits. Carroll's nephew, Daniel Carroll of Duddington, owned much of this property, thus causing complications that resulted in the dismissal of Pierre Charles L'Enfant, the architect of the capital. Carroll resigned in May 1795, because of poor health. He died the next year.

He is depicted in the painting *Adoption of the Constitution* on the Constitution Sesquicentennial stamp issued September 17, 1937.

John Carver

Scott 550
Born: circa 1576, Nottinghamshire, England
Died: April 1621, Plymouth, Massachusetts

John Carver left England in 1609 and went to Holland to join the Separatists living in Leiden. He became a deacon of the church. In 1617, the Separatists were considering going to America to seek religious freedom. Carver returned to England in 1617 with Robert Cushman to negotiate with the Virginia Company of London for financial support for the voyage. The Virginia company gave them nothing. Carver and Cushman returned to Leiden empty-handed. In 1619, Carver again went to England with Cushman. This time they obtained financial support from Thomas Weston, who headed a group of English merchants willing to invest in the Pilgrims' venture.

Cushman did not sail with his friend Carver. Carver boarded the *Mayflower* with his wife Catherine and six servants. Cushman boarded the *Speedwell*. When the *Speedwell* proved unseaworthy and returned twice, Cushman remained behind. In November, the *Mayflower* arrived in America and anchored near the site of what is today Provincetown, and after a month moved across the bay to a more favorable location. The Pilgrims named their village Plymouth in honor of the port from which they sailed.

The Pilgrim colony is deserving of fame, not because of its numbers, but because of the political ideals of its people. Unlike the colony in Virginia, the Plymouth colony had no charter. The Pilgrims organized themselves into a self-governing community. They announced that they would make their own laws, and they promised to obey the laws they made in the Mayflower Compact, which Carver and 40 of the other family heads signed. Their doctrine of home rule was destined to become the dominant political belief in the Colonies.

Carver was elected the first governor of the Plymouth Plantation in November 1620. He organized the colony. During the first winter, many colonists died from illness and the severe weather. Carver was so weakened from illness that he never recovered. In April 1621, he died.

Carver is one of the signers of the Mayflower Compact depicted on the 5¢ stamp of the Pilgrim Tercentenary issue of December 21, 1920.

Giuseppe Ceracchi

Scott 143
Born: July 4, 1751, Rome, Italy
Died: January 30, 1802, Paris, France

Giuseppe Ceracchi was among those sculptors who in the late 19th century imparted the neoclassic genre in Rome. He was inspired by Roman imperial portraits and executed busts of contemporary figures, such as the one of Johann Joachim Winklemann, now in the Roma Museo Capitolium. He also created the busts of notable personages for the U.S. Capitol. The Library of Congress (located in the Capitol from 1800 to 1895) was almost totally destroyed by an accidental fire on December 24, 1851. More than three-fifths of the books were burned, and many paintings, portraits and busts were lost. At least four sculptured busts attributed to Ceracchi were destroyed: Christopher Columbus, Americus Vespucius, Thomas Jefferson and George Washington.

Ceracchi studied with Tommaso Righi in Rome. When he was about 24, he went to London. He rendered busts of Sir Joshua Reynolds, Lord Shelburn, Viscount Keppel and others. On the facade of Sommerset House, he created the statue *Strength and Temperance*. It won wide acclaim.

In the early days, the United States could not boast of any native sculptors until William Rush began working as a carver of ship figureheads in Philadelphia. Two academies of art were founded, in Philadelphia and New York. Both imported collections of plaster casts of Greek and Roman sculpture from the Musee Napoleon. The enthusiastic and eccentric Ceracchi visited Philadelphia from 1791 to 1794 and made busts of several notables, including George Washington, Alexander Hamilton, Benjamin Franklin and Thomas Jefferson. He had hoped to incorporate these portraits into a marble monument to Liberty.

Ceracchi returned to Milan and modeled several busts of Napoleon, who invited him to Paris. His allegiance to Napoleon must have been seriously thwarted, for he turned against the emperor and joined in a conspiracy to assassinate Napoleon. Ceracchi was captured and imprisoned. On January 30, 1802, he was executed by the guillotine.

His bust of Alexander Hamilton was selected for the 1870 30¢ stamp.

Jean-Baptiste Simeon Chardin

Scott 1535
Born: November 2, 1699, Paris, France
Died: December 6, 1779, Paris, France

Jean Baptist Simeon Chardin was the son of master carpenter Jean Chardin of Paris. By the time young Jean was 30 years of age, he was admitted to the Royal Academy of Painting and Sculpture (1728). He studied with Pierre Jacques Cazes, known for his renditions of scenes of historical interest, and with Noel Nicolas Coypel, whose interest was mainly mythological subjects. Chardin focused on pictures of inanimate objects and animals. In 1728, he painted *The Rayfish*. The painting is in the Louvre in Paris.

Still life continued to be his forte, along with paintings that depicted scenes and events from the everyday life of ordinary people. Chardin followed the style of the masters in the Low Countries, including Pieter de Hooch and Gabriel Metsu. He incorporated arrangements that would stand alone as a painting of still life, such as the inkwell and quill in *Boy with a Top*. His paintings capture touching events, as exemplified by the mother and her two children saying grace in *Le Benedicte*.

In 1740, Chardin was awarded an audience with King Louis XV, who so admired his work that he added two of Chardin's works to his own collection. These were *Benediction* and *Industrious Mother*. Both now hang in the Louvre.

When Chardin was about 60, he won the right to a private apartment in the Louvre. He obtained lucrative commissions from the Marquis de Marigny to decorate the interior of the Chateau de Choisy and the Chateau de Bellevue, panels of which are housed in the Louvre. Engraved copies of his works were printed by Charles Nicolas Cochin. Even when his eyesight began to fail in his later years, Chardin painted pastels that were among the best of the century.

A Chardin painting appears on a 1974 stamp honoring the Universal Postal Union and letter writing.

Charles II of Great Britain

Scott 1230
Born: May 29, 1630, Whitehall Palace, London, England
Died: February 6, 1685, London, England

Charles was the son of Charles I and Henrietta Maria. At age 8, he began his education under the Duke of Newcastle. At age 15, to escape the civil war, he went to the west of England under the governorship of Sir Edward Hyde. In July 1646, he joined his mother in Paris. He studied two years in Paris under Thomas Hobbes. Charles I was executed January 30, 1649. Young Charles was proclaimed king of Scotland, parts of Ireland and the Channel Islands.

At age 20, he pledged himself to the Presbyterian faith, thus strengthening the Loyalists. He was defeated by Oliver Cromwell at the Battle of Worcester and sailed for France on October 15, 1651. He was advised by loyalists, the Duke of Ormonde (Hyde) and, in 1654, by Sir Edward Nicholas. Charles next escaped to Germany. In 1656, he was in Belgium living on a small pension from Spain. Cromwell died in 1658.

In 1659, Charles went to Fuenterrabia in northern Spain to acquire military aid, but for naught. A Loyalist uprising in England also failed. Through the efforts of the Duke of Albemarle (George Monck), power was restored for the Independents of the Presbyterians. Charles followed Monck's advice and issued the Declaration of Breda on April 4, 1660, and on May 8, 1660, at age 30, he was proclaimed the king of England. His council consisted both of Loyalists and former rebels. Order was returned, and a government was organized. Hyde, now Earl of Clarendon, continued to be Charles' adviser. The Navigation Act of 1651 was re-enacted. The Indemnity Bill was disputed by the king, and 25 of the people involved in the execution of Charles I were executed.

On April 23, 1661, Charles was crowned. This was followed by the realignment of church and state. He settled many foreign affairs, especially with Spain. In 1662, Charles married Catherine of Braganze, Portugal, drawing England closer to France.

On March 24, 1663, the proprietors of Carolina were put in control of what is now North and South Carolina, Georgia and part of Florida. Among the proprietors were Hyde and Monck. The domain that had been chartered by Charles lasted until it became a royal colony in 1729. Charles II's name is on the first page of the Carolina Charter that is depicted on a 1963 stamp.

Samuel P. Chase

Scott 1691
Born: April 17, 1741, Princess Anne, Maryland
Died: June 19, 1811, Washington, D.C.

Samuel Chase's parents moved to Baltimore when he was 2 years old. Chase was admitted to the bar at Annapolis in 1761. Three years later he took his seat in the Maryland Colonial legislature, from 1764 to 1776, and continued in the state legislature from 1776 to 1785. In 1765, he was a leader against the Stamp Act. He twice served as a delegate to the Continental Congress.

In 1776, Chase joined Benjamin Franklin, Charles Carroll and Bishop John Carroll on a trip to Canada seeking aid, but to no avail. He returned in time to sign the Declaration of Independence.

His resignation from the Congress in 1778, after serving on several committees, came about because of unscrupulous dealings in the flour market, brought to light by Alexander Hamilton. Chase returned for a year in 1784 and attended the conferences organizing the Constitutional Convention. He did not attend the convention. When it came time for Maryland to ratify the Constitution, Chase voted against it.

In 1788, he was appointed chief judge of the criminal court of Baltimore. In 1791, he was chief judge of the Maryland general court, holding both positions at the same time. In 1796, President Washington appointed him to the Supreme Court. Chase was quite conspicuous for the next five years. When John Marshall was appointed chief justice in 1801, Chase's position waned. His partisan and pugnacious actions made him a target for impeachment.

Thomas Jefferson pressured the House of Representatives into voting for impeachment of Chase in 1804. Charges were heard in the Senate in February 1805, and on the phrase "high crimes and misdemeanors," the Senate, by construing the expression strictly, found Chase not guilty. Chase was the only Supreme Court justice to be impeached. He stayed on the bench until he died.

Of the men standing in the first stamp on the four se-tenant series of July 4, 1976, Chase is standing second from the left.

Dennis Chavez

Scott 2185
Born: April 8, 1888, Los Chavez, New Mexico
Died: November 18, 1962, Washington, D.C.

Dennis Chavez was born of Spanish-American parents in the village of his own name, Los Chavez, in Valencia County, New Mexico. Los Chavez was a town of fewer than 500 people, located some 30 miles south of Albuquerque.

Chavez quit school at age 13 to work in politics. He helped a local Democratic office-seeker, even though Chavez himself was too young to cast a vote. For his work, Chavez was awarded a clerkship in Washington, D.C., to assist Senator Andrieus A. Jones, who needed a Spanish-speaking interpreter in his 1916 campaign. This experience encouraged Chavez to pursue the fields of law and political science.

Chavez attended Georgetown University from 1917 to 1920 and was awarded a bachelor of laws degree. He was admitted to the bar. He returned to Albuquerque to begin his practice and to serve in the state legislature. He represented New Mexico in the U.S. Congress for two terms, from 1931 to 1934. In 1935, he was appointed to fill a vacant seat in the Senate, which made up for his senatorial election loss in 1934. In 1936, he was elected to return to that seat, and was re-elected in 1940, 1946 and 1952.

In the mid-1950s, his Senate seat was challenged because of supposed voting irregularities in New Mexico. Chavez was not charged, however, and he did not lose his position. He was again re-elected in 1958.

Chavez was a staunch Democrat and supported Franklin D. Roosevelt's New Deal bills. He fought to develop resources in the West and in support of the causes of native Americans. He likewise championed Latin American affairs, especially in Puerto Rico. He was dubbed "Puerto Rico's Senator" for his support of reciprocal trade agreements.

Chavez served as chairman of the Senate Public Works Committee and as second-ranking member of the Appropriations Committee. His diligent work led to the establishment of the federal Fair Employment Practices Commission. He also labored on behalf of federal aid to the needy and child welfare programs. He was the champion of the poor.

In 1991, a 35¢ Great Americans stamp was issued to honor Chavez.

Abraham Clark

Scott 1692
Born: February 15, 1726, Elizabethtown, New Jersey
Died: September 15, 1794, Elizabethtown, New Jersey

Abraham Clark spent his youth in Elizabethtown, New Jersey, where he studied civil law and mathematics. He served the people of New Jersey by arbitrating land disputes for those in need. He became known as the "poor man's counselor." He drew up deeds, leases and other writings for transferring titles to property. He made use of his mathematic studies in surveying.

He was known as "Congress Abraham" for his participation in several congresses. In 1775, he served in the New Jersey provisional congress. From 1784 to 1787, he was elected to the state legislature. He was a delegate from New Jersey to the Annapolis Convention, which served as a forerunner to the Constitutional Convention. He served in the U.S. Congress from 1791 to 1794.

At the Annapolis Convention in 1786, only New York, Pennsylvania, Delaware, Virginia and Clark's own New Jersey were represented. Nine states had accepted the original invitation from Virginia. The purpose of the call was to settle interstate commerce and arbitrate a system of uniform commercial regulations for all states. Twelve commissioners attended, including Alexander Hamilton and James Madison. John Dickinson was chairman. Their proposal was approved by Congress on February 21, 1787. The Constitutional Congress met on May 2 in Philadelphia. Because of ill health, Clark was unable to attend.

Clark served as clerk of the New Jersey Colonial assembly and was appointed high sheriff of Essex County. He was a Whig.

In June 1776, he went to the general Congress, voted for separation from England and signed the Declaration of Independence. He was elected to Congress eight times. It was Clark who made the motion to activate the Federal Constitution. Clark was appointed by the state legislation during the winter season of 1789-1790 to arbitrate the war debts New Jersey had contracted.

In the row of men seated in the second stamp of the four Declaration of Independence stamps issued July 4, 1976, Clark is the sixth from the left.

Shobal Vail Clevenger

Scott 152
Born: October 22, 1812, Butler County, near Middletown, Ohio
Died: September 23, 1843, near Gibraltar, Atlantic Ocean

Shobal Clevenger worked in Cleveland, Ohio, at Dorfeuille's Western Museum, making wax figures of grotesque characters in the Chamber of Horrors, as well as representations of criminals and celebrities in the museum. He received instruction from Eckstein, a German modeler.

Clevenger first worked with David Guion in the early 1830s in Cincinnati. Cincinnati was rapidly becoming an art center, due partly to the patronage of Nicholas Longworth. Longworth encouraged Clevenger to go to Washington, D.C., and New York City.

Clevenger went to Washington to sculpt portraitures. He also worked in New York City and Boston. His busts were among the strongest and most direct of any of the earlier American sculptors.

He sculpted political leaders and literary figures. One portrait he executed was that of Washington Allston, a painter from South Carolina. At the time Clevenger was rendering Allston's portrait sculpture, the ailing artist was working on a painting titled *Belshazzar's Feast*. Clevenger represented the moribund artist so realistically that he was commissioned after Allston's death to produce a bust not showing so much of Allston's physical deterioration.

Clevenger sailed in 1840 to Florence, Italy, to join Hiram Powers. He worked with fine Italian white Carrara marble and created *The North American Indian*, a full-length statue that was called the first distinctive American sculpture. He became ill in 1843 and began his journey to America. One day out from Gibraltar, he died.

He left *The North American Indian* in Rome. It is presumed to have been destroyed. A collection of his busts are in the Pennsylvania Academy of Fine Arts, the New York Historical Society, the Boston Athenaeum and the Metropolitan Museum in New York City.

The portrait bust of Daniel Webster by Clevenger was selected for the 15¢ definitive issued in April 1870.

George Clinton

Scott 1691
Born: July 26, 1739, Little Britain, New York
Died: April 20, 1812, Washington, D.C.

George Clinton was the son of an Irish immigrant, Charles Clinton, who came to America in 1729 and commanded a regiment of provincial troops in the French and Indian War. At age 18, George went to sea. He returned and joined his father's regiment as a lieutenant in the French and Indian War. He practiced law in Ulster County and entered the New York Provincial Assembly. He was elected to the Continental Congress. He voted for the Declaration of Independence. He left Philadelphia before the signing of the document.

Clinton was appointed brigadier general of the state militia. As a general, he was inept. Realizing this, he offered his resignation. Congress recommissioned him. He took part in the Battle of White Plains, New York, on October 28, 1776. He was directed to defend Highland on the west bank of the Hudson but could not withstand the advances of Sir Henry Clinton.

In 1777, he was elected to the dual position of the first governor and lieutenant governor of New York. He settled for governor only on July 30, 1777, and kept that seat until 1795. As an independent state, New York was governed by the provincial congress from 1776 to 1777.

George Clinton opposed the Constitution and made every effort to block its ratification as he presided over the ratification convention. When nine states had ratified the document, the required number for approval and acceptance, Clinton conceded. New York became the 11th state to ratify the Constitution.

In 1790, Clinton declared himself a Democratic-Republican. He retired from the gubernatorial seat in 1795. However, he was re-elected in 1800.

In 1804, he was elected vice president of the United States under Thomas Jefferson. In 1808, he ran for president but lost to James Madison. He served as Madison's vice president. He died before his term of office had expired.

Clinton is shown as the third man from the left seated before the men standing in the first of the four 1976 Declaration of Independence stamps.

49

George Clymer

Scott 1692
Born: March 16, 1739, Philadelphia, Pennsylvania
Died: January 23, 1813, Morrisville, Bucks County, Pennsylvania

George Clymer was an ardent patriot. Though he was not present when the Declaration of Independence was adopted, he realized his "dearest wish" when he signed that document. His business wisdom was used on various committees in both the Continental and first U.S. congresses. He signed the Constitution. He fulfilled two successive commissions to which George Washington appointed him and retired from public life July 31, 1796, after an almost unbroken service of more than 20 years.

Clymer's grandfather, Richard Clymer, was an immigrant from Bristol, England. His father, Christopher Clymer, and his mother, Deborah of the Philadelphia Fitzwater family, both died in 1740, when George was an infant. He was taken in by his uncle, William Coleman, a friend of Benjamin Franklin.

Clymer was educated at the College of Philadelphia (now the University of Pennsylvania). He later became a partner of Reese Meredith and Son. He married Elizabeth Meredith, Reese Meredith's daughter, in 1765. With the Merediths, he formed the company of Merediths and Clymer. After Reese Meredith died, Clymer continued as a partner with his brother-in-law.

Clymer was captain of volunteers in General Cadwalader's brigade and acted as chairman of the Boston Tea Party. He was one of two First Continental Congress treasurers. He entered Congress as a Pennsylvania delegate.

On a detour from their march to Philadelphia, the British, after their victory at Brandywine, wrecked Clymer's home and terrorized the family as retribution because Clymer had been heavily involved in the cause against the British.

At the end of his career, he actuated community interests in banking, the arts and agriculture. He remained in these positions until his death.

Clymer is the third from the left of the three men standing behind the row of men seated on the second stamp of the se-tenant Declaration of Independence stamps issued July 4, 1976.

David Cobb

Scott 1686d
Born: September 14, 1748, Attleborough, Massachusetts
Died: April 17, 1830, Taunton, Massachusetts

David Cobb was an Army officer, a congressman and a jurist. He was the son of Thomas and Lydia Leonard Cobb. He grew up in and received his elementary education in Attleborough, Massachusetts, located in the southeastern part of the state in Bristol County, just north of Providence, Rhode Island, at the end of the old Ten Mile Road. Today it is spelled Attleboro.

Cobb graduated from Harvard College, in Cambridge, Massachusetts, in 1766 at age 19. In 1775, he was a delegate to the Massachusetts Provincial Congress. Two years later, he was commissioned a lieutenant colonel in the Massachusetts militia and was present at the surrender of the British at Yorktown. In 1783, he was brevetted a brigadier general, and three years later he was commissioned major general.

He was a member of the U.S. House of Representatives from Massachusetts' third congress as a Federalist. From 1802 to 1805, he was president of the Massachusetts Senate, and in 1812, he was a member of the Massachusetts Board of Military Defense.

He died in Taunton, Massachusetts, April 17, 1830, and was buried in the Plain Cemetery of that town located just 10 miles southeast of his birthplace, Attleborough.

On the 1976 American Bicentennial souvenir sheet of 13¢ stamps, Cobb is shown on the fourth stamp from the left, mounted on a horse with John Trumbull to his left. Trumbull was a colonel and aide to General Washington in the American Revolution and obtained firsthand knowledge of the war, as well as of the officers and men in Washington's command. It is believed that he faithfully depicted their true visage and stature in his paintings. He eventually secured a commission to provide paintings of events of the Revolution for the Rotunda of the nation's Capitol.

51

Bartholomew Columbus

Scott 242
Born: circa 1456, Genoa, Italy
Died: 1514, Santo Domingo, Hispaniola, West Indies

Bartholomew Columbus was the third son of Domenico and Susanna Colombo (or Columbus). He was a chartmaker and went to Lisbon, Portugal, to ply his trade. In 1476, he was in Lisbon when his brother, Christopher, came ashore at Lagos from the wrecked Bechalla. Christopher visited Bartholomew, who was working in the Genoese community. The two brothers began working together and conceived the idea to sail west to China.

Christopher went to Spain to seek support, and Bartholomew went to England to seek the support of Henry VII. Bartholomew was unsuccessful. He went to France, where Anne de Beaujeu, Charles VII's sister, set him up as a chartmaker at Fontainebleau. Christopher sailed west and discovered America.

News traveled slowly across the Alps, finally reaching Bartholomew at Fontainebleau. Christopher was already on his second voyage.

Bartholomew favorably impressed Isabella and Ferdinand, who gave him command of three caravels to take provisions to Hispaniola. Bartholomew's arrival at the settlement of Isabela was good news to Christopher. The new colony needed a leader.

Christopher sailed for Spain in the *Nina* on March 10, 1496, and left Bartholomew in command. Bartholomew moved the colony to a new location and called it Santo Domingo. Isabella and Ferdinand sent Bobadilla to the island with unlimited power. When Christopher returned, he, Bartholomew and their brother, Diego, were shackled and returned to Spain. They were pardoned and freed once they reached Spain.

Bartholomew and Christopher embarked on a fourth voyage in 1503 to continue their search for China. At Belem, Bartholomew was wounded. They sailed to Jamaica and were marooned for a year before they were rescued.

The two brothers sailed home after two and a half years. Christopher died. Bartholomew returned to Santo Domingo in 1509 with Christopher's son, Diego, who aided him in the administration of the colony until Bartholomew died in 1514.

Bartholomew is seen standing in chains with his brothers Christopher and Diego on the $2 Columbian stamp issued January 2, 1893.

52

Diego Columbus

Scott 242
Born: circa 1468, Genoa, Italy
Died: February 21, 1515, Seville, Spain

Diego was the son of Domenico Colombo, a wool weaver, and Susanna, whose father was also a wool weaver. Cristoforo (Christopher) was the oldest of the Colombo (Columbus) children. Diego was 17 years younger than Christopher, who was born in 1451.

When Christopher Columbus returned from his first voyage, the 25-year-old Diego joined his illustrious older brother on his journey to fullful his religious vows for the successful return from the Indies. It was June 1493. Five converted Indians also returned with them.

Diego went with Columbus on his second voyage. At the colony of Isabela, things were not going well, but the crew continued to cling to the hope of finding gold. With his crew near mutiny, Columbus put all arms and munitions in the flagship with Diego in command. While Columbus left to explore Cuba, Diego was in charge of the settlement of Isabela. Las Casa says of Diego that he was "a virtuous person, very discreet, peaceable and simple," who really intended to be a bishop. He was incapable of controlling the colonists.

Bartholomew Columbus was in Isabela when Christopher returned from Cuba. Ferdinand and Isabella had given Bartholomew command of three caravels to take provisions to Hispaniola. Bartholomew gave up Isabela and established the colony of Santo Domingo.

Francisco Roldan, whom Christopher had appointed chief justice of Hispaniola, stirred up rebellion. The sovereigns in Spain sent Francisco de Bobadilla with unlimited powers, and in early October 1500, Christopher and his brother Diego were shackled and placed on a ship destined for Spain.

In Spain, the prisoners were freed. Christopher planned his fourth and last voyage, and Diego entered the priesthood. Diego was with Christopher at the time of Christopher's death in Valladolid, May 20, 1506. He sailed with his nephew, the young Diego, to Santo Domingo but very soon returned home. He lived quietly and died in Seville.

Diego Columbus is seen standing with his brother Christopher in chains on the $2 stamp of the Columbian series issued January 2, 1893.

Diego Columbus (son of Christopher)

Scott 239
Born: 1480, Porto Santo, Madiera Islands, Portugal
Died: February 23, 1526, La Puebla de Montalban, Toledo, Spain

Christopher Columbus married Dona Felipa Perestrello e Moniz, daughter of Bartholomew Perestrello of one of the first families of Portugal. The couple lived with her mother in Lisbon. They later moved to Porto Santo to live with Dona Felipa's brother, the governor. Into this illustrious family in 1480 was born the future Don Diego Colon, second admiral and viceroy of the Indies.

When Diego was age 2, the family moved to Funchal in Madiera. From here, Christopher sailed the seas. When Diego was 5, his mother died. Columbus took Diego to Huelva, Spain. They landed in Palos. Columbus took Diego to the monastery, Santa Maria de Rabida, Diego's new home. Five years later, when Diego was 10, Columbus came to La Rabida to get him.

Queen Isabella financed a voyage to the Indies by Christopher Columbus. In 1493, at age 13, Diego was living in the city of Cordova with Columbus' mistress, Beatriz Enriquez, and Diego's 5-year-old half brother, Ferdinand.

Columbus made his second voyage. Upon Columbus' return, Diego and Ferdinand were serving as pages to the queen at Valladolid, where Diego served as attendant to Prince Juan in the Spanish court. Christopher Columbus returned from his third voyage in chains and disgrace. In 1500, he was ready for yet another voyage, his fourth and last. He sailed from Seville, April 3, 1502. Young Ferdinand accompanied him. Christopher and Ferdinand returned to Seville on November 9, 1504. Isabella was ill and died on November 26. Columbus fell ill and died a year and a half later on May 19, 1506.

Diego married Dona Maria de Toledo of royalty. Three years after Christopher Columbus' death, King Ferdinand appointed Diego governor of Hispaniola and gave him his father's title, admiral of the Indies.

Diego sailed to the New World in 1509. King Ferdinand died in 1516. His successor was Charles V. In 1523, Charles recalled Diego to Spain. Upon Diego's return, Charles gave him no recognition. On February 23, 1526, at the age of 46, Diego died.

Young Diego is seen sitting on the stool next to Fray Juan Perez at the left end of the table in the 30¢ Columbian stamp issued January 2, 1893.

John Singleton Copley

Scott 1273
Born: July 26, 1738, Boston, Massachusetts
Died: September 9, 1815, London, England

John Copley's father was Richard Copley, and his mother was Mary Singleton Copley, emigrants from Ireland. While John was yet a boy his father died. In 1748, his mother married Peter Pelham, who was a master engraver of messotint portraits. It was his stepfather's profession that launched young Copley on a career of portraiture.

In 1766, Copley painted a picture of his half brother, Henry Pelham, titled *The Boy with a Squirrel*, and sent it to London to be exhibited in the Society of Artists. It was that picture that stimulated Benjamin West to invite Copley to England. West was constantly on the lookout for promising student artists.

Copley spent some 21 years in Boston as a portrait painter, painting his subjects as they really were, not exaggerated as was the custom. He had a successful career in Boston. Even though Joshua Reynolds and West urged him to come to Europe to work and study, he stayed on in his estate on Beacon Hill.

He married Susanna Clarke in 1769. When the political situation became precarious, he finally left for Europe in the spring of 1774. He was in Rome when the War of Independence began, and he joined his family in London in 1775. He continued to paint portraits while in London, but his ambition was to paint historical subjects, the most highly regarded aspect of his field.

After he did well with *Watson and the Shark* (1778), he received wide recognition for *The Death of the Earl of Catham* (1779-1781), which is considered by many as his masterpiece. For the *Corporation of London*, he won the commission to paint *The Siege of Gibraltar* (1784-91).

Realism in the representation of historical events in paintings was revolutionary, and it was Copley and West who together brought this to the fore.

Copley was commemorated on a 1965 5¢ issue depicting the portrait of his daughter Elizabeth.

55

Lou Costello

Scott 2566
Born: March 6, 1908, Paterson, New Jersey
Died: March 3, 1959, Beverly Hills, California

Louis F. Cristillo began his acting career as a derelict comedian performing in vaudeville as a roly-poly buffoon. He met fast-talking, hawklike, know-it-all William A. Abbott. They complemented each other so well the two New Jerseyites teamed up in 1931. They formed what would become an internationally famous comedy duo, Abbott and Costello. It was a two-man team of the straight guy and the foil. Billed as Lou Costello, he was, by contrasting with Abbott, the foil. He portrayed a personality of a childish gracioso, voicing the punch lines to his partner Abbott, asking and getting the answers to his never-ending childlike questions of who? what? where? when? and why?

This type of banter led to the famous baseball dialogue "Who's on First?" It evolved into a rapid-fire set of puns and mix-ups. They repeated this skit hundreds of times on stage and in nightclubs. "Who's on First" is inscribed on a plaque in the National Baseball Hall of Fame in Cooperstown, New York.

For the first eight years as a team, they played, vaudeville circuits. They appeared at Loew's State Theater in New York City in 1938 and on the Kate Smith radio show until 1940. They also performed in the Broadway review *Streets of Paris* in 1939 and 1940.

These successes were a natural stepping-stone to Hollywood. In 1940, they starred in their first motion-picture success, *One Night in the Tropics*. In the film *The Naughty Nineties*, Abbott and Costello keep the laughs flowing on a Mississippi showboat. They were two of the most highly paid performers of their time. From 1941 to 1956, they completed 35 films. Moviegoers filled the theaters to see such slapstick and foolishness as *Buck Privates* and *In the Navy*, films that helped to soften the pain of young men being drafted into the service for World War II. Later came *Rio Rita, Lost in a Harem, Jack and the Bean Stock, The Time of Their Lives* and *Abbott and Costello in Hollywood*. In 1956, they ended their film career with *Dance with Me Henry*.

The team dissolved their partnership in 1957. It was an amicable separation. Costello was not well. Two years later he died.

Costello appears with Abbott in the 1991 booklet of comedian caricatures by Al Hirschfeld.

Nathaniel Currier

Scott 1551
Born: March 27, 1813, Roxbury, Massachusetts
Died: November 20, 1888, New York, New York

Nathaniel Currier began his lifework in lithography as an apprentice to the pioneer lithographer John B. Pendleton in Currier's hometown of Roxbury, Massachusetts. When Pendleton moved to Philadelphia in 1829, Currier went along. After four years in Philadelphia, Pendleton moved to New York, and young Currier stayed with him.

In 1834, Currier had fulfilled his apprenticeship. He left Pendleton and set up his own lithography house in New York in association with the artist J.H. Bufford. Currier's new firm was located at 1 Wall Street. The first print that was of any success by this partnership was the *Ruins of the Merchant's Exchange,* done four days after the building burned on December 16-17, 1835.

In additon to spectacular current-event scenes, Currier made prints of war heroes and the wars they fought, as well as of boxing, fishing, horse racing and the new ships that ran by steam. He also made prints of city scenes, country scenes, drawings of frontier growth, and pictures of townscapes of European villages — the places that were home to immigrants who came to America.

In 1852, Currier hired James Merritt Ives as a bookkeeper. Ives had married Currier's sister-in-law. Ives had a well-rounded education, including a knowledge of libraries and art galleries.

After five years, Currier and Ives became partners. Henceforth all prints were signed "Currier and Ives" and sold from about 10¢ to $3.50. The partners had branch offices in Europe. They produced posters and handbills. P.T. Barnum was one of their most famous customers. Over the span of 70 years, they printed some 7,000 different pictorial prints. To hasten the work, a production line of women meticulously applied the color.

Currier retired in 1880, and his son, Edward West Currier, continued in his stead. Ives' son, Chauncy, had also entered the firm. James Ives died in 1895. In 1902, Chauncy bought out Edward, but photography and advanced technology, as well as Ives lack of enthusiasm led to the firm's closing in 1907.

Currier and Ives' *The Road —Winter* appears on a1974 Christmas stamp. Currier's *Winter Pastime* was also chosen for a 1976 Christmas stamp.

Gerard David

Gerard David: National Gallery
Christmas USA 15c

Scott 1799
Born: circa 1460, Oudewater, Holland
Died: August 13, 1523, Bruges, Belgium

Gerard David presumably went from his birthplace Oudewater, Utrecht, to Haarlem, Holland, where he learned from the paintings of Dirck Bouts and Geertge. He studied painting under the direct tutilage of A. van Ouwater before going to Bruges, Belgium, in 1483. He established himself as a master of the use of color. He especially emphasized tones of blue and green.

In 1484, he joined the Guild of St. Lukes. In 1896, he married Cornelia Cnoop, the daughter of the dean of the goldsmiths' guild. He studied the works of the masters, especially Van der Weyden, Van der Goes and the Van Eycks. He was a contemporary of Bruges' famed Hans Memling and was influenced by him directly. In 1501, David became the dean of the Guild of St. Lukes.

From Memling, he acquired the technique of rendering his compositions in accordance with the technical principles of architecture. He also learned to paint the human form realistically. He painted great alterpieces during this period. Notable examples are: *The Marriage of St. Catherine* (National Gallery), the *Annunciation* (Sigmaringen collection), and especially *Madonna with Angels and Saints* (Rouen, France). In 1515, David spent time in Antwerp studying the delicate sacred themes of Quentin Massys, which showed more intimately human aspects of life and movement in religious paintings. The results of this study are such examples as his *Pieta* (National Gallery) and the *Descent from the Cross* (Cavallo collection, Paris).

David influenced his pupils in Bruges. Isenbrandt, Cornelis and Ambrosius Benson gained recognition. Others who paid attention to David's works were Jan Mabuse and Joachim Patinir. David was probably the last great master of the 15th century's Flemish school. Dutch painters took a backseat once the Italian paintings achieved an influence in northern Europe.

Bruges was David's home and where he died on August 13, 1523. His remains were interred in the Church of Our Lady at Bruges.

David's *The Virgin and Child* (National Gallery) was reproduced on the traditional Christmas stamp for 1979.

Alexander Jackson Davis

Scott 1841
Born: July 24, 1803, New York, New York
Died: January 14, 1892, West Orange, New Jersey

In 1829, Alexander Jackson Davis became a partner of Ithiel Town, with whom he worked and studied for nearly 15 years. He was involved in the building of state capitols and government buildings. During their partnership, Davis excelled in the so-called Greek Revival style. He was involved building the state capitol of North Carolina (1831), the New York Customs House (1832), the Patent Office in Washington, D.C. (1832), the Indiana state capitol (1832-35), the Illinois state capitol (1837) and the Ohio state capitol (1839).

Much of his work was done independently, such as the Lyndhurst, which was the first of a series of houses in the style called the Hudson River Gothic. It is a classic example of the American Gothic Revival style. This mansion is located at 635 S. Broadway, in Tarrytown, New York, overlooking the Hudson River. It was built for former New York Mayor William Paulding in 1838. It was constructed of marble quarried by the convicts of Sing Sing Prison. The house was sold to George Merritt, a New York merchant. In 1865, Davis doubled the size of the original mansion. The mansion was purchased by railroad tycoon Jay Gould in 1880.

Much of the furniture within the house is also Gothic and was designed by Davis. The interior has such Gothic details as ribbed and vaulted ceilings, figures bosses and walls painted to resemble dressed stone, as well as a large number of stained-glass windows and panels. It sits on a 67-acre site surrounded by picturesque landscaping, overlooking the Hudson from the rear.

From 1843, Davis worked independently, producing such structures as the Assembly Hall of the University of North Carolina (1844) and buildings for the Virginia Military Institute (1852, 1859), Lexington, Virginia. He was one of the co-founders of the American Institute of Architects in 1857.

Davis is honored on the fourth stamp of the American Architecture series of 1980. The stamp shows the Lyndhurst mansion.

Stuart Davis

Scott 1259
Born: December 7, 1894, Philadelphia, Pennsylvania
Died: June 24, 1964, New York, New York

Stuart Davis was a painter of colorful, collagelike abstracts that fit well into the pop-art vogue of the 1960s. He was commissioned by the U.S. Post Office Department to design a painting especially to commemorate fine arts in America. The stamp was issued six months after his death.

Davis studied in New York City from the time he was 16 years of age until he was about 20. He learned from Robert Henri, the leading advocate of realism in the tradition of Thomas Eakins. Henri was a member of the realistic group known as "the Eight." In the book *Art —America in Modern Times* by Holger Cahill and Alfred Barr (1934), these painters were dubbed the "Ashcan" painters because they painted such motifs as backyards and garbage cans. John Frederick Peto (1854-1907) may well have been their inspiration.

Davis exhibited watercolors in the Armory Show in 1913 and viewed abstract art, which stimulated his interest. He began to work in that direction even though he was called for duty in World War I as a mapmaker. He painted still lifes consisting of nothing but an eggbeater, an electric fan and a rubber glove repeatedly for a year (1927-28). In the 1930s, his work became more intense in color, and the shapes became smaller.

He taught and painted for the government program during the Great Depression of the early 1930s, executing murals. By 1950, his work had culminated in the use of bizarre shapes. Even letters and numbers were included in his designs. Examples of his works are *Visa* in the Museum of Modern Art, New York City, in which words make up the entire composition, and his *Colonial Cubism* in the Walker Art Center, Minneapolis, which shows his bold simplicity. An abstract painting that is a typical grouping of colorful scraps is *Ready to Wear*, painted in 1955, now in the Art Institute of Chicago. Two major exhibits of his work were held in New York City in 1946 and 1957.

Davis died in New York City at the age of 69. The special red, white, blue and black collagelike abstract design used for the Fine Arts stamp is labeled "to the Fine Arts."

Stephen Daye

Scott 857
Born: 1594, London, England
Died: December 22, 1668, Cambridge, Massachusetts

Stephen Daye was an apprentice locksmith in London. He may also have had some training in printing. He was 44 years old when he came to America in mid-1638 with the Reverend Jose Glover. In September, he set up his printing press. The Reverend Glover was a wealthy dissenting minister who financed Daye's printing business in the English Colonies in America. One might surmise that the Reverend Glover saw the advantages of spreading his preachings through the printed word.

Daye set up his printing press in Cambridge, Massachusetts. This was the first press in the Colonies. Daye's son, Matthew, worked with him and carried on the occupation. Eventually their press came under the control of Harvard College. The Daye press is today in the Harvard University museum.

Records show that the first two pieces printed by their press were the *Freeman' Oath* and *An Almanac for 1639, calculated for New England by Mr. William Pierce, Mariner.* Copies of these and most of their works have been lost. The earliest known printing in North America by Daye that is in existence is the *Bay Psalm Book* or *The Whole Booke of Psalms, faithfully translated in English Metre.* It is dated 1640.

From the Daye press came *A list of Theses at Harvard Commencement in — 1643,* printed that year, and *A Declaration of Former Passages and Proceedings betwixt the English and the Narrowgansetts, with their confederates, Wherein the grounds and justice of the ensuing warre are opened and cleared.* This wonderful old lengthy title was printed in 1645. Another book of unusual interest is a bible translated into Indian by a missionary, the Reverend John Eliot, and printed at Cambridge in 1663 by Samuel Green and Marmaduke Johnson using Daye's press.

The Daye press is shown on a stamp issued September 25, 1939.

Jonathan Dayton

Scott 798
Born: October 16, 1760, Elizabeth, New Jersey
Died: October 6, 1824, Elizabeth, New Jersey

Jonathan Dayton was one of eight children of Elias and "Miss Rolfe" Dayton. Jonathan was educated at Princeton University (then the College of New Jersey). After graduating in 1776, he joined his father's unit in the war. He saw action in most of the New York and New Jersey campaigns. At Yorktown, in 1781, he was a captain. He returned to his studies of law in 1783 and was admitted to the bar. He sat on the New Jersey Assembly in 1786 and 1787. His father was elected to the Federal Convention but declined the appointment in favor of Jonathan, who at 27 became the youngest member of the Constitutional Convention. Dayton frequently opposed some elements of the document, but on September 17, 1787, he signed it.

Though appointed, he declined to serve on the First Congress under the Constitution. He served the New Jersey Council in 1789 and the Assembly in 1790 as the speaker. He was chosen for the Second, Third, and Fourth Congresses, and served as speaker in the Fifth Congress. He favored having the secretary of war and treasury in the House. He supported the administration in its report on the Whiskey Rebellion of November 1794.

He served as a member of the Senate from 1799 to 1805. He visited New Orleans in July 1803 and was in favor of the Louisiana Purchase. He opposed the 12th Amendment concerning the electoral vote by ballot for president and vice president. He also opposed the impeachment of Justice Samuel Chase.

Dayton was involved in the proposed building of a canal around the Ohio Falls and held title to some 250,000 acres between the Big and Little Miami rivers. He was a friend of Aaron Burr and was involved in Burr's expedition down the Ohio. For this, he was charged with high treason and misdemeanor on June 1807. His case never came to trial. He later held local offices and served two terms in the New Jersey Assembly, 1814-15. Layfayette visited him in the fall of 1824. Dayton died a few days later.

In 1795, a group of Revolutionary soldiers bought a site in Ohio on the Great Miami River from John C. Symmes. It was laid out as a town in 1796 by Israel Ludlow, one of the owners, who named it Dayton after Jonathan Dayton.

Dayton is depicted on the 1937 Constitution Sesquicentennial stamp.

Henry Dearborn

Scott 644
Born: February 23, 1751, Hampton, New Hampshire
Died: June 6, 1829, Roxbury (Boston), Massachusetts

Henry Dearborn was the son of Simon and Sarah Marston Dearborn. Henry attended elementary school, then studied medicine with Dr. Hall Jackson of Portsmouth, New Hampshire. He entered practice at Nottingham Square, New Hampshire, in 1772. When trouble began with England, he became a captain with the local militia. He took 60 men to Cambridge when the Lexington and Concord fighting began. He joined Colonel John Stark's regiment in the fighting at Bunker Hill.

In 1775, he joined Benedict Arnold's expedition to Quebec and took part in the assault on Quebec on December 31, 1775. He was taken prisoner and was released in a prisoner exchange in March 1777. He was appointed major of the 3rd New Hampshire Regiment commanded by Colonel Alexander Scammell.

In September 1777, he was transferred to the 1st New Hampshire Regiment and took part in the battles against General John Burgoyne's forces in the fighting at Ticonderoga and Freeman's Farm. He was present at the surrender of Burgoyne at Saratoga. Dearborn was at Valley Forge the winter of 1777-78 and took part in the Battle of Monmouth the following June. He was in the battle with General John Sullivan from Wyoming Valley against the Six Nations in the Genesee Valley. Later, he joined Washington's staff at Yorktown. Dearborn became a brigadier general (later major general) of the militia and, in 1790, was appointed marshal for the district of Maine. He represented his district as a Republican in the Third and Fourth Congresses. President Jefferson appointed him secretary of war. He served through both of Jefferson's terms.

President Madison appointed him major general in the U.S. Army in command of the important north sector. Dearborn proved to be an imcompetent leader. He captured Toronto (York) with heavy losses. He also captured Fort George, but again his troops suffered heavy losses. Dearborn became ill. Morgan Lewis relieved him. Dearborn was given command of New York City.

Dearborn was given an honorary discharge on June 15, 1815. In 1822, President Monroe made him minister to Portugal. He later retired.

On the stamp issued August 3, 1927, picturing the *Surrender of Burgoyne*, Dearborn is the second person from the far left. Only his head is visible.

Lee De Forest

Scott C86
Born: August 26, 1873, Council Bluffs, Iowa
Died: June 30, 1961, Hollywood, California

Lee De Forest is known as the "father of radio" for his invention of the Audion tube, a three-element (triode electron) tube. The tube has vast potential as a generator, detector and amplifier of radio signals. The Audion was perhaps the most important invention in the field of electronics.

De Forest attended school in Council Bluffs. He attended Talladega College in Alabama. His father was president of the school. Young De Forest graduated from the Scheffield Scientific School of Yale University in 1896. In 1899, he received his doctorate at Yale, then went to the Western Electric Company in Chicago. He researched radio and radio broadcasting projects.

His first patent was granted for an electrolytic detector used in radio headphones. His Audion patent of 1907 was hotly contested because it was said that it was an extension of John S. Fleming's diode electron tube. The litigation continued for years. Not until 1934 did the U.S. Supreme Court uphold De Forest's claim to the invention. He was awarded more than 300 patents. In 1909, De Forest demonstrated on radio the first broadcast of music. It was the singing voice of Enrico Caruso performing at the Metropolitan Opera. The first newscast was broadcast in 1916.

De Forest founded several companies: the De Forest Wireless Telegraph Company, the Radio Telephone Company and the De Forest Radio Company. He published his book, *Television Today and Tomorrow*, emphasizing the use of televison as an educational and cultural medium. He sold his rights to the Audion in 1918, then turned his attention to producing sound for motion pictures. In 1923, he founded the De Forest Phonofilm Company.

Among his contributions to the fields of telecommunications and motion pictures were innovations for the electric phonograph, long-distant telephony and facsimile transmission (FAX). In 1948, he contributed to color television and, in 1957, the automatic telephone dialing device.

His autobiography, *Father of Radio*, was published in 1940. He was awarded the Edison Medal in 1950 and the National Association of Broadcasters Award in 1958. He was elected president of the Institute of Radio Engineers.

His Audion is depicted on a 1973 Electronic Progress airmail stamp.

Andrea Della Robbia

Andrea della Robbia: National Gallery
Christmas USA 15c

Scott 1768
Born: October 20, 1435, Florence, Italy
Died: August 4, 1525, Florence, Italy

Andrea Della Robbia was the nephew and pupil of Luca Della Robbia and the son of Marco, Luca's brother. Andrea added five sons to the family, three of whom carried on a prolific production of enameled reliefs.

Andrea's work was equal to Luca's, but their sons' works were never equal to that of Andrea or Luca. Of Andrea's sons, the youngest, Girolamo, worked mostly in France, spending nearly 40 years in the service of the French royal family. He was also an architect and built the Chateau de Madrid (now destroyed) in the Bois de Boulogne for Francis I. Luca II worked in Florence and Rome. He was with Raphael at the Vatican in 1518, and his beautiful tile flooring in the upper story of Raphael's loggie at the Vatican still exists. Giovanni, the eldest of the three, worked closely with his father, mostly in Florence. His works are difficult to distinguish from that of Andrea's.

The family called themselves the Atelier, French for "artists' workshop." Their work extended from Florence to France and Rome. Their works remain in churches and other buildings of Italy. An altar in Santa Maria Della Grazie near Arezzo is the only marble sculpture work by Andrea known to be in existence. One of the most noteworthy renditions by Andrea is the group of medallions with reliefs of infants in white on a blue ground set on the front of the foundling hospital at Florence.

Andrea produced a large number of reliefs of the Madonna and Child. Typical are the main reliefs left in the original white with the framing decorated with garlands of lifelike fruit and flowers painted with colored enamels. In the elaborate frameworks rising behind the altar in the Arezzo Cathedral is Andrea's enamel work. In the chapel of the Campo Santo is a fine relief of the Madonna and Child with four saints at the sides. In Grado is a standing Madonna and angels in the Santa Maria Church. One of his latest works was a relief representing the *Adoration of the Magi* in the little church, Santa Maria, in Pian di Mugnone, near Florence.

An example of Andrea Della Robbia's terra-cotta work, *Madonna and Child with Cherubim*, was chosen for the 1978 traditional Christmas stamp.

Luca Della Robbia

CHRISTMAS

USA 22

Luca della Robbia. Detroit Institute of Arts

Scott 2165
Born: 1399 or 1400, Florence, Italy
Died: September 22, 1482, Florence, Italy

The name Della Robbia stands with the great Italian sculptors of the Renaissance period, who prospered under the patronage of the court of the Medici family. Luca Della Robbia was the son of Simone di Marco Della Robbia. Luca's brother was Marco, whose son Andrea was Luca's pupil. Andrea and three of his sons carried on Luca's work.

Luca Della Robbia was supposedly apprenticed to the great silversmith Leonardo di Ser Giovanni (famous for his cross of 1459), but more likely it was Ghiberti. Della Robbia created beautiful pieces of sculpture in marble and bronze. His most famous work in marble is the *Singing Galleries*, or *Cantorio*, the reliefs of 10 panels representing angels and boys singing and playing on various instruments. It was sculptured for the Cathedral of Florence and can be viewed today at the Bargello in Florence.

In 1439, along with Donatello, he completed two marble altars for chapels in the cathedral, one of which is now in the Bargello. In 1446, along with Michelozzo and Maso di Bartolomeo, he cast the bronze door for the sacristies of the cathedral. It is divided into 10 square panels of small heads projecting from the frames. Luca finished the last two panels in 1467 himself.

One of his marble works existing today is the elaborate tomb of Benozzo Federighi, bishop of Fiesole, now in the church of SS. Trinita in Florence. In his final years of work, he concentrated on the production of enameled terra-cotta reliefs. Della Robbia perfected this work in terra-cotta so that it is now known as "Della Robbia ware." Most existing reliefs are the works of the younger members of the Della Robbia family, who carried on the tradition.

In 1471, Luca Della Robbia was elected president of the Florentine Guild of Sculptors, but declined to serve because of his advanced age and poor health. His work, the *Genoa Madonna Enameled Terra-Cotta*, is reproduced on the 1985 traditional Christmas stamp.

John Dickinson

Scott 1687e
Born: November 8, 1732, Talbot County, Maryland
Died: February 14, 1808, Wilmington, Delaware

John Dickinson was know as the "penman of the Revolution." Despite the numerous pamphlets, letters and papers he composed that had a resounding effect upon the colonists, he opposed open confrontation. He held out for non-separation from Britain. He did not sign the Declaration of Independence. Nevertheless, his writings influenced the Colonies to strike for independence. When he was 8, his family moved to Kent County, Delaware. He studied law in Philadelphia and in London at the Middle Temple. He began his law practice in 1757. He wrote pamphlets on both the Stamp and Sugar acts. This won him a position on the Pennsylvania legislature in the Stamp Act Congress in 1765.

In one of his *Letters from a Farmer in Pennsylvania*, published in newspapers during 1767 and 1768, he describes himself: "I am a farmer, settled after a variety of fortunes near the banks of the river Delaware in the province of Pennsylvania. I received a liberal education and have been engaged in the busy scenes of life, but am now convinced that a man may be as happy without bustle as with it. My farm is small; my servants are few and good; I have a little money at interest; I wish for no more; my employment in my own affairs is easy; and with a contented, grateful mind . . . I am completing the number of days alloted to me by divine goodness."

Dickinson aided in the drafting of the Articles of Confederation. When war with Britain was inevitable, he served in the Delaware militia. He represented Delaware in Congress in 1779 and was elected president of the Supreme Executive Council of Delaware in 1781 and of Pennsylvania in 1782. In 1786, he was present at the Annapolis Convention. In 1787, he was a member of the Constitutional Convention. Through his efforts, Delaware and Pennsylvania were the first two states to ratify the Constitution.

In 1783, he was one of the founders of Dickinson College at Carlisle, Pennsylvania, and was the first president of its board of trustees.

Dickinson is the second person from the left in the fifth 18¢ stamp of the second American Bicentennial souvenir sheet issued May 29, 1976.

John Donne

Letters mingle souls
Donne
Raphael
10c US

Scott 1530
Born: 1572, St. Nicholas Olave Parish, London, England
Died: March 31, 1631, London, England

John Donne was born into a well-to-do family with staunch Catholic roots. His father died in 1576. John's Catholic stepfather, Dr. John Syminges, was president of the Royal College of Surgeons. Donne entered Hart Hall, Oxford, in 1584 and transferred to Cambridge in 1587. In 1591, he attended Thavies Inn, a London law school. The following year he transferred to Lincoln Inn.

He met Thomas Egerton, the son of the lord keeper, and was able to gain a position as secretary. In October 1601, he became a member of Parliament. In 1600, Egerton's niece, Ann More, came to live with the lord keeper after Lady Egerton's death. Donne and More were secretly married in 1601. More's father, Sir George More, had Donne imprisoned. Donne was discharged from his duties. The next eight years were spent in poverty.

Donne traveled to Europe with Sir Walter Chute in 1605 and 1606 as an interpreter. From 1606 to 1610, he worked for Thomas Morton. Donne wrote *Biathanatos*, exploring suicide. In 1610, he entered the employ of Sir Robert Drury. In 1614, he again became a member of Parliament. Urged by King James I, Donne took the Anglican order in 1615. He was given an honorary doctor of divinity degree from Cambridge. He was vicor of parishes in Rent.

On August 1617, his wife died from the birth of their 12th child (only seven survived their first years). In 1619, he composed his poem, *A Hymn to Christ at the Authors last going into Germany*. In 1621, he was appointed dean of St. Paul's in London. In 1631, he preached his great sermon, "Death's Duell," before the king. It was Donne who penned the words "Ask not for whom the bell tolls, it tolls for thee," words that were quoted by Hemingway in his book *For Whom the Bell Tolls*.

Donne's name and lines from one of his poems occur on every other stamp in the 1974 Universal Postal Union series.

William Edward Burghardt DuBois

Scott 2617
Born: February 23, 1868, Great Barrington, Massachusetts
Died: August 27, 1963, Accra, Ghana

William DuBois made good use of his extensive education as a writer, teacher, philosopher, organizer and diplomat. He received his bachelor of arts degree from Fisk University, Nashville, Tennesee, in 1888. He went to Harvard for his master of arts degree in 1891 and his doctorate in 1893. He taught first at the African Methodist Episcopal University of Wilberforce, Ohio, as professor of Greek and Latin from 1894 to 1896. On May 12, 1896, he married Nina Gomer. He was an assistant instructor at the University of Pennsylvania. He was professor of economics and history at Atlanta University.

In 1909, Du Bois co-founded the National Association for the Advancement of Colored People (NAACP) and was the editor of its organ, *The Crisis*, until 1932. He left the association and *The Crisis* because of a disagreement over policy matters. In 1944, he rejoined as director of research. Four years later he permanently disassociated himself from the NAACP. In New York City, he joined the United Nations Council on African Affairs, serving as its chairman. In 1951, he was on the leftist Peace Information Bureau.

In 1950, his wife died. The couple had two children, Burghardt Gomer and Nina Yolande. In 1951, Du Bois married Shirley Graham. With the United Nations during the 1950s, he traveled extensively in the Communist Bloc. He was awarded the Lenin Peace Prize in 1959. At age 93, he moved to Accra, Ghana, to direct and edit the *Encyclopedia Africana*. He joined the Communist Party in 1961 and became a citizen of Ghana in 1963.

A Creole, Du Bois was the son of Alfred and Mary Burghardt Dubois. His writings reflect his philosophy. Best known are *Souls of Black Folk*; *John Brown*; *Quest of the Silver Fleece*; *Darkwater*; *The Gift of Black Folk*; *Dark Princess*; *Color and Democracy*; *The World of Africa*; *In Battle for Peace*; and *Worlds of Color*. He was the editor in chief of the *Encyclopedia of the Negro*.

He is honored on a 29¢ Black Heritage stamp issued January 31, 1992.

Harvey T. Dunn

Scott 2154
Born: March 8, 1884, Manchester, South Dakota
Died: October 29, 1952, Tenafly, New Jersey

Harvey T. Dunn was born in a sod house in the Red Stone Creek Valley, a feeder of the James River, in east central South Dakota. His birth is registered in the town of Manchester, located 25 miles directly east of Huron. He was the son of Thomas and Bersha Dow Dunn. After high school, he was inspired to paint the prairie scenes he knew so well. He grew up with the pioneering homesteaders. He preferred drawing and painting the homesteaders rather than the more dashing cowboys and Indians that most western artists chose.

Dunn began his studies at the South Dakota State College in Brookings. He attended the Art Institute of Chicago from 1902 to 1904. He was invited by Howard Pyle, America's foremost illustrator at the time, to study at Pyle's school in Wilmington, Delaware. Pyle deeply influenced him, as did his early teacher, Ada B. Caldwell, who helped cultivate his technique and style.

On March 12, 1908, Dunn married Johanne Krebs, with whom he had a son and a daughter. His painting of early South Dakota life established him as a Western illustrator, muralist and portraiture painter. He illustrated leading publications. He taught at the Grand Central School, New York City. In his paintings, he focused on the head as the point of greatest interest. He used the brightest shades for the head, adding the overall design in dark tones.

During World War I, Dunn was a captain assigned to the American Expeditionary Forces (AEF) as an illustrator (official war artist). After the war, he joined Charles S. Chapman at Leonia, New Jersey, in the Dunn School of Illustration. In 1952, he was awarded a Doctor of Fine Arts by the South Dakota State College. He was a member of the National Academy of Design and the Society of Illustrators, for which he was their president in 1948-49. He was a Mason. He also belonged to the Artist Guild of Salmagundi. He wrote *Evening in the Classroom*, published in 1934.

The South Dakota Memorial Art Center, at South Dakota State College, Brookings, acquired 40 of his works. His work is also in the National Gallery of Art, Washington, D.C., and the Delaware Art Museum, Wilmington.

Dunn's charcoal drawing, *The Battle of Marne, France*, was chosen for the 1985 stamp honoring World War I veterans.

70

Thomas Cowperthwait Eakins

Scott 1335
Born: July 25, 1844, Philadelphia, Pennsylvania
Died: June 25, 1916, Philadelphia, Pennsylvania

Despite his exacting and detailed talents as a painter and sculptor, Thomas Eakins was given little recognition during his lifetime. He was a teacher, photographer and sculptor with interests in anatomy and mathematics. To him, painting was a science. He used rudamental motion pictures to study the movements of men and animals in action.

After studying at the Pennsylvania Academy of Fine Arts, he went to Paris and spent three years of intense training at the Ecole des Beaux-Arts (1866-69) under J.-L. Gerome and Leon Bonnat. He took a quick trip to Spain to view the works of Goya and Velasquez and to study the works of the 17th-century painters. In 1870, he returned to Philadelphia and set up a studio in his father's home. He studied anatomy at the Jefferson Medical College. While at the college, he painted the now famous *The Gross Clinic* (1875), depicting the celebrated surgeon Samuel D. Gross operating before his students. Equally famous is *The Agnew Clinic*, painted in 1889. He painted sports scenes showing athletes in action. *Max Schmitt in a Single Scull* (1871) and *Between the Rounds* (1899) are prize examples.

In 1886, he was dismissed from his teaching position at the Pennsylvania Academy of the Fine Arts (where he became a lecturer in 1873) for bringing a nude model before a class of both men and women. Nevertheless, many of his students supported him and formed the Art Students League of Philadelphia. For the next six years, Eakins headed the group with no financial remuneration.

His sculpture *The Prophets* is in the Witherspoon Building in Philadelphia. He sculpted the figures for a battle monument in Trenton, New Jersey, and in Brooklyn, New York, for the Soldiers' and Sailors' monument.

He painted scenes of life around him, and his realism was almost shocking. Even people who sat for portraits complained that they "showed too much." His paintings were, for the most part, done for his own amusement. He never achieved real success during his lifetime. In the 1880s, he devoted most of his paintings to portraitures of his friends and admirers.

The 1967 stamp issued to honor the work of Eakins shows one of his sports scenes titled *The Biglin Brothers Racing*.

Seth Eastman

Scott 287
Born: Januury 24, 1808, Brunswick, Maine
Died: August 31, 1875, Washington, D.C.

Seth Eastman attended the U.S. Military Academy at West Point from 1824 to 1829. His first assignments were to Fort Crawford, Wisconsin, and Fort Snelling, Minnesota, between 1829 and 1831. He spent the next three years as a topographer with the Army Topographical Corps.

He spent seven years at West Point as an assistant teacher in drawing, where he further sharpened his skills at architectural renderings of buildings and landscapes. The result of this practice can be seen in the 17 paintings of historic forts now hanging in the center building, first floor, west corridor of the nation's Capitol. The paintings were executed under a special order from President Andrew Johnson. Eastman painted these scenes between 1870 and the time of his death in 1875. Fort Sumpter, South Carolina, was painted in three aspects: before the war, after the bombardment, and after the war when the fort had been rebuilt.

Eastman served in the Florida War in 1840 and 1841. He returned to Fort Snelling in 1841 and stayed until 1848. He went to Texas for two years. He served in Texas from 1855 to 1856. Between his Fort Snelling duty and his assignment in Texas, he illustrated Henry R. Schoolcraft's treatise, *History and Statistical Information Respecting the Indian Tribes of the United States.*

Following his Texas stint, he was in the Office of the Quartermaster General, Washington, D.C. He retired in 1863 but returned to service in 1866 and was brevetted a brigadier general in the U.S. Army by President Andrew Johnson and commissioned to paint Indian scenes. Nine paintings were executed between 1867 and 1869: *Buffalo Chase, Death Whoop, Dog Dance of the Dakotas, Feeding the Dead, Indian Council, Indian Mode of Traveling, Indian Woman Dressing a Deer Skin, Rice Gathering* and *Spearing Fish in Winter.* These paintings hung in the House Indian Affairs Committee room in the Capitol. When the committee moved to the Longworth House Office Building, Eastman's paintings went along.

The scene from Eastman's painting *Buffalo Chase* was chosen for the 4¢ stamp of the Trans-Mississippi Exposition issue of June 17, 1898.

William Ellery

Scott 1692
Born: December 22, 1727, Newport, Rhode Island
Died: February 15, 1820, Newport, Rhode Island

William Ellery's great-grandfather came to America and settled in Gloucester, Massachusetts. His grandfather moved to Bristol, Rhode Island, and then to Newport, where his parents, William and Elizabeth (Almy) Ellery made their home. Young William Ellery graduated from Harvard in 1747 and returned to Newport. He was involved in business as a merchant, served as a naval officer and served two terms as clerk of the General Assembly. In 1770, he began practicing law, 23 years after he had graduated from Harvard.

In 1776, he took his seat in Congress. He retained his seat every year except 1780 and 1782. He served until 1786. In 1779, he was appointed as a congressional member of the Board of Admiralty. In 1780, he was given an office by Congress and served as a non-congressional member of the board.

When the British occupied Newport during the war, they burned Ellery's property in revenge for his activities. In 1785, he was elected chief justice of the superior court of Rhode Island, but rejected this position in order to continue serving in Congress.

Ellery retired from Congress in 1786 and became commissioner of the Continental Loan Office for Rhode Island. He held this position until January 1, 1790. He was appointed by President George Washington as collector of the customs for the district of Newport and held this position for 30 years. He was one of the few Federalists retained by Thomas Jefferson, James Madison and James Monroe, which speaks for his character and Revolutionary War record.

When he signed the Declaration of Independence, he positioned himself near the secretary so he could watch the faces of the others who signed "their death warrant." "All displayed undaunted resolution," he said.

Of the three men standing behind the row of men seated on the second stamp of the Bicentennial issue of July 4, 1976, William Ellery is the man in the center, as depicted on Trumbull's painting *Declaration of Independence*.

Rodrego de Escobedo (Escobar)

Scott 118
Born: circa 1470, Huelva Province, Spain?
Died: circa 1530, Palos, Huelva Province, Spain?

Aboard the *Santa Maria,* the flagship under the command of Christopher Columbus, was the pilot, Peralonzo Nino of the Nino maritime family of Palos; Juan de la Cosa, who had captured the *Santa Maria* and was thus her owner; several civilians; an interpreter; a royal comptroller; a steward; and a master-at-arms. Also aboard was a legal officer or notary by the name of Rodrego de Escobedo or Escobar, who was to witness any discoveries, to make proper records and deeds, and to make official all transactions in the name of Spain.

The ships *Santa Maria, Nina* and *Pinta* sailed on September 6, 1492, from the old world to the new, arriving at Guanahani Island on October 12. Escobedo duly witnessed the great event. Three launches were lowered, and men from each ship were taken ashore. The site was called Fernandez Bay.

Escobedo was at Columbus' side to draft all deeds and notarize all transactions. According to records, Columbus claimed the island for Spain, gave thanks to the Lord, knelt down and kissed the earth and proclaimed the island to be San Salvador in the name of the holy Savior. Everything that Columbus proclaimed was written down by Escobedo and made official. All present signed the deed as witnesses. The natives watched as though the Christians were performing some magical rite.

On the fourth voyage, Columbus sailed along the coast near the area that today is Panama. It is recorded that on January 24, 1503, Columbus had retreated to Chief Quibian's village. His men were making a nuisance of themselves, and the natives were restless. Diego Mendez and Rodrego de Escobar pulled off a head-shaving prank. This amazed the natives, who were presented with the shears, mirror and comb. It is not known if this was the same notary Rodrego de Escobedo or Escobar of Columbus' first voyage.

Escobedo is seen in the center of the painting *Landing of Columbus* by John Vanderlyn. He is standing directly behind Columbus, which indicates his importance. The painting was selected for the 15¢ Columbian stamp issued April 2, 1869.

Jan van Eyck

Scott 1363
Born: circa 1385, Maaseik, Limburg Province, Belgium
Died: 1441, Bruges, Belgium

Jan van Eyck may have been a younger brother of Hubert van Eyck (1366-1426), although this is not known for certain. Jan was raised under the protection of the Benedictine convent. When the schools of painting in Maaseik degenerated so that nothing much was flourishing, Van Eyck moved to Flanders. He was under the sponsorship of Philip of Charolais until Philip's court was dissolved.

At this time, John of Bavaria was in residence at the Hague as Count of Holland. He hired Van Eyck as his painter. Van Eyck worked for the Count of Holland until 1424, when he returned to the employ of Philip, who was then the Duke of Burgundy. He remained in Philip's service until his death. He received his salary at Bruges, but he resided at Lille. For extra pay, he went on missions for Philip the Good to Lisbon to seek favors from Isabella of Portugal. In the Spanish provinces, he studied landscape paintings. When he returned, he settled at Bruges and married. He had a daughter.

Van Eyck painted altarpieces and portraits. An excellent example is the *Annunciation* on the outer panel of the altarpiece in Ghent, painted in 1432. Of his portraits, *Young Man* in 1432 and *Man in a Red Turban* in 1433 are realistic.

Jan van Eyck's paintings are not as masculine as those of Hubert van Eyck, and his religious paintings are not as stern. For Rollin, chancellor of Burgundy, Jan van Eyck painted the *Madonna* in 1433. It is now in the Louvre, Paris. In the same year, he painted the *Virgin and Child* that is housed in the National Gallery, Melbourne, Australia. In 1435, he painted the *Madonna and Child*, now in the Stadelsches Kunstinstitut, Frankfurt, Germany.

The angel Gabriel from *The Annunciation* by Van Eyck was chosen for the traditional Christmas stamp in 1968.

Ferdinand II of Aragon

Scott: 234
Born: March 10, 1452, Sos del Rey Catolica, Aragon, Spain
Died: January 23, 1516, Madrigalejo, Spain

Ferdinand was the son of King John II of Aragon and Juana Enriquez. In 1468, at the age of 16, he began negotiating for a marriage with his cousin, Princess Isabella, sister of Henry IV of the Kingdom of Castile and Leon. On October 19, 1469, they were married. They had five children: Isabella, the heir apparent John, Juana, Catalina and Maria.

In 1474, Isabella's brother died, and she proclaimed herself queen. Henry's daughter, Juana la Beltraneja, claimed she was the queen. Civil war broke out. Ferdinand's skillful military leadership put the uprising to rest. In 1479, John II died, and Ferdinand became king of Aragon. Ferdinand played the dual role of Ferdinand II of Aragon and Isabella's consort, establishing the basis for national unity in Spain. Though Isabella was energetic and a devout Catholic and Ferdinand an unscrupulous politician, the couple were nevertheless confirmed the "Catholic kings" by Alexander VI at the suggestion of Innocent VIII, primarily for political reasons. The Muslim kingdom in Spain was expelled in the 1480s, ending with the fall of Granada in 1492 after 11 years of war. With this menace over, Christopher Columbus was finally sanctioned to find India by sailing westward to Christianize the heathen world.

In 1493, Ferdinand took back the provinces of Cerdagne and Roussillon from France. In 1494, he expelled the French from Naples and, in 1504, took over the Kingdom of Naples.

On November 26, 1504, Isabella died. Their only daughter, Juana la Loca ("The Insane"), could not rule. Ferdinand had been named her regent by Isabella. By that time, the heir apparent and their eldest daughter had both died. Juana was insane.

In his last years, Ferdinand's Italian holdings were being threatened by Italy. He died in 1516, and his grandson, Charles I (later Charles V of the Holy Roman Empire), became king of a united Spain.

Ferdinand is seen seated on the throne with Queen Isabella on the 15¢ stamp of the Columbian Exposition issue of January 2, 1893.

William Few

Scott 798
Born: June 8, 1748, near Baltimore, Maryland
Died: July 16, 1828, Fishkill-on-the-Hudson, New York

The family of William Few's father (also named William) emigrated from England to Pennsylvania in 1682. His father moved to Maryland to become a tobacco planter. He married Mary Wheeler. Tobacco raising proved unprofitable, and the family moved in 1758 to North Carolina to live in the frontier. Young William had no formal schooling.

About 10 years before the Revolution, citizens of North Carolina organized, calling themselves the Regulators. They wanted to enforce respect for life and property. Governor William Tryon led a force against the Regulators and defeated them in a bloody battle along Alemance Creek on May 16, 1771. Six of the vigilantes were accused of treason and hanged. One was James Few, William's brother. This battle could be considered the beginning of the Revolutionary War. Those who survived became Sons of Liberty.

Immediately following the Alemance Battle, the British destroyed the Fews' farm. This created a financial burden for the family. The father left with the family and joined a Quaker settlement in Georgia, leaving young William behind to settle matters. William joined the family in 1776 and became an ardent Revolutionist as a lieutenant colonel. In addition to his field duty, William was twice a member of the General Assembly of Georgia and a member of the state executive council. He was state surveyor-general, commissioner to the Indians, and twice a delegate to the Continental Congress. He was elected to the General Assembly in 1783.

In 1787, he was one of six delegates from Georgia to be sent to the Philadelphia Convention that drafted the U.S. Constitution. He and Abraham Baldwin stayed to the end, and both signed it. In 1788, he was a member of the state convention that ratified the Constitution and was one of the first U.S. senators from Georgia. He served a fourth term in the Georgia Assembly, and in 1796, he was appointed judge of the second federal judicial court.

In 1799, he moved to New York City, served four years on the General Assembly and other city offices. From 1804 to 1814, he was a director in the Manhattan Bank and president of the City Bank, when his career ended.

Few is depicted on the 1937 Constitution Sesquicentennial stamp.

Sir Luke Fildes

Scott 949
Born: October 18, 1844, Liverpool, England
Died: February 27, 1927, London, England

Samuel Luke Fildes received his art training in the South Kensington and Royal Academy schools. This English genre painter and illustrator is usually referred to as Sir Luke Fildes. He is generally known for the pictures he painted of Venetian life and the many notable portraits he rendered.

Among his most famous are the coronation portraits of King Edward VII and Queen Alexandra and of King George V.

The Casual Ward, painted in 1874, is at the Royal Holloway College. But his most famous picture is *The Doctor*, painted in 1891. It hangs in the National Gallery of British Art (Tate Gallery) in London.

Fildes was elected to the Academy of Royal Artists in 1879 and the Royal Academy (of Arts) in 1887. He was knighted in 1906. He is noted for the sentimentality reflected in his paintings.

Fildes's painting *The Doctor* is most significant for the year it was painted, 1890. That year Emil von Behring observed the existence of the curative properties in the serums of animals that had recovered from diphtheria.

The therapeutic value of the serum was established beyond doubt in 1894, when the death rate from the disease in Paris was cut in half using the serum. It also was used in Copenhagen in the Blegsdam Hospital in 1898.

It was in 1826 that Pierre Bretonneau of Tours made a classic description of the disease, giving it the present name, and then 57 years later, Edwin Klebs of Konigsberg, Prussia, demonstrated the diphtheria bacillus in 1883.

Actually diphtheria was known from antiquity. It was Aretaeus the Cappadocian who first described diphtheria, called ulcera Syriaca in the 3rd century A.D.

But, as Sir Luke Fildes shows in his painting, doctors were no better off in 1890 than Aretaeus was in the 3rd century and for centuries before that. They could only sit and watch the child die, as sadly depicted on the stamp honoring physicians. The stamp was issued July 9, 1947.

Thomas Fitzsimons

Scott 798
Born: 1741, Ireland
Died: August 26, 1811, Philadelphia, Pennsylvania

When Thomas Fitzsimons signed the U.S. Constitution at Philadelphia in 1787, he signed it "FitzSimons." He came from Ireland when he was a youth and made Philadelphia his home. He went into the mercantile business. On November 23, 1763, he married Catharine Meade, whose father, Robert Meade, was an influential merchant. Robert Meade was the great-grandfather of General George G. Meade, who defeated General Robert E. Lee in the Battle of Gettysburg 100 years after Catharine and Thomas were married. Fitzsimons went into partnership with his wife's brother, George. Together they formed George Meade & Company, specializing in trade with the West Indies.

Fitzsimons was a staunch backer of the cause for independence. After the Battle of Lexington and Concord, he raised a company of militia and, as their commander, took part in several meaningful campaigns. He also served on the Council of Safety and the Navy Board. Fitzsimons agitated the government to pay the soldiers their back pay before they were sent home.

In 1783, he was a member of the Philadelphia Board of Censors. He was elected to the state legislature. He was a member of the Federal Constitution of 1787 and, on November 17, put his "ThoS FitzSimons" to this document. In 1789, he was elected to the first House of Representatives and served until 1795. He wholeheartedly supported Hamilton's fiscal policies, and wanted to retire the debt and level a protective tariff.

When he was defeated for re-election in 1794 by Democrat John Swanwick, he returned to full-time private life, except for a position on a commission to fulfill the Jay Treaty. In 1781, he helped establish the Bank of North America. He was also a founder and director of the Insurance Company of North America. He was president of the Philadelphia Chamber of Commerce. He took an interest in education and was a trustee of the University of Pennsylvania.

Despite his successes, he, along with Robert Morris and other business associates, went into bankruptcy. He never fully recovered financially. He nevertheless was always a philanthropist.

He is one of the signers on the 1937 Constitution Sesquicentennial stamp.

William Floyd

Scott 1691
Born: December 17, 1734, Brookhaven, Long Island, New York
Died: August 4, 1821, Westernville, New York

William Floyd's great-grandfather, Richard Floyd, came to the Colonies from Wales in the 1600s and settled in Long Island. William was the eldest son of Nicoll and Tabitha Smith Floyd. The elder Floyd died when William was 18, and young Floyd took over the proprietorship of the family's land and wealth. He had limited schooling. He did not attend college.

Floyd capitalized on the family wealth and long-standing high social position in the community, which won him important positions in civic affairs and in the military. He was an officer in the Suffolk County militia and was elevated to major general. He heartily supported the Revolution.

From 1774 to 1777, he served in the Continental Congress from the New York delegation and again from 1778 to 1783. He served on the committees of clothing, in 1776, and the admiralty and treasury, in 1779. He was dependable but neither brilliant nor aggressive. When the British invaded Long Island, they took possession of Floyd's property. His militia drove the enemy off, but in 1776, the Redcoats drove Floyd's harassed family to Connecticut. By the end of the war, his estate lie in ruins.

He served in the New York State Senate. From 1789 to 1791, he was in the First Congress but failed in his bid for re-election for the second term.

In 1784, he purchased land on the headwaters of the Mohawk River near Rome, New York. He ran for lieutenant governor against Stephen Van Rensselaer in 1795, and in 1801, he was a delegate to the New York state constitutional convention. He served as presidential elector in 1792, 1800, 1804 and lastly in 1820. In 1808, at the age of 74, he was again state senator.

Floyd had married twice. Isabella Jones of Southhampton was his first wife and Joanna Strong of Setauket his second.

On the first stamp of the four Declaration of Independence stamps issued July 4, 1976, Floyd is the fifth from the left of the men standing.

80

John Forbes

Scott 1123
Born: 1710, Fife County, Scotland
Died: March 11, 1759, Philadelphia, Pennsylvania

John Forbes was born into the military profession. His father was Colonel John Forbes, who steered him into purchasing a cornet's commission in the Second North British Dragoons, the Scots Greys, when he was 25 years of age. He served in the War of the Austrian Succession and distinguished himself in the Battle of Fontenoy in 1745 and the Battle of Dettingen in 1748.

Colonel Forbes served as adjutant general to the Earl of Loudoun in the 17th Foot at Nova Scotia in the spring of 1758. By year's end, he was promoted to brigadier general, assigned to lead troops against the French and Indians at Fort Duquesne, the gateway to the west. He spent most of 1758 clearing the way from Bedford, west of Somerset and over Laurel Hill.

He had inadequate equipment and lacked funds. He had difficulty getting his artillery to keep up with him. His troops were harassed by the Indians. His troops were made up of about 6,500 officers and men, including Colonel Henry Bouquet's battalion of Royal Americans, Montgomery's Black Watch Hylanders and about 5,000 men from Maryland, Pennsylvania, North Carolina and Virginia, the latter with a detachment led by Colonel George Washington. They reached Fort Duquesne in late November. The French garrison had abandoned the fort. They had too few men to guard the approaches. The Indians had fallen away from them and transferred their uncertain loyalty to the English. The local manpower had returned to their farms where they were needed.

Forbes became desperately ill and was hauled along on a litter. He commanded the group with his usual vigor until he reached his goal. He promptly changed the name of the fort to Fort Pitt in honor of William Pitt, who had been named chief minister of England in June 1757 and had directed the affairs in the decisive theater in America. It was the beginning of the end of the French domination in America and the beginning of British eminence. It was also the beginning of the end of Forbes. He was taken to Philadelphia critically ill. He died the following March. The name Fort Pitt was retained, and the site later became the city of Pittsbourgh (today, Pittsburgh).

Forbes is seen lying on the litter on the 1958 Fort Duquesne stamp.

Frank Heyling Furness

Furness 1839-1912 Penn Academy Philadelphia
Architecture USA 15c

Scott 1840
Born: November 12, 1839, Philadelphia, Pennsylvania
Died: June 27, 1912, Philadelphia, Pennsylvania

In the obituaries of Frank Furness in the Philadelphia newspapers, much was said about his war record and the lives of his father and brother, but there was hardly a mention of the more than 300 buildings he designed and built in and around Philadelphia. Today, more than half of his buildings have been demolished, but he did much to shape Philadelphia in the 19th century.

He had a knack for drawing caricatures. He preferred to be called "Captain" and strode around town in a domineering military manner. He dressed in loud plaids to go with his red beard and drooping mustache. It is said that he could draw and swear at the same time. This impressed no one except young Louis Sullivan who worked in his office as a draftsman in 1873. Furness had several partners over the years, but none lasted more than a few years.

Furness was the last child of a Unitarian minister. Furness quit school early and went to work for Philadelphia architect John Fraser. He studied under Richard Morris Hunt (1827-95). When the Civil War broke out in 1861, he enlisted in the Union cavalry, rising to the rank of captain and receiving the Medal of Honor.

After the war, he returned to Hunt's office for about a year and became thoroughly indoctrinated in the eclectic Beaux Arts-inspired architecture of which Hunt was the acknowledged American master. Furness stuck to the Gothic-derived style of the Victorian era. When tastes changed, he did not change with them. His commissions declined. His crowning point was the Library of the University of Pennsylvania (1891), renamed the Furness Building. He also designed the Pennsylvania Academy of Fine Arts (1876) and the Entrance Pavilions to the gardens of the Zoological Society.

Furness is honored on a stamp in the 1980 American Architecture series. The stamp with his name features the Penn Academy building in Philadelphia.

Johann Fust

Scott 1014
Born: circa 1400, Mainz, Germany
Died: October 30, 1466, Paris, France

Johann Fust, or Faust, was a lawyer, banker and money-lender of Mainz, Rhineland-Palatinate, Germany. He is best remembered for advancing Johannes Gutenberg money for his work on a printing press with movable type. In 1450, Fust advanced the sum of 800 guilders to Gutenberg. He loaned him additional moneys in 1452. Apparently Gutenberg had not made payments, and in 1455, Fust brought suit to collect the sum of 2,026 guilders for principal and interest. Gutenberg was to have made payments of 300 guilders a year but fell in arrears.

The suit was tried by the Barefoot Friers of Mainz, and it was decided in Fust's favor on November 6, 1455. Some historians say that Fust settled by taking printing equipment from Gutenberg in the value owed, and others say this is not so. Nevertheless, Fust, with the aid of his son-in-law Peter Schoeffer of Gernsheim, who had been a scribe in Paris in 1449, set up a printing press. By August 14, 1457, they had completed a Psalter of 350 leaves. It was especially remarkable because each paragraph began with a letter printed in two colors, blue and red. These letters were printed from two-piece type.

Fust and Schoeffer in 1459 printed a folio of 160 leaves by Durandus titled *Rationale divinorum officorum* and the 51-leaf book of the *Clementine Constitutions*. In 1461 and 1462, these printers published several papal bulls, proclamations of Adolf of Nassau, and other matters. In 1462, they printed the two-volume *Biblia Sacra Latina* on Andreae gloss. Another with Andreae gloss is the *Sixth Book of Decretal*, a folio of 141 leaves dated December 17, 1465. Fust and Schoeffer are given credit for producing the first book of the Latin classics, *Cicero's De officiis*, in 1465. In an inscription placed at the end of the book, Fust wrote, for the first time, referring to Peter Schoeffer, "puerum suum" (my son). This book was reprinted February 4, 1466, and was the first to contain Greek characters.

The *Gramatica rhytmica* came out in 1466, a folio of 11 pages. This could well have been Fust's last work. In the fall, he was in Paris at the time of the plague that struck the city. It is believed that Fust died of the disease.

On the 1952 3¢ stamp, Fust is seen standing behind Gutenberg as Gutenberg is showing a vellum of print to the elector of Mainz.

James Gadsden

Scott 1028
Born: May 15, 1788, Charleston, South Carolina
Died: December 25, 1858, Charleston, South Carolina

James Gadsden was the grandson of Christopher Gadsden (1724-1805). Christopher Gadsden made himself known at the Continental Congress at Carpenter's Hall in Philadelphia in 1774. At the Stamp Act Congress, Christopher Gadsden said, "There ought to be no New England men, no New Yorker, known on the continent, but all of us Americans."

James Gadsden grew up in Charleston. He studied at Yale, graduating in 1806. He went into the merchandising business in Charleston. He joined the Army and served through the War of 1812. He held the rank of lieutenant.

During the first period of the Seminole War in Florida, he served as aide to General Andrew Jackson. In 1818, Jackson ordered the execution of two British traders, Robert Ambrister and Alexander Arbothnot. It was Gadsden who had uncovered the evidence that convicted them. By 1820, he had risen to the rank of colonel. While he was acting adjutant general in 1822, he resigned from the Army. He was well-acquainted with the Florida gulf coast region.

He settled on a plantation in Florida. President James Monroe assigned him the job of relocating Seminole Indians on reservations in southern Florida. Gadsden remained on this assignment until 1832, when the Seminoles were ordered to go West. This led to the second Seminole War of 1834-35. In 1842-43, about 3,800 Seminoles joined as part of the Five Civilized Tribes removed to Indian Territory in Oklahoma. Many, however, remained in Florida.

Gadsden returned to Charleston,where, in 1840, he was made president of the Louisville, Cincinnati & Charleston Railroad, which two years later became the South Carolina Railroad Company. He advocated a large transcontinental line. In 1853, he was appointed minister to Mexico by Secretary of War Jefferson Davis. He negotiated with Mexican President Antonio Lopez de Santa Anna for the purchase of land south of the Gila River that was Mexican land according to the 1848 Treaty of Guadalupe Hidalgo. On April 25, 1854, the Senate approved a little less than 30,000 square miles of what is now the southern quarter of New Mexico and Arizona. It was called the Gadsden Purchase to honor Gadsden's efforts.

The Gadsden Purchase is honored on a 3¢ stamp issued in 1953.

Thomas Gainsborough

Scott 1536
Born: spring 1727, Sudbury, Suffolk, England
Died: August 2, 1788, London, England

Thomas Gainsborough painted about 500 pictures and sketched some 18 plates. The most well-known is *Blue Boy*, a painting of Master Buttall, in the Huntington collection, San Marino, California. He painted George III eight times. He made his living painting portraits, but he told the king he preferred landscapes. He would often place a landscape in the background of a portrait.

From 1780, he gave vent to his desires and painted pictures of peasants, combining figures with his beloved landscapes. From 1784 until his death four years later, he exhibited his paintings in his home in the Schomberg House, Pall Mall, after withdrawing from the Royal Academy.

His portraits were good likenesses, paint and powder, silks and satins not withstanding. A beautiful example is the painting of *The Hon. Mrs. Graham* in the National Gallery, Edinburgh. The earliest examples are *The Road Through a Wood*, 1747, in Philadelphia's Museum of Art; *Cornard Wood*, National Gallery, London; and *The Charterhouse*, Founding Hospital, London.

Gainsborough's father was a manufacturer of crepe. Thomas was the youngest of nine children. When he was 14, he went to London and received instruction from Hubert Gravelot in etching. He studied at the Academy in St. Martin's Lane. He returned to Sudbury and married Margaret Burr in 1745. Philip Thickness, governor of Landquart Fort, obtained commissions for him. Thickness wrote *Sketch of the Life and Paintings of Thomas Gainsborough*.

In 1759, Gainsborough went to Bath. He entered his paintings in exhibitions in London. He finally settled in London in 1774. He was a charter member of the Royal Academy. He died at age 61 and was buried at Kew.

One of Gainsborough's portraits, that of Mr. John Douglas, was chosen to represent letter writing in the Universal Postal Union issue of 1974.

Elbridge Gerry

Scott 1692
Born: July 17, 1744, Marblehead, Massachusetts
Died: November 23, 1814, Washington, D.C.

Elbridge Gerry graduated from Harvard in 1762. He worked with his father in the mercantile business. In 1772, he became a member of the Massachusetts General Court and served on the Committee of Correspondence. He was in the provincial congress and was a member of the Committee on Safety in 1774 and 1775. In 1776, he entered the Continental Congress. Because of illness, he was unable to sign the Declaration of Independence until September. He was a staunch supporter of the Revolution. He remained in Congress until 1781, then returned to the mercantile business. He again returned to Congress in 1783.

President John Adams, in 1797, appointed Gerry to accompany John Marshall and Charles C. Pinckney on a commission to France to settle smoldering disputes. The XYZ (as Adams called the three outside agents) Affair involving the commission was rebuffed. All efforts to negotiate a treaty of commerce and friendship with France, which involved a $250,000 bribe, ended in the two nations at loggerheads. It nearly culminated in war. Marshall and Pinckney left in disgust, but Gerry stayed on. Adams labored for a peaceful settlement. Eventually the dispute ended with the Treaty of Montefontaine.

Each year from 1800 to 1803, Gerry unsuccessfully ran for governor of Massachusetts. In 1810, he ran again and was elected. During his second term of office, the senatorial district boundaries were redrawn to favor Republican domination and restrict the Federalists in subsequent elections. Some of the districts appeared grotesque on the maps. One was likened to a salamander and called a "gerrymander." The process of redistricting to serve political purposes is known today as "gerrymandering."

In 1812, Gerry won the vice-presidential seat as James Madison's running mate. Two years later he died in office.

Of the men seated on the second stamp of the signers of the Declaration of Independence stamps issued in 1976, Gerry is the fourth from the left.

Domenico Ghirlandajo

Scott 1579
Born: 1449, Florence, Italy
Died: January 11, 1494, Florence, Italy

Domenico (di Tommaso Bigordi) Ghirlandajo was the son of Tommaso Bigordi, a goldsmith. He worked with his father as an apprentice but changed to painting and mosaic work under the tutelage of Alesso Baldovinetti. His earliest work now existing is the fresco at San Gimignano, Siena Province. Here, in 1475, he was commissioned to decorate the chapel of St. Fina in the Collegiate. These frescoes commemorate the deaths of local saints.

In 1480, he decorated the wall of the Ognisanti Church in Florence with a painting of St. Jerome. In the refractory is his *Last Supper*. In 1481, he received a commission from Pope Sixtus IV to go to Rome to paint frescoes in the Sistine Chapel along with Cosimo Roselli and Sandro Botticelli. Only the *Christ Calling the First Apostles* survives.

From 1482 to 1485, he painted frescoes in the Sala della Orologio in the Palazo Vecchio. From the study of architecture of the ancient city of Rome, he was inspired to paint the *Apotheosis of St. Zenobious*. He was commissioned to paint scenes from the life of St. Francis in the chapel of the Sassetti family in the Church of Santa Trinita. With several assistants, he was commissioned by Giovonni Novella to restore the frescoes in the choir of St. Maria Novella. Only the *Birth of the Virgin* was solely Ghirlandajo's.

Ghirlandajo flourished in Florence at the time of Lorenzo il Magnifico of the House of Medici. He painted the portraits of Florentine dignitaries in his frescoes. The altarpiece of St. Maria Novella, the *Virgin in Glory*, is now in Munich. The *Virgin and Saints* is in the Uffizi Gallery, Florence. The *Adoration of the Magi* is in the Innocenti in Florence; the *Visitation* is in the Louvre, Paris; and *Christ in His Glory* is in the Badia of Volterra. Michelangelo spent three years under his guidance. Ghirlandajo died of a fever at age 45.

His *Madonna and Child* appears on the 1975 traditional Christmas stamp.

Nicholas Gilman

Scott 798
Born: August 3, 1755, Exeter, New Hampshire
Died: May 2, 1814, Philadelphia, Pennsylvania

Nicholas Gilman was the son of Nicholas and Ann Taylor Gilman of Exeter, New Hampshire. Young Nicholas grew up and received his elementary education in Exeter, New Hampshire. Exeter, at the falls of the Squamscott River, was settled in 1638 by the Reverend John Wheelwright, whose individualism seemed to have set the tone for the community. Revolutionary attitudes and politics characterized the town from the start. It was one of the first towns to defy royal commands, to flaunt talk of liberty and to burn in effigy British Lords Bute and North. Revolution became the talk of the town, and Exeter claimed to have only one Tory — the town printer.

When the Revolution erupted, the capital at Portsmouth, which was heavy with Tories, was moved to Exeter. New Hampshire signed the first state constitution in Exeter in 1776. It was the first of the 13 Colonial states to do so. This was the atmosphere that surrounded young Gilman. When the war broke out, he entered the Army. He was commissioned captain in the New Hampshire line, and later transferred to the adjutant-general's staff and served until the war ended. He returned to Exeter and became active in politics.

He was a delegate to Congress from 1786 to 1788 and, with John Langdon of Portsmouth, represented New Hampshire in the Constitutional Convention of 1787. Both signed the Constitution as representatives of the state. Gilman understood the importance of its adoption by the state and was anxious and concerned when New Hampshire was slow to ratify it.

He served in the new Congress as a Federalist from 1789 to 1797. His only contribution during this time was a plea for a post office in Exeter. He accepted a minor position offered to him by Thomas Jefferson in 1802. He switched from a Federalist to a Jeffersonian Republican. He ran for the U.S. Senate that year but was defeated. He left politics until 1804, when he served in the state Senate for a year. When he ran for the U.S. Senate in 1804, he was elected. He held that seat until his death on May 2, 1814, in Philadelphia. While on his way home from the capital, he suddenly died. Gilman never married.

He is depicted on the 1937 Constitution Sesquicentennial stamp.

Il Giorgione (Zorzi da Castelfranco)

Scott 1444
Born: circa 1478, Castelfranco Veneto, Treviso, Italy
Died: September or October 1510, Venice, Italy

Giorgione, also known as Zorzi, Zorzo or Zorzon of Castelfranco, was probably the son or grandson of a person called Zorzon, a native of the neighboring town of Vedelago, who was living in Castelfranco in 1460. Another story of Georgione's birth was that he was the son of a peasant girl in the neighboring town of Vedelago by one of the members of the great Barbarelli family. This was a fabrication simply to tie the Barbarelli family to the great painter, since the story came some years later. It is groundless.

Early in his life, Georgione went to Venice as an apprentice to Giovanni Bellini. He remained in Venice. He received commissions from the Doge Agostino Barberigo and the condottere Consalvo Ferrante as early as 1500.

In 1504, he received a commission to paint an altarpiece in the Cathedral of Castlefranco in memory of Matteo Costanzo. In 1507, he worked on a picture for the hall of the ducal palace. This commission came from the Council of Ten. He also worked on the frescoes on the exterior of the Fondaco di Tedeschi or German Merchant's Hall at Venice in 1507 and 1508. He worked on the Cas Soranz, the Casa Grimani alli Servi and other palaces in Venice.

He died of the plague at the young age of 32. He had gained great fame by then. He introduced new innovations in art. His treatment of light and shadows was significant. The arrangement or treatment of the light and dark parts of his pictorial work is seen clearly in the painting *Adoration of the Shepherds* or *Allendale Nativity* in the National Gallery, Washington, D.C.

Experts say only 10 to 12 works by Giorgione are now in existence. Much of his work has been lost. The *Sleeping Venus* in the Gemaldegalerie, Dresden, is an example of his work, as is the *Concert Champetre* in the Louvre, Paris.

Giogione's *Adoration of the Shepherds* was chosen for the traditional Christmas stamp of 1971.

Nathaniel Gorham

Scott 798
Born: May 27, 1738, Charlestown, Massachusetts
Died: June 11, 1796, Charlestown, Massachusetts

The historic town of Charlestown, Nathaniel Gorham's birthplace and home, is located on Boston Harbor between the mouths of the Mystic and Charles rivers. Today, it is the site of the Boston Naval Shipyard. The *Constitution* (*Old Ironsides*) is docked in Charlestown. The *Constitution* was launched the year after Gorham died.

When Gorham was 15 years old, in 1753, he was sent to New London, Connecticut, to apprentice to a merchant. He did not return until 1759. He promptly went into business on his own and also took part in civic affairs.

During 1774-75, he was a delegate to the provincial congress, and from 1778 to 1781, he sat on the Board of War. He served in the Massachusetts Constitutional Convention in 1779 and 1780. He was elected to the state Senate in 1780 and to the House in 1781, where he served for six years. He was the speaker for three years.

Gorham was a delegate to the Continental Congress in 1782, 1783 and the 1785-87 session, and served as president from June 1786. He was presiding officer of the convention. He, along with Rufus King, signed the U.S. Constitution on September 17, 1787, and a year later, Gorham was a staunch member of the Massachusetts ratifying convention.

He continued to be active in state politics. From 1785, he was the judge of the Middlesex Court of Common Pleas and a member of the governing council from 1788 to 1789.

In 1788, he joined with Oliver Phelps of Connecticut and purchased a large tract of land extending over some six million acres. It was land that had been ceded to Massachusetts from New York following the Revolution. It was a grandiose land speculation scheme, but it went sour. Within two years, Gorham and his partner were bankrupt. Gorham owed the state a huge sum. The sale of land to the settlers did not materialize at a time of post-war depression. He could not meet his payments.

He spent the last six years of his life at Charlestown in retirement. Gorham and the other signers of the Constitution are memorialized on the Constitution Sesquicentennial stamp issued September 7, 1937.

Francisco Jose de Goya y Lucientes

Scott 1537
Born: March 30, 1746, Fuendetodos, Aragon, Spain
Died: April 16, 1828, Bordeaux, France

The village of Fuendetodos was in the semi-desert area around Saragossa, Spain. It was Goya's mother's home. The family had gone there for financial help. His father was a master gilder in Saragossa. By 1760, the family returned to Saragossa, where Goya went to school in the studio of Jose Luzan Martinez. It was here that he met Francisco Bayeu and his lifelong friend, Zapater.

When he was 19, Goya made a hasty trip to Madrid after a brawl between church rivals in which three youths were killed. He ended up destitute in Rome.

He returned to Saragossa that fall and obtained a commission to paint frescoes in the famous cathedral El Pilar and in the Carthusian church Aula Dei. He married Bayeu's sister and, in 1775, returned to Madrid. Bayeu was working at the royal palace under Antony Raphael Mengs, who had obeyed the call to Spain to paint for Charles III. Through Bayeu's influence, Goya took a job painting cartoons for tapestries in the crown prince's residence until 1780.

In 1785, Goya was appointed director of the Academy of Arts and became the court painter the following year. In the Prado, he painted *The Family of Charles IV, Queen in a Mantilla* and *King in Uniform*. He created a gallery of portraits of famous men and women, the *Duchess of Alba* being one of his best.

With the French invasion, Goya worked with Joseph Bonaparte and joined the Josefinos. When the French fled Madrid, Goya went into hiding. The painting in 1808 of the *Dos de Mayo* massacre convinced the people that he was a patriotic Spaniard, which was reinforced by his *Disasters of War* etchings.

When he was 78, he settled in Bordeaux, where he painted *Water Carrier, Knife Grinder* and *Milkmaid*. He was mentally tormented in his final years. His home was decorated with nightmarish scenes that are now in the Prado.

His *Portrait of a Gentleman Holding a Letter* was chosen for one of the Universal Postal Union stamp issues of 1974.

John Greaton

Scott 644
Born: March 10, 1741, Roxbury (South Boston), Massachusetts
Died: December 16, 1783, Roxbury, Massachusetts

John Greaton, or Graeton, was the son of John and Catherine Lenton Greaton, proprietors of Roxbury's well-known Greyhound Tavern. His father also carried on a merchandising trade. Greaton grew up in picturesque Roxbury and attended the free Latin School. He went into trading with his father.

He joined the patriots' cause early as one of the Sons of Liberty. On December 26, 1774, he was one of the 15 in Roxbury to establish the non-importation agreements. He was made a lieutenant of the militia in the first parish of Roxbury. When the British marched to Lexington, Greaton greeted them with his gun. He was one of the first to enlist in the Continental Army.

By July 1, 1775, he was a colonel of the regiment of General Heath's Division. During the British siege of Boston, Greaton directed his men to capture and destroy stores of British supplies. He went on an expedition to Canada and suffered hardships in that campaign. On January 1, 1776, he was commissioned colonel of the 24th Continental Infantry and returned to join Washington at Morristown. He took part in the battles of Trenton and Princeton. In the campaign against General John Burgoyne, he was with Nixon's brigade.

He was promoted to senior officer at Albany and commanded the Northern Department in the capacity of brigadier general. His advancement to brigadier general did not come about until January 7, 1783, because of personality conflicts in the Continental Congress, though he was a capable military leader.

While he was awaiting his appointment, he joined with officers of adjoining states to register to Congress their dissatisfaction concerning back pay. Congress finally heeded their demands with concessions of full pay for five years instead of half-pay for life. The Army was disbanded, and Greaton returned to Roxbury, where he died a few months later at age 42.

He had led and commanded his regiment throughout the war, beginning with the Battle of Lexington, and was at the surrender of Burgoyne at Saratoga. He had married Sara Humphreys in 1760.

On the 1927 stamp issued picturing the *Surrender of Burgoyne*, Greaton is the first person pictured to the far left. Only his head is visible above the neck of Captain Seymour's mount of the Shelton Horse Brigade.

Walter Gropius

Scott 2021
Born: May 18, 1883, Berlin, Germany
Died: July 5, 1969, Boston, Massachusetts

Walter A. Gropius is often remembered as the founder and first director of the Bauhaus in Weimar (later moved to Dessau), Germany, which lasted until the Nazi takeover in 1933. It had a revival in Chicago as the New Bauhaus, which evolved into the Chicago Institute of Design.

Gropius began his architectural studies at Charlottenburg-Berlin and Munich universities from 1903 to 1907, then joined the firm of Peter Behrens. Behrens was one of the early modern designers of industrial buildings. His designs range from such simple items as miners' lamps to the complex German AEG Electrical Company building. Gropius, as well as Ludwig Mies van der Rohe and Le Corbusier (Charles Edouard Jeanneret), were greatly influenced by Behrens' building innovations and architectural designs.

Gropius won the competition to build the Fagus Shoe Last Factory at Alfeld an der Leine (1911) in collaboration with Adolf Meyer. This was the first glass-walled building with internal framing that was to become today's international style, a style that eliminates all decorations, even moldings, resulting in a severe, cold, but sternly impressive structure.

Gropius' methods were not pleasing to Hitler, who considered himself the ultimate critic of architectural design. Hitler called these buildings "blocks of ice." In 1928, Gropius resigned the leadership of the Bauhaus and turned it over to Meis van der Rohe.

In 1934, Gropius fled to England and collaborated with Maxwell Fry in designing Impington College, Cambridge. From 1937 to 1952, he headed the Department of Architecture in Harvard University's Graduate School of Design. Gropius designed the dormitories and social rooms of the Graduate Center. After his retirement, he formed TAC (The Architects Collaborative). He designed the U.S. Embassy in Athens (1960), the University of Baghdad (1961), and, with Pietro Belluschi, the Pan Am Building in New York City.

The Gropius House, Lincoln, Massachusetts, is shown on a stamp in the American Architecture series issued in 1982.

Thomas Grosvenor

Scott 1361
Born: September 20, 1744, Pomfret, Windham County, Connecticut
Died: January 11, 1825, Pomfret, Windham County, Connecticut

Thomas Grosvenor was the youngest of four sons of John and Hannah Dresser Grosvenor. He graduated from Yale. He returned to Pomfret to practice law. When Connecticut raised its first seven regiments of minutemen, he was commissioned a second lieutenant in the first company of the 3rd Regiment.

The Americans sent 1,200 men under Colonel William Prescott to occupy Bunker Hill. Prescott's command went beyond Bunker Hill to Breed's Hill. British General Thomas Gage ordered a direct assault up the hill. Twice American lines held, and twice the British, after heavy losses, retreated from their lines. On the third assault, the Americans gave way, for they had run short of ammunition. In the battle, Grosvenor was stationed on the rail fence running from the redoubt to the Mystic River. He received a wound that pierced his right hand, but saw his rifle shots drop nine British soldiers. In John Trumbull's painting *The Battle of Bunker Hill*, he is seen in the right foreground standing with sword in hand. The painting is reproduced on a 1968 stamp.

Grosvenor was promoted to captain and served at the Battle of Long Island, August 27, 1776. He took part in the battles at Brandywine, Germantown and Monmouth. In 1777, he was promoted to major in the 2nd Connecticut Regiment. On March 13, 1778, he was commissioned lieutenant colonel of Durkee's Regiment and served in the Battle of Monmouth on June 28, 1778. Following the death of Durkee, Grosvenor was appointed lieutenant colonel, commandant of the 1st Connecticut Regiment. He served as sub-inspector under Baron Friedrich Willhelm von Steuben and as assistant adjutant general.

After January 1, 1783, he retired to Pomfret and resumed practicing law. He married Ann Mumford, with whom he had five children. He was a member of the Connecticut Governor's Council for more than 20 years, and judge of probate and chief justice of the Court of Common Pleas of Windham County.

Johannes Gutenberg

Scott 1014
Born: 1397? (1394-1399), Mainz, Germany
Died: February 3, 1468, Mainz, Germany

Johannes Gutenberg took his last name from the birthplace of his mother Elsgen Wyrich zum Gutenberg. His father's name was Friel zum Gensfleisch. The family was prosperous. They moved to Strasbourg. Johannes began his early life working with a goldsmith. In the late 1430s, he began a printing operation with Andreas Dritzehn and the Heilmann brothers. It is believed they were working on a secret invention of movable type. Dritzehn died in 1438, and his brothers wanted part of the operation. Gutenberg prevented it, even though the brothers sued. In 1448, Gutenberg returned to Mainz. In Mainz, he demonstrated printing from movable type.

Apparently Gutenberg got the idea from a type of printing used in making playing cards and prints from woodblocks. A well-to-do Mainz banker, Johann Fust, joined Gutenberg about 1450 and gave him financial support. The result of their operation was the so-called 42-line Bible. Their printing had 42 lines per column. This was probably the first real worthwhile printing to come from such a device. The Bible was completed in August 1456. Fust then sued Gutenberg for the moneys owed him. In November 1455, Fust repossessed the printing shop. Fust's son-in-law, Peter Schoeffer, had worked with Gutenberg as an associate. Fust and Schoeffer operated the shop

Gutenberg opened another shop elsewhere in Mainz. Several books — especially the printing of the *Catholicon* of Johann Balbus — are thought by many authorities to have been printed by Gutenberg, though no markings were made in the books to indicate this. He also had ties in Strasbourg. The registers of St. Thomas Church of Strasbourg show that Gutenberg had borrowed money from the chapter of the church on November 17, 1442, and made payments regularly until 1457. This loan had been underwritten by Martin Brechter. After 1458, the payments, either by Gutenberg or Brechter, were in arrears.

In October 1462, Adolphus II, elector of Mainz, suspended all printing and expelled Gutenberg from the city. Gutenberg returned in 1465 after the archbishop made amends and granted him a pension and exemption from taxes.

Gutenberg is shown on the right on the 1952 3¢ Gutenberg Bible issue.

John Hancock

Scott 1687d
Born: January 12, 1737, Braintree (now Quincy), Massachusetts
Died: October 8, 1793, Quincy, Massachusetts

John Hancock was, on August 2, 1776, the first to sign the Declaration of Independence. With a theatrical flourish, he said, "There, I guess King George can read that!" His father, the Reverend John Hancock, died when John was young. His brother Thomas had no children and adopted young John, who suddenly found himself under the paternality of the wealthiest merchant trader in the American Colonies. Young Hancock was sent to the Boston Latin School, then to Harvard, where he graduated in 1754. He studied English merchantilism in London and returned to America in 1761. In two years, he was a full partner of Thomas Hancock and Company. The next year Thomas Hancock died of a stroke. At the age of 27, John was head of the company.

In 1763, he was a member of the Massachusetts General Assembly. The Townshend Acts bore heavily on Massachusetts. When a tidewaiter was forcibly detained while collecting duty from Hancock for the Madeira wine on his sloop, *Liberty*, disturbances broke out. Hancock's ship was confiscated and later burned at Newport.

In March 1770, the Boston Massacre infuriated Hancock. For his generosity, he was made treasurer of Harvard College in 1773, at which job he proved most incompetent. He was soon replaced.

Hancock and Samuel Adams led the patriots. General Gage sent British troops to Concord to destroy war supplies and capture Hancock and Adams. The two were warned in time and fled to Philadelphia.

Hancock served twice as president of the Continental Congress from 1775 to 1777. He served in the Massachusetts Constitutional Convention in 1780. He was governor of Massachusetts from 1780 to 1785. In 1787, he replaced Governor Bowdoin as an aftermath of the Shays' Rebellion.

Hancock is shown sitting by Charles Thomson on the fourth 18¢ stamp of the second souvenir sheet issued May 29, 1976.

Walter Kirtland Hancock

Scott 1408
Born: June 28, 1901, St. Louis, Missouri

Two monumental works of sculpture were started by Gutzon Borglum but finished by others — Mount Rushmore and the memorial to the Confederate Army on Stone Mountain near Atlanta. The Stone Mountain memorial features three colossal equestrian figures, Jefferson Davis, Thomas "Stonewall" Jackson and Robert E. Lee, sculpted on Stone Mountain's shear northern face.

The United Daughters of the Confederacy proposed a huge statue on Stone Mountain in 1915. Originally, the monument was to be just of General Lee, but Borglum proposed three figures on horseback. Borglum began the memorial. He and his sponsors then came to a serious disagreement, and Borglum quit. Another sculptor, Augustus Lukeman, worked on the project from 1923 to 1928, when the owners reclaimed the mountain, and work stopped.

The Stone Mountain project lay fallow from 1928 to 1964 and wasn't finished until 1970. Its completion was made possible in 1958 when the state legislature created a memorial association to buy the land. Walter Hancock was commissioned and finished the project as it stands today.

Hancock was from Gloucester, Massachusetts. He was born in St. Louis, the son of Walter Scott and Anna Spencer Hancock. He studied at the school of fine arts at Washington University in St. Louis, at the University of Wisconsin and the Pennsylvania Academy of Fine Arts. He was granted a fellowship at the American Academy of Rome. He was head of the sculpture department of the Pennsylvania Academy of Fine Arts from 1929 to 1968.

He was the designer of several medals, including the Eisenhower inaugural medal and the Air Medal for both the Army and Navy. In St. Louis, he sculpted the exterior relief at Forest Park. In Kansas City, his work is seen at City Hall and, in Philadelphia, the War Memorial at the Pennsylvania Railroad 30th Street Station. He completed many statues, including those of Douglas McArthur, John Paul Jones, Chief Justice Earl Warren, Chief Justice Warren E. Berger, Robert Frost, Hubert Humphrey, Gerald R. Ford and Abraham Lincoln. Hancock was awarded numerous prizes for his creations and was awarded an honorary doctor of fine arts degree from Washington University. He served as a captain in the Army from 1942 to 1946 as archives officer.

The Stone Mountain colossus is pictured on a 1970 stamp.

Oliver Nowell Hardy

Scott 2562
Born: January 18, 1892, Harlem, Georgia
Died: August 7, 1957, Hollywood, California

Oliver Hardy started his career as a law student at the University of Georgia. He gave up the legal field for the stage and screen. He made his first film in 1913 and directed several short comic films. He moved to Hollywood, arriving at about the same time as Stanley Laurel and Charles Chaplin.

Laurel played parts in movies but was not outstandingly successful. He did some writing and stage directing. He worked in about 60 short films in which he played the comic villain. However, he was quite obscure as a film personality. At the Hal Roach studio in 1926, he teamed up with Stanley Laurel, who had come from England with the Fred Karno vaudeville troupe as Charlie Chaplin's understudy.

It was when these two comedians made the film *Putting Pants on Philip* that they became enthusiastic about teaming up with each other. For the next 25 years, they produced about 200 films, always billed as Laurel and Hardy. Stan was the skinny, whiny-voiced, always smiling (but never laughing), excuse-making sidekick of Hardy, who was always getting the two into what Ollie called "a fine mess!"

They dressed in various manners but almost never without their hats. Laurel usually wore a large bow tie of wild colors and garish design.

Their comedy was a psychological necessity throughout the Depression years of the 1930s and the war years of the 1940s. They were beloved by audiences around the world. Today their films are often replayed on television and special theaters. Look-alikes have appeared on television advertising skits aping the Laurel and Hardy acts. From *Soup to Nuts* (1928) to *The Bullfighters* (1945), just two examples of their best, they never failed to portray classic slapstick comedy.

Hardy appears with Laurel in the 1991 booklet of five different stamps by cartoonist Al Hirschfeld depicting famous American comedians in caricature.

98

William M. Harnett

Scott 1386
Born: August 10, 1848, Clonakilty, County Cork, Ireland
Died: October 29, 1892, New York, New York

The Harnett family emigrated from Ireland to the United States when William was a small boy. They settled in Philadelphia. William learned silver engraving as his trade. When he was about 19, he became interested in painting, spending his spare time at the Pennsylvania Academy of the Fine Arts. When he was of age, he moved to New York City to study at the National Academy of Design and at Cooper Union. He continued his trade as an engraver for a jewelry firm. When he was 27, he devoted his full time to painting, and exhibited his work at the National Academy of Design.

His paintings were precise still life renditons in the tradition of the American painter Raphael Peale and the 17th-century Dutch realists. His paintings reflect the deception-of-the-eye (trompe l'oeil) technique. Harnett was the leader in this style. He grouped together guns, pipes, books, sheet music, busts, musical instruments and other common items on a background of an old wooden door and proceeded to render them in photographic clarity even more realistic and detailed than a camera could accomplish.

His chief follower was John Frederick Peto, also of Philadelphia, who differed markedly in his preoccupation with objects that were used, worn, or discarded, in his humor and in his concern with the dramatic effects of light.

Harnett lived and worked in New York City. He traveled in Europe from 1880 to 1886 and again in 1889. He attracted many followers and imitators, but after his death at the early age of 44, critics looked upon his work as visual trickery. In the early 1940s, however, his style was revived, especially by the surrealists. His paintings *Emblems of Peace*, *After the Hunt*, and *The Old Violin* have established him as one of the leading American artists of the 19th century.

Harnett is honored on the American Painting stamp of 1969 showing his still life painting *Old Models*.

Benjamin Harrison

Scott 1691
Born: 1726, Berkeley, Charles City County, Virginia
Died: April 24, 1791, Berkeley, Charles City County, Virginia

Benjamin Harrison's third son, William Henry Harrison, and his great-grandson and namesake Benjamin Harrison, became the ninth and 23rd presidents of the United States, respectively.

Benjamin Harrison was born in Berkeley mansion in Charles City County, Virginia. He was the son of Benjamin Harrison and Anne Carter. He was the fifth Benjamin in direct line to a Benjamin Harrison who came to the Colonies sometime before March 1633. To distinguish him from the others, historians have dubbed him "the Signer." Harrison was a student at William and Mary College in 1745 when his father died. He did not finish college. He returned home, married Elizabeth Bassett and took charge of Berkeley.

In 1749, he was elected to the House of Burgesses and continuously served there until 1775. He opposed the Stamp Act in 1764, as did others of the planter aristocracy. He likewise opposed Patrick Henry's Stamp Act resolutions as lacking in policy. As a member of Virginia's Committee of Correspondence in 1773, Harrison helped formulate the program of resistance. When the Earl of Dunmore dissolved the House of Burgesses, Harrison was elected to the general congress of the Colonies. He returned to the Congress in 1775 and was retained until 1778, though he resigned in 1777. He was elected to the new House of Delegates and returned successively until 1781. Harrison took an active part in Congress, especially in the Committee for Foreign Affairs and the Marine Committee, helping establish the departments of state, war and navy. He signed the Declaration of Independence and the Articles of Confederation.

In 1781, he took over as governor of Virginia when Thomas Nelson Jr. resigned, and was twice re-elected, serving through 1784. He was again elected to the House of Delegates, where he served until his death.

On the first of the four 1976 Declaration of Independence stamps, Harrison is foremost on the left of center, seated at the table.

100

John Hart

Scott 1692
Born: circa 1711, Stonington, Connecticut
Died: May 11, 1779, Hopewell, New Jersey

John Hart was the son of Edward and Martha Hart. In 1712, when John was yet an infant, the family moved from Stonington, Connecticut, to west-central New Jersey. They settled at Hopewell, just six miles northwest of Princeton. Hart grew up with little or no formal education but learned to farm. In time, he acquired considerable property. In addition to farmland, he invested in fulling mills at nearby Glen Moore and a grist mill and fulling mill in Rocky Hill. In 1740, he married Deborah, the daughter of Richard and Hannah Reeder Scudder of Ewing (Trenton), New Jersey. The Harts had a large family.

Hart was appointed justice of the peace of Hunterdon County in 1755. In 1761, he was elected to the Twentieth Assembly and remained a member until it was dissolved in 1771. He opposed the Stamp Act of 1765 because he felt that rights to tax the Colonies were vested in the Colonies only.

In 1775, he was serving as judge of common pleas of New Jersey. He was elected to the First Provincial Congress of New Jersey on July 8, 1774. He was re-elected and served until June 1776, when he was sent to the Continental Congress. In January 1775, he was chairman of the Township Committee of Hunterdon County and was appointed to the Committee of Correspondence and then to the Committee of Safety on August 17, 1775.

On June 15, 1776, he was elected a delegate to the Continental Congress. On August 2, 1775, he signed the Declaration of Independence and was elected to the first Assembly under the new state constitution of New Jersey.

During the war, as a member of the Council of Safety from March 18, 1777, to October 8, 1778, his farm and mills were laid to waste by the British armies. After the battles of Princeton and Trenton, he returned to his farm. Late in 1778, he retired from public service. He died the following year.

Of the row of men seated in the second stamp of the Declaration of Independence set issued July 4, 1976, Hart is the second from the right.

George P.A. Healy

Scott 1113
Born: July 15, 1813, Boston, Massachusetts
Died: June 24, 1894, Chicago, Illinois

George Healy was the eldest son of a sea captain, William Healy. His mother was Mary Hicks. He had younger brothers and a sister. His father died when George was quite young, and it fell upon him to support the family.

Early in life, Healy showed artistic talent. He was influenced by Thomas Sully. Mrs. Harrison Gray Otis, the wife of a U.S. senator, sat for Healy for a portrait. She recommended his work to other wealthy patrons. By 1834, he had earned enough money to go to Paris.

In Paris, though he spoke no French, he was admitted to the studio of Baron Antoine Jean Gros shortly before the despondent Gros committed suicide. Gros had gained fame for his flattering paintings of Napoleon. Healy became friends with Thomas Couture, who also studied under Gros. Couture was appointed official court painter by Emperor Napoleon III.

Healy remained in Paris and became very adept at painting portraits, which included such notables as King Louis-Philippe, Lewis Cass, Marshal Soult, Francois Guizot, and Leon Gambetta. He was awarded a medal at the Universal Exposition in 1855 for his *Franklin Urging the Claims of the American Colonies before Louis XVI* that he exhibited along with several of his portraits.

He returned to the United States and set up a studio in Chicago. In 1857, he moved into the country. He was a member of the National Academy of Design. He painted more than 500 portraits, including several U.S. presidents. His best, *Webster Replying to Hayne,* now hangs in Faneuil Hall, Boston.

At the end of the Civil War, he returned to Paris. He contributed a self-portrait for the Uffizy Gallery collection in Florence, the first American to be so honored. He returned to Chicago in 1892 and died two years later.

Healy's portrait of the young Abraham Lincoln was chosen for the 1¢ Lincoln Sesquicentennial stamp issued February 12, 1959.

Joseph Hewes

Scott 1692
Born: January 23, 1730, Kingston, New Jersey
Died: November 10, 1779, Philadelphia, Pennsylvania

Joseph Hewes was raised by his Quaker parents, Aaron and Providence Worth Hewes, in Kingston, New Jersey, three miles northeast of Princeton. He attended elementary school in Kingston. He apprenticed himself to a merchant in Philadelphia. He went into business for himself, did well and amassed a considerable fortune. Even though he was in the City of Brotherly Love, his Quaker faith waned, especially when he moved to Edenton, North Carolina, one of the oldest towns in the state.

Hewes had resisted the independence movement, though he had been instructed by the North Carolina provincial congress to support it. It is reported that when he was convinced by John Adams that North Carolina strongly supported it, he "startled suddenly upright, and lifted up both his hands to Heaven, as if he had been in a trance, cried out 'It is done! and I will abide by it.'" He denounced his Quakerism and signed the Declaration of Independence.

He became engaged to Isabella Johnston. A few days before the wedding ceremony was to take place, she died. Hewes remained a lifelong bachelor.

In 1766, he became a borough member of the Colonial Assembly and remained a member until the assembly was dissolved in 1775. He was a member of the Committee of Correspondence. He was a delegate to all five provincial congresses.

In 1774, Hewes was elected to the Continental Congress and served until 1777. He was a borough member of the House of Commons until 1778 and, in 1779, was again elected to Congress. According to the records, overwork caused him to collapse and die. He is buried in Christ Church, Philadelphia.

On the second stamp of the four 1976 Declaration of Independence stamps, Hewes is the fourth man from the right.

103

Thomas J. Heyward

JULY 4,1776

Scott 1691
Born: July 28, 1746, St. Helena's Parish (St. Luke's), South Carolina
Died: March 6, 1809, St. Luke's Parish, South Carolina

Because others in the Heyward family bore the name Thomas, this patriot was referred to as Junior. In 1920, the General Assembly of South Carolina appropriated $2,500 to erect a monument over his grave on his father's plantation. Thomas Heyward Jr. was the eldest son of Colonel Daniel Heyward, one of the wealthiest planters of colonial South Carolina, and Mary Miles Heyward. He was born on the family plantation, "White Hall."

When the British blocked the port of Boston, a provincial congress met on July 6, 1774, at Charleston. Thomas Heyward was a delegate. He was selected as one of the 13 members of the Council of Safety. Heyward was elected to the second provincial congress that met on November 1, 1775, and again on February 1, 1776. He helped prepare the state constitution.

He was chosen by the provincial congress as one of the five delegates from South Carolina to the Second Continental Congress. He signed the Declaration of Independence. He served in the Congress until late 1778. He returned to South Carolina to serve as a circuit judge.

He served in the state militia as a captain of a batallion of artillery in Charleston and saw action in Moultrie's defeat of the British on February 4, 1779, on Port Royal Island, where he was wounded. He also took part in Charleston's defense and was defeated. He was a paroled prisoner of war. His parole was canceled. He was sent to St. Augustine, Florida, and held prisoner until exchanges were made in July 1781. He represented Charleston in the legislature from 1782 to 1784 and continued as a circuit judge until 1789.

Heyward was twice married, first to Elizabeth Mathews in 1773 and, after her death, to Susanna Savage in 1786.

Of the five men seated before the six men standing in the first stamp of the four 1976 Declaration of Independence stamps, Heyward is fourth from left.

Enos Hitchcock

Surrender at Saratoga 1777 by Trumbull

US Bicentennial 13 cents

Scott 1728
Born: March 7, 1744, Springfield, Massachusetts
Died: February 26, 1803, Providence, Rhode Island

Enos Hitchcock's ancestry in America dates to Luke Hitchcock (1606-59), who took the Freeman's oath in New Haven in 1644. Hitchcock moved from New Haven to Wethersfield, Connecticut. Through the years, his descendants moved northward. By 1744, Hitchcock's grandson, Peletiah, was living in Springfield, Massachusetts, where Enos was born. His mother was Sarah Parsons Hitchcock. After his elementary education in Springfield, Enos went to Harvard. He graduated in 1767. He continued his theological studies and, in 1771, was ordained associate pastor to the retiring pastor of the Second Church in Beverly, Massachusetts, where he remained until April 6, 1780.

During the Revolutionary War, Hitchcock served as chaplain in the Revolutionary Army. He shared the hardships of the retreat from Ticonderoga and the triumph of Burgoyne's surrender. He witnessed the execution of Andre, the patriot's vindication of the hanging of Nathan Hale by the British. He often dined with Thaddeus Kosciusko. He preached to the Society of Free Masons on the Feast of St. John with General Washington as a worshiper, and was invited to Washington's headquarters for worship service.

Hitchcock corresponded with the Reverend Joseph Willard, who was later president of Harvard College. He was the guest of Ezra Stiles, president of Yale University. Stiles had been pastor of the Second Congregational Church in Newport, Rhode Island, then served two years at Portsmouth, New Hampshire. He may have been influential in getting Hitchcock established in Providence, Rhode Island, on October 1, 1783, as pastor of the Benevolent Congregational Church, where Hitchcock spent the remainder of his years.

Hitchcock had married Achsah Upham Jordan of Truro, Barnstable County, Massachusetts, on January 13, 1771. The Hitchcock's had one daughter, Achsah. Both his wife and daughter preceded Hitchcock in death. His adopted daughter survived him.

On the 1977 Surrender of Burgoyne stamp, Hitchcock is depicted as the second man from the right.

Katsushika Hokusai

Universal Postal Union 1874-1974   Hokusai   10c US

Scott 1531
Born: October-November 1760, Tokyo, Japan
Died: May 10, 1849, Tokyo, Japan

Color prints, Nishiki-ye, or brocade pictures, so-called from their brilliant coloring, are products of Ukiyo-ye or "passing-world pictures," a genre painting school depicting the everyday life and customs of ordinary people. These pictures were not highly regarded in artistic circles of Japan. They were taken to Europe by the Dutch. They appeared in the Parisian Porte Chinoise, and marvelous specimens were purchased in these shops for a few sous. In time, the mongraphs on Hokusai and Utamaro by Edmond de Concourt attracted public attention to Japanese color prints, and the demand grew. Today, these prints sell for hundreds and even thousands of dollars.

The greatest of all Ukiyo-ye painters, Hokusai, was born in Yedo (Tokyo). At age 5, he was adopted by Nakajima Issai. Most of his family were artisans. Hokusai studied wood engraving, but before he was 20 years of age, he began the study of painting color prints with the famous Kasugawa Shunsho. He was expelled because he showed disrespect for the master and his work.

Henceforth Hokusai lived in extreme poverty, making just enough from his prints to exist. He obtained commissions to illustrate books such as the *Manga*, a 15-volume encyclopedia on Japanese daily life. Hokusai's most famous works are the color prints of the *Thirty-six Views of Fuji*, drawn and colored between 1823 and 1829. He produced a series of color prints, *Views of Famous Bridges, Waterfalls* and *Views of the Lu-chu Island*.

He worked against such famous contemporaries as Hiroshige (Andro Tokitaro); Sharaku, whose prints are rare today; and Kitagawa Utamaro, who gained the title Ukiyo-ye Chuukoo-no-so or "Great Master of the Popular School." Hokusai produced about 30,000 designs.

Five Feminine Virtues by Hokusai depicts a woman reading a letter. It is shown on one of the eight stamps of the 1974 Universal Postal Union issue.

106

Winslow Homer

Scott 1207
Born: February 24, 1836, Boston, Massachusetts
Died: September 29, 1910, Prout's Neck, Maine

Born to be an artist, Winslow Homer painted scenes of people in action and the sea. He was self-taught until he apprenticed himself to a Boston lithographer when he was 19. Two years later, he was an illustrator for *Balluo's Pictorial* in Boston and the *Harper's Weekly* in New York City. When the Civil War broke out, *Harper's* sent Homer to Virginia to sketch scenes of the war and army life, an experience that greatly influenced his life. Earlier he had sketched Abraham Lincoln at the president's inauguration in Washington, D.C.

Late in 1866 he went to France for nearly a year to paint. He had used oil primarily, and in 1873, he began to use watercolor as well as oil. From 1881 to 1882, he lived in England near Tynemouth, a fishing village on the North Sea. This experience influenced him to paint the sea and fishermen in action. In these paintings, he preferred watercolor to oil.

In 1883, he settled in Prout's Neck, Maine, a lonely point of land on the Atlantic Coast. He lived alone. He never married. His subjects from this time on were the seas, the forest, the mountains and the sturdy men who worked in these rugged environs. This resulted in such pictures as *The Life Line* in the Philadelphia Museum of Art, *Eight Bells* in the Addison Gallery, Andover Massachusetts, and *The Fog Warning* in the Boston Museum of Fine Arts.

In the picture *Eight Bells*, painted in 1886, two mariners, dressed for rain with navigation instruments, are contemplating the weather and calculating their position. The clouds are as ominous as is the foaming sea. Homer's later works were almost entirely of the sea. Each winter he visited the Bahamas, Cuba or Florida. He was always searching for scenes of the sea, examples of which are *Rum Cay, Mending the Nets, Searchlight, Harbor Entrance* and *Santiago de Cuba.*

Homer went on hunting and fishing trips to the Adirondacks and the wilds of Quebec, where he caught the emotions that went into his compositions. He captured his feeling of the ocean in *The Gulf Stream*, one of his most famous works. It hangs in the Metropolitan Museum of Art, New York City.

His well-composed picture *Breezing Up* hangs in the National Gallery, Washington, D.C. This painting is reproduced on a 1962 stamp.

William Hooper

Scott 1692
Born: June 17, 1742, Boston, Massachusetts
Died: October 14, 1790, Hillsboro, North Carolina

William Hooper was the eldest child of the Reverend William and Mary Dennie Hooper. His elementary education was at the Boston Latin School in preparation for Harvard College. He entered the college in his sophmore year and graduated in 1760. He returned to Boston and began reading law in the office of the colorful James Otis, a 1743 Harvard graduate.

While Hooper was studying law with Otis in 1761, Otis was elected to the Massachusetts General Court, where his eloquence shaped the Colonial opinion preceding the Revolutionary War. It was these associations that no doubt shaped young Hooper's liberal ideas, though his parents remained staunchly loyal to the mother country throughout the Revolution.

Hooper was admitted to the bar in 1764 and went to Wilmington, North Carolina, to practice and live. He married Anne Clark, whose family was among Wilmington's early settlers.

Hooper became active in local politics. In 1773, he was elected to the Assembly. When the royal government was overthrown, he became a leader in the Popular Party. He was placed on the Committee of Correspondence. He was elected to all five of the provincial congresses. He also was elected to the Continental Congress. Though he was not present to vote for independence, he returned in time to sign the Declaration of Independence.

He returned in 1777 to his home, "Finian," in Masonboro Sound (near Wilmington). He was a borough member of the House of Commons and practiced law. His wealth had been lost while he was giving public service to the cause. He had to flee Wilmington when the British threatened its capture. He was suffering from malaria. He moved to Hillsboro, North Carolina, and lived to see the Federal Constitution ratified. He died soon thereafter.

On the second stamp of the 1976 Declaration of Independence series of four stamps, in the row of men seated, Hooper is the seventh from the left.

Stephen Hopkins

Scott 1692
Born: March 7, 1707, Providence, Rhode Island
Died: July 13, 1785, Providence, Rhode Island

Stephen Hopkins was the son of William and Ruth (Wilkinson) Hopkins. The Hopkins family trace their ancestry in America to Thomas Hopkins, who came to Providence in 1638 from England and associated with Roger Williams. Stephen Hopkins grew up on a farm in the area of Cranston and Scituate. Later he did surveying. In 1726, he married Sarah Scott, with whom he had seven children. His wife died in 1753, and he married Anne Smith.

As the oft-elected governor of Rhode Island, he alternated with William Greene and Samuel Ward between the years 1755 and 1768. His political jockeying with Ward bordered on tribal feuding.

When Scituate became a town in 1731, Hopkins was moderator of the first town meeting. The next year he was elected town clerk. He was president of the town council and represented Scituate in the General Assembly. He served in the General Assembly off and on until 1752. He served as a justice of the Court of Common Pleas. He moved to Providence. He was assistant justice of Rhode Island's Superior Court and, in 1751, became chief justice.

In 1755, he won the gubernatorial seat over Greene, and served until 1757, when Greene defeated him for the office. In 1758, Hopkins won the seat again and held it until 1762, when Ward won the election. Hopkins won the governorship for the third time in 1763. He held it until 1765, when he was defeated by Ward. Hopkins won for the fourth time in 1767. He represented Providence, and Ward represented Newport. Hopkins was sent to the general congresses of 1754, 1755 and 1757. He signed the Declaration of Independence and was involved in the Articles of Confederation. In 1776, the year Rhode Island became a state, he retired.

On the second Declaration of Independence stamp of 1976, of the three men standing behind the men seated, Hopkins is the first on the left.

Francis Hopkinson

Scott 1692
Born: October 2, 1737, Philadelphia, Pennsylvania
Died: May 9, 1791, Philadelphia, Pennsylvania

Francis Hopkins was a lawyer, author, artist, musician, poet, essayist and patriot. He was the son of Thomas and Mary Johnson Hopkinson. Thomas came to Philadelphia from London in 1731. He was one of the founders of the College of Philadelphia. Francis was awarded the college's first diploma in 1757.

Francis Hopkinson studied law in the office of Benjamin Chew, the provincial attorney general. He also studied the harpsichord. In 1761, he was admitted to the bar of the Supreme Court of Pennsylvania.

He spent a year abroad. On September 2, 1768, he married Ann Borden of the Quaker town of Bordentown, New Jersey. On May 1, 1772, they moved to nearby New Castle, Delaware, where Hopkinson became collector of customs. They then moved to Bordentown, where Hopkison practiced law.

In 1774, he was appointed to the governor's council. He supported the Whigs. He wrote poems and political essays, including "A Prophecy," which predicted the Declaration of Independence. He represented New Jersey in the Continental Congress. He signed the Declaration of Independence. He was chairman of the Continental Navy Board. In 1779, he became judge of the admiralty for Pennsylvania. He became treasurer of loans in July 1781.

During the war, he put his talents to work writing pamphlets and celebrated historical events with allegorical cantatas. He directed a performance attended by George Washington and other notables. He put his artistic talents to use by designing state seals. In 1777, he designed the American flag.

When the Admiralty Court was abolished in 1789, Washington appointed Hopkinson judge of the U.S. Court of the Eastern District of Pennsylvania. He died suddenly of apoplexy on May 9, 1791.

In the row of men seated in the second stamp of the Declaration of Independence, issued July 4, 1976, Hopkinson is the first on the far right.

110

Edward Hopper

Scott 1391
Born: July 22, 1882, Nyack, New York
Died: May 15, 1967, New York, New York

Edward Hopper was a student of Robert Henri, the founder of the so-called "ashcan school." Hopper sold his first painting at the Armory Shows, the celebrated International Exposition of Modern Art held at the 69th Regiment Armory in New York City in 1913. This show included 1,500 paintings and sculptures, about 1,000 of which were executed by American artists and 500 by Europeans. The show opened the door to modern art in America, dealing a heavy blow to academic art in the United States.

Hopper was not recognized as a first-rate artist until about 1920, when he exhibited at the Brooklyn Museum and sold another picture in the watercolor division. In the 1930s, he became one of the leading exponents of realism. This was somewhat in opposition to the influence of the French artists on American art. Hopper advanced beyond the "ashcan school" of his early teachings, which rendered art of social realism depicting such everyday sights as garbage cans, backyard clotheslines and old wooden doors. Hopper's paintings depicted American scenes. His works first gained major recognition in the art world with a one-man show at the Museum of Modern Art, New York City. A retrospective exhibit was shown at the Whitney Museum of American Art in New York City in 1964. An exhibit at the Art Institute in Chicago in 1964 and 1965 covered 55 years of his work. Many of his paintings, such as *Early Sunday Morning*, painted in 1930, and *Night Hawks*, painted in 1960, are considered classics in American Art.

As the "ashcan school" attempted to create a feeling for the less fortunate and represented social realism, Hopper said in 1960 that his art had no motif at all. Thirty years earlier he had said, "My aim in painting has always been the most exact transcription possible of my most intimate impressions of nature."

In 30 years, his paintings increased in formal precision and in intensity of a purely visual statement, which was progressively brought out in his paintings.

Hopper's *The Lighthouse at Two Lights, Maine*, now in the Metropolitan Museum of Art, New York City, was chosen for the stamp to celebrate the Maine Statehood sesquicentennial. The stamp was issued on July 9, 1970.

Jean Antoine Houdon

Scott 64
Born: March 20, 1741, Versailles, France
Died: July 15, 1828, Paris, France

By a stroke of circumstances, Jean-Antoine Houdon's father, who was a wine merchant, took a position as concierge of the Ecole Royale des Eleves Proteges, a preparatory school for the French Academy in Rome. At age 12, Jean-Antoine entered the Ecole Royale de Sculpture. He grew up in the artists' work rooms. At age 20, he had absorbed all he could from his masters, Michel Ange Slodtz, Jean Baptiste Lemoyne and Jean Baptiste Pigalle. He left France for Italy for eight years of intensive study and work. One of his masterpieces executed during this time was *St. Bruno* for the Carthusian monastery Santa Maria degli Angeli. The painting so struck Pope Clement XIV that the pope nearly broke the rules of silence. To this day, Houdon's *Flayed Man* (1767) is a model of anatomical perfection for sculpting students.

Houdon returned to France in 1769. He entered the Academy in 1777 on the strength of his *Morpheus,* now in the Louvre. He spent the rest of his life working out of the ateliers of the Royal Academy and its successor, the Institut de France. The nobility were his patrons, including Catherine the Great of Russia, who owned his famous *Diana.* The Dutch East India Company commissioned a bust from him, and the princes of Mecklenburg-Schwerin sat for him. He sculpted portrait busts of Cagliostro, Diderot, Gluck, Voltaire, Jean Jacques Rousseau (Louvre) and Lafayette. By the mid-1780s, he was acknowledged as the leading portrait sculptor in the world.

Houdon made a bust of Benjamin Franklin, who accompanied Houdon to the United States in 1785. Houdon completed a bust of Washington, then returned to Paris to complete a statue of Washington, which now stands at the State Capitol, Richmond, Virginia. Though meticulously timely in detail, it has a classic pose and displays the fasces, the bundle of rods that symbolizes union.

Houdon survived the Napoleonic era, even counting Napoleon as one of his subjects. For the most part, he lived out the rest of his life quietly.

Houdon's portrait bust of George Washington was selected for the 3¢ definitive stamp issued August 18, 1861.

Henry Hudson

Scott 372
Born: date unknown, England
Died: probably soon after June 22, 1611, near James Bay, Canada

Nothing is known of Henry Hudson prior to 1607, the year he was employed by the Muscovy Company. The company was looking for a shorter route to Japan and China by way of a passage across the north pole. Hudson sailed the *Hopewell* to the Shetland Islands, then to the east coast of Greenland. He traveled east to Spitsbergen (Norway), discovering Jan Mayen Island in the the Greenland Sea. Finding it impossible to skirt the ice pack, he returned to England. In 1608, he made a second voyage attempting to skirt the ice pack and find a way to the east between Norway and Russia, but none was found.

In 1609, he was hired by the Dutch East India Company. He left Amsterdam in April in the *Half Moon*. He entered the Barents Sea, but severe weather hampered his progress. He headed for America, reached Newfoundland by July, coasted south as far as Chesapeake Bay, and turned north and into Delaware Bay. On September 3, he entered what is now New York Harbor. He sailed up the great river (now the Hudson), believing he was headed for Japan and China. He got as far as the site of Albany and realized that it was a river and not a passage to the east. He sailed back to what is today known as Manhattan.

He returned to Dartmouth, England, in November. Records of the voyage were kept by mate Robert Juet.

In June 1910, a group of promoters sent him on an expedition in the *Discovery*. Hudson passed south of Greenland through the great strait (later named for him). On August 3, he sighted Hudson Bay, which he was certain was the "Sea to the Westward." In November, the *Discovery* was frozen in at the south end of a large bay (now James Bay).

In June, Hudson took his ship out of anchor. Mutiny broke out. Hudson, his son, and seven others were set adrift, without provisions, in a small boat. No trace of them was ever found. The crew headed for England. On the way, some of the men were killed by Eskimos. Nine members of the crew survived. Juet died on the return voyage. After five years, six of the nine men were brought to trial for the murder of Hudson. No record of the results of that trial exists.

Hudson is honored on a 1909 Hudson-Fulton stamp.

Hubert Horatio Humphrey

Scott 2190
Born: May 27, 1911, Wallace, South Dakota
Died: January 13, 1978, Waverly, Minnesota

Hubert Humphrey grew up in Doland, South Dakota. After high school, he attended the University of Minnesota, but quit because of the Depression. He later finished at the Denver College of Pharmacy. He worked as a pharmacist. In 1936, he married Muriel Buck. They had four children.

Humphrey returned to the University of Minnesota and earned a degree in political science in 1939. In 1940, he earned a master's degree from Louisiana State University at Baton Rouge. He taught at both institutions and at Macalester College in St. Paul, Minnesota. He headed the Minnesota branch of the Works Progress Administration. In 1943, while he was the assistant regional director of the War Manpower Commission, he ran for mayor of Minneapolis and lost.

In 1943 and 1944, he was professor of the Army Air Force training program at Macalester College. In 1945, he ran successfully for mayor, and was re-elected in 1947. He was deeply involved in founding Americans for Democratic Action, a national, liberal, anti-communist organization.

In 1948, Humphrey became the first Minnesota Democrat elected to the U.S. Senate. He was re-elected in 1954 and 1960. He served as the U.S. delegate to the United Nations in 1956-57. He was the U.S. delegate to the UNESCO Conference in Paris and the Nuclear Test Suspension Conference in Geneva.

From 1961 to 1964, Humphrey was the assistant majority leader in the Senate. From 1965 to 1969, he reached the zenith of his career as the 38th vice president of the United States under President Lyndon B. Johnson.

In 1968, he lost his bid for the presidency. His ticket, running under the slogan "Opportunity for Justice," was thwarted by Richard M. Nixon's "Dump the Hump" campaign. Humphrey returned to the University of Minnesota as a professor of political science. He served on the board of *Encyclopedia Britannica*.

In 1970, he returned to the Senate. He was re-elected in 1976. In 1977, his colleagues elevated him to deputy president pro tempore of the Senate, a position created to honor him.

He died from cancer in 1978. He was honored in 1991 with a 52¢ stamp.

Richard Morris Hunt

Richard Morris Hunt 1828-1895 Biltmore Asheville NC

Architecture USA 18c

Scott 1929
Born: October 31, 1827, Battleboro, Vermont
Died: July 31, 1895, Newport, Rhode Island

Richard Hunt and his elder brother, William Morris Hunt, were both artists. William studied with Thomas Couture in Paris and also came under the direct influence of Jean Francois Millet. He introduced the Barbizon school to America. He painted the images of many important people of America. Most of his work was destroyed in the great fire of Boston in 1872.

Richard turned his attention to architecture. He graduated in 1843 from the Boston Latin School and went to Geneva, Switzerland, where his mother had taken all five of the Hunt children after the death of their father. He continued his basic schooling, then entered the Ecole des Beaux-Arts in Paris in 1846. While he was in Paris, he designed the Pavillon de la Bibliotheque.

Richard and William returned to the United States in 1855. William opened a studio in Boston in 1860, after working in Newport, Rhode Island, for five years. Richard worked on the U.S. Capitol additions in Washington, D.C. William drowned at the Isles of Shoals, off the New Hampshire coast.

Richard opened his studio in New York City in 1858 but returned to Europe for more study. In the 1860s, commissions began to come to him. He designed the Lenox Library and the Tribune Buildings in New York City, the Theological Library and Marquand Chapel at Princeton, the Divinity School and the Scroll and Key Building at Yale, and the base of the Statue of Liberty for Frederic Auguste Bartholdi's "Liberty Enlightening the World." He designed such famous residences as the Marble House and the Breakers at Newport, and George W. Vanderbilt's Biltmore estate near Ashville, North Carolina.

His design for the Administration Building for the World's Columbian Exposition in Chicago in 1893 won him a gold medal from the Royal Institute of British Architects. He was a co-founder of the American Institute of Architects and president in 1888-91. A memorial to Hunt, designed by Daniel French and Bruce Price, is on a wall in Central Park in New York City.

Hunt is honored with a stamp in the 1981 American Architecture series. It shows the Biltmore House, Ashville, North Carolina.

Samuel Huntington

Scott 1687c
Born: July 3, 1731, Windham, Connecticut
Died: January 5, 1796, Norwich, Connecticut

Samuel Huntington had a sporadic and scanty elementary education, but he was an avid reader. He was the son of Nathaniel and Mehetable Thurston Huntington. When he was 16, he was apprenticed to a cooper. In his free time, he studied law and Latin. His self-education paid off. He was admitted to the Connecticut bar in 1758. He made Norwich, Connecticut, his home and place of practice from 1760 until his death in 1796.

He married Martha Devotion of Windham, the daughter of the Reverend Ebenezer Devotion. The Huntingtons had no children, but Samuel's brother, Joseph, had married Hannah, Martha's sister. Samuel and Martha took two of Joseph and Hannah's children and raised them. The boy, Samuel II, became a distinguished Ohio state senator, Supreme Court judge and governor.

Samuel Huntington began his political career in 1764 in the Connecticut legislature. He served for 20 years. He represented the British crown as attorney to the king for Connecticut affairs from 1765 to 1774. In 1774, he was appointed associate justice of the Supreme Court of Connecticut. In 1775, he became a member of the Connecticut Council of Safety.

When he entered the Continental Congress in 1776, he was an avid supporter for independence. He voted for and signed the Declaration of Independence. He remained a member of the congress and followed John Jay as its president, serving from September 1779 to July 1781.

In 1783, he returned to Connecticut to serve as chief justice of Connecticut's Supreme Court. In 1785, he was elected as the state's lieutenant governor, and in 1786, he was elected the third governor of Connecticut. He was the state's first Federalist governor. He held the office until his death.

He is the fourth person from the left on the third 18¢ stamp of the American Bicentennial souvenir sheets issued on May 29, 1976, at Philadelphia.

Jared Ingersoll

Scott 798

Born: October 27, 1749, New Haven, Connecticut
Died: October 31, 1822, Philadelphia, Pennsylvania

Jared Ingersoll's parents were Jared and Hannah Whiting Ingersoll of New Haven, Connecticut. Jared Ingersoll was living in New Haven, where his father had been serving since 1768 as judge of the vice-admiralty court for the Philadelphia district. Three years later, in 1771, they moved to Philadelphia to be at the seat of the court. When the British army approached the city in 1777, the elder Ingersoll, as a Loyalist, was paroled by the patriots to Connecticut. Young Jared took over his father's affairs.

Young Jared Ingersoll graduated from Yale College in 1766. In July 1773, the year he was admitted to the bar in Philadelphia, he went to England to study law at Middle Temple, London, at which time he switched from his father's Loyalist support to join the patriots' cause. He left England in 1776 and traveled on the continent, leaving for America from Paris in 1778.

In 1781, he married Elizabeth Pettit, daughter of Colonel Charles Pettit of Philadelphia. His first experience in law practice was taking over for Joseph Reed, president of the newly created supreme executive council of Pennsylvania. In 1791, Ingersoll was admitted to the bar of the U.S. Supreme Court. He was an outstanding lawyer.

In 1796, he opposed Alexander Hamilton in the case involving the question of the constitutionality of an act of Congress. In 1797, he was the attorney for Senator William Blount, against whom impeachment proceedings were brought. Blount was the first U.S. senator to be impeached, though the charges were dismissed in 1799.

In 1780, Ingersoll was elected a member of the Continental Congress. He was a delegate to the Federal Convention of 1787. He was one of the eight from Pennsylvania to sign the U.S. Constitution. He was active in local politics, a member of the Philadelphia common council, and was city solicitor, attorney-general of Pennsylvania and U.S. district attorney for Pennsylvania.

In 1812, he was nominated for the vice presidency with DeWitt Clinton on the unsuccessful Federalist ticket. Until his death, he was presiding judge of the district court for the city and county of Philadelphia.

Ingersoll is depicted on the 1937 Constitution Sesquicentennial stamp.

Henry Inman

Scott 263
Born: October 28, 1801, Utica, New York
Died: January 17, 1846, New York, New York

William Inman came to America in 1792 from England at the age of 30. He settled at Whitestown, near Utica, New York. With his wife Sarah, he had four sons. His son Henry was born in 1801. When Henry was 9, his father moved his family to New York City.

Henry received an appointment to the U.S. Military Academy at West Point, but met artist John Wesley Jarvis and decided to become a portrait painter. Jarvis counted such persons as Andrew Jackson, Henry Clay and Thomas Paine as his clients. At the begining of his apprenticeship, Inman was painting the backgrounds of the portraits for Jarvis, but soon he, too, was painting portraits. In 1822, he opened his own studio on Vesey Street, New York. Many eminent persons sat for him. He was one of the founders of the National Academy of Design.

In 1832, he married Jane Riker O'Brien and moved to Philadelphia. He was the director of the Pennsylvania Academy. He became associated with Colonel C.G. Child in a lithographing business at the same time Nathaniel Currier was apprenticed to John B. Pendleton in the same city. Inman also painted country scenes and landscapes, but his clients bought mostly portraits.

He returned to New York. Friends commissioned him to go to England and paint portraits of the 1843 poet laureate of England, William Wordsworth; essayist Thomas Babington Macaulay and the Reverend Doctor Thomas Chalmers, the first moderator of the Free Church of Scotland in Edinburgh. During his visit, Inman painted *View of Rydal Water*.

He returned to New York in 1845. He was given a commission by Congress to paint a series of historical scenes for the Capitol at Washington, D.C. Hardly had he begun when he died of a heart attack at the age of 45. His portraits included Chief Justice John Marshall, President Martin Van Buren, William H. Seward, DeWitt Clinton, John James Audubon, Nathaniel Hawthorne, Clara Barton, Lafayette and William Penn.

Inman's portrait of Marshall was chosen for the 1894 $5 definitive stamp.

James Benson Irwin

Scott 1435
Born: March 17, 1930, Pittsburgh, Pennsylvania
Died: August 8, 1991, Glenwood Springs, Colorado

James Benson Irwin attended school in Salt Lake City. The family later moved to San Jose, California. Here Irwin first met his future wife, Mary Ellen Monroe, a photographer's model. Irwin received his bachelor of science degree from the U.S. Naval Academy in 1951. At the University of Michigan, he received his master of science degree in aeronautical and instrumentation engineering in 1957. He attended test pilot school and was chosen in the fifth group of astronauts in 1966, having first applied in 1964.

Irwin was backup lunar module pilot for *Apollo 12* and lunar module pilot for *Apollo 15*, becoming the eighth man to set foot on the moon. The *Apollo 15* mission was launched July 26, 1971, the fourth lunar landing and the first to use the Lunar Rover. The lunar landing was on July 30. David R. Scott and Irwin spent 18 hours exploring the area around the Apennines and along the rim of Hadly Rill. One trip brought them to the foothills of the Apennines to obtain crystalline rock samples thought to have been the original crust of the moon. In the lunar module *Falcon*, they rejoined Major Alfred M. Worden in the command module *Endeavour,* circling the moon. They circled the moon once more, then headed for Earth, splashing down on August 7 in the Pacific Ocean with only two of the three parachutes performing properly. They landed safely.

Irwin, Scott and Worden admitted carrying 400 unauthorized stamped and canceled envelopes to the moon. They planned to sell the covers after their return. The covers were destroyed, and the three astronauts were reprimanded.

Two years later, while playing handball, Irwin suffered a heart attack. He had resigned from NASA and the Air Force in July 1972 to form a religious organization, High Flight Foundation, with Baptist pastor William H. Rittenhouse in Colorado Springs, his home. To share his experiences as an astronaut, he wrote a book, *To Rule the Night*. He twice led expeditions to Mount Ararat in Turkey in search of evidence of Noah's Ark. In 1982, he reached the summit, where he fell and received painful injuries. He carried on his mission vigorously until he died at the age of 61 from a heart attack.

Irwin is seen riding over the moon surface in the *Lunar Rover* on the Space Achievement stamp issued August 2, 1971.

119

James Merritt Ives

Scott 1551
Born: March 5, 1824, Belleview, New York, New York
Died: January 3, 1895, Rye, New York

James Ives' father was the superintendent of the grounds of Belleview. It is reported that James was born in a cottage on the grounds. He grew up in New York and went to work at the age of 12, which interrupted his formal education. He spent much of his time in the libraries and art galleries studying and reading. In 1852, he married Caroline Clark, the sister-in-law of Nathaniel Currier. Currier took him into his lithographing firm as the bookkeeper.

Ives demonstrated his knowledge of art that he had gained in his self-educating efforts at the public libraries. He seemed to know what the public wanted in pictures. He was a perfectionist for detail and demanded technical exactness. He was able to direct the production of fine and excellent prints.

In 1857, five years after joining the firm, he was made a partner, and the name of the house was changed to Currier & Ives. Ives became the general manager. In addition to his ability to direct the activities of the staff of artists whom Currier & Ives employed, Ives was able to create excellent drawings as well. Several lithographs published by Currier & Ives were Ives' creations.

In 1865, Ives moved from Brooklyn to Westchester, and in 1867, he moved again to Rye, New York, his home for the remainder of his life. This was at the end of the Civil War. During the war, he organized and served as captain of Company F of the 23rd Brooklyn regiment, which became involved when the Confederates invaded Pennsylvania.

Ives never ceased to be involved in lithographing. In 1880, Currier's son, Edward West Currier, succeeded when the elder Currier retired. Ives died in 1895, and his son Chauncy carried on in his place. Ives bought out Currier in 1902. Chauncy Ives carried on until 1907, when he sold out to Daniel W. Logan, who soon disposed of the remaining stock and the equipment.

Currier and Ives produced more than 7,000 different pictures. Their work covered nearly every subject imaginable. In addition to nostalgic items, they covered the newsworthy subjects, including sports and tragedies. They hired a team of women to apply the color to the prints in an assembly-line manner.

An example of a Currier and Ives work is the *The Road — Winter* chosen for the contemporary Christmas stamp of 1974.

120

Iwo Jima Marines

Scott 929
Iwo Jima, U.S. Marines raising flag on captured island
Date: February 23, 1945, Mount Suribachi, Japan

Joe Rosenthal, an Associated Press photographer, captured a historic event when, on February 23, 1945, several Marines climbed to the top of Mount Suribachi, Iwo Jima (Sulfur Island), and planted the U.S. flag. In Rosenthal's picture, from left to right are Private 1st Class Ira H. Hayes, Arizona Pima Indian; Private 1st Class Franklin R. Sousley, Kentucky; Sergeant Michael Strank, Jamestown, Pennsylvania; Pharmacist's Mate 2nd Class John H. Bradley, Antigo, Wisconsin; Private 1st Class Rene A. Gagnon, Manchester, New Hampshire; and Corporal Harlon H. Block, Weslaco, Texas. Only Hayes and Rene Gagnon came through the battle unscathed. Bradley was wounded and evacuated. Sousley, Strank and Block were killed on Iwo Jima.

This flag-raising was a repeat performance. An earlier photograph showed three men holding a flag upright, a Marine standing on the summit and, in the foreground, a Marine holding a rifle and sitting and acting as guard. It was snapped by Sergeant Louis R. Lowery, photographer for the official Marine Corps magazine *Leatherneck*. The men tied a flag on a seven-foot piece of iron pipe and raised it. This realistic photo is in the Marine Corps archives. The four flag raisers were 1st Lieutenant Harold Schrier, Platoon Sergeant Earnest I. Thomas, Corporal Charles W. Lindberg and Private 1st Class James R. Nicel. The flag was handed to Schrier by Lieutenant Colonel Chandler W. Johnson.

Thomas went aboard the *Estes* and, on an NBC broadcast, told the world of company E's accomplishment. He was killed nine days later.

Rosenthal missed the real flag-raising, but he had a keen eye for a good picture. A larger flag was secured from the LST 779 on the beachhead. A longer piece of pipe was found, and the six Marines started shoving the pipe into the ground when Rosenthal snapped the famous picture.

His Iwo Jima flag-raising picture is shown on the U.S. Marines stamp.

William Jackson

Scott 798
Born: March 9, 1759, Cumberland, England
Died: December 18, 1828, Philadelphia, Pennsylvania

William Jackson was left an orphan as a young boy. He was taken from England to South Carolina to be raised by Owen Roberts of Charleston.

At the outbreak of the Revolutionary War, he obtained the commission of subaltern in Gadsden's regiment. Two years later, he became a lieutenant. He took part in the incompleted expedition against St. Augustine, Florida.

When Major-General Benjamin Lincoln took command of the Southern Department, Charles Cotesworth Pinckney recommended Jackson as an aide. Jackson saw action at Tullifiny Bridge, Stono Ferry, Savanna and, with Laurence and Henderson, at the Battle of Charleston. He went with John Laurens to France as Laurens' secretary in 1781. He was responsible for shipping supplies, obtained by Laurens, to the Continental Army. When he returned to the United States in February 1782, Secretary of War Benjamin Lincoln assigned him to the War Department. In 1783, Jackson resigned.

When the Constitutional Convention met in Philadelphia in 1787, Jackson and William Temple Franklin applied for the position of secretary. Jackson was nominated by Alexander Hamilton and won the position. He served faithfully, though, according to its order, the records were burned at the end of the session.

In 1788, Jackson was admitted to the Pennsylvania bar. He was a candidate for secretary of the U.S. Senate in 1789 against Samuel Allyne Otis. Otis won the job. Washington appointed Jackson as one of his personal secretaries. Jackson resigned in December 1791. Washington offered him the job of adjutant-general of the U.S. Army, but Jackson declined.

On November 11, 1795, at the age of 36, he married Elizabeth Willing of Philadelphia, the daughter of Thomas Willing, president of the Bank of North America. One of Washington's final official acts was to appoint Jackson to the post of U.S. surveyor of customs at Philadelphia.

Jackson became editor of the *Political & Commercial Register* of Philadelphia. He was the secretary of the Society of the Cincinnati his last 28 years.

Jackson attained the rank of major. Throughout his post-war lifetime, he was referred to as "Major Jackson." He is depicted on the 1937 Constitution Sesquicentennial stamp.

Lou Jacobs

Scott 1309
Born: 1903, Bremerhaven, Germany
Died: September 13, 1992, Sarasota, Florida

Jacob Ludwig, born in Bremerhaven, Germany, first witnessed a clown act at age 11 and decided that's what he wanted to be. He practiced acrobatics and clowning antics at the age of 15.

At the age of 20, he came to the United States. He turned his name around from Jacob Ludwig to Lou Jacobs. Two years later, John Ringling of the Ringling Brothers and Barnum and Bailey Circus hired him.

Jacobs was the world's most dedicated clown, if not the most famous, along with Emmett Kelly, Otto Griebling and Felix Adler. He performed before millions of people over a span of 60 years.

He never changed his facial makeup that was characterized by a huge perpetual laugh painted on his shadowed face, a rubber-ball nose and high arching eyebrows. Atop his egg-shaped bald head sat a small hat. His face was the emblem of the Ringling Circus.

His clown suit was colorful and bulky, making him look larger than he was. It was especially effective when he stepped out of a small comical car that appeared to be half his size, or when he was in a motorized bathtub, or sliding around on water skis. He had a little chihuahua called Knucklehead. He dressed him as a rabbit or a tiny elephant or a turkey, then chased him with a huge blunderbuss.

With his wife, the former aerialist Jean Rockwell, he had two daughters, Lou Ann Barreda and Dolly Jacobs, who both starred as circus aerialists.

In his later years, he became professor of Clown College of the Ringling Circus in Venice, Florida. In 1992, he died of heart failure at the Sarasota Memorial Hospital at the age of 89.

Jacobs' famous clown face appears on the 1966 Circus stamp honoring John Ringling's birth centenary.

Daniel of St. Thomas Jenifer

Scott 798
Born: 1723, Charles County, Maryland
Died: November 16, 1790, Annapolis, Maryland

The origin of the unusual name St. Thomas Jenifer is not known. Daniel of St. Thomas Jenifer's father, who also was named Daniel, was a physician of English ancestry. His mother was of Swedish ancestry, the daughter of Samuel and Elizabeth Hanson and the sister of John Hanson, the presiding officer of Congress under the Articles of Confederation.

The younger Daniel of St. Thomas Jenifer was wealthy and lived on an estate called "Stelpney," located in Charles County, Maryland. He held several offices of public trust, including agent and receiver general for the last two lord proprietors of Maryland. In his early 20s, he was entrusted with the office of justice of the peace of Charles County and later of the western circuit of the province. In 1760, he was involved with settling boundary disputes between Delaware and Pennsylvania. In 1766, he was appointed to the provincial court. From 1773 to 1775, he sat on the governor's council.

At first he was not in favor of a revolution, hoping for a peaceful solution to the friction between Britain and the Colonies. By the time the Revolution broke out, he was firmly behind the Colonists. He was chosen president of the Council of Safety for Maryland, and he worked diligently for the cause. When the state government was established in 1777, he was made president of the Senate. The following year he was elected to the Continental Congress and was a member until 1782. He served on several important committees. In 1785, he was one of the commissioners who met in Alexandria and then at Mount Vernon to settle with Virginia the question of navigation of parts of Chesapeake Bay and the Potomac River.

In 1787, he was sent as a delegate from Maryland to the Federal Convention in Philadelphia. He served but made no notable indent in the framing of the new Constitution. He signed the Constitution.

Jenifer never married. He lived at "Stelpney" in a happy and comfortable state of bachelorhood, exchanging many visits with George Washington, with whom he had cultivated a close and enjoyable friendship.

Jenifer is depicted on the 1937 Constitution Sesquicentennial stamp.

Jesus of Nazareth

Scott 1321
Born: circa 6 B.C., Bethlehem, Judaea
Died: circa A.D. 30, Calvary, Jerusalem, Judaea and Sumaria

According to the Gospel of Luke, "The angel Gabriel was sent from God to a city of Galilee named Nazareth, to a virgin betrothed to a man whose name was Joseph of the House of David; and the virgin's name was Mary. And he came to her and said:'Hail, O favored one, the Lord is with you.' "

At the time of Jesus' birth, Mary and Joseph went to Bethlehem in response to the demands of the Roman census, because it was Joseph's home city. Jesus was born in a cave in a manger. King Herod heard of the prophesy of the three wise men who had followed a star to Bethlehem. The prophesy stated that a new King of the Jews had been born there. Fearing a challenge to his throne, Herod ordered that all children 2 years old or younger who had been born in Bethlehem be put to the sword. Joseph, Mary and the baby Jesus fled to Egypt. Soon thereafter Herod died, and the family returned to Nazareth.

Jesus' childhood and youth were spent with his carpenter father, doing the chores of any child. The only story recorded from his youth concerns Jesus running off to the temple while his parents were in Jerusalem. When found by them, Jesus said, "I must be occupied with my Father's affairs." Jesus was known as the carpenter, the son of Mary, and the brother of James, Joses, Judas, Simon (Mark) and two sisters.

Jesus also learned from the rabbis, from whom the children of every town learned the law and its meaning, Hebrew history and the Hebrew language. Jesus was educated. Jesus (from the Hebrew, meaning "God is salvation") is universally recognized to have been the Jewish rabbi who, in the period before the destruction of the temple by the Roman armies, gathered disciples by his teaching and was condemned as a troublesome impostor by priests and other leading men among the Jews of Jerusalem. His own disciples believed him to be the Messiah of the Jews and the Son of God. His teachings and the story of his life are the basis of the Christian faith.

In 1966, the United States issued a 5¢ Christmas stamp with a foreshortened reproduction of Flemish artist Hans Memling's *Madonna and Child*.

125

William Samuel Johnson

Scott 798
Born: October 7, 1727, Stratford, Connecticut
Died: November 14, 1819, Stratford, Connecticut

William Samuel Johnson received his early education from his father, Samuel Johnson, the first president of King's College, New York. His mother was Charity Floyd Nicoll, widow of Benjamin Nicoll and daughter of Colonel Richard Floyd, prominent New Yorkers. William graduated from Yale in 1744 and received his master's degree from Harvard in 1747. He represented his hometown in the House of Representatives. He was the first Episcopalian in the Connecticut council. On November 5, 1749, he married Anne Beach.

Johnson was opposed to parliamentary taxation. He was given an honorary doctor of laws degree from Oxford in 1766, the year he was appointed Colonial agent in London, yet he remained moderately Whig.

Upon his return home in 1771, he was publicly thanked for his service, re-elected to the Council and made a judge of the superior court. In 1772, he was an aspirant for office under the Crown. In 1774, he was a delegate to the Continental Congress but declined because of a private engagement.

When fighting broke out at Lexington and Concord, the Connecticut Assembly chose Johnson and Erastus Wolcott to encourge General Gage to call a halt to the fighting, but the radical elements refused to stop. When Johnson returned, he was dropped from the council. He retired from politics for a few years. In 1779, his Stratford neighbors asked him to persuade British commanders, who were raiding the Connecticut coasts, to cease their attacks. Johnson was arrested. He conferred with Governor Trumbull, and after stating his case and then taking the oath of fidelity to the state, he was released.

In 1781, he was involved in the Susquehanna dispute with Pennsylvania. In 1784, Johnson was elected to the Confederation Congress. He was in the Federal convention from June 2 to June 27 and, with Roger Sherman, signed the U.S. Constitution for the state of Connecticut.

He was one of the first senators from Connecticut, but when the capital was moved to Philadelphia, he resigned to be close to his position at Columbia College. He was the college's first president from 1787 to 1800.

His wife died, and in 1800, he married Mary Brewster Beach.

Johnson is shown on the 1937 Constitution Sesquicentennial stamp.

Joseph, husband of Mary

Scott 1444
Born: circa 50 B.C., Bethlehem, Judaea (?)
Died: circa A.D. 20, Nazareth, Galilee (?)

Biblical accounts of Matthew and Luke disagree as to the original home of Joseph and even in their genealogies. In Matthew he is the son of Jacob and the grandson of Matthan. His genealogy is traced from Abraham to King David, and from David to Joseph, the "husband of Mary, of whom Jesus was born, who is called Christ" (Matthew 1:1-17). In Luke, Jesus is "the son (as was supposed) of Joseph, the son of Heli, the son of Matthat" and so on to "Shem the son of Noah" and so on to "Seth, the son of Adam, the son of God" (Luke 3:23-38).

Most artists depict Joseph as being much older than Mary, who was about 16 when they married. One may guess that Joseph was about 50. If he lived a normal lifespan, he may have died about age 70.

About 6 B.C., Joseph and Mary went to Bethlehem to be counted in the census. They went to Bethlehem because it was the home of Joseph, the city of David. One can assume it was Joseph's birthplace. At this time, Jesus was born (Luke 2:1-8). It may be assumed that the genealogy according to Matthew is the correct one, or at least the one given to connect Jesus with the House of David (Matthew 1:18-25; Luke 1:26-38).

Sometime thereafter, Joseph and his family fled to Egypt because of the treachery of King Herod, who ordered that all boys born within the last three years be killed. Joseph again is alluded to in the Gospel of Luke when Jesus was 12 years old. Jesus went to the temple where Mary found him. According to Luke 2:51, Mary was to have told Jesus, "Your father and I have been looking for you anxiously." According to the Gospel of Mark, Jesus was a carpenter, a trade he learned from his father. No more mention of Joseph is made. He was not present at the Crucifixion. How, when and where he died is only conjecture.

Joseph is depicted in the Nativity scene by Lorenzo Lotto on the traditional Christmas stamp of 1970.

Theodore von Karman

Scott 2699
Born: May 11, 1881, Budapest, Hungary
Died: May 6, 1963, Aachen, Germany

Theodore von Karman enhanced American technology as an emigre scientist from Europe. He graduated in 1902 from the Budapest Royal Technical University in mechanical engineering. He taught there for two years, worked two years as a mechanical engineer, then went to Goettingen, Germany. He received his doctorate in 1908 after two years of graduate study and was an instructor until 1912. The Aeronautical Institute at the University of Aachen sought the services of Karman. He made Aachen his home until 1930, except for a short stint in the Austrian air force during World War I.

In 1930, he joined the California Institute of Technology (Caltech), heading the Guggenheim Aeronautical Laboratory. He announced, at the Fifth Volta Congress in Italy, his theory of air resistance of bodies moving with speed faster than sound waves, known as the Karman vortex trail. His work with this laboratory, later called the Jet Propulson Laboratory, led to supersonic aircraft rocket flights and guided missiles. His work in World War II led to the development of the Bell X-1 plane, the first plane to break the sound barrier.

Karman chaired the advisory group for aeronautical research and development (AGARD) for the North Atlantic Treaty Organization (NATO), which he helped found. He formed the Aerojet Engineering Corporation (later Aerojet-General), a manufacturer of rockets and missiles. He served on the scientific advisory board of the Air Force. He joined General Dymanics Corporation as a consultant on nuclear research and guided missile development.

In 1936, he became a U.S. citizen. Karman's research at Caltech resulted in the development of the wind tunnel to aid in the study of ballistic missiles. He was awarded the Wright Brothers Memorial Trophy. In 1963, President Kennedy presented him with the first national Medal of Science. That same year Karman died in Aachen, and Kennedy was assassinated in Dallas.

Karman is portrayed on a 29¢ commemorative issued in 1992.

Rufus King

Scott 798
Born: March 24, 1755, Scarboro, Massachusetts (now Maine)
Died: April 29, 1827, Jamaica, Long Island, New York

Rufus King was the eldest son of Captain Richard and Isabella Bragdon King. He was educated at Drummer Academy, South Byfield, Massachusetts. He graduated from Harvard, then studied law under Theopilius Parsons.

King was admitted to the bar in 1780 and practiced law in Newburyport. He was a delegate to the Massachusetts General Court in 1783, 1784 and 1785. From 1784 to 1786, he was elected by the legislature as a delegate to Congress. He served in the Constitutional Convention at Philadelphia as chairman of the Committee on Finance and on the commission to adjust the boundary between Massachusetts and New York. In the Constitutional Convention, King was considered its most eloquent orator. He, along with Nathaniel Gorham, signed the Constitution for Massachusetts. As a delegate from Newburyport, at the Massachusetts convention for ratification, he strongly advocated its adoption.

On March 30, 1786, King married Mary Alsop. He quit his law practice, moved to New York City and was elected to the New York Assembly. In July 1789, he was elected to the U.S. Senate along with General Philip Schuyler. He joined Alexander Hamilton and John Jay in publishing papers explaining Hamilton's financial measures. King wrote under the name "Camillus."

King was an authority on maritime law and commercial matters. In 1795, he was elected a director of the Bank of the United States and was elected to a second senatorial term in January 1795. In 1796, Washington appointed him plenipotentiary to Great Britain to succeed Thomas Pinckney. In London, he concluded two important conventions with the Addington ministry in 1803.

He returned to the United States. He was the Federalist candidate for vice president with Charles C. Pinckney. They were defeated by Jefferson and Clinton. In 1808, Pinckney and King were again nominated for the presidency, but again were defeated. King opposed the War of 1812. In 1813, he was again elected to the Senate from New York. In 1821, he was a member of the New York constitutional convention. He opposed the Missouri Compromise.

King accepted the ministry to St. James's Court. He arrived in Liverpool, June 26, 1825, was taken ill and returned home, where he died within a year.

King is depicted on the 1937 Constitution Sesquicentennial stamp.

John Langdon

Scott 798
Born: June 26, 1741, Portsmouth, New Hampshire
Died: September 18, 1819, Portsmouth, New Hampshire

John Langdon's roots in America can be traced to his great-grandfather, Tobias, who emigrated sometime before 1660. His grandfather settled in Portsmouth, New Hampshire, in the latter part of the 1600s. Langdon grew up in Portsmouth and attended grammar school, then apprenticed as a clerk in a counting house. He went to sea. He engaged in diverse commercial ventures on his own. By the time the Revolutionary War broke out, he was quite wealthy.

In 1774, he took part in the raid on British war supplies in the Portsmouth fort. He was speaker in the legislature and attended the Continental Congress. On June 25, 1776, he was appointed agent for Continental prizes in New Hampshire. He profited in securing lead, powder and other military supplies.

On February 2, 1777, he married John Sherburne's daughter, Elizabeth, who was 20 years younger than he. That same year he entered the legislature as speaker and also financed General Stark's expedition against General Burgoyne, pledging 70 hogsheads of Tobago rum as security. He led a body of militia in the fighting around Saratoga. When General Burgoyne surrendered, he witnessed the event. He also took part in the Rhode Island campaign.

In 1783, he was a delegate to Congress, in 1784 state senator and, in 1785, he followed Meshech Weare as state president. From 1786 to 1787, he was again speaker of the legislature and later attended the Constitutional Convention in Philadelphia. He signed the U.S. Constitution.

Langdon served again as state president as a Democratic-Republican. He was a member of the New Hampshire Convention that ratified the Constitution on July 21, 1788. He resigned the state presidency to enter the U.S. Senate and to take part in organizing the new U.S. government.

In 1801, President Thomas Jefferson offered Langdon the position as secretary of the Navy, but Langdon declined in order to organize the Republican Party in New Hampshire. He served in the legislature from 1801 to 1805. From 1806 to 1809, he was governor. He was elected again from 1810 to 1812, when he retired. He was nominated for vice president on the Democratic-Republican ticket but declined.

Langdon is depicted on the 1937 Constitution Sesquicentennial stamp.

Benjamin Henry Latrobe

Scott 1780
Born: May 1, 1764, Fulneck, near Leeds, Yorkshire, England
Died: September 3, 1820, New Orleans, Louisiana

Benjamin Latrobe was educated in the classics. When he was 22, he began studying engineering and architecture under the distinguished architect S.P. Cockerell. Ten years later, he sailed for Richmond, Virginia, where he designed the penitentiary. He also worked on the Virginia state capitol.

After completing the Virginia capitol, he moved to Philadelphia, where he supervised the construction of the Bank of Philadelphia, a building representative of Greek Revival architecture. In 1801, he was charged with the construction of a water-supply system for Philadelphia.

In 1803, Latrobe accepted the task of overseeing the construction of the south wing of the Capitol in Washington for President Jefferson, who had appointed him to the newly created post of surveyor of public buildings. Latrobe moved to Washington. Latrobe's years in government service were his most productive. He designed and oversaw the building of several public structures, performed engineering tasks for canal companies and contributed designs for several educational buildings. From 1805 to 1818, the Baltimore Roman Catholic Cathedral occupied his time. He asked no pay for this project.

In 1813, Latrobe moved to Pittsburgh and became involved with Robert Fulton in steamboat building. This project was unsuccessful, and Latrobe lost everything. The burning of many buildings by the British in the War of 1812 necessitated his return to Washington in 1814, primarily to rebuild the Capitol. Later, he designed the portico and terrace as additions to the White House.

In 1820, his son Henry died in New Orleans of yellow fever while working on that city's water system. Latrobe went to New Orleans to complete the project. In September, he, too, died from the disease.

In Baltimore, the Basilica of the Assumption of the Blessed Virgin Mary at the corner of Cathedral and Mulberry streets is the oldest cathedral in the United States. It is noted for its nine striking stained-glass windows and the south tower's clock and bells, which sound the "Angelus" three times a day. It was designed by Latrobe. It was dedicated in 1821, a year after his death.

Latrobe is honored on the second stamp of the 1976 American Architecture issue showing the famous Baltimore cathedral.

Arthur Stanley Jefferson (Stan) Laurel

Scott 2562
Born: June 16, 1890, Ulverston, England
Died: February 23, 1965, Santa Monica, California

Like many other successful stage personalities, Arthur Stanley Jefferson Laurel was born into a theatrical family and grew up with the smell of the greasepaint and the sounds of music and applause. At age 25, Laurel came to the United States from England with Fred Karno's vaudeville troupe, which included Charlie Chaplin, an artist whom Laurel never ceased to greatly admire. Like Chaplin, Laurel made his way to Hollywood, where the greatest future seemed to lie for all types of theatrical endeavor.

He first joined the Hal Roach studio in 1917, working as a writer and director. At the Hal Roach studio, Laurel teamed up with Oliver Norvell Hardy in 1927 to make the film *Putting Pants on Philip*. After that film, Laurel and Hardy never again worked apart.

The two relied mostly on the make-it-up-as-you-go-along technique and did not rely on scripts. They would put their film together, editing it as they progressed. Laurel did most of the editing.

On film, Hardy was the larger, dominant member of the duo — easily irritated, and blaming Laurel for all the messes they got into and somehow got out of. Even if Laurel was the hero of the situation, Hardy took all the credit. Such was the format of their comedies, but the viewer got the impression that the two could not possibly get along without each other. So it was in real life.

However, it was Laurel who dominated affairs off screen. His theatrical background prevailed in the final analysis of their productions.

The best works of Laurel and Hardy were created in the 1920s and '30s. They began in short comedies, such as *From Soup to Nuts* in 1928, and later made feature films, such as *Way Out West* in 1937.

Hardy died August 7, 1957, and Laurel was seldom seen in public after that. He enjoyed some rejuvenation of income when their films were rerun on television in the early 1960s. Laurel died February 23, 1965, in Santa Monica, California. He was 74 years of age.

The inseparable team of Laurel and Hardy, which was the first of many comedy pairings to achieve cinematic success in this country, was jointly commemorated with a 29¢ stamp in the 1991 Comedians booklet.

132

John Laurens

Scott 1686e
Born: October 28, 1753, Charleston, South Carolina
Died: August 27, 1782, Combahee River, South Carolina

John Laurens was the son of the illustrious Henry Laurens. His father engaged in trading and farming at Charleston, South Carolina, until 1771, when he retired to take up service for the state.

In August 1780, Henry was detailed to negotiate a loan of $10 million in Holland. The British captured him off the coast of Newfoundland and imprisoned him in the Tower of London. On the last day of 1781, he was paroled. When the Revolutionary War ended, Cornwallis was given his freedom in exchange for Henry Laurens. Henry was then appointed as one of the negotiators of the Treaty of Paris, and arrived in time to sign it along with Adams, Franklin and Jay. He did not remain to sign the definitive treaty.

John Laurens had returned from England in 1777 and at once joined Washington's staff as a confidential secretary. He participated in all the battles from Brandywine to Yorktown. For his gallantry, he was dubbed "the Bayard of the Revolution," which is synonymous with the perfect knight.

When the British captured Charleston, Washington sent Laurens to induce the king of France to send supplies to American soldiers. The French fleets were put into action, as were the land forces in Virginia. Cornwallis was defeated at Yorktown as a result. Laurens had returned to Yorktown in time to lead the Army that captured the forward unit and ended the war. With the Vicomte de Noailles, he set up the terms of the surrender at Yorktown.

Washington said of him, "He had not a fault that I could discover, unless it were intrepidity bordering upon rashness." It was this rashness that ended a promising career. In a skirmish with the British just before peace was formally concluded, his luck ran out. It occurred on the Combahee River. On August 27, 1782, at the age of nearly 29, this meaningless skirmish proved to be his demise.

Laurens is shown standing second from the left on the fifth 13¢ stamp of the first American Bicentennial souvenir sheet issued May 29, 1976.

Richard Henry Lee

Scott 1691
Born: January 20, 1732, Stratford Hall, Westmoreland County, Virginia
Died: June 19, 1794, Chantilly, Westmoreland County, Virginia

Thomas and Hanna Ludwell Lee had 11 children. Richard Henry was the seventh child. His early education came from private tutors, and then at the academy at Wakefield, in Yorkshire, England. He graduated in 1751 and returned home the following year. He set his sights for the House of Burgesses, which he attained in 1758. First, however, he became justice of the peace of Westmoreland County in 1757. In December 1757, he married Ann Aylett.

In the House of Burgesses, Lee advocated checking the growth of slavery. He was involved with Patrick Henry in the Two Penny Act. When he vigorously opposed Parliament's plan to tax the Colonies in 1764, he was recognized as an important Colonial-rights defender.

Lee's wife died in December 1768. In 1769, he married Thomas Pinckard's widow, Anne, the daughter of Colonel Thomas Gaskins. For five years he tended to his plantation, shipping tobacco to his brother William in London.

In 1773, he organized the plan for intercolonial committees of correspondence. He became a close friend of Samuel Adams. On June 7, 1776, speaking for Virginia at the Continental Congress, he moved that "these United Colonies are, and of right ought to be, free and independent states." And thus, except for his signature on the Declaration of Independence, Lee's part was essentially finished. He resigned his seat in Congress in May 1779.

He was elected to the Virginia House of Delegates in 1780. In 1784, he was again elected as a delegate to Congress. He was chosen for the Constitutional Convention but declined. He opposed the Constitution for lack of a bill of rights and insisted on amendments before adoption. He was chosen a senator in the new state government. He retired from the state Senate in 1792.

Of the five men seated before the six men standing in the first stamp of the 1976 Declaration of Independence stamps, Lee is the first on the left.

Francis Lewis

Scott 1687c
Born: March 21, 1713, Llandaff, Glamorganshire, Wales
Died: December 31, 1802, New York, New York

Francis Lewis sold cloth to the British army during the French and Indian War (1756-63). He had established successful businesses in both New York and Philadelphia. He was an aide to General Mercer at Fort Oswego in 1756 and was captured by the Indians and taken to France for prisoner exchange.

Lewis was the only child of the Reverend Francis Lewis, rector of Llandaff Glamorganshire, Wales, and Amy Pettingal of Caernarvon. His parents died when he was young. He was raised by his mother's relatives. He became an apprentice in London at a mercantile house. This prepared him for his career.

In 1738, at the age of 25, Lewis chose New York City as the place to ply his trade. He returned to England for two years and made several voyages back to America. In June 1745, he married Elizabeth Annesley of New York. He accumulated considerable wealth and retired in 1765 at age 52, the year he was a member of the Stamp Act Congress.

In 1774, he served as a delegate to New York's Provincial Convention, and in 1777, he helped draft the first constitution of New York. He served as a member of the Continental Congress from May 1775 to November 1779. He signed the Declaration of Independence belatedly on August 2, 1776.

Among his many duties, he was a member of the Committee of 51 and 60, and such semi-administrative groups as the Marine, the Secret, and the Commercial committees. He was a member of the Board of Admiralty.

In 1776, during the British Long Island campaign, Lewis' home in Whitestone was burned down and demolished. His wife was taken prisoner. She died in 1779 from the rigors of imprisonment. Impoverished from large contributions to the cause, Lewis lived with his sons' families until he died.

He is shown second from the left on the third stamp of the second American Bicentennial souvenir sheet issued May 29, 1976.

Morgan Lewis

Scott 644
Born: October 16, 1754, New York, New York
Died: April 7, 1844, New York, New York

Morgan Lewis was the second son of Francis Lewis, New York merchant and signer of the Declaration of Independence. Morgan's mother was Elizabeth Annesley Lewis, who died in 1779 as a result of the rigors of imprisonment when the British took her captive. Morgan was a graduate of the College of New Jersey (now Princeton University) with the class of 1773. He studied law. The Revolution interrupted his studies.

He volunteered for service in 1775 at Cambridge and in New York City. He attained the rank of major in 1776 in the 2nd Regiment of the New York Line. He served as deputy quartermaster-general for the New York Department and was chief of staff for General Horatio Gates at Ticonderoga and Saratoga. He was present at the surrender of Burgoyne at Saratoga on October 17, 1777.

He resumed his legal studies and was admitted to the bar. On May 11, 1779, he married Gertrude Livingston, the daughter of Robert R. and Margaret Beekman Livingston of Clermont. He was elected to the Assembly in 1789-90 and again in 1792. Between these assemblies, he served as attorney general. After the second session, he was appointed third justice of the Supreme Court of New York from December 1792 to October 1801, when he was promoted to chief justice. In 1804, he won the governorship over Aaron Burr. He represented the Democratic-Republicans, backed by DeWitt Clinton.

Lewis was not able to shoulder the gubernatorial position well, and Clinton removed his support. Both the Livingstons (known as the "Quids") and Clintonians threatened to become Federalists. As a result, Lewis was not elected in 1807. Approaching 1812 and with war again threatening, Lewis returned for terms in the state Senate and for a seat on the Council of Appointment. During the War of 1812, he was quartermaster-general on the Niagara frontier. He served without distinction. He was placed in command of the region around New York City in 1813.

He acted as landlord of the Livingston estates and took part in local societies. He was one of the founders of New York University.

In the painting *Surrender of Burgoyne* by John Trumbull, reproduced on the stamp issued August 3, 1927, Lewis is the fourth man from the left.

Benjamin Lincoln

Scott 1686a
Born: January 24, 1733, Hingham, Massachusetts
Died: May 9, 1810, Boston, Massachusetts

Benjamin Lincoln grew up on a prosperous farm southeast of Boston. He served in the Massachusetts legislature from 1772 to 1773 and was a member of the provincial congress from 1773 to 1775. In 1775, he was made adjutant of a militia regiment. The next year he was named major general and subsequently became one of George Washington's most reliable lieutenants.

With a force of New England militia, he cut Burgoyne's communications with Canada in the fall of 1777. He was severely wounded at Saratoga but recovered. In August of 1778, his next commission from General Washington was to take command of the troops in the south. In Savannah, Georgia, however, his army was unable to rout the British troops. When he was backed into Charleston, he surrendered to Sir Henry Clinton, who took him prisoner.

Lincoln was released and returned to General Washington in 1781 in time to be present at the surrender of the British on October 19 at Yorktown. Washington honored him by appointing him to receive the surrender sword.

Lincoln held the post of secretary of war from October 1781 to 1783, then returned to the farm in Hingham.

Postwar deflation, declining farm prices, heavy and unjust taxes and much indebtedness resulted in an uprising mainly by the farmers. Daniel Shays was the reluctant leader of the rebellion, which took place in Springfield and counties to the west. Lincoln relieved General Shepherd and chased Shays and his followers through the snow to the middle of Worcester County at Petersham, where on February 4, 1787, the rebels surrendered. Shays retreated to Vermont.

As collector of the Port of Boston in 1789, Lincoln again became financially sound and lived out his life in comfort.

He is depicted astride the white horse in the second 13¢ stamp of the first American Bicentennial souvenir sheet, issued May 29, 1976.

Charles Augustus Lindbergh

Scott C10
Born: February 4, 1902, Detroit, Michigan
Died: August 26, 1974, Kipahula, Hawaii

When Charles Lindbergh successfully flew the Atlantic Ocean alone May 20-21, 1927, some 100,000 Parisians jammed into the tarmac of Le Brouget Airport to welcome him. When he returned to New York, he was welcomed again with a ticker-tape parade. He was dubbed the "Lone Eagle" and "Lucky Lindy." His luck was the result of hard work and determination.

Lindbergh attended the University of Wisconsin for two years, then went to Lincoln, Nebraska, to a flying school. He bought a used Curtiss "Jenny" and took up barnstorming. He trained at the Army flying school at Brooks Field, Texas, completing a year's training in 1925. Lindbergh was ready to make his living flying. He flew mail from St. Louis to Chicago in 1926.

Raymond Orteig offered $25,000 to anyone who could fly the Atlantic non-stop alone from New York to Paris. With help from St. Louis businessmen, Lindbergh purchased a Ryan monoplane, which he christened *The Spirit of St. Louis*. Before attempting a wide ocean flight, he tested his plane on May 10, 1927, by flying from San Diego to Curtis Field on Long Island, New York. This flight established a transcontinental record. Ten days later, on May 20, he took off from Long Island's Roosevelt Field, and 33½ hours and 3,600 miles later, he landed at Le Bourget airfield near Paris. He collected his prize plus fame and glory and a Medal of Honor.

In December 1927, he flew to Mexico City, where he met Anne Spencer Morrow, the U.S. ambassador's daughter. They were married in 1929. In 1932, their 2-year-old son was kidnapped and murdered. A carpenter, Bruno R. Hauptmann, was convicted of the crime and executed.

Between 1935 and 1939, the Lindbergh's lived in Europe, where Charles was twice invited to inspect the German Air Force. In the early 1940s, he warned the United States of Germany's air power. President Franklin D. Roosevelt rebuked him. Lindbergh resigned his Air Corps Reserve commission. Nevertheless, he flew 50 combat missions in the Pacific theater.

Lindbergh was a consultant to the Pan American Airways and, in 1954, was named a brigadier general in the Air Force Reserves. For his book, *The Spirit of St. Louis*, he won the Pulitzer Prize.

Lindbergh is honored for his Atlantic flight on the 1927 airmail stamp with his name. The stamp pictures his plane, *The Spirit of St. Louis*.

Jean-Etienne Liotard

Scott 1533
Born: 1702, Geneva, Switzerland
Died: 1789, Geneva, Switzerland

Jean-Etienne Liotard's early training was much influenced by the works of Jean Petitot, the painter of miniature portraits in enamel. Liotard may have studied under an artist named Gardelle in his early life.

Liotard went to Paris in 1723 to further his studies under the tutilage of J.B. Masse and F. le Moyne. His success with this school earned him the privilege of going to Naples with the Marquis Puysieux and then to Rome in 1735. In Rome, he painted the portaits of several cardinals and of Pope Clement XII.

In 1738, Liotard traveled to Constantinople with Lord Duncannon and then to Vienna in 1743, where he was engaged to paint the portraits of the imperial family. While in Constantinople, he took to dressing in the Turkish oriental style, an eccentricity for which he was dubbed "the Turkish painter."

He continued to receive commissions and support from distinguished persons, which led him to Paris in 1744, and then to London. In England, he painted the portrait of the princess of Wales, dated 1753. In 1756, he went to Holland. At the age of 55, he married Marie Fargues. In 1772, Liotard was back in England, where he painted and exhibited his works at the Royal Academy. In 1776, he returned to Geneva, where he lived quietly until his death.

His portrait is in the Uffizi Gallery, Florence, Italy. In the Victoria and Albert Museum, London, is a picture of a seated Turk. His portrait of General Herault is in the Louvre, Paris. The Louvre also possesses 22 of his drawings. Most of his works, paintings and pastel drawings are in Amsterdam, Bern and Geneva. In Dresden are examples of his pastels, *La Liseuse, Chocolate Girl*, and *La Belle Lyonaise*. He was a collector of the masters and wrote a treatise on art and painting. He worked diligently and showed great versatility.

An example of his portraiture is represented on the fourth stamp of the 1974 Universal Postal Union issue. The portrait is titled *The Lovely Reader*.

Fra Filippo Lippi

Christmas USA 20c

Fra Filippo Lippi, National Gallery

Scott 2107
Born: circa 1406, Florence, Italy
Died: October 8 or 10, 1469, Spoleto, Italy

At age 15, Filippo Lippi took the vows of a Carmelite monk in the monastery of St. Maria del Carmine, Florence. Ten years later he finished a fresco for the monastery and departed. In 1434, he painted in the Basilica of St. Antonio and the Capella del Podesta in Padua. His earliest known work is the *Madonna and Child* of 1437. It was formerly in the Museum of Tarquina, but now is in Rome at the Galleria Nazionale. The capitani of Orsanmichele hired him to paint a panel for the Barbadori Chapel in St. Spirito, Florence. The panel is now in the Louvre. *The Coronation of the Virgin* was begun in 1441 and was completed in 1447. It is in the Uffizi at Florence. *St. Bernard's Vision of the Virgin* was also finished in 1447. It is now in London's National Gallery.

In 1452, Lippi was in Prato painting the choir for the proveditor of the cathedral. It was finished in 1464. Lippi was appointed chaplain to the nuns of St. Niccolo de Frieri in Florence in 1452. He was also the rector of the Church of St. Quirico at Leganaia, near Florence.

His next position was that of chaplain of the nuns at St. Margherita at Prato in 1456. The Virgin in the beautiful picture in the Pitti Palace Gallery is said to be Sister Lucrezia Buti, who sat for him. He eloped with her, and in 1457, she bore him a son, Philippino. Lucrezia Buti and her sister Spinetta renewed their vows in 1459. In 1461, Lippi and a notary friend from Prado were accused of immoral behavior with the two sisters. The Medici family, who were staunch patrons of Lippi, persuaded Pope Pius II to release Lucrezia from her vows and let her live with Lippi as his rightful wife.

In 1463, Lippi painted *The Adoration of the Child*, now in the Uffizi. He was painting frescoes in the apse of the Cathedral of Spoleto when he died. The archives of Spoleto recorded his death as October 10, 1469. The necrology records in Carmine record it as October 8. He lies buried at Spoleto.

Lippi's painting *Madonna and Child* is shown on a 1984 Christmas stamp.

140

Philip Livingston

Scott 1694
Born: January 15, 1716, Albany, New York
Died: June 12, 1778, York, Pennsylvania

Philip Livingston was the fifth son of Philip and Catherine Van Brugh Livingston. The elder Philip was the second lord of the Livingston manor. Young Philip was raised in landed luxury. He received his A.B. degree at Yale.

He became wealthy through importing and privateering during the French wars. On April 14, 1740, he married Christina Broeck of Albany, the daughter of Colonel Dirck Ten Broeck. They lived on an estate in Brooklyn Heights, New York. They maintained a comfortable town house on Duke Street.

Livingston became increasingly busy in local civic affairs. He helped organize the New York Society Library in 1754 and the St. Andrew's Society, an early benevolent group. He was one of the first to organize the New York Chamber of Commerce in 1768 and the New York Hospital in 1771.

On the political scene, he first served on the board of aldermen, representing the East Ward from 1754 to 1763. In 1758, he was elected to the Assembly. He was a member of the Stamp Act Congress.

Livingston was elected to the Assembly in 1768 for the third time and was the speaker of the House. He served on the Committee of Fifty-One, which named the New York delegates to the First Continental Congress. He was one of the five chosen to attend the sessions at Philadelphia. He became a member of the Committee of Sixty to enforce the terms of the association. He was a member of the New York congress and the Second Continental Congress. He signed the Declaration of Independence in August 1776. He served on numerous important committees. In 1777, he was chosen as one of the senators in the upper house of the new legislature. In 1778, he returned to the Continental Congress meeting in York, Pennsylvania.

On the fourth stamp of the Declaration of Independence se-tenant series issued July 4, 1976, Livingston is the first on the right.

William Livingston

Scott 798
Born; November 30, 1723, Albany, New York
Died: July 25, 1790, Elizabethtown, New Jersey

William Livingston was a grandson of Robert Livingston (1654-1728). Robert Livingston was the founder of the family and first lord of the Livingston Manor, New York. He came first to Massachusetts in 1675 and later settled in Albany. He had acquired 160,000 acres of land along the Hudson River through marriage to Alida Schuyler Van Rensselaer.

William was the son of Catherine (Van Brugh) Livingston and Robert's son Philip. He was well-tutored under the care of his maternal grandmother Sara Van Brugh and, by design, spent a year with the Mohawk Indians with a missionary. He graduated from Yale in 1741. He chose law instead of the mercantile business of his brothers. He read law in the office of James Alexander of the Zenger trial fame. Before he had finished his law studies, he married Susanna French in 1745. He was admitted to the bar in 1748.

Livingston contributed to the *Independent Reflector* and the *New York Mercury*, attacking the faction headed by Lieutenant Governor James de Lancey, who Livingston accused of favoring the union of church and state. He was in oppositon to Parliamentary interference in provincial affairs. Through his writings, he became quite popular.

In the election of 1769, however, the De Lancey faction won a decisive victory and secured a majority in the Assembly. Livingston then retired to his estate near Elizabethtown and built his home called "Liberty Hall."

He became a member of the Essex County Committee of Correspondence and rose to a position of leadership. He was one of the province's delegates to the First Continental Congress. He was a deputy to the Second Continental Congress, serving until June 5, 1776, when he assumed command of the New Jersey militia. He served until the legislature, under the new Constitution, elected him first governor of the state. For the next 14 years, he bore the responsibilities of the governorship.

He called for a revision of the Articles of Confederation at the Federal Convention of 1787. He was one of the signers of the new U.S. Constitution.

He is depicted on the Constitution Sesquicentennial stamp issued in 1937.

James Barton Longacre

Scott 300
Born: August 11, 1794, Delaware County, Pennsylvania
Died: January 1, 1869, Philadelphia, Pennsylvania

James Barton Longacre's father was Peter Longacre, whose friend, John W. Watson, the owner of a bookstore and who wrote the annals of Philadelphia, noted the boy's artistic talents. Watson apprenticed him into the bookstore. Later, he arranged with Philadelphia engraver George Murray to teach Longacre the art of engraving. Longacre stayed with Murray until 1819.

At the age of 25, he was already regarded as one of the nation's best engravers. While he was still with the firm of Murray, Draper, Fairman & Company, he rendered portraits of such notables as George Washington, Thomas Jefferson and John Hancock on the facsimile of the Declaration of Independence. This facsimile was published by John Binns of Philadelphia in 1820. The plate was one of the largest single engravings ever executed in the United States up to that time. It measured 35 inches by 25 inches in size. The remainder of the plate was engraved by John Vallance, and the finished product was an exact likeness of the Declaration of Independence at a cost of $9,000.

John Sanderson's *Biography of the Signers of the Declaration of Independence* was illustrated by Longacre's engravings. In 1826, Longacre provided the portraits for actors illustrated in *Acting American Theatre*, edited by Lopez and Wemyss. In association with James Herring of New York, he contributed to *The National Portrait Gallery of Distinguished Americans*. Between 1834 and 1839, four octavo volumes were produced. Some of the portraits he made were from paintings he had made from life. He contributed to other publications as well, especially children's books of the American Sunday School Union of Philadelphia.

Longacre was appointed chief engraver of the U.S. Mint on September 16, 1844. He designed the first double-eagle coin in 1849. In 1854, he engraved the first $3 gold piece and the gold dollar. In 1867, just two years before he died, he completely reworked the coinage of the Republic of Chile.

The engraving of Benjamin Franklin by Longacre was chosen for the 1¢ stamp of the 1902-03 definitive series.

Lorenzo Lotto

Scott 1414
Born: circa 1480, Venice, Italy
Died: September 1556, Casa Santa of Loreto, Italy

Lorenzo Lotto was a deeply religious, lonely man whose paintings much reflected his own inner character. He moved from city to city, fulfilling commissions to paint, and thus made his living. He apparently never had a wife or any family life. Near the end of his career, the Counter Reformation disturbed him deeply. He settled at the Casa Santa of Loreto as an Oblate of the Blessed Virgin, where he spent the last few years of his life.

Lotto considered himself a Venetian, although he spent most of his life elsewhere. He lived and worked at the time of the great Titian. His portraits express the profound character of the people he portrayed with expressions that are marked by insight and sensitivity. An example of his portrait painting, *Gentleman with Gloves,* is in the Pinacoteca di Brera, Milan. *Ser Giovanni della Volta and His Family* is in the National Gallery, London.

Lotto began his early life in Venice, studying and working under Alvise Vivarini of the famous family of painters who originated in Padua. Giovanni Bellini undoubtedly influenced Lotto.

One of Lotto's earliest works of note (about 1500) is the *Danae*, now in the National Gallery, Washington, D.C. In the Pinacoteca Civica, Recanati, Italy, is an example of his work on the folding panels of an altarpiece, completed in 1508. From 1508 to 1512, he was in Rome and may have painted with Raphael. He went to Tuscany and Lombardy. From 1513 to 1525, he was in Bergamo, where he painted the fresco *Lives of the Saints.*

From 1526 to 1529, he was back in Venice. In 1538, he was in Ancona. At this time, he started an account book in which he recorded most of his paintings until the time of his death. Lotto's life ended in solitude and poverty. Today he is recognized as one of the greatest painters of the 16th century.

His *Nativity* was chosen for the 1970 traditional Christmas stamp.

Thomas Lynch Jr.

JULY 4,1776

Scott: 1691
Born: August 5, 1749, Prince George Winyah Parish, South Carolina
Died: late 1779, at sea, Bermuda Triangle?

Thomas Lynch Jr. was the only son of Thomas and Elizabeth Allston Lynch. He was educated at the Indigo Society School, Georgetown, South Carolina, and at Eton and Cambridge in England. He studied law at the Middle Temple of the Inns of Court, London, from 1764 to 1772. He returned to South Carolina in 1772. He did not pursue law as a career. To introduce his son to public life, Lynch's father purchased for him Peach Tree Plantation in St. James Parish, where young Lynch became a member of the landed gentry.

In May 1772, he married Elizabeth Shubrick. Through his father's influence, he was appointed to several civil offices. He became a member of the first and second provincial congresses. He was appointed a member of the first state General Assembly and the Second Continental Congress. The provisional congress elected him a captain in the 1st South Carolina Regiment. Young Captain Lynch went to North Carolina in July 1775 to recruit his line company. While he was fulfilling this duty, he contracted bilious fever (probably viral hepatitis) that debilitated him for the rest of his life.

Lynch helped organize the General Assembly of South Carolina under the Constitution and was thereby elected to the Continental Congress as a sixth delegate so he could be close to his ailing father. His own health was such that he could do little. He signed the Declaration of Independence. Soon thereafter, he began the trip home with his failing father, who died on the way.

In 1779, he was in poor health. He elected to take passage from South Carolina to the West Indies and then to France. After he and his wife sailed, the ship was never heard of again. According to legend, it joined the ships and galleons that lie on the bottom of the sea in the infamous Bermuda Triangle.

On the first of the four 1976 Declaration of Independence stamps, Lynch is the fourth person from the left of the four men seated.

Mary Hays McCauley (Molly Pitcher)

Scott 646
Born: October 13, 1754, Trenton, New Jersey
Died: January 22, 1832, Carlisle, Pennsylvania

Mary "Molly" Ludwig was the daughter of a German emigrant who came to the Colonies in 1730. She grew up on a small dairy farm until her father arranged with a doctor in Carlisle, Pennsylvania, for her to be a household domestic. In 1769, she married John Caspar Hays.

During the Revolutionary War, Hays joined the 7th Pennsylvania regiment. In June 1778, the British army, under Sir Henry Clinton, evacuated Philadelphia and marched towards New York. General Washington, from Valley Forge, followed the British. The retreating enemy was overtaken at the Monmouth Court House, New Jersey.

During the battle, Hays was manning an artillery gun, and Molly was with him. It was a hot day, so Molly assisted the artillerymen by bringing them drinking water in a large pitcher. The soldiers called her "Molly Pitcher," a sobriquet that went down in history. Hays collapsed from fatigue and the heat. Molly stepped in and manned the gun in his place and served heroically for the remainder of the battle.

Because of the conduct of General Charles Lee, nothing was gained by the battle. General Washington, ignorant of Lee's treasonable intentions, had entrusted the attack to him. Lee was just beginning a needless retreat when Washington arrived. He ordered Lee to the rear and averted disaster.

Molly returned to Carlisle and lived a quiet life until Hays' death in 1789. She later married a man named McCauley. This unhappy marriage ended in dissolution. Molly was soon living in poverty.

In 1822, when she was about 68 years of age, the General Assembly of Pennsylvania, cognizant of her plight, awarded her an annual stipend of $40 in recognition of her heroism.

She is honored on the 2¢ Washington stamp of 1926-34 with an overprint of her sobriquet "Molly Pitcher" in bold capital letters. The stamp was issued in memory of the Battle of Monmouth and of the heroine of the battle.

James McHenry

Scott 798
Born: November 16, 1753, Ballymena, County Antrim, Ireland
Died: May 3, 1816, Baltimore, Maryland

At the age of 18, James McHenry came to America with a group of immigrants who left Ireland for Philadelphia in 1771. The next year his family established an importing business in Baltimore that ultimately resulted in a considerable estate, which he inherited in 1790. McHenry was educated first in Dublin, then attended the Newark Academy. He studied poetry but turned instead to study medicine under Dr. Benjamin Rush in Philadelphia.

In 1775, he displayed his ardent patriotism by rushing to Cambridge to offer his services to the military. In January 1776, he was assigned to the medical staff of the military hospital in Cambridge. In August, he was named surgeon of Colonel Robert Magaw's 5th Pennsylvania Battalion.

When Fort Washington fell in November, McHenry was taken prisoner, and paroled to Philadelphia and Baltimore in January 1777. He returned to service following a prisoner exchange in March 1778. In May, he was secretary to General George Washington. He ended his medical career. In August 1780, Washington assigned him to Lafayette's staff. When Lafayette was taken prisoner in Belgium in 1792, ending up in Olmutz, Moravia, McHenry pleaded with Washington to intervene. Lafayette was released in 1797.

In May 1781, McHenry was commissioned a major, serving until he was elected to the Maryland Senate in September. He served in the Senate for five years. In May 1783, he was appointed to Congress and served until 1786.

In 1787, he was a Maryland delegate to the Constitutional Convention. He served as a member of Maryland's ratification committee and was with the committee that welcomed Washington to New York for inauguration in 1789.

In January 1796, he was selected as secretary of war, replacing Timothy Pickering, who was taking the position of secretary of state. John Adams was not happy with McHenry as war secretary and demanded his resignation. McHenry prepared an elaborate defense that was read from the floor of the House on December 1802. He then retired to his estate in Lafayette near Baltimore and lived with his wife, Margaret Allison Caldwell. Fort McHenry was named for McHenry to honor his service as secretary of war.

McHenry is depicted on the 1937 Constitution Sesquicentennial stamp.

Thomas McKean

Scott 1694
Born: March 19, 1734, New London, Chester County, Pennsylvania
Died: June 24, 1817, Philadelphia, Pennsylvania

Thomas McKean's ancestors were Scotch-Irish. His father was William McKean, a farmer and tavern proprietor. His mother was Letitia Finney McKean, daughter of a prominent Pennsylvania Scotch-Irish family.

Thomas McKean attended the New London Academy under the Reverend Francis Allison, then went to New Castle, Delaware, to read law in the office of his cousin, David Finney. He was chief clerk and recorder for probate for New Castle County. He was admitted to the bar in the Lower Counties at age 20. He was appointed deputy attorney-general in 1756, clerk of the Delaware Assembly from 1757 to 1759 and, from 1762, served the assembly for 17 years.

He was a delegate to the Stamp Act Congress. He served as collector of the port of New Castle in 1771 and speaker of the Assembly, 1772-73. He married Mary Borden of Bordentown, New Jersey, in 1763. Ten years later, she died.

On September 3, 1774, he married Sarah Armitage of New Castle. The couple and his six children moved to Philadelphia. He led a movement in Delaware for a Colonial Congress and represented that Colony in the Continental Congress until 1783. He promoted a popular movement in Pennsylvania for a new state government. He signed the Declaration of Independence.

His brief military service was as a colonel commanding a battalion of Philadelphia contingents at Perth Amboy, New Jersey, in July and August 1776. From September to November 1777, he was acting president of Delaware. On July 28, 1777, he was commissioned chief justice of Pennsylvania.

In Congress from 1778 to 1783, he supported the Articles of Confederation. In mid-1781, he was president of Congress. He accepted the chief justiceship of the Supreme Court and served for 22 years. He was nominated for governor in 1799 and served for eight years, succeeding Thomas Mifflin.

On the fourth stamp of the Declaration of Independence set issued on July 4, 1976, McKean is the second from the right.

148

Guglielmo Marconi

Scott 1500
Born: April 25, 1874, Bologna, Italy
Died: July 20, 1937, Rome, Italy

Guglielmo Marconi's father, Guiseppe, was a well-to-do businessman. His mother, Annie Jameson Marconi, was the daughter of Andrew Jameson of County Wexford, Ireland, a wealthy gentleman as well. Marconi studied in Bologna, then in Florence. He attended a technical school in Leghorn, where he met Vincenzo Rosa. With Rosa, he studied physics, particularly the Hertzian (electromagnetic) wave technique that followed the formulas of J.C. Maxwell.

He experimented with using Hertzian electromagnetic waves for communication. He was able to greatly increase the frequency of the megahertz waves from seven to 50. The key element was the coherer that functioned as a radio wave detector. Later, he was able to transmit signals from one end of his house to the other. This feat was the beginning of wireless telegraphy.

In 1896, he went to England with the intention of putting his findings to use in communicating from ship to shore. He rigged up an experiment on Salisbury Plain. He set up a new station at The Needles on the Isle of Wight. In 1898, he sent a message to William Thomson (Baron Kelvin). The message was called a Marconigram. It went a distance of nine miles across the Bristol Channel.

In June 1897, Marconi went to La Spezia on the Gulf of Genoa, Italy, where he set up a ship-to-shore station that covered 12 miles. He formed the Wireless Telegraph and Signal Company Ltd. In 1900, the name was changed to the Marconi Wireless Telegraph Company Ltd.

In 1899, a wireless station was established in South Foreland (Dover) that reached into France, 31 miles away. By year's end, Marconi had extended it to 75 miles, exchanging messages with a ship. In 1900, he received the now famous patent number 7777 to operate on different wavelengths. On December 1901, at St. John's, Newfoundland, he picked up signals from Poldhu in Cornwall, England, the first transatlantic communication by wireless.

Ship-to-shore communication became more frequent, which was immeasurably important to ships in distress. In 1909, Marconi, with Karl Ferdinand Braun of Germany, won the Nobel Prize for Physics. Marconi delved into shortwave radio and microwaves.

The Marconi wireless apparatus is shown on a 1973 stamp.

Mary, Mother of Jesus

Christmas USA 1981

Botticelli: Art Institute of Chicago

Scott: 1939
Born: ?
Died: ?

Mary was the daughter of Joachim and Anna, who were well into their middle age and who very much desired a child. Anna's prayers were answered by an angel who informed her that "a daughter will be born unto you who shall be called Mary . . ." Mary's family relationship is recorded in the New Testament, Luke 1:36. Her exact birthplace is not known for certain; an early 2nd-century apocryphal document says it is Jerusalem, while another early apocryphal writing says her birthplace was Sepphoris in Galilee. The Gospel of Luke indicates that Mary went to Nazareth to live. She went one day to the town's only well to get water, where the angel Gabriel spoke to her. She was frightened and ran home. The angel came again to her and bade her not to be afraid and told her that she was with child, even though she was a virgin.

Mary was betrothed to the village carpenter, Joseph, who was of the House of David. According to Scriptures, the child was "to be called Jesus who would be great and the Son of the Most High . . . the Son of God."

Jesus was born in Bethlehem while Mary and Joseph were responding to the requirements of a Roman census, since Bethlehem was the City of David and Joseph was of the House of David. The child was born in a stable.

The family went south to escape an order by Herod that all boys born in the City of David within the past three years should be killed. When Herod died, the family was free to return to Nazareth. Jesus was the older brother of James, Joses, Simon (Mark), Judas and two sisters.

Mary was at the wedding at Cana, where Jesus turned water into wine. She followed Jesus as much as possible while he was teaching. Mary was apparently at the crucifixion of Jesus. Tradition and religious art have portrayed Mary holding Jesus after he was taken down from the cross — the pitiful Pieta.

Mary lived her last years at Mount Zion in the house of John of Zebedee, the wealthy fisherman. John of Zebedee died a martyr about A.D. 44. Mary may have died soon thereafter.

One of many stamps portraying Mary is the 1981 Christmas stamp.

Jan Ernst Matzeliger

Scott: 2567
Born: September 15, 1852, Paramaribo, Dutch Guiana
Died: August 24, 1889, Lynn, Massachusetts

Jan Matzeliger's father was a Dutch colonial engineer in 1852 in Dutch Guiana (now Surinam), where Matzeliger was born. His mother was a black woman. Dutch Guiana was located on the northeastern coast of South America. More than a third of the people of Dutch Guiana were Creoles, people of mixed black, native and colonial ancestry. These people spoke Sranan Tonga, although Dutch was the official language.

When Matzeliger, a Creole, was 10 years old, he worked as an apprentice in a government machine shop. When he was 18 or 19, Matzeliger came to the United States, working at various jobs and becoming an apprentice cobbler in Philadelphia. By 1877, he was in Lynn, Massachusetts, cutting and sewing leather in a shoe factory.

Matzeliger soon realized that the machines he was using could, and should, be greatly improved upon. He worked alone at night on different designs. By 1880, he had a workable lasting machine, but he needed money. By 1883 — two revisions later, and with outside financing — he had constructed a design good enough to be patented and commercially manufactured.

Matzeliger's Consolidated Hand Method Lasting Machine Company was ready to make fame and fortune for him, but, at the age of 37, illness stopped his progress. He died of tuberculosis in 1889.

The United Shoe Machinery Company acquired Matzeliger's patent and all the company stock. Thanks to his lasting machine, shoe production increased a thousandfold. More importantly, the much more efficient production of high-quality footwear made possible by his machine resulted in such a substantial decrease in price that many more people could afford to own well-made and stylish shoes.

Matzeliger was honored with a 29¢ Black Heritage stamp in 1991.

151

Bernard Ralph Maybeck

Scott 1930
Born: February 7, 1862, New York, New York
Died: October 3, 1957, Berkeley, California

Bernard Ralph Maybeck received his early education at private and public schools. He studied in Paris at the Ecole Nationale et Speciale des Beaux Arts, the Ecole des Beaux Arts et Metier, Louvre and Sorbonne. He undertook special courses at the University of California from 1894 to 1896 and again from 1898 to 1900. He received several honorary degrees.

In 1890, he married Anna White. He was an instructor of drawing and descriptive geometry and architecture at the University of California. He was selected originator and manager of the Phoebe A. Hearst competition for architectural design for the University of California. He designed the Phoebe A. Hearst Memorial at the University of California in 1899.

Maybeck was a member of the Berkeley City Planning Commission and the founder of the Council of Allied Arts. He was also a member of the San Francisco Society of Architects and the Societe des Eleves de M. Andre, Paris. He was voted an honorary member of the San Francisco chapter of the American Institute of Architecture.

He designed the Packard Building in San Francisco and the Palace of Fine Arts at the Golden Gate Bridge. The Palace of Fine Arts is the last remaining structure of the 1915 Panama-Pacific Exposition. The palace is now a park.

In 1900, four important architects appeared in California: Bernard R. Maybeck, Charles S. and Henry M. Green, and Irving Gill. However, the Spanish baroque designs of Bertram G. Goodhue dominated most of California. Maybeck survived with his bold innovations. Many critics consider the First Church of Christ Scientist in Berkeley as Maybeck's masterpiece. The Outdoor Art Club House in Mill Valley, California, and the many Berkeley houses ranging over several decades before and after 1915 proved Maybeck to be a true innovator and one of considerable versatility.

Maybeck's Palace of Fine Arts is depicted on a stamp in the American Architecture series of 1981.

Hans Memling

Scott 1321
Born: circa 1430, Seligenstadt, Mainz, Germany
Died: August 11, 1494, Bruges, Belgium

Hans Memling's worldwide reputation lies in his successful portraitures and his classic rendition of the Virgin Mary. He is thought to have studied under Rogier van der Weyden in Brussels.

The female saints in Memling's paintings look so much like princesses that serious but unsuccessful attempts have been made to identify some of them with actual persons. Patrons are frequently seen kneeling on either side of the central religious subject, usually with their families. The resemblance between King Balthasaar and Charles the Bold of Burgundy in both *Adorations of the Magi* is undeniable. The only figure clearly unique is that of the Virgin. Memling's treatment of the Virgin Mary is the finest aspect of all his work. The artist invariably gave her the same face — bland, meditative and spiritual.

Memling was recorded as a citizen of Bruges on January 30, 1465. He made this his home until his death. He married Anne de Valkenaere circa 1480. She died in 1487. His career in Bruges was very successful. He was able to lend a large sum to Maximilian I to cover expenses of the war with France and was wealthy enough to buy three houses in the port area.

Many panels that appear in numerous churches and museums throughout the world were attributed to Memling's studio, where he employed apprentices in the 1480s. His earliest work is in London, the *Donne Triptych*. His last work is in Lubeck, Germany. Despite the fact that Italy had its own great painters, Memling received commissions from Italy, especially through the Medici representatives. The Hospital of St. Jean in Bruges houses the Musee Memling. When he was buried at the Church of St. Gilles in Bruges, he was said to be the "best painter in all Christendom."

Memling's art depicting the Virgin and Child is represented on the 1967 traditional Christmas stamp.

Michelangelo

Letters
mingle souls

Raphael

Donne

10c US

Scott 1530
Born: March 6, 1475, Caprese Michelangelo, Toscan, Italy
Died: February 18, 1564, Rome, Italy

In the autumn of 1474, Ludovico Buonarroti, and his wife, Friancesca dei Neri, went to Caprese Michelangelo to serve as resident magistrate. While in Caprese Michelangelo, their second son was born. He was named Michelangniolo Buonarroti, but to all he is known as Michelangelo. At the age of 13, Michelangelo went to work for Florence's foremost painter, Domenico Ghirlandajo. He studied at the Brancacci chapel. Michelangelo became embroiled in a scrap with a student, who hit him in the nose, leaving it deformed.

His earliest work, *Madonna of the Stairs*, completed when he was 17 and now in the Casa Buonarroti, Florence, exemplifies his impending genius. This was followed by *Battle of the Centaurs and Lapiths* in 1492, also in the Casa Buonarroti. Of all his art, the perfect human body in expressive motion was his genius. He displayed it to its most possible perfection.

His work in Rome from 1496 to 1501 launched his career. His *Bacchus* is in the Museo Nazionale in Florence, and the beautiful *Madonna with the Dead Christ*, also called the *Pieta*, is in St. Peter's Basilica, Rome.

From 1501 to 1504, he created *David*, the nude young male now in the Academia, Florence. The frescoes on the ceiling of the Sistine Chapel in the Vatican took Michelangelo four years of strenuous work while painting on his back. The ceiling features a series of scenes, from the "Act of Creation" to the "Drunkeness of Noah."

In 1536, he painted the *Last Judgement* on the altar wall of the Sistine Chapel. This is probably the single most famous picture in the world. In the adjoining Capella Paolina, he painted the *Conversion of Saul* and the *Crucifixion of Peter* in 1542 to 1550.

Michelangelo is depicted in *School of Athens* painted by Sanzio Raphael, The painting is reproduced on a stamp in the 1974 Universal Postal Union set.

154

Arthur Middleton

Scott 1691
Born: June 26, 1742, Middleton Place, Charleston, South Carolina
Died: January 1, 1787, Goose Creek, South Carolina

Arthur Middleton was the son of Henry (1717-84) and Mary Williams Middleton of Middleton Place, located northwest of Charleston. Arthur inherited the Middleton home from his mother, who died while he was in England.

His main education was procured in London, first at the academy in Hackney, then at the famous Middle Temple, where he studied law. In 1764, he married Mary Izard, daughter of Walter Izard. They had eight children.

In the fall, he was elected to the Colonial House of Assembly. He corresponded with the agent in London as a member of the Committee of Correspondence. In 1768, his last year on the committee, he went to London with his wife. While in London, their first son, Henry, was born. Benjamin West painted a picture of the young family. They returned in September 1771.

In 1772, Middleton was again elected to the House of Assembly and sat in the first provincial congress. He was among the citizens who seized weapons and gun powder from the public storehouse on April 21, 1776. He helped raise money for the cause. On June 14, 1776, he became a member of the first Council of Safety that governed the Colony. He was a member of the second provincial congress and, on February 11, 1776, was on the committee to prepare the constitution for South Carolina.

Middleton's father was in the Continental Congress in 1776 but when he became ill, he gave his son his position. Arthur Middleton signed the Declaration of Independence. He declined re-election in 1778.

When John Rutledge resigned the presidency of the state, Middleton was chosen his successor but declined. During the seige of Charleston in 1780, he was in the militia, taken prisoner and was sent to St. Augustine. He was released in the prisoner exchange in July 1781.

In the first stamp of the 1976 Declaration of Independence issue, of the six men standing, Middleton is the sixth from the left and is seen leaning forward.

155

Ludwig Mies van der Rohe

Mies van der Rohe, 1886-1969 Illinois Inst Tech Chicago

Architecture USA 20c

Scott 2020
Born: March 27, 1886, Aachen, Germany
Died: August 17, 1969, Chicago, Illinois

Ludwig Mies van der Rohe, the son of a stonemason, finished his basic schooling by age 15. He went to Berlin to work with Bruno Paul, the furniture designer. He was an apprentice for industrial architect Peter Behren.

In 1907, he designed the Riehl house in Berlin. In Holland, in 1912, he studied the work of L.P. Berlage. At Stuttgart, in 1927, the Deutsche Werkbund exposition displayed his Glass Industry exhibit. He introduced designs of a glass skyscraper as early as 1921.

Mies van der Rohe was of the famous purist school of design, the Bauhaus, founded in Weimar in 1919 by Walter Gropius. The school moved to Dessau in 1925. Mies van der Rohe succeeded Gropius as its director during the crucial years of 1930 to 1933. Nazi pressure forced it to close in 1933.

Mies van der Rohe designed the German Pavilion at the International Exposition in Barcelona in 1929 and the Tugendhat house in Czechoslovakia.

He emigrated to the United States in 1937 and was appointed professor of architecture at the Illinois Institute of Technology, where he taught until 1958. He received his U.S. citizenship in 1944. He designed the new campus for the institute. In 1950, he created the Farnsworth House in Plano, Illinois, which transformed the concept of his pavilion at Barcelona into an all-glass house.

While with the Illinois Institute, he designed some 20 building for the 100-acre campus, including the boxlike Minerals and Metals Research Building and the Crown Hall. These exemplify his ideal, "less is more." This concept led him to simplify his forms and concentrate his full attention on the specific details.

In Chicago and elsewhere, he began to receive large commissions for skyscrapers. In 1951, he completed the twin-tower 26-story apartment building at 860 Lakeshore Drive and, in 1964, the Chicago Federal Center. In 1956-59, with Philip Johnson in New York City, he designed the most impressive Seagram building. He again left his mark in Europe with the Schaefer Museum in Schweinfurt, West Germany and the National Gallery in Berlin.

One of Mies van der Rohe's buildings on the Chicago Illinois Institute of Technology campus is shown on a 1981 American Architecture stamp.

Thomas Mifflin

Scott 798
Born: January 10, 1744, Philadelphia, Pennsylvania
Died: Janury 20, 1800, Lancaster, Pennsylvania

Thomas Mifflin was born to a Quaker family. He was the first son of John and Elizabeth Bagnell Mifflin. He attended a Quaker school and went to the College of Philadelphia, graduating in 1760. He went to Europe for a year.

In 1772, he was elected to the provincial assembly. He was an ardent patriot and a Whig. He was elected to the Second Continental Congress. After the Battle of Lexington and Concord, he became an active soldier. He was appointed a major, and the Quakers read him out of their meetings.

On June 25, 1775, he was appointed Washington's aide-de-camp, and by August, he was quartermaster general. He served until March 1778. He led an attack on a British foraging expedition at Lechmire's Point on November 9, 1775, and the next month he was commissioned colonel. On May 16, 1776, he was appointed a brigadier general.

He resigned as quartermaster and led a covering party in the withdrawal from Long Island. He was present at the battles of Trenton and Princeton and was appointed major-general. He assisted in the defense of Philadelphia.

In the summer of 1777, he resigned his commissions of quartermaster and as major-general. He was deeply involved in the "Conway Cabal." It was largely on his recommendations that General Gates became president of the Board of War. On discovery of the cabal, he disavowed having any part of it. He left the Board of War and rejoined the Army but was inactive. On August 17, 1778, Congress accepted his resignation. From 1782 to 1784, he was again in Congress and was elected president.

Ironically, when Washington returned his commission, it was Mifflin who accepted it. Mifflin was a member of the Federal Convention in 1787 and signed the Constitution. He was elected to the Supreme Executive Council of Pennsylvania in 1788, serving as president until 1790. He was chairman of the state Constitution Convention, and president of the convention in 1789 and 1790. He was the first governor of Pennsylvania, serving from 1790 to 1799.

He borrowed heavily and went into debt. He had to leave Philadelphia. He later died penniless. The state paid his burial expenses.

Mifflin is depicted on the 1937 Constitution Sesquicentennial stamp.

Peter Minuit

Scott 836
Born: circa 1580, Wesel, Duchy of Cleves, Rhenish Prussia
Died: June 1638, St. Christopher, Leeward Islands, West Indies

Peter Minuit, or Minnewit (the Dutch spelling), was probably of Walloon or French ancestry, but some say he was originally Dutch. In 1625, he went to New Netherlands with a group of colonists and returned. He again went to New Netherlands in January 1626 aboard *The Sea Mew* (*Het Meeuwitje*) with another group of colonists. They landed at Manhattan Island on May 4, 1626.

The first director of the colony, Cornelius May, had been replaced by Willem Verhulst. Verhulst was recalled to the Netherlands, and Minuit took his place. He established himself as the first director general of the colony. He acquired the rest of the island of 22 square miles from the Algonquin Indian chief for the price of trinkets valued at the time at about $24 or 91¢ a square mile.

He changed the name of the island from Manhattan to New Amsterdam and built a fort by the same name at the southern end of the island. He made the fort the seat of government and home for the people. He treated the Indians kindly but was severe with the colonists. He granted liberal trading privileges to the Dutch patroons. In 1631, the West India Company recalled Minuit, fearing his policies would endanger the company's monopoly.

In Amsterdam, Samuel Blommaert recommended Minuit to the Swedish chancellor, Axel Oxenstierna, to lead a contingent of colonists to America. In 1638, Minuit was in the employ of Sweden. He commanded two ships of Swedish and Finnish settlers, who, in March 1638, landed on the coast of the Delaware River near the present site of Wilmington. In 1638, he bought land from the Delaware Indians and built a fort. He called it Fort Christiana, after the child queen of Sweden. He claimed the land along the river between what is now Fort Mifflin down to what is now Bombay Hook National Wildlife Refuge. He called it New Sweden.

He sailed for St. Christopher, one of the Leeward Islands, to trade tobacco. He went to visit the captain of a Dutch ship. A hurricane struck, capsized the ship, and Minuit was drowned.

The "Landing of the First Swedish and Finnish Settlers in America," led by Minuit, is honored on a stamp issued June 27, 1938.

Clement Clarke Moore

Scott 1472
Born: July 15, 1779, New York, New York
Died: July 10, 1863, Newport, Rhode Island

Clement Clarke Moore was an educator, lexicographer and poet. His life spanned two great wars. He was born during the Revolutionary War and died during the Civil War. He was a 1798 graduate of Columbia College, where his father, Benjamin Moore, had been president and professor of logic. His father was consecrated the second bishop of New York in 1801 by the American Protestant Episcopal church. His father had also graduated from Columbia College in 1768, when it was known as King's College.

The elder Moore wanted his son to follow in his footsteps and become a priest in the American Protestant Episcopal church. However, Clement was scholarly and concentrated on studies of the Hebrew language. In 1809, he completed and published his *A Compendious Lexicon of the Hebrew Language in Two Volumes*, as an aid to those who studied Hebrew.

In addition to his lexicographic endeavors, he was an authority on Oriental and Greek literature. From 1823 to 1850, Moore was professor at the General Theological Seminary, an institution for which he had donated 60 lots of valuable New York City property for the erection of this facility.

It was not the thousands of hours Moore spent in arduous teaching and exacting writing that made him famous. Nor was it his generous gift of land to the Theological Seminary. What made his place in history was a simple and delightful Christmas poem written for his children that begins, "Twas the night before Christmas when all through the house, not a creature was stirring, not even a mouse..." He titled it *A Visit from St. Nicholas*. The poem was published anonymously on December 23, 1823, in the *Troy Sentinel*, Troy, New York.

In 1844, 21 years later, it was again published in Moore's own collection of *Poems*. It has been republished thousands of times since.

The first line of Moore's famous Christmas poem was selected for the contemporary Christmas stamp issued October 9, 1972.

159

Daniel Morgan

Surrender at Saratoga 1777 by Trumbull

US Bicentennial 13 cents

Scott 1728
Born: 1736, Bucks County, Pennsylvania
Died: July 6, 1802, Winchester, Virginia

Daniel Morgan was the son of James and Eleanora Morgan. Some historians place his birthplace at Hunterdon County, New Jersey. Morgan went to the Shenandoah Valley in Virginia. He signed on as a wagoner for General Edward Braddock's ill-fated expedition, ending at Fort Duquesne in 1755. He was a lieutenant in Pontiac's War. In 1774, he accompanied Lord Dunmore's expedition to western Pennsylvania. He married Abigail Bailey.

On July 22, 1775, he was commissioned a captain of a company of Virginia riflemen, and from Winchester, Virginia, he took his men to Boston. He volunteered to serve with Benedict Arnold on his expedition to Quebec through the Maine wilderness. He participated in the December 31 battle. He assumed command when Arnold was wounded but had to surrender and was taken prisoner. He was released. On November 12, 1776, he was commissioned a colonel to raise a regiment in Virginia.

He joined George Washington in April 1777, participating in New Jersey. He assisted General Gates against Burgoyne, fighting bravely at the battles of Freeman's Farm and Bemis Heights. After Burgoyne's surrender, Washington recalled Morgan to assist in the Philadelphia campaign of 1777. Morgan resigned in 1779 and retired to Virginia to build his mansion, "Saratoga."

In 1780, Morgan was recalled to duty after Gates was defeated at Camden. Nathaniel Greene, succeeding Gates, sent Morgan to command the forces in western North Carolina, as a brigadier general. Morgan was forced to retreat but fought back and won a decisive victory at Cowpens. He retreated again to join Greene's troops at Guilford Court House. He joined Lafayette for a short term of duty in July, defending Virginia.

Morgan again retired to "Saratoga" and by 1796 had acquired a great tract of land on the Monongahela and Ohio rivers. He returned to duty in 1794 to suppress the Whiskey Insurrection in western Pennsylvania. He served one term in Congress in 1797, then retired to Winchester.

On the Surrender of Burgoyne issue of October 7, 1977, Morgan is seen prominently in the foreground, standing fifth from the right.

Giovanni Battista Moroni

Scott 2367
Born: circa 1525, Albino, Bergamo, Italy
Died: February 5, 1578, Brescia, Italy

Giovanni Battista Moroni was born in the village of Albino, Italy. When he was 20 years of age, he became a student of Alessandro Buonvicino, who was known as Moretto da Brescia, or Il Moretto. Moroni was also influenced by Lorenzo Lotto and the aging Titian.

Moroni painted a number of altarpieces in the span of his 35-year career in the midst of the High Renaissance of the 16th century. His portraits were his best and most notable works. Even such later greats as Sir Anthony Van Dyck, the Flemish painter, were impressed and influenced by Moroni's style.

Moroni's portraits were different in that they did not embellish the background with landscape or architectural displays. His backgrounds were neutral, giving the full emphasis to the subject. His subjects were usually attired in the dark clothing that was the fashion of the time. His portraits usually showed three-quarters of the upper figure or the entire figure.

His religious subjects were painted only in the last few years of his life. Representative works of Moroni's are scattered around the western world in prestigious galleries and museums. In the Johnson Collection is the *Portrait of a Seated Man* displayed in the Philadelphia Museum of Art. His *Portrait of a Young Man* is in the Berlin City Museum. *Portrait of a Gentleman* is in Milan and *Man with a Sword* is in the Uffizi, Florence. A self portrait and a portrait of Conte Secco Suardo are also in the Uffizi. A portrait of Bartolomeo Bongo is in the Metropolitan Museum of Art, New York City. *The Magistrate Antonio Navagero* is at the Brera Palace, Milan, and *Paolo Vidoni Cedrelli* is in Bergamo, Italy. *A Tailor* hangs in the National Gallery, London. *A Gentleman in Adoration Before the Madonna* is in the National Gallery, Washington, D.C.

His paintings took on a silvery look and appeared monochromatic. His religious themes showed the direct influence of Il Moretto. Moroni's portraits followed Lotto but lacked the romantic air rendered by him.

The Moroni *Madonna and Child* was chosen for the 1987 traditional Christmas stamp.

Gouverneur Morris

Scott 798
Born: January 31, 1752, Morrisania, Westchester County, New York
Died: November 6, 1816, Morrisania, Westchester County, New York

Gouverneur Morris was the younger half-brother of Lewis Morris and Richard Morris. The Morrises acquired large tracts of land in New York (Bronx) and New Jersey (Monmouth County). They named their New York estate "Morrisania" in 1697. The desendants were known as the lords of the manor. Gouverneur Morris was the son of Lewis Morris, second lord. His mother, Sarah Gouverneur Morris, was his father's second wife.

Gouverneur Morris graduated from Kings College, New York, in 1768 at age 16. He studied law in the office of William Smith and, at the age of 19, was admitted to the bar. In 1774, he was all for "reunion with the parent state" to keep things at a status quo. When the Revolution broke out, Morris and his half-brothers Richard and Lewis were patriots but his other half-brother, Staats Long Morris, joined the British army.

On May 22, 1775, Gouverneur Morris took his seat on the provincial congress, representing Westchester County. He sat in the Constitutional Convention, which met in July 1776. With John Jay and Robert R. Livingston, he drafted the frame of government. He was a member of the Council of Safety.

Morris made an official visit to George Washington at Valley Forge in 1778. From 1778 to 1779, he sat in the Continental Congress but was defeated for re-election in late 1779. He transferred his citizenship from New York to Philadelphia, where he began law practice and wrote for the *Pennsylvania Packet* under the name "An American."

From 1781 to 1785, he served with Robert Morris as an assistant in finance. In 1787, he was elected to the Constitutional Congress as a Pennsylvania delegate. He was one of the six from Pennsylvania to sign the Constitution. After the convention, he returned to "Morrisania." He went to France as agent for Robert Morris. He became involved with the court in the French Revolution.

In 1792, Washington named Gouverneur Morris minister to France. He represented the United States admirably between 1792 and 1794. He filled an unexpired term in the U.S. Senate in 1800. He was not re-elected in 1802. He became involved in the Erie Canal project as chairman of the commission.

Morris is depicted on the 1937 Constitution Sesquicentennial stamp.

Lewis Morris

Scott 1691
Born: April 8, 1726, Morrisania, Westchester County, New York
Died: January 2, 1798, Morrisania, Westchester County, New York

As with Benjamin Harrison, the dubbing "Signer" must be added to Lewis Morris' name to distinguish him from the other Lewis Morrises of Colonial history. The Morris family was descended from Richard and Lewis Morris, emigrants from England to Barbados and then to New York.

They were successful merchants and acquired large tracts of land in New York (Bronx) and New Jersey (Monmouth County). Their New York estate was known as "Morrisania." They referred to the heads of the estate as lords.

Lewis "The Signer" Morris was the brother of Richard and half-brother of Gouverneur Morris, who was 26 years his younger. He became the third lord of the famous Morris manor, "Morrisania."

Morris led the delegation from Westchester to the New York Provincial Congress and was selected for the Second Continental Congress. He was instrumental in obtaining supplies and munitions for the Revolutionists.

Morris was appointed brigadier general in command of his home militia. He was absent for the signing of the Declaration of Independence in July 1776, but signed it later in the year.

During the war, "Morrisania" was ruined by the British. Morris was later elected a New York state senator and became a member of the Board of Regents of the New York State University.

Lewis was a strong supporter of the ratification of the U.S. Constitution by New York.

Of the six men standing, pictured on the first stamp of the Declaration of Independence set of four stamps issued July 4, 1976, Lewis Morris is the fourth from the left.

Anna Mary Robertson Moses

Scott 1370
Born: September 7, 1860, Greenwich, New York
Died: December 13, 1961, Hoosick Falls, New York

Anna Mary Robertson was educated during the summer while she was growing up on the farm. At 17, she married Thomas Moses. The young couple settled on a farm near Eagle Bridge, Rensselaer County, New York. She worked as a diligent farmwife until her husband died in 1927.

Moses, who became known as Grandma Moses, kept busy embroidering pictures in worsted until she was about 80 years old. Her hands had become too arthritic to handle the needle, so she began painting pictures. She had done some painting as early as 1918, but her paintings did not gain national recognition for another 20 years. She had shown a talent for drawing when she was a young girl. She used old postcards and Currier & Ives prints as a guide.

She gave away many of her paintings as gifts or sold them for small sums at the local drugstore in Hoosick Falls. To save paint, she would paint several paintings at one time. In all, she completed more than 2,000 pictures.

In 1939, art collector Louis Caldor, bought four of Grandma Moses' pictures at the drugstore. He was so impressed that he drove to her farm and bought an additional 15. That same year, three of those paintings were in an exhibition, "Contemporary Unknown Painters," in the Museum of Modern Art in New York City. In October 1940, the Galerie St. Etienne in New York City held a one-person showing of 35 of her "American primitive" works. In November, Gimbel's department store brought her to New York for a Thanksgiving exhibition of her paintings. Her oils of "rural American scenes of times gone by" were exhibited in Europe and the United States.

Grandma Moses never moved from her white farmhouse and did not stop painting until she was 100 years old. She wrote about her life in a book published in 1952 titled *My Life's History*.

Her painting *Fourth of July* is reproduced on a 1969 commemorative.

164

Myron

Scott 719
Born: circa 500 B.C., Eleutherai, Attic-Boeotian Territory, Greece
Died: circa 430 B.C., Athens, Greece

Myron received commissions for his sculptures in bronze in sanctuaries throughout the ancient Greek world. The use of bronze in casting was discovered and developed a generation before his time. He was taught by Hagelada of Argos of the Argive metal-casting school. By casting in Aegina bronze, a wide variety of new compositions were created. Myron became a master at this new art. His work was well-known. He created statues and groups for wealthy patrons and city-states, especially on the Athenian Acropolis.

Recorded history by ancient authors (Pliny and Pausanias) mention his works of art with great praise. Myron's versatility is represented in bronzes of the pagan Hellenic gods, lesser dieties, heroes, athletes and animals, examples of which were *Athena and Marsyas* (dieties), *Discobolus* (athlete), and *Cow* (animal). His *Discobolus* (*Discus Thrower*) is his most celebrated. He made statues of Olympic victors Thimanthin in 456 B.C., Lydinos in 448 B.C. (the second time), Philippos about 450 B.C., and the famous runner and Olympic victor, Ladas, who died of his own exertion.

At least 21 works are ascribed to Myron. Many more are lost. The *Cow* or *Heifer* was created for the city of Athens. During the 1st century, it was taken to Rome, where it stood for 500 years. The *Cow* sparked some 36 witty epigrams in the *Greek Anthology*, which ran from 700 B.C. to A.D. 1000, now about 16 books. These epigrams relative to the *Cow* are the only link to its identity and possible authenticity. Many copies of these works have been made in marble. Several copies of *Athena and Marsyas* were made, but the best is now divided. One half (Athena) is in the Liebieghaus at Frankfurt am Main, Germany, and the other half (Marsyas) in the Museo Laterano in Rome. Fortunately a marble copy of *Discobolus* is in the National Museum, Rome. The bronze, originally in Delphi (circa 440 B.C.), is lost.

Myron was a contemporary of Pheidias (middle 5th century B.C.) and Polykleitos. Pythagoras of Samos (or Rhegion), also an athlete sculptor, was his rival. His only student was his son, Kydics.

The *Discobolus* was chosen for the 1932 5¢ Olympic Games stamp.

165

James A. Naismith

Scott 1189
Born: November 6, 1861, Almonte, Ontario, Canada
Died: November 28, 1939, Lawrence, Kansas

James Naismith graduated from McGill University in Montreal in 1887. He had worked in a logging camp before entering college. He was an athletic and well-bred young man. He believed in developing young men through proper exercise and competitive games. After graduating from McGill, Naismith continued as that school's director of physical education and attended Presbyterian College of Montreal with the intention of going into the ministry.

Through the Young Men's Christian Association, Naismith decided to make physical education his life's endeavor. He went to the YMCA Training School (now Springfield College) at Springfield, Massachusetts. In 1891, the school's superintendent, Luther H. Gulick, saw the need for a competitive sport between the football and baseball seasons. Naismith created such a sport.

At either end of an exercise court, Naismith mounted peach baskets on the rim of an elevated running track 10 feet above the central court. With a soccer ball he developed a tossing game. Originally, Naismith had 18 players at his disposal, and his first rule was "There shall be nine players on each side." Shortly thereafter, the number was made optional, depending on the size of the available court and the number of players available. Later, when the popular game spread over the country, the number of players was standardized to five on each team — two guards, a center and two forwards. The improvised baskets were improved upon, as was the ball, and the court size and markings were standardized. The game spread rapidly throughout the world.

Naismith attended the Gross Medical College in Denver during 1895-98, and received his medical degree. He later became professor of physical education at the University of Kansas at Lawrence, a position he held until his retirement in 1937.

The man and his creation were honored with a 4¢ stamp in 1961.

Thomas Nelson

Scott 1686d
Born: December 26, 1738, Yorktown, Virginia
Died: January 4, 1789, Hanover County, Virginia

Thomas Nelson was the son of William Nelson, who was governor of Virginia from 1770 to 1771. The family lived in Yorktown. Thomas was sent to Cambridge, England, and studied at Christ's College. He returned to Yorktown. He was elected to the House of Burgesses and served for several terms. He sat in the provincial conventions of 1774-76. It was his instructions that prompted the Virginia delegates sitting in the Continental Congress to move for the Declaration of Independence. He was one of the signers, along with his fellow Virginia delegates, George Wythe, Richard Henry Lee, Thomas Jefferson, Benjamin Harrison, Francis Lightfoot Lee and Carter Braxton.

Poor health plagued Nelson, and he had to resign from the Congress. His illness was not so severe that he could not accept the post as commander in chief of the military forces of Virginia in 1777. He returned to Congress in 1779, but his health again failed him. He resigned. Nelson raised public money to pay for Virginia's military debts. He pledged his own assets as security.

In 1781, he followed Thomas Jefferson into the gubernatorial seat of Virginia. As head of the Virginia militia, he joined Washington at the siege of Yorktown in September. Lord Cornwallis had supposedly set up headquarters in Nelson's Yorktown mansion. Without tergiversation, Nelson ordered his gunners to fire away at the homestead, but for naught. Little damage was done.

The war was over, and again Nelson's health was poor. He resigned as governor of Virginia. He was relieved by Benjamin Harrison, who completed the term in 1784, turning it over to Patrick Henry. The time came for Nelson to make good his indebtedness incurred as his contribution to the cause. His property had to be sold, and he spent the remainder of his life in poverty.

Nelson is shown as first equestrian on the left on the fourth 13¢ stamp of the first 1976 American Bicentennial souvenir sheet.

Alonso de Ojeda

Scott 118
Born: circa 1465, Cuenca, Spain
Died: circa 1515, Santo Domingo (Dominican Republic)

Alonso de Ojeda sailed with Columbus in 1493 on Columbus' second voyage. Ojeda remained on the islands for two years.

Ojeda sailed again in 1499 and 1500, along with Amerigo Vespucci and Juan de la Cosa. Vespucci had been a pilot for Columbus and was an able geographer, cosmographer and astronomer to the king of Spain. Juan de la Cosa was the navigator and mapmaker, who had sailed on the *Nina* in 1493. He was an able seaman but, in 1509, while exploring the Pearl Coast of Venezuela under the command of Ojeda, he was killed by an Indian's poison arrow.

On the 1499-1500 voyage, they explored the coast of South America as far north and west as the Gulf of Venezuela. In 1502, Ojeda again visited this coast, but the Portuguese claimed he was trespassing. He was fined, censured and imprisoned for debt. In 1505, he sailed into the Gulf of Darien. In 1508, the king of Spain made him governor of Nueva Andulucia, which extended from the Gulf of Darien to the Gulf of Venezuela.

Ojeda was commissioned to form a colony near what is today Cartagena, but failed. In 1509, he sailed from Santo Domingo to settle a colony. He again met with failures but finally settled at San Sebastian in what is now northwestern Columbia on the east side of the Gulf of Uraba.

His colony was running short of supplies, so he left it in the hands of Francisco Pizarro and sailed for Hispaniola. He was wrecked off the coast of Cuba but finally arrived in Santo Domingo. The colony did not wait for Ojeda to return and instead moved to the gulf's west side. They renamed it Santa Maria la Antiqua del Darien under the leadership of Vasco Nunez de Balboa, who had arrived at the gulf settlement as a stowaway. The settlement thrived. Ojeda remained in Santo Domingo until he died in obscurity.

He is pictured in John Vanderlyn's *Landing of Columbus* painting on the 15¢ Columbian stamp issued April 2, 1869. He is standing behind and to the left of the flag, wearing a feather in his hat and shouldering a gun.

168

William Owen 'Buckey' O'Neill

Scott 973
Born; February 2, 1860, St. Louis, Missouri
Died: July 1, 1898, San Juan Hill, Cuba

A monument to William Owen "Buckey" O'Neill stands on the Yavapai County Courthouse Plaza in Prescott, Arizona. It was unveiled July 3, 1907, by Captain O'Neill's adopted son Maurice and Kate Hicky, the daughter of O'Neill's best friend. The statue was created by Solon H. Borglum. It pays tribute to the First United States Volunteer Cavalry (Theodore Roosevelt's Rough Riders) and Captain O'Neill, the organizer of the Rough Riders.

O'Neill grew up in Washington, D.C. He was nicknamed "Buckey" because of his ability to go against the odds or "buck the tiger" in the game of faro, and not because he is riding a bucking horse on the statue.

O'Neill came to Prescott in 1881 as a court reporter for Judge Deforest Porter. In the fall of 1885, he attended a medicine show where he met Pauline Marie Schindler. On April 27, 1886, they were married. On November 15, 1893, the young couple moved into the house built by W.B. Jones on the corner of Sheldon and Mount Vernon streets. O'Neill had an office upstairs to publish the *Hoof and Horn*, a stockman's paper. He contributed to the *San Francisco Chronicle*. O'Neill was also probate judge and sheriff, a reporter, a mining promoter, candidate for delegate to Congress in 1894 and mayor of Prescott.

He was the mayor of Prescott when he left for Cuba to fight in the Spanish-American War with the Arizona Volunteers. On May 4, 1898, the Prescott volunteers met at the Plaza to bid their good-byes to friends and family. The train headed for the regimental rendezvous at San Antonio, Texas.

The regiment that Captain O'Neill commanded was officially called the First United States Volunteer Cavalry. Colonel Theodore Roosevelt said he was joining a regiment of "rough riding men." The sobriquet stuck, and they were known in the history books as the Rough Riders.

Captain O'Neill was the only regimental officer killed from among the Arizona volunteers. He was supposedly shot by a sniper. He was buried on the battlefield, and on May 1, 1899, his remains were returned to the United States and laid to rest with the nation's honored dead at Arlington National Cemetery.

Solon Borglum's statue of the Rough Riders is shown on the 1948 3¢ stamp marking the 50th anniversary of the Rough Riders.

Elisha Graves Otis

Scott 2254
Born: August 3, 1811, Halifax, Windham County, Vermont
Died: April 8, 1861, Yonkers, New York

Elisha Graves Otis was the son of Stephen and Phoebe Glynn Otis, who were farmers. Otis was never in robust health. He went to school in Halifax. At the age of 19, he went to Troy, New York, to work in the building trade. About 1833, he acquired a hauling wagon and trucked goods to and from Troy and Battleboro, Vermont. He acquired land in Green River, Vermont, where he built a gristmill that he converted to a sawmill. He made wagons and carriages.

On February 25, 1842, his wife, Susan, died, leaving him with two sons, Charles Rollin, age 7, and Norton Prentice, age 2. In 1845 his health began to fail again. He moved his family to Albany, New York, to work as a master mechanic for a bedstead factory. That same year he married Elizabeth A. Boyd.

In 1848, he established his own shop, doing machine work and producing a turbine waterwheel he had invented. The power for his shop was from the current of Patroon's Creek. When the city of Albany took over the creek for its water supply, Otis closed his shop. In 1851, he returned to the bedstead work, this time at Bergen, New York. Again he was the master mechanic.

In 1851, the company built a new factory at Yonkers. Otis was put in charge of constructing the machinery. To accomplish this an elevator was needed. Otis built one. He incorporated a number of his own devices, especially an automatic safety device to check the fall in case the lifting chain broke.

The elevator attracted the attention of other New York builders. Otis soon had commissions to build three more elevators. He began his own elevator business. In 1854, he exhibited his elevator at an exposition, the American Institute Fair, in New York and demonstrated its safety device by deliberately cutting the lifting cable and walking out of the elevator uninjured.

Commissions were not rushing in, so he supplemented his work by manufacturing other items he had invented, such as railroad car trucks and brakes in 1852, a steam plow in 1857, and a bake oven in 1858. In 1861, the year he died at age 50, he invented a steam elevator.

The Otis elevator is depicted on the 1988 5.3¢ Transportation coil.

Samuel Allyne Otis

Scott 854
Born: November 24, 1740, Barnstable, Massachusetts
Died: April 22, 1814, Washington, D.C.

Samuel Allyne Otis traces his ancestry from a Glastonbury yeoman's family. The family emigrated from Somerset, England, to America in 1631 and settled first in Hingham, Massachusetts. Samuel was the son of Colonel James and Mary Allyne Otis. His father was the son of John Otis, who moved to Barnstable from Hingham, commanded the militia of Barnstable County, served as a judge for 25 years and as councillor of the province for 19 years. The Otis home was in Great Marshes, near West Barnstable.

Samuel Allyne Otis' brother, James, was a lawyer, admitted to the bar in Plymouth. James coined the phrase, "Taxation without representation is tyranny." He became mentally deranged in his later years. While visiting a friend in Andover, he was killed by a bolt of lightning.

Samuel married Elizabeth Gray, who was the daughter of Harrison Gray, treasurer of the province of Massachusetts Bay and a refugee Loyalist in the Revolution. Otis graduated from Harvard in 1759 and engaged in the mercantile business in Boston. He became a member of the Massachusetts House of Representatives in 1776 and was a member of the Board of War that year. He was charged as collector of clothing for the Continental Army in 1777.

He attended the Massachusetts Constitution Convention and was a member of the Massachusetts House of Representatives from 1784 to 1787. He was its speaker the first year. He was a member of the Continental Congress from 1787 to 1788 and secretary of the U.S. Senate from 1789 to 1814.

He died in Washington, D.C., on April 22, 1814, and was buried in the Congressional Cemetery in Washington, D.C.

Otis was in attendence at the inauguration ceremonies at the Federal Building, New York City, the sesquicentennial of which was memorialized by a stamp issued on April 30, 1939.

William Paca

Scott 1691
Born: October 31, 1740, near Abingdon, Harford County, Maryland
Died: October 13, 1799, Wye Hall, Talbot County, Maryland

William Paca was the son of the well-to-do planter John Paca and Elizabeth Smith Paca. William Paca was educated at the College of Philadelphia, graduating in 1759 with a master of arts degree. He practiced law in the lower courts in 1761. He then studied law at the Inner Temple in London and was admitted to the bar of the provincial court in 1764.

Paca married Mary Chew, the daugher of wealthy Samuel and Henrietta Maria Lloyd Chew of Annapolis, on May 26, 1763. Mary died 11 years later. They had five children; only one lived to adulthood. In 1777, Paca married Anne Harrison of Philadelphia, who died in 1780.

In 1768, Paca was first elected to the provincial legislature. While in the provincial assembly, he served on the committee that directed the construction of the State House at Annapolis. He served on the Maryland Committee of Correspondence and was sent to the First Continental Congress in June 1774. In Annapolis, he represented the city in the provincial convention that met in November. He served on several important committees in the Second Continental Congress. He voted for and signed the Declaration of Independence.

In August 1776, Paca was in the convention that framed the Maryland constitution and was elected one of the first of 15 state senators. He was appointed chief judge of the Maryland General Court in 1778. In 1780, Congress appointed him chief justice of the Court of Appeals in admiralty and prize cases. From 1782 to 1785, he was governor of the State of Maryland.

He took an active interest in establishing Washington College, Chestertown, Maryland. He was an honorary member of the Society of Cincinnati. In 1788, he was a delegate in the Maryland convention that adopted the U.S. Constitution. George Washington appointed him federal district judge in 1789.

On the first stamp of the 1976 Declaration of Independence set, of the six men standing, Paca is the first on the left.

Robert Treat Paine

Scott 1692
Born: March 11, 1731, Boston, Massachusetts
Died: May 11, 1814, Boston, Massachusetts

Robert Treat Paine was the son of the Reverend Thomas and Eunice Treat Paine. His ancestors were prominent leaders in politics and the ministry. Paine was baptized at the Old South Church at the foot of Beacon Hill. He entered the ministry and studied in the Boston Latin School. He graduated from Harvard in 1749. He taught for awhile, then returned for additional study in theology.

Paine served as chaplain of the New England troops on the Crown Point Expedition of 1755. He then sailed the Atlantic, ending with a whaling expedition to Greenland. He gravitated from theology to law, studying with Benjamin Pratt. He was admitted to the bar in 1757. He began practice in Portland. In 1761, he moved to Taunton. As an associate prosecuting attorney in the celebrated Boston Massacre trial, his zeal turned to the Patriots' cause.

In 1770, he married Sally Cobb, sister of General David Cobb. They had eight children. He represented Taunton in the provincial assembly in 1773, 1774, 1775, 1777 and 1778. He was chosen as one of the Massachusetts delegates to the Continental Congress meeting in Philadelphia. In the second Congress after the Battle of Bunker Hill, he voted for George Washington as the commander-in-chief of the Army. He signed both the Olive Branch Petition, an appeal to the Crown, and the Declaration of Independence.

In 1777, he remained in Massachusetts as the speaker of the House of Representatives, though he had been elected to the Congress in Philadelphia. In December 1777, he was chosen by Congress to inquire into the failure of the Rhode Island Expedition. He was chosen the first attorney general of Massachusetts. He was a judge of the state Supreme Court from 1790 to 1804, when he retired because of increasing deafness. He had moved to Boston in 1780, the year he co-founded the American Academy of Arts and Sciences.

Of the row of men seated in the second 1976 Declaration of Independence stamp, Paine is the fifth from the left.

Dorothy Parker (Campbell)

Scott 2698
Born: August 22, 1893, West End, Monmouth County, New Jersey
Died: June 7, 1967, New York, New York

Dorothy Rothchild grew up in New York, went to a Catholic convent school in Manhattan and Miss Dana's School in Morristown, New Jersey. Her mother was of Scottish ancestry, and her father was Jewish. Dorothy felt a constant resentment at being Jewish. Her mother died when she was yet an infant, and her father remarried.

Her first success in writing came when she sold verses to editor Frank Crowninshield of *Vogue* magazine. She was hired by *Vogue* for $10 a week to write captions. Crowninshield was also the editor of *Vanity Fair*. A year later, sensing her talents, he gave her a job on this magazine. She worked with Robert Benchley and others known as the "Algonquin Round Table."

At this time, she married a handsome Hartford man, Edwin Pond Parker II. Though this marriage was dissolved by divorce a few years later, it was his name she preferred to use as her nom de plume rather than Rothchild.

Contrary to her off-handed wit, Parker took her work seriously. Her first book of satyrical verse, *Enough rope*, published in 1926, included the oft-quoted couplet "Men seldom make passes/At girls who wear glasses."

Shortly after *The New Yorker* magazine was established in 1925 by Harold Ross, Parker left *Vanity Fair* to write short stories for *The New Yorker*. She also contributed numerous book reviews, covering such authors as Nan Britton, Upton Sinclair, Emily Post, Sinclair Lewis and Ernest Hemingway. Parker contributed book reviews to *Esquire* magazine for which "Best Fiction of 1957" covered Ellery Queen, Truman Capote and James Thurber.

Parker married Alan Campbell, whose father was Scottish and mother Jewish. The couple went to Hollywood as a screenwriting team. He joined the Army during World War I. They were divorced in 1947, but remarried in 1950, separated in 1952, then reunited in 1956. Campbell died in 1963.

Parker is depicted on a 29¢ Literary Arts stamp issued August 22, 1992.

John Parker

Scott 617
Born: July 13, 1729, near Lexington, Massachusetts
Died: September 17, 1775, near Lexington, Massachusetts

John Parker's parents were Josiah and Anna Stone Parker. John Parker served his military apprenticeship in the French and Indian War and fought at Louisburg and Quebec. He was probably a member of the noted company of rangers commanded by New Hampshire soldier and author Robert Rogers. The company was known as "Rogers' Rangers." They fought gallantly during the French and Indian War.

When Parker was not involved in battles, he was a farmer and mechanic and held various offices in Lexington. He married Lydia Moore on May 25, 1755, with whom he had seven children.

By 1775, in Massachusetts, the authority of Governor Gage was openly defied. Parker helped form a company of minutemen. He also helped set up stores of munitions at strategic spots. Gage dispatched troops to Concord on the night of April 18, 1775, to arrest Samuel Adams and John Hancock and to seize the munitions. It was intended to be a surprise attack, but Paul Revere and others alerted the countryside. Parker became one of the foremost figures in the action that was soon to take place. He ordered 130 men to guard the house where Adams and Hancock were hiding. He then dismissed them, but as the British advanced, he gathered about 70 men. He issued the order: "Stand your ground. Don't fire unless fired upon. But if they mean to have a war, let it begin here."

Some 700 British forces under the command of Gage advanced to Lexington and Concord to arrest Adams and Hancock and seize any stores of ammunition they could find. About 50 minutemen met them. Shots were exchanged. When the shooting stopped, eight minutemen were dead, and 10 were wounded. The British retreated. The minutemen fired shots, picking off so many Redcoats that the retreat to Boston was a humiliating rout. Parker was in the thick of it. The Revolutionary War had begun.

Two months later, the provincials gathered for the siege of Boston. Parker was much too ill to take part in the Battle of Bunker Hill, which took place on June 17, 1775. Exactly three months later he died.

In an engraving on the 1¢ stamp issued April 4, 1925, Parker is shown standing facing his troops before the shooting started.

William Paterson

Scott 798
Born: December 24, 1745, County Antrim, Ireland
Died: September 9, 1806, Albany, New York

William Paterson's parents, Richard and Mary Paterson, came to New Castle on the Delaware River in October 1747. William Paterson entered the College of New Jersey (now Princeton) and graduated in 1763. He read law in the office of Richard Stockton in 1764 and, in 1766, received his master of arts degree from the college. He passed the bar examination in 1768. He practiced law in New Bromley, Hunterdon County, then returned to Princeton in 1772. He went to South Branch, Somerset County, to practice. About 1779, he purchased a farm he called "Raritan," on the north bank of the Raritan River.

He attended the New Jersey Provincial Congress as a deputy from Somerset County on May 11, 1775, and was re-elected the following year. In 1776, he was a member of the convention that formed the state constitution and was chosen attorney general in 1776. The next year he was a member of the legislative council of the state of New Jersey.

He was an officer in the Somerset County battalion of minutemen and a member of the Council of Safety in 1777. He was elected to serve in the Continental Congress in 1780 but declined because of the pressures of his office. He continued as attorney general of New Jersey until 1783, when he resigned to give his full time to private practice.

In 1779, he married Cornelia Bell. They had three children. His wife died following the birth of their third child. He later married Euphemia White.

Paterson was chosen for the Federal Convention at Philadelphia in May 1787 and signed the Constitution. He was chosen senator from New Jersey and was in New York on March 19, 1789, to greet George Washington. When Governor William Livingston died in 1790, Paterson completed his term.

In 1793, Washington appointed Paterson associate justice of the U.S. Supreme Court. In the summer of 1806, his health was failing. He started for Ballston Springs, New York, to "take the cure." He made it to Albany, where his daughter, Cornelia, the wife of Stephen van Rensselaer, resided. Paterson died and was buried in the manor house vault.

Paterson, New Jersey, was so named to honor Paterson. He is depicted on the 1937 Constitution Sesquicentennial stamp.

Juan Perez

Scott 239
Born: circa 1455?, Old Castile, Spain
Died: circa 1515?, La Rabida, Huelva Province, Spain

From what little is known of his life, one can only surmise the approximate birth date and death date of Fray Juan Perez. Queen Isabella and Christopher Columbus apparently were the same age, both recorded to have been born in 1451. In his youth, Juan Perez had belonged to the Crown's contadores, the state accounting office. Queen Isabella had retained him as a page; therefore, it can be assumed that he may have been a few years younger than the queen. He probably was born somewhere in Castile.

Perez became a friar, and Isabella granted him the privilege of being her personal confessor, a largely honorary position. The position nevertheless conferred prestige on the friar because of his long-standing familiarity with the court and his extraordinary flair for politics. By 1490, Perez was in the monastery of Santa Maria de Rabida in Huelva Province, Andalusia, Spain, when Columbus visited La Rabida. Perez was fascinated with Columbus. Also at La Rabida was Father Antonio de Marchena, a cosmographer and humanist well known at court. The priest was familiar with the fact that the earth is round.

Perez was instrumental in introducing Columbus to the wealthy Alonso de Quintanilla, who managed the property of the Crown. Perez had worked in Quintanilla's office in his younger days when still a contador. In January 1486, Perez was rector of La Rabido. Later in 1491, he again was active in Seville, when he made it known to the queen that if Spain did not support Columbus perhaps France or Portugal would. Perez and other influential members of court persuaded Isabella to give support. She agreed.

In the negotiations that followed, Perez drew up the early drafts of the text. Columbus made a public appearance at the Church of St. George, Palos, on May 23, 1492, with his friend Perez, while a notary read the royal order of the first voyage. On his return from the first voyage, Columbus went to Santa Clara de Moguer near Palos and spent two weeks with Perez at La Rabida. On Palm Sunday, March 31, 1493, Columbus entered Seville.

On the 30¢ stamp of the 1893 Columbian issue, Perez is shown at the table on the extreme left.

Pietro Perugino

Born: circa 1450, Citta della Pieve, Umbria, Italy
Died: February/March 1523, Fontignano, Perugia, Umbria, Italy

Perugino was the son of Cristoforo Vannucci. His given name was Pietro Vannucci, though he called himself Pier della Pieve and Il Perugino. At the age of 10, he became a student of Florenzo di Lorenzo. He studied at the workshop of Andrea del Verrocchio alongside Leonardo da Vinci. His earliest works, dated 1478, are a fresco of St. Sebastian in the Church of Castel Cerqueto near Perugia and a small panel with the *Annunciation of Conte Ronieri* in Perugia.

He went to Rome and painted in the Sistine Chapel. His works were destroyed to make room for Michelangelo's *Last Judgement*. The works that now remain in the Chapel by Perugino are the *Baptism of Christ* and *Christ Giving the Keys to Peter*. He left Rome, visited Perugia and went to Florence in 1486. In 1493, he married Chiara Fancelli. They had three sons.

Perugino resided mostly in Florence until 1499. He painted a lovely altarpiece for Cardinal Guilano della Rovere, a half figure of the Madonna in 1480. It is now in the National Gallery. *The Madonna With Saints and Angels* is now in the Louvre, Paris, and the *Crucifixion* is in the Uffizi, Florence. In 1495, he painted the *Pieta*, now in the Pitti Palace, Florence.

From 1496 until 1498, he worked on the 15-panel altarpiece for St. Pietro of Perugia. The panels were confiscated by the French in 1797 and are now in the galleries of several French cities. Others are in the Vatican gallery.

In 1499, the bankers of Perugia commissioned him to paint their hall. It was an extensive undertaking featuring the seven planets and the signs of the zodiac on the vault and the *Nativity* and *Transfiguration* on the walls. He had several pupils who were instrumental in carrying out this project, including Raphael.

A few years later Perugino was called to Rome by Pope Julius II to paint the Stanza in the Vatican but was replaced by Raphael. Perugino's last work was created for the Church of Castello di Fontignano near Perugia. He died of the plague in February or March of 1524. His body was buried without rites in a common grave of the plague victims.

Perugino's *Madonna* was chosen for the 1986 Christmas stamp.

John Frederick Peto

Letters mingle souls
Peto
Donne
10c US

Scott 1532
Born: May 21, 1854, Philadelphia, Pennsylvania
Died: November 23, 1907, Island Heights, New Jersey

John Peto lived with his grandmother until he was 25. He was a student at the Pennsylvania Academy of Fine Arts in Philadelphia, where he met William Michael Harnett. Peto opened a studio in Philadelphia and exhibited his work at the academy. He was an avid follower of Harnett, the trompe-l'oeil still-life painter. However, Peto's paintings represented objects that are homely and worn, very different from Harnett's shiny, elegant bric-a-brac. Peto's dark tonalities were more like the paintings of Thomas Eakins and Albert Ryder.

Peto worked in obscurity. He refused to make his objects neat and attractive or to evoke nostalgic sentiment of pretty objects that appealed to the eye. Nevertheless, the quality of pathos and tenderness are in Peto's works, as seen especially in the well-known *Poor Man's Store*, painted in 1885 and now in the Museum of Fine Arts, Boston. The scene shows an array of simple wares in a battered storefront window bathed in soft yet subtle direct light.

Peto was an expert painter of trompe l'oeil. His still-life paintings showed objects cluttered on the shelf or fastened to an old board or weathered door. He was a master at the "rack picture," such as *Old Souvenirs*, painted in 1881. He began painting these rack pictures in Philadelphia to decorate offices. They represented illusions of bulletin boards.

Old Souvenirs was attributed to Harnett until the fake signing was exposed in the late 1940s. Peto's technique was so close to that of Harnett's that an unscrupulous Philadelphia art dealer accumulated several Peto paintings and faked Harnett's signature on them. These faked paintings fetched high prices.

In 1889, Peto moved to Island Heights, New Jersey, where he remained until his death at age 53 of Bright's disease. He sold his painting to the tourists.

Peto's trompe-l'oeil still-life painting *Old Scraps* is reproduced on a stamp in the 1974 Universal Postal Union set.

William Phillips

Surrender at Saratoga 1777 by Trumbull
US Bicentennial 13 cents

Scott 1728
Born: circa 1731, England
Died: May 13, 1781, Petersburg, Virginia

William Phillips spent his lifetime in military uniform from the age of 15 until he died at age 50. In 1746, he accepted his appointment to the Royal Military Academy at Woolwich. In five months, he achieved the rank of lieutenant fireworker. He was quartermaster of the royal regiment of artillery and reached the grade of lieutenant on April 1, 1756. He was appointed aide-de-camp to Sir John Ligonier, lieutenant general of the ordinance.

He advanced to captain on May 12, 1756, and was given a company of miners for service in Minorca. Minorca was being besieged by the French. Phillips' company was not needed and was converted to a company of artillery in which he retained the grade of captain over the ranking seniors in the artillery.

Phillips went to Germany in 1758 to command a brigade of British artillery attached to Allied troops serving under Prince Ferdinand of Brunswick. He was in the Battle of Minden in 1759. He was promoted to brevet major and then to lieutenant colonel.

In 1776, Phillips was in Canada under Lieutenant General Sir Guy Carleton and John Burgoyne. In April 1777, Phillips was promoted to regimental major, and in August 1777, he was a major general of the British army. At Stillwater, near Saratoga, on September 19, 1777, Captain Thomas Jones and all his commissioned officers and men, except five, were killed.

Then came the Battle of Saratoga on October 7, 1777. Phillips conducted the retreat from Saratoga. At the Council of War on October 13, he was the second senior at the surrender and was taken prisoner. Early in 1781, he was exchanged for American General Benjamin Lincoln and rejoined the British army under Lieutenant General Sir Henry Clinton at New York.

He participated in the campaigns in Petersburg, Chesterfield and along the James River, where he shelled American ships at a place called Osborne's. He marched to Manchester then back to Osborne's. He became ill with a fever. He returned to Petersburg on May 13 and died that day.

On the 1977 Surrender of Burgoyne stamp, Phillips is the first on the left.

Charles Pinckney

Scott 798
Born: October 26, 1757, Charleston, South Carolina
Died: October 29, 1824, Charleston, South Carolina

Charles Pinckney went to school in Charleston. He studied law and was admitted to the bar in 1779. In 1779 and 1780, he was a member of the South Carolina House of Representatives. His father was Colonel Charles Pinckney, a wealthy lawyer and planter. His mother was Frances Brewton Pinckney.

In 1779, he enlisted in the American Army as a lieutenant of the Charleston regiment of militia in time to see action at the siege of Savanna, Georgia. He was taken prisoner, along with 5,000 men under General Benjamin Lincoln, when Charleston surrendered to Sir Henry Clinton on May 12, 1780. In June 1781, Pinckney was released.

From 1784 to 1787, he was a delegate to Congress under the Articles of Confederation. His efforts led to the Constitutional Convention in Philadelphia. He presented his draft of some 32 provisions that were incorporated in the final adoption. He signed the document.

He returned to Charleston and led the fight for South Carolina to ratify the new Constitution. This was accomplished May 23, 1788. On April 27, 1788, he had married Henry Laurens' daughter, Mary Eleanor. Pinckney was the elected governor in January 1789, succeeding his second-cousin, Thomas Pinckney. He served until 1792. In 1790, he presided over the state constitutional convention. His wife died in 1794, leaving him with three children.

Until 1798, Pinckney was a Federalist. He was disappointed in not receiving a satisfactory post, so he turned to support Thomas Jefferson's Democratic-Republican Party. He was again elected governor in 1796. He was elected to the U.S. Senate, representing South Carolina.

For his support of Thomas Jefferson, he was awarded the position of U.S. minister to Spain in 1801. He tried to persuade Spain to sell or cede Florida to the United States, but was unsuccessful. In 1805, he returned to Charleston.

Pinckney was elected governor again in 1806. He brought about the ratification of the Bill of Rights, while he was a member of the legislature. From 1814 to 1818, he practiced law. In 1818, he was elected to the House of Representatives. He opposed the Missouri Compromise of 1820.

Pinckney is portrayed on the Constitution Sesquicentennial stamp of 1937.

Charles Cotesworth Pinckney

Scott 798
Born: February 25, 1746, Charleston, South Carolina
Died: August 16, 1825, Charleston, South Carolina

Charles Cotesworth Pinckney, lawyer, statesman and signer of the U.S. Constitution, was the son of Charles Pinckney, chief justice of South Carolina, and Elizabeth Lucus Pinckney. He and his younger brother, Thomas, grew up in Charleston. They were educated in England. Charles entered Westminster School in 1761, Christ Church College, Oxford, in 1764, and was admitted to Middle Temple. In 1769, he was admitted to the English bar. He studied botany, chemistry and military science at the Academy at Caen in France.

He returned home and was admitted to the South Carolina bar on January 19, 1770. He served in the state legislature between 1769 and 1778. On September 28, 1773, he married Sarah, daughter of Henry Middleton and sister of Arthur, a signer of the Declaration of Independence.

At the outbreak of the Revolution, Pinckney became captain of the 1st Regiment of South Carolina troops in 1775. He was promoted to major, then to colonel in September 1776. His regiment took part in the defense of Fort Sullivan in June 1776. He served as aide to George Washington and was present at the battles of Brandywine and Germantown. He returned to his regiment and served in the Florida campaign in 1778 and in the seige of Savannah in 1779.

When Charleston capitulated in 1780, Pinckney was taken prisoner. He was paroled in Philadelphia with his brother. They were exchanged in 1782. Pinckney rejoined the Army. Shortly before his discharge in November 1783, he was brevetted a brigadier general. He returned to practice law. His wife died in 1784, and he married Mary, the daughter of Benjamin Stead, in 1786.

In 1787, he was a delegate to the federal Constitutional Convention, and with John Rutledge, Pierce Butler and his second-cousin Charles Pinckney, he signed the U.S. Constitution. He worked for its ratification in 1788.

He was minister to France in July 1796 and was part of the XYZ Affair. War with France seemed imminent, and Pinckney was made major general in charge of all forces south of Maryland. He was discharged in 1800 and ran for vice president with John Adams as president. In 1804 and 1808, he was unsuccessful as the Federalist candidate for the presidency.

Pinckney is depicted on the 1937 Constitution Sesquicentennial stamp.

Martin Alonso Pinzon

Scott 118
Born: circa 1440, Palos, Huelva Provence, Spain
Died: circa 1493, Palos, Huelva Provence, Spain

Three prominent maritime families of Palos — the Quinteros and especially the Ninos and the Pinzons — made it possible for Christopher Columbus to outfit and man his ships for the great voyage west. Martin Alonso Pinzon commanded the *Pinta* and took his younger brother Francisco Pinzon on as the ship's master. The *Nina* was commanded by Pinzon's brother, Vincente Yanez Pinzon, whose master-owner was Juan Nino. The *Santa Maria* was the flagship commanded by Columbus, whose pilot was Peralonso Nino, Juan's brother.

For the *Pinta*, Martin Alonso Pinzon recruited 26 men from the Andelusian towns of Seville, Cordova and Jerez de la Fontera. It was at the conference held by Fray Juan Perez of La Rabida that Pinzon decided to give aid to Columbus. On September 6, 1492, the fleet of three ships set sail for the Indies.

At 2:00 a.m. on October 12, Rodrigo de Triana, the lookout on Pinzon's *Pinta*, spotted the moonlight reflecting off the white cliffs of land. The *Santa Maria* came alongside, and Columbus reportedly shouted, "Senor Martin Alonso, you did find land!" Columbus went ashore with the royal standard of Castile, and the Pinzons flew the white standards displaying the green crowned cross. Columbus named the island San Salvador.

On November 20, Pinzon left the fleet and set off on his own. On January 4, 1493, Columbus sailed for Spain in the *Nina*. The flagship had been wrecked on Christmas day at Navidad. The *Pinta* was spotted sailing downwind also for Spain. Pinzon came aboard and reported to Columbus where he had been.

The two ships sailed the rough trip homeward but were separated by heavy weather. The *Pinta* made port at Bayona near Virgo in northern Spain at the end of February and immediately sent a message across Spain to Ferdinand and Isabella who were in Barcelona. Pinzon was attempting to garner for himself the glory of the great discovery. The sovereigns refused the message.

Pinzon then sailed to Palos. The *Nina* had arrived in Palos and was moored in. Rebuffed by the king and queen, old, sick and tired after 224 days of a tortuous journey, Pinzon took to his bed and died. He is depicted in the center of the 15¢ 1869 stamp. He is holding the second flag.

Vincente Yanez Pinzon

Scott 231
Born: circa 1460, Palos, Huelva Province, Spain
Died: circa 1524, Palos, Huelva Province, Spain

Vincente Yanez Pinzon was the younger brother of Martin Alonso Pinzon. If history's calculations are correct, Martin was 20 years his senior. Vincente was a member of the famous maritime family of Pinzons of Palos de la Frontera. This family, the Ninos and the Quinteros were instrumental in furnishing ships for Christopher Columbus' first voyage in search of the Indies. Vincente was in charge of the *Nina*. Juan de la Cosa furnished the flagship *Santa Maria*.

Upon arriving at the West Indies island of Guananani, which Columbus named San Salvadore, or Holy Savior, Pinzon went ashore as a flag bearer and as a witness to the great event. When his elder brother Martin Alonso Pinzon left the fleet at Cuba with the *Pinta* for two months to search the islands on his own, Vincente remained faithful to Columbus. When the *Santa Maria* became tangled on the coral reef off the northwestern coast of La Isla Espanola (Haiti), he assisted Columbus. After the *Santa Maria* was wrecked, he turned the *Nina* over to Columbus for the return voyage to Spain.

Vincente Pinzon matured into an adventurous seaman. In December 1497, he sailed with four ships southwest to the easternmost projection of South America. He started south, then turned and followed the coast to Central America at Costa Rica. He investigated the mouth of the Amazon. He returned to Haiti, where he lost two of his four vessels, then sailed for Palos, reaching home in September 1500. Ferdinand and Isabella appointed him governor of his newly discovered lands — in name only, for he could not govern such land.

Seven years later he returned to the coast of Central America with Juan Diaz de Solis. They sailed into the Gulf of Honduras. These same two explorers set out again in 1509 to sail along the coast of South America and coasted as far south as the estuary of Rio de la Plata (the site of Buenos Aires), still looking for an opening to Asia. According to Antonio de Herrera y Tordesillas, the Spanish historian and first historiographer of the Indies, Pinzon may have sailed as far as 40 degrees south to Bahia Blanca, passing by La Plata.

Pinzon faded into history's oblivion about 1523. He is seen in the left center of the 2¢ Columbian stamp. He is holding the first flag to the left.

184

William Thomas Piper

Scott C129
Born: January 8, 1881, Knapp Creek, New York
Died: Janaury 15, 1970, Lock Haven, Pennsylvania

William T. Piper is best known for his manufacturing genius of the Piper Cub, an outgrowth of a glider he had developed while associated with Taylor Brothers Aircraft Corporation. The original name of the Cub was the "Brownbach Tiger Kitten." It was a two-cylinder, two-cycle plane and was first flown on September 2, 1930. It was too flimsy. Piper's 37-horsepower E-2 Cub was approved for flight June 15, 1931.

In 1936, Piper acquired the Taylor Corporation, which was on the verge of bankruptcy. In 1937, he produced a record 687 Cubs. During World War II, the U.S. Army purchased more than 5,600 Piper Cubs. The Army used them for special personnel planes, for photoreconnaissance, and as spotters of enemy artillery. Because they were highly maneuverable, the Piper Cub easily eluded enemy planes. The remarkable Cub could land at the slow speed of 20 miles per hour. Piper was dubbed "the Henry Ford of Aviation."

In the 1950s, he built a twin-engined Cub, popular with business and professional men, and in the 1970s, he developed the Super Cub as well as 16 other types of aircraft. The giant Piper Aircraft Corporation, established in 1929, built more planes than any other plane manufacturer in the world.

Piper was the son of Thomas and Sarah Maltby Piper. He was born in Knapp Creek, New York, a mile from the Pennsylvania border. In 1898, Piper served as a private in the Pennsylvania Volunteer Infantry. He graduated from Yale University in 1903 with a bachelor of science degree. He worked as a construction engineer until 1914, when he became a partner in the Dallas Oil Company of Bradford, Pennsylvania.

On July 30, 1910, he married Marie Vandewater, with whom he had five children. In World War I, he was a captain in the Army Engineers. After the war, he joined the Taylor Brothers Aircraft Corporation. He learned to fly in 1931.

On December 22, 1943, he married Clara S. Taber, his second marriage. In 1954, at the age of 73, he received certification to fly twin-engined aircraft. He served as the president and director of the Piper Aircraft Corporation until his death in 1970 at the age of 89 at his home in Lock Haven.

Piper was portrayed on a 1991 airmail stamp also showing his Piper Cub.

John Pitcairn

Scott 618
Born: 1722, Dysart, Fifeshire, Scotland
Died: June 17, 1775, Boston, Massachusetts

John Pitcairn was the son of the Reverend David Pitcairn and Katherine Hamilton Pitcairn. Early in life, he joined the Royal Marines. He was commissioned captain on June 8, 1756, and received his majority on April 19, 1771. He married Elizabeth Dalrymple. Two of their children gained prominence. Robert Pitcairn was a midshipman on the *Swallow* commanded by Philip Carteret. Pitcairn was the first to site the Pacific island that now bears his name. David Pitcairn gained prominence as a physician.

John Pitcairn was sent to Boston as an officer of the garrisoned troops. On the night of April 18, 1775, he was ordered by General Gage, under the command of Lieutenant Colonel Francis Smith, to destroy the stores of ammunition stashed around Lexington and Concord and to capture Samuel Adams and John Hancock, who were hiding in the area. The mission was to be a surprise attack, but Paul Revere, Samuel Prescott and William Dawes rode out to warn the people and to allow Hancock and Adams to escape to Woburn.

The minutemen, under Captain John Parker's command, had gathered to meet the Redcoats. Pitcairn, in command of the British, rode forward and, with sword drawn, ordered the minutemen to disperse. Parker ordered his men to withdraw, being outnumbered 700 to 70. The rebels then played havoc with the Redcoats retreating to Boston, and the Revolutionary War was under way.

Two months later, on June 17, 1775, General Gage ordered troops to occupy the hills outside of Boston and gain the high ground before the Americans used the hills for cannon fire on the city. Again, the Americans anticipated Gage and, with 1,200 men under Colonel William Prescott, headed for the hills. They went beyond Bunker Hill to Breed's Hill, where the battle was fought. While storming the American redoubt, Major Pitcairn was mortally wounded. The fatal shot was supposedly fired by Peter Salem, who was standing behind Lieutenant Thomas Grosvenor. Pitcairn was taken to a house in North End, where he died. Gage dispatched a surgeon, but it was too late.

Pitcairn is seen with sword drawn astride his horse on the far right in the painting *Birth of Liberty* by Henry Sandham. The painting is reproduced on the 2¢ Lexington-Concord stamp issued April 4, 1925.

Cole Porter

Scott 2550
Born: June 9, 1891, Peru, Indiana
Died: October 15, 1964, Santa Monica, California

Cole Porter learned to play the violin at age 6 and the piano at 8. When he was 10, he wrote and vanity published *The Bobolink Waltz*. This song convinced his grandfather that Porter should study law instead of music. He was a top student at Worcester Academy and a popular student at Yale University. While at Yale, he composed the school songs, *Bingo Eli Yale* and *Bulldog*. After graduation in 1913, he enrolled in Harvard Law School. A semester of law school convinced the dean that Porter should return to music.

Porter's grandfather sent him to Paris. He studied under Vincent d'Indy and had a composition performed at the Paris Conservatoire. His talents lay in light popular music. He and his classmate, T. Lawrence Riggs, composed the musical *See America First*. It was produced on Broadway in 1916 but was no hit. It has been reported that Porter joined the French Foreign Legion as a romantic gesture of renunciation following the failure of the musical.

Porter married Linda Lee Thomas. He composed for Hitchy Koo in 1919 and Greenwich Village Follies in 1923. He was moderately successful, but Broadway producers considered him a rich playboy and not a serious artist. He went to Italy to paint. In Italy, he met Ray Goetz, a well-known Broadway producer who hired Porter to compose a light score in the American jazz style for his musical play *Paris*. It was produced in 1928 and was successful.

Porter's formula was to choose a title of a song and then write the words and music to suit it. His harmonies were complicated. His tunes had a soft beat of quiet sophistication and elegance. His theme was love. *Night and Day, I Get a Kick out of You*, and his masterpiece, *Begin the Beguine*, are examples.

In 1937, Porter was injured in a fall from a horse. Despite numerous operations, the man who composed *Don't Fence Me In* became dependent on a wheelchair and crutches.

Porter was honored on June 8, 1991, on a Performing Arts stamp.

Hiram Powers

Scott 139
Born: July 29, 1805, near Woodstock, Windsor County, Vermont
Died: June 27, 1873, Florence, Italy

Hiram Powers learned of his talents for sculpting while working in the waxwork department of a Cincinnati museum, where he learned to model in clay. Powers was the eighth child of nine children of Stephen and Sarah Perry Powers. He was born on a farm near Woodstock, Vermont. His father was poor.

The family moved to outstate New York then to Ohio. Powers' father died of malaria. Powers worked as a tavern boy, a bill collector and, in 1823, in Cincinnati at a clock and organ factory. At the age of 24, he took a job at the waxworks of Dorfeuille's Western Museum in Cincinnati.

In 1832, he married Elizabeth Gibson of Cincinnati. She worked with him in the museum's Chamber of Horrors. Powers work was noticed, and he received orders to make portrait busts from casts of the human face. At this time, he worked with Kirke Brown and Shobal Vail Clevenger.

In 1834, he went to Washington, D.C., and found work in portraitures. He made portrait busts, in white Carrara marble, of Chief Justice Marshall, Andrew Jackson, John C. Calhoun and Daniel Webster. After two years, he was eager to go to Italy and learn serious sculpting. He received financing from three patrons, whom he later repaid. He departed with his wife and two young children. His wife contracted smallpox aboard the ship, and they were delayed in Paris. He studied the masters of sculpting in Paris.

The Powers arrived in Florence in the fall of 1837. As did William Story, Powers spent the rest of his life in Florence. At first he was poor, but his talent won him fame and fortune in time.

In his late 1860s, he sustained a disastrous fall that left him infirm, hastening his death. Powers' most notable work was the *Greek Slave*, a nude female full-length statue that created much notoriety. It was exhibited in the Crystal Palace, London, in 1851. A copy is in the Corcoran Gallery, Washington, D.C. The original was sold in England for several thousand dollars.

Powers' portrait bust of Thomas Jefferson appears on the 10¢ stamp of the 1870-71 definitive series.

Powhatan (Chief Wahunsonacock)

Scott 328
Born: circa 1550, Powhatan Indian Territory
Died: 1618, Powhatan, near Jamestown, Virginia

Powhatan was the name of a confederation of 32 Algonquin tribes of about 200 villages, nearly 10,000 people. More significantly it was the name of an Algonquin village that once stood at the falls of the James River, in the present area of Richmond, Virginia. Powhatan is the Algonquin name for "Falls in a Current of Water." The person called King Powhatan by the British settlers was Chief Wahunsonacock (Wa-hun-sen-a-cawh). He was, as the settlers soon learned, a strong and wise leader.

It was starvation and disease, not Indians, that reduced the colonists from 300 to 150 in the first three years of settlement in America. The Indians at first did not consider the Pilgrims invaders. They not only permitted the fledgling Virginia colony along the James River to survive but helped them through the first desperate winters by bringing them corn and vegetables.

Powhatan probably had never seen white men before 1607, when Captain John Smith and his group established their colony. Some years earlier Jesuit missionaries had visited but did not stay.

Powhatan became chief when his father died. He became the economic and political leader of a territory that embraced most of tidewater Virginia and the eastern shore of the Chesapeake Bay. His military force consisted of some 2,000 warriors and braves. Captain Smith was saved from execution by Powhatan, according to legend, when his daughter, Pocahontas (Matoaka), intervened. When Smith went up the river to barter for corn, he was surrounded by several hundred warriors directed by Opechancanough, Powhatan's half-brother. Smith used his wit and his gun to stave off a possible slaughter. Pocahontas was seized by a deceptive act of a colonist, Samuel Argall, in 1613. The following year she became the wife of John Rolfe.

King Powhatan is depicted in the upper-right cameo of the 1¢ Jamestown Exposition stamp of April 26, 1907.

Louis Prang

Scott 1580
Born: March 12, 1824, Breslau, Prussian Silesia
Died: June 14, 1909, Los Angeles, California

Louis Prang's father, Jonas Louis Prang, operated a factory for dyeing and printing calico in Breslau. His mother was Rosina Sherman Prang. He apprenticed to his father, then went to Hagen, Westphalia, Germany, to study printing and dyeing. He went to Bohemia and worked with Peter Walzel for five years. After working as a journeyman, he toured Vienna, Switzerland, Alsace, Rouen and Great Britain. Prang returned to Prussia and found himself under a ban for holding liberal opinions. He fled to Bohemia, then to Switzerland.

From Switzerland, he emigrated to the United States. He arrived in New York City, where he formed a printing venture to publish architectural material. The business was short-lived. He made leather goods but was unsuccessful. He turned to wood engraving. He worked as a journeyman under Frank Leslie, the head of the art department of *Gleason's Pictorial*, until 1856. On November 1, 1851, he married Rosa Gerber, with whom he had a daughter.

In 1856, he formed a partnership in lithography with Julius Meyer. The partnership was known as Prang & Meyer and, after 1859, as L. Prang & Company. The company printed business cards, announcements and various forms of small advertising. During the Civil War, Prang printed maps and battle plans. Prang produced prints of famous works of art.

In 1867, he established a printing shop in Roxbury, Massachusetts. He printed Christmas cards. He established the Prang Educational Company in Boston and published drawing books for schools.

Prang's wife died in 1898. He retired to California in 1899. In April 1900, he married Mary Amelia Dana Hicks, teacher and author of a number of books for art instruction. He died in June 1909.

An example of Prang's Christmas cards was selected as the contemporary Christmas stamp of 1975.

William Prescott

Surrender at Saratoga 1777 by Trumbull

US Bicentennial 13 cents

Scott 1728
Born: February 20, 1726, Groton, Massachusetts
Died: October 13, 1795, Pepperell, Massachusetts

William Prescott's forebear, John Prescott, came to America from England as early as 1640. By 1643, the family was settled in Lancaster, Worcester County, Massachusetts. They moved northward a few miles to the town of Groton, Middlesex County, where William was born. He was the son of Benjamin and Abigail Oliver Prescott. William Prescott grew up in Groton and married Abigail Hale of Sutton, Worcester County, on April 13, 1758. He became a farmer in Pepperell, Massachusetts.

When the Boston port was closed by an act of Parliament in 1774, Prescott saw to it that the people of Boston received food. Soon thereafter, he was a colonel in charge of a regiment of minutemen and led a contingent of soldiers to Concord to aid in the fighting. By the time he had traversed the 35 miles, the Redcoats had retreated to Boston, and he missed the actual battle. Prescott then went to the headquarters of the provincial army in Cambridge and was appointed to the council of war.

On the night of June 16, 1776, General Artemas Ward ordered Prescott to Bunker Hill near Charlestown. Ward was commanding the American troops in the area. Prescott took about 1,000 men to Charlestown and, after conferring with the other officers, decided to fortify Breed's Hill instead of Bunker Hill. In the night, he moved out. When morning came and the Redcoats arrived, to their surprise the patriots were digging in and organizing for defense. The British opened fire. Prescott defied the bullets and paced back and forth atop the entrenchments, directing and emboldening his men to fight with everything they had as he bravely commanded the redoubt. They lost to the British.

Prescott took part in the evacuation of New York in 1776 and was present at the surrender of Burgoyne in 1777. Because of his age of 50 years and some infirmities, he retired from military service. He returned home to farm and to serve his city as selectman and representative in the general court.

On the 1977 Surrender of Burgoyne at Saratoga stamp, Prescott is the sixth man from the right.

Harriet Quimby

Scott C128
Born: May 1, 1875, Coldwater, Michigan
Died: July 12, 1912, Boston, Massachusetts

Harriet Quimby was the daughter of William and Ursula M. Cook Quimby. She grew up in California and was educated by private tutelage in America and France. She began her career as a writer for the *San Francisco Dramatic Review* in 1902 and contributed to the Sunday editions of the *San Francisco Chronicle* and the *San Francisco Call*. She joined the staff of the popular *Leslie's Weekly* in 1906. With this popular publication, she contributed to the women's page and edited the aviation section of the paper. She traveled extensively to Egypt, Africa, Europe, South America and the West Indies. She was a venturesome, self-reliant career woman, somewhat ahead of her time.

Quimby made her home in New York City and never married. In 1910, she became fascinated with aviation while covering an air meet at Belmont Park, New York. She began training to be the first woman aviator. In 1910, she was the first person to be given a license to pilot a monoplane under the revised rules of the International Aero Club of America and France.

In September 1910, Blanche Stuart Scott made her first solo flight. On August 1, 1911, Quimby became the first American woman to receive an airplane pilot's license. It was license number 37. With this distinction, she made barnstorming tours of exhibition flights in the United States and Mexico and teamed up with Mathilde Moisant, the second U.S. woman to hold an American airplane pilot's license.

In March 1912, Quimby went to France to be the first woman to fly over the English Channel. She achieved this feat on April 16. Three months later, on July 12, 1912, back in the United States, Quimby and an aviator friend, William Willard, were cruising over Dorchester Bay, at the mouth of the Neponset River, south of Boston Harbor, before a large crowd of awe-inspired onlookers. Their Bleriot monoplane suddenly nosed over in midair, hurling the two fliers some 2,000 feet to their deaths.

Quimby is portrayed on a 50¢ Pioneers in Aviation airmail stamp issued April 17, 1991.

Raphael

Christmas USA 20c

Raphael, 1483-1983, National Gallery

Scott 2063
Born: April 6, 1483, Urbino, Papal States, Italy
Died: April 6, 1520, Rome, Italy

Like Mozart, Raphael showed great genius in his early life and was given close and intensive guidance by his father, Giovanni Santi. Santi was a highly regarded painter in Urbino and a court painter for the dukes of Urbino and Mantua, both centers of the arts. In 1494, when Raphael was 11, his father died. His mother had died a few years earlier, so Raphael was an orphan. Raphael was not trained by the apprenticeship system. Instead, he learned to paint at home.

While still a teenager, he produced works that are today considered masterful, such as the *Creation of Eve* and the *Trinity*, now in the Pinacoteca in Citta di Castello. Other early works are in the Pinacoteca Vatican and the Pinacoteca di Brera, Milan. In 1504, Raphael went to Florence, where he painted the *Madonna del Branuca*, now at the Pitti Palace Gallery. *Madonna di Cas Tempi*, now in Munich, was painted during this time, as was *La belle jardiniere*, in the Louvre in Paris.

Raphael went to Perugia and back to Urbino during this four-year Florentine period, but he was never truly accepted as more than a guest painter. He learned from the works of Leonardo da Vinci and Michelangelo.

He went to Rome in 1509 to work for Pope Julius II, painting a suite of rooms in the Vatican known as the Stanze della Signatura, the pope's library. He completed *Theology*, *Jurisprudence*, *Philosophy*, and *Poetry* personifications on the ceiling with the *Judgment of Solomon* in the middle. Also in the Vatican is *The School of Athens*, long acknowledged as Raphael's masterpiece and the perfect embodiment of the classical spirit of the High Renaissance. The central figure in the foreground is a representation of Michelangelo. Raphael had the task of designing a set of 10 large tapestries to complete the decoration of the Sistine Chapel, representing the story of Saints Peter and Paul.

Raphael's *The Small Cowper Madonna*, now in the National Gallery, Washington, D.C., was chosen for the 1983 traditional Christmas stamp.

George Read

Scott 1687e
Born: September 18, 1733, North East, Cecil County, Maryland
Died: September 21, 1798, New Castle, Delaware

George Read was born in North East in Cecil County, Maryland. His father was an Irish landowner. His mother was the daughter of a Welsh planter. Read attended school in Chester, Pennsylvania, and at the Reverend Francis Alison's academy in New London, Pennsylvania. He then studied law. In 1753, he was admitted to the bar in nearby Philadelphia, and settled in New Castle, Delaware, for legal practice. From 1763 to 1774, he was the attorney general for Delaware, Kent and Sussex counties.

In 1763, he married Gertrude Ross Till, the widowed sister of George Ross, another signer of the Declaration of Independence. The Read's had four sons and a daughter.

Read was a member of the First Continental Congress, though he at first opposed the Declaration of Independence. Seeing no other way, he signed the petition to King George III. He later signed both the Declaration of Independence and the federal Constitution. He signed three of the most basic documents of the United States. He drafted the new constitution of Delaware in 1776 and presided over the convention that adopted it. He codified the laws of Delaware while acting as president-governor of the state.

In 1782, Read was judge of the U.S. Court of Appeals for the Admiralty Cases. In 1786, he was a delegate to the Annapolis Convention, and the following year he was a delegate to the Constitutional Convention, where he was a stalwart champion for the smaller states.

Read was elected to the U.S. Senate in 1789 and 1791. He resigned in 1793 to become chief justice of Delaware. He served in this office until his death.

Read is shown as the first person to the left on the fifth 18¢ stamp of the second American Bicentennial souvenir sheet issued May 29, 1976.

James Renwick

Scott 1838
Born: November 1, 1818, (Bloomingdale) New York, New York
Died: June 23, 1895, New York, New York

Architect James Renwick was a direct descendant of James Renwick (1662-88), the Scottish covenanter, who was hanged as the last of the martyrs of the Scottish National Covenant. When architect Renwick's father, James Renwick (1792-1863), was a child, he was brought to America by his parents and grew to be an educator and engineer. He was a friend of Washington Irving and toured Europe with Irving.

He graduated from Columbia College in 1807 and, by 1820, was professor of natural philosophy and experimental chemistry at the college. He retired in 1853 as Columbia's first professor emeritus.

As an engineer, he carried out the construction of the Morris Canal and surveyed the boundary between the United States and Canada, resulting in the Webster-Ashburton (boundary) Treaty.

Coming from such an illustrious family and being a graduate of Columbia College in 1836, where his father was a professor in the height of his career, young Renwick began his career as an engineer. However, in 1843, he began to pursue a career in architecture after he won the design for the new Grace Church at Broadway and 10th Street, New York City.

He designed several other churches. In 1853, his design was chosen for St. Patrick's Cathedral, now a popular tourist attraction, in New York City. He designed many buildings and residences and was the city's official architect responsible for hospitals and other buildings, including Vassar College. His architecture represents Gothic Revival style.

He designed hotels and bank buildings, as well as the facade for the New York Stock Exchange. In Washington, D.C., he designed the Corcoran Gallery of Art and the Smithsonian Institution, called the "Castle."

Renwick is honored on the first stamp of the American Architecture series of 1980. The stamp features the Smithsonian Institution "Castle," so-called because it resembles a castle with its steeples and central tower.

195

Jan Ribault

Scott 616
Born: circa 1520, Dieppe, France
Died: October 12, 1565, northeastern Florida

Jan Ribault was a French navigator. When Ribault was in his early 40s, he was commissioned by Admiral of France Gaspard il de Coligny to take the French Protestants, the Huguenots, to America. Ribault sailed February 18, 1562. On May 1, he landed at the mouth of what is now the St. John's River, which he christened Riviere de Mai, in honor of the month of their arrival. (The site is today called Mayport, and is part of Jacksonville, Florida.) Ribault settled his colonists at Port Royal Harbor (now Paris Island, South Carolina), in the estuary of Port Royal Sound. He built a fort, called Fort Charles. He then returned to France. The colonists ran low on supplies, revolted against their governor and seized a small boat with intentions of crossing the Atlantic and returning home. Luckily, an English ship rescued them.

Ribault was in England in 1563. He published a treatise, *True and Last Discoverye of Florida*. In April 1564, Admiral Coligny sent an expedition under Rene Goulaine de Laudonniere. The expedition established a colony, Fort Caroline, at the mouth of the Riviere de Mai, in the jaws of the Spaniards.

Pedro Menendez de Aviles was a one-time captain of a Spanish treasure fleet, who had a falling out with the governing board and was imprisoned. However, Philip II of Spain commissioned him to take an expedition to Florida. Menendez outfitted a ship, sailed in 1565 and landed in a wide inlet of the Tolomato River. There he established the Spanish colony of St. Augustine.

While Ribault's ships were in the mouth of the Riviere de Mai, Menendez slaughtered nearly everyone in the colony. Ribault's son and a few survivors escaped in two ships and sailed to safety. Ribault was sailing toward St. Augustine for revenge when a storm drove him to seek shelter in the Matanzas Inlet, where his ships were wrecked. Forced to abandon his ships, Ribault and the survivors attempted to return to Fort Caroline overland. He and his men were surrounded by the Spanish and induced to surrender when they received assurances of safe conduct. They were betrayed and killed October 12, 1565.

The 5¢ 1924 Huguenot-Walloon stamp shows the monument dedicated to Ribault at Mayport (Jacksonville), Florida. The statue was moved to Fort Caroline in Jacksonville. It was dedicated at the new site in 1958.

Henry Hobson Richardson

Richardson 1838-1886 Trinity Church Boston
Architecture USA 15c

Scott 1839
Born: September 29, 1838, Priestley Plantation, St. James Parish, Louisiana
Died: April 27, 1886, Boston, Massachusetts

Different regions of the world have evolved different styles of buildings. Be they romanesque or nipponese, all are basically shelters. Architects study them all. Architect Henry Hobson Richardson was the son of a well-to-do cotton-industry executive. He was well-educated. He attended private schools in New Orleans, doing well in mathematics. He enrolled in Harvard University to study civil engineering, but he changed his major to architecture.

Following his graduation from Harvard, Richardson went to Paris to study. He worked with architects in the daytime and studied at the Ecole des Beaux Arts at night. In 1866, he settled in New York City.

He designed many churches, his first being the Church of the Unity in Springfield, Massachusetts. He also designed the Grace Church in West Medford, Massachusetts, the Battle Street Church in Boston and the North Church of Springfield. Perhaps his best design was Trinity Church in the Back Bay of Boston (1872-77) on the east side of Copely Square.

Richardson used colored stones for the exterior of Trinity Church. The design of the church, with its dominant central tower, round arches, and compact, massive shape, was insprired by the 11th-century romanesque buildings that preceded the emergence of the Gothic style in Europe. On the west and opposite side of Copely square is the Boston Public Library, designed in classical simplicity by architects McKim, Mead and White to harmonize with the Trinity Church.

Richardson designed two halls at Harvard University. He also designed Pittsburgh's courthouse and county jail, and, in Chicago, the Marshall Field Building. His skillful handling of materials both for strength and for beauty influenced men like Louis H. Sullivan, who worked with him, and Frank Lloyd Wright, who worked with Sullivan.

Richardson is honored on the second stamp of the American Architecture series of 1980. The stamp features the Trinity Church in Boston.

Friedrich Adolph von Riedesel

Surrender at Saratoga 1777 by Trumbull
US Bicentennial 13 cents

Scott 1728
Born: June 3, 1738, Lauterbach, Hesse, Germany
Died: January 6, 1800, Braunschweig, Germany

Charles (1670-1730) of Hesse-Kassel, Germany, was the first to adopt the system of hiring out his soldiers as mercenaries to help the national finances. The landgrave of Hesse-Kassel was married to the daughter of George I. Because of this tie, England asked Hesse-Kassel to furnish troops to fight in the American Revolution. Hesse-Kassel furnished some 22,000 troops, and thousands more were furnished by neighboring German States. The Hessians fought well in the battles of Long Island, Fort Washington, Brandywine, White Plains, Newport and Charleston, but were defeated at the Battle of Trenton.

Friedrich Adolph von Riedesel enlisted in a Hessian infantry regiment soon bound for England. He was given the grade of vice ensign. His unit was made part of the British army and was billeted in a town near London.

The American Revolution broke out when Riedesel was in his late 30s. Riedesel was promoted to major general and placed in command of the Braunschweig infantry troops. His contingent landed in Quebec on June 1, 1776. He studied the Colonial troops' tactics of rapid firing and their way of fighting, using strict military discipline in their training.

He had the misfortune of being with General Burgoyne at Saratoga. He had distinguished himself at Ticonderoga and Hubbardtown. His Braunschweiger contingent saved Freeman's Farm on September 19, 1777. If Burgoyne had heeded Riedesel's advice on October 7, a safe retreat to Canada would have prevailed. Instead, they were taken prisoner at Saratoga on October 17.

Two years later, Riedesel was freed in a prisoner exchange and was appointed to a command on Long Island. He returned to Germany in 1783 and continued in the military service. He rose to the grade of lieutenant general in 1787. In 1789, he was commander of the Braunschweig contingent of the Hessian army farmed out to assist the stadtholder of the Netherlands. He also was commandant of Braunschweig.

Of the two small figures between and behind Burgoyne and Gates on the 1977 Surrender of Burgoyne stamp, Riedesel is the man on the left.

John Ringling

Scott 1309
Born, May 2, 1866, Baraboo, Wisconsin
Died: December 3, 1936, Sarasota, Florida

Ringling, the greatest name in circus business, spanned 85 years and two generations. Four Ruengeling brothers, Albert (1852-1916), Otto (1858-1911), Alfred (1861-1919) and Charles (1863-1926), were born in the Mississippi River town of McGregor, Iowa. John was born in Baraboo, Wisconsin. The boys grew up in Iowa. The older brothers were successful with a song and dance troupe called the Classic and Comic Concert Company. In 1882, Charles and John joined the troupe, and the name was Anglicized to Ringling.

The brothers went on the road. Within a year, they added circus acts. John played the clown. In 1884, they added a bear and used their work horse in their acts. Charles became the manager. In 1888, they acquired their first elephant.

The brothers expanded by acquiring other small circuses, including the John Robinson show and the well-known Foresaugh-Sells show. In 1907, they acquired the "Greatest Show on Earth," the Barnum and Bailey Circus. After 1919, the Ringling Brothers used the "Greatest Show on Earth" subtitle after their circus' name. They traveled the country as Ringling Brothers and Barnum and Bailey, "the Greatest Show on Earth." The show needed nearly 250 railroad cars to move it from city to city. It employed 5,000 people. The "Big Top" seated 10,000 spectators.

Charles speculated in Florida real estate and acquired land in Sarasota, which became the Ringling's home and museum. When Charles died on December 3, 1926, John took charge. He died on December 3, 1936. The management then fell to nephews John Ringling North and Robert E. Ringling, until the firm was sold in 1967. It survived the Depression years and the disasterous fire in Hartford, Connecticut, in July 1944, when 163 people died. From 1957 on, the show was booked mainly in large indoor arenas.

John Ringling was honored with the 1966 Circus stamp.

Norman Percevel Rockwell

Scott 1238
Born: February 3, 1894, Manhattan, New York, New York
Died: November 9, 1978, Stockbridge, Massachusetts

Norman Percevel Rockwell was born a few blocks west of Central Park on Amsterdam Avenue. His mother, Nancy Hill Rockwell, claimed a relative by the name of Sir Norman Percevel. Norman dropped the Percevel as soon as he was on his own.

He inherited artistic talent from his father, Waring Rockwell, a cotton-goods merchant who was an amateur sketcher, and from his grandfather, Thomas Hill, an English artist who emigrated to America. Rockwell said his own passion for exactness could be traced back to his grandfather.

At age 15, he left high school to attend the Chase School of Art in New York City and then the National Academy School. At age 16, he enrolled at the Art Student League. It was his friend Clyder Forsythe who directed him to the *Saturday Evening Post*. Rockwell's first cover design appeared May 20, 1916.

He married Irene O'Connor in the fall of 1916. In 1918, he joined the Navy and worked on a camp newspaper, *Afloat and Ashore*. After the war, he lived in New Rochelle, New York. It was during the 1920s that he became a leading *Post* cover illustrator and tasted prosperity. After 13 years of marriage, his wife left him.

Rockwell and Mary Rhodes Barstow were married on April 17, 1930. They lived in Arlington, Vermont. They had three sons, Thomas, Jarvis and Peter. In 1953, they moved to Stockbridge, Massachusetts. In 1959, Mary died of a heart attack. On October 25, 1961, Rockwell married Molly Punderson.

Rockwell is best known for his more than 300 *Saturday Evening Post* covers depicting common people doing common things. He finished the last of the *Four Freedoms Paintings* in the spring of 1943, reproductions of which ran into the millions. He painted portraits of many famous people.

Rockwell's illustration *Letter Carrier, 1863* is reproduced on the 1963 City Mail Delivery stamp.

Benjamin Rush

Scott 1692
Born: January 4, 1746, Byberry (near Philadelphia), Pennsylvania
Died: April 19, 1813, Philadelphia, Pennsylvania

Benjamin Rush graduated from the College of New Jersey (now Princeton University) in 1760. He studied at the University of Edinburgh and was awarded his doctor of medicine degree in 1768. He began his practice in Philadelphia and took a position as professor of chemistry at the College of Philadelphia. He chaired this department until 1789, when he took the position of professor of practice at the University of Pennsylvania. He attained the chair of institutes of medicine when this department was merged into the University of Pennsylvania. Rush was also physician to the Pennsylvania Hospital, the chief founder of the Philadelphia Dispensary (the first in this country) in 1786 and treasurer of the U.S. Mint.

Rush was a staunch patriot. He served in the provincial congress, which replaced the Colonial Assembly. He was chosen a member of the Continental Congress in July 1776, just in time to sign the Declaration of Independence.

He was surgeon general for the Middle Department under Surgeon General William Shippen from 1776 to 1778. He deserted General George Washington at Valley Forge to join the infamous Conway Cabal against Washington's overly cautious and defensive strategy or Fabian tactics.

Rush was a typical 18th-century theorist, a man whose social propagandism against war, slavery, alcoholism and the death penalty was perhaps not entirely disassociated from a personal interest in increasing his practice. He was the ablest American clinician of his time. He described cholera infantum (1773) and dengue (1780). His greatest failing was his adherence to blood-letting. He has been likened to Sangrado, but he saved many patients. He rightfully looked upon inflammation as the effect rather than the cause of disease.

Of the row of men seated on the second stamp of the 1976 Declaration of Independence set, Rush is the third from the left.

Charles Marion Russell

Scott 2401
Born: March 19, 1864, St. Louis, Missouri
Died: October 24, 1926, Great Falls, Montana

Separately, Frederick Remington and Charles Marion Russell went west to be cowboys and to paint action pictures of the wild new frontier. Remington, fresh from Yale, was 19. Russell, fresh from military school, was 16. Both were essentially self-taught. Russell drew pictures for the amusement and amazement of his friends — scenes of cattle, camps, Indians, and the rough frontier life they were living. Gradually painting became his main endeavor in life.

He grew up at the family estate "Oakhill." At age 15, he was enrolled at a military school in New Jersey. In 1880, he went west to a Montana ranch to paint. At the age of 32, and after cowpoking for 16 years, Russell married 18-year-old Nancy Cooper, who had a great influence on him in developing and promoting his art. The couple moved to Great Falls, Montana.

Russell's climb to success was slow. He sold his pictures and drawings in saloons and local stores. Some began to show up in Eastern magazines. In 1904, he exhibited at the St. Louis World's Fair. The Russells went to New York City to sell some of his work. Collectors of Western art purchased his work, and his pictures were reproduced on calendars.

In 1914, Russell went to England and had a successful exhibit at the famous London Dore Galleries. He had shows in New York, Boston, Chicago, Los Angeles and elsewhere. He was an ambitious and prolific painter and sculptor. In all, he produced more than 2,500 pictures.

By 1920, he was realizing top prices for his paintings and sculptures and was gaining recognition as a serious painter and sculptor. Russell also modeled in wax. In 1904, his wax models were cast in bronze and sold by Tiffany & Company of New York City. His sculptures number about 100, depicting mounted cowboys, Indians and animals.

Like Remington he too showed much action in his pictures. He was a stickler for authenticity, and recorded much for history that otherwise would have been lost. He remained a cowboy at heart, wrote illustrated letters and verse filled with chawbacon pragmatism and branding-iron philosophy. The letters and verse were collected in his posthumous book *Good Medicine*.

Russell's painting *C.M. Russell and Friends* was shown on a 1989 stamp.

Edward Rutledge

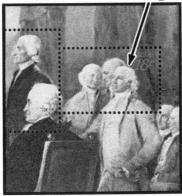

Scott 1687e
Born: November 23, 1749, Charleston, South Carolina
Died: January 23, 1800, Charleston, South Carolina

Edward Rutledge was the youngest of seven children born to Dr. John and Sarah Hext Rutledge. His illustrious brother, John Rutledge, was the oldest. Both brothers died in 1800, within seven months of each other.

Edward Rutledge began his studies at the Middle Temple, England, in 1767. He was admitted to the English bar in 1772 and returned to South Carolina the following year as a barrister. In 1774, he married Henrietta Middleton, with whom he had three children.

From July 1774 to 1777, he was a member of the Continental Congress and served as a member of the first Board of War. After his brother John and Christopher Gadsden left the Congress, Rutledge was the delegation's leader. On July 2, 1776, he voted for the resolution of independence, and on July 4, he signed the Declaration of Independence.

From 1775 to 1776, he was a member of the first and second provincial congresses of South Carolina. In 1776, he was commissioned a captain in the South Carolina Artillery group and saw action at Beaufort in 1779. He was captured at the fall of Charleston, was imprisoned by the British and was one of the so-called St. Augustine exiles. He was exchanged and freed in time to take his seat in the House of Representatives in 1782. He served until 1796.

He had a successful legal practice and held influential political positions. He made wise investments in land. He was active in the state conventions of 1788 and 1790. He was presidential elector, as a Federalist, in 1788, 1792 and in 1796, the year he voted for Thomas Pinckney and Thomas Jefferson.

He served two terms in the state Senate, from 1796 and from 1798, and also served as governor of South Carolina from 1798. His wife, Henrietta, died on April 22, 1792. He married Mary Shubrick Eveleigh on October 28, 1792.

Rutledge is the third person from the left on the fifth 18¢ stamp of the second American Bicentennial souvenir sheet issued May 29, 1976.

John Rutledge

Scott 798
Born: September 1739, Charleston, South Carolina
Died: July 18, 1800, Charleston, South Carolina

John Rutledge was the first child born to Dr. John and Sarah Hext Rutledge. Edward was his younger brother. His father taught John at home but died when John was 11. Rutledge finished his undergraduate learning at the Latin School in Charleston. He studied law at the Middle Temple, London, was admitted to the English bar in February 1760 and returned to Charleston.

In 1763, he married Elizabeth Grimke. They had 10 children. He was a committee chairman in the Stamp Act Congress in 1765. He was sent to the first Continental Congress in 1774. He was elected to the Council of Safety. He was a member of the committee that wrote the South Carolina constitution of 1776 and was elected president of the General Assembly. The following December he was re-elected for the regular term of two years. He was South Carolina's first statehood governor with the title of president.

Rowlins Lawndes served as governor for a year, and when the state faced invasion in January 1779, Rutledge was again elected governor and took the field in a desperate effort to supply Generals Benjamin Lincoln and William Moultrie with troops. When the British commander slipped behind Lincoln in a dash upon Charleston, Rutledge proposed a parley and made an offer of neutrality. In March 1780, Charleston was beseiged by land and sea. A month before the fall of Charleston, Rutledge slipped out and strove to gather militia for its relief, but in May, it was surrendered. Rutledge retired to North Carolina. In 1781, he returned to South Carolina with military supplies.

He took a seat in the House as a member from St. Andrew's Parish. He was in the House of Representatives from 1784 to 1790. With Charles Cotesworth Pinckney, Charles Pinckney and Pierce Butler, he was elected to the Federal Convention of 1787. He became chairman of the Committee of Detail. With his three South Carolina peers, he signed the U.S. Constitution.

Rutledge was appointed to the U.S. Supreme Court in 1789 but resigned to accept the office of chief justice of South Carolina. He was appointed chief justice of the U.S. Supreme Court. After one session, he retired. He began to show signs of insanity after the death of his wife in 1792.

Rutledge is depicted on the 1937 Constitution Sesquicentennial stamp.

Eero Saarinen

Eero Saarinen 1910-1961 Dulles Airport Washington DC
Architecture USA 20c

Scott 2022
Born: August 20, 1910, Kyrkslatt (Kirkkonummi), Finland
Died: September 1, 1961, Ann Arbor, Michigan

Eero Saarinen was the son of Finnish-American architect Gottlieb Eliel Saarinen. Eliel designed the Finnish Pavilion at the 1900 Paris Exposition and the League of Nations Building in Geneva. When he came to America in 1923, bringing with him his son Eero, he was recognized as one of Finland's foremost architects. In America, he designed the Christ Lutheran Church in Minneapolis and the Tabernacle Church of Christ in Columbus, Indiana.

Eero was 13 when he came to America. He finished high school, then attended Yale School of Architecture, graduating in 1934. The Saarinens formed a partnership until the elder Saarinen's death in 1950. They received awards from the American Institute of Architects in 1948 for the design of a new annex to enlarge the Smithsonian Institution in Washington, D.C.

Eero Saarinen became an American citizen in 1940. In 1948, he won the competition for the Jefferson National Expansion Memorial in St. Louis with a design of an arch that is an inverted catenary curve of 886 tons of gleaming stainless steel, 630 feet high, dominating the riverfront and signifying a gateway to the West. The arch was completed in 1964.

Saarinen designed the Kresge Auditorium for the Massachusetts Institute of Technology, as well as the adjacent chapel. In 1959, he designed the Ingalls Hockey Rink at Yale University, featuring a roof suspended from steel cables and hanging from a parobolic arch 228 feet long, as if it were an extension of a skaters stride. The Trans World Airlines Terminal at Kennedy International Airport, New York, is sensational as is the Dulles International Airport terminal building with its swooping roof paralleling an airplane's takeoff pattern. The Vivian Beaumont Repertory Theater for the Lincoln Center for Performing Arts in New York is partially underground, but scraping the sky is the CBS building, the first reinforced concrete tower in New York. For a finish on the John Deere building, Moline, Illinois, Saarinen turned to unfinished Cor 10 steel in which its own rust will provide a protective coating.

Saarinen is honored on a stamp in the 1982 American Architecture set.

Arthur St. Clair

Scott 854
Born: March 23, 1736, Thurso, Caithness County, Scotland
Died: August 31, 1818, Chestnut Ridge, Pennsylvainia

Arthur St. Clair was the son of William and Elizabeth Sinclair. He entered the University of Edinburgh but did not complete the term. In 1757, he was an ensign in the British army and served in Canada. On May 15, 1760, he married Phoebe Bayard. He was advanced to lieutenant, then resigned from the army.

His wife inherited £14,000 that he was able to add to his own military service claims. With this windfall, he purchased 4,000 acres in the Ligonier Valley of western Pennsylvania. Because of this large estate, Deputy Governor John Penn made him the agent of Colonial government in this frontier country.

In 1773, the county of Westmoreland was formed, and St. Clair was its justice. When the Revolutionary War began, he was a member of the Committee of Safety of Westmoreland County, but he lost control of the Pittsburgh area to the Virginians. He was relegated to a minor role.

In the winter of 1775-76, he was a brigadier general with George Washington in the battles of Trenton and Princeton. In 1777, as major general, he was ordered to defend Fort Ticonderoga, but he evacuated the post, resulting in a court martial, from which he was exonerated.

St. Clair was a delegate to the Continental Congress, and in 1787, he was its president. He was appointed governor of the Northwest Territory. His raw dealings with the Indians and their treaties resulted in war. As major general, he was commander of the Federal Army. He was defeated on November 4, 1791, on the banks of the Wabash, about a day's march from the site of Fort Wayne. He was ordered to construct military posts, which he failed to do. He was freed of blame and resigned his command but continued as territorial governor until 1802, when he was removed from office by President Jefferson.

As governor of the Northwest Territory, St. Clair is shown attending Washington's inauguration on a stamp issued April 30, 1939.

Rodrego Sanchez

Scott 118
Born: 1448, Helmantica, Salamanca Province, Spain
Died: 1513, Valladolid, Valladolid Province, Spain

The persons sailing on Christopher Columbus's first voyage to discover a new route to China and Japan were mostly enlisted sailors, stewards, boatswains, caulkers, able seamen and ship boys recruited from the Andalusian towns of Seville, Cordova and Jerez de la Frontera. The only foreigners besides Columbus were one other Genoese, one Portuguese and a Venetian.

In addition to the maritime personnel aboard the three ships, the *Santa Maria*, the *Nina* and the *Pinta*, were several civilians with various offices. Most of these civilians were aboard the flagship with Columbus. Two of the civilians were from the royal court representing the Crown. One was Pedro Gutierrez, a major domo or repostero of the king. He may have been sent by the king to keep watch over the other members of the Crown. The other was Rodrego Sanchez, the royal comptroller, whose office it was to see to it that an accounting was made of all the riches acquired from the East.

Sanchez was to make certain that Columbus adhered to the capitulations made between the sovereigns and himself in April 1492. Columbus was to get 10 percent of the gold, gems, spices or other merchandise produced or obtained by trade within the domains of the lands he encountered.

He was to establish a trading post on one of the islands below Japan. Sanchez would be instrumental in setting up the accounting of these acquisitions and gleening the king's 90 percent.

On Thursday night October 11, 1492, Columbus was sure he saw a flickering light ahead. "It was like a little wax candle whose flame went up and down," he wrote. He was sure it was people with torches on land. He called Sanchez to verify the sightings, but he could not do so. On Friday, October 12, at 2:00 a.m., land was sighted by Martin Alonso Pinzon on the *Pinta*. Columbus named the island San Salvador. When the sun was high, the landing party went ashore. Sanchez was at Columbus' side.

Sanchez is depicted as the first person to the right of the center flagbearer (Martin Alonso Pinzon) in John Vanderlyn's painting *Landing of Columbus* on the 15¢ stamp issued April 2, 1869.

Henry Sandham

Lexington & Concord 1775 by Sandham

US Bicentennial IOcents

Scott: 1563
Born: May 24, 1842, Montreal, Canada
Died: June 21, 1910, London, England

Henry Sandham's father, John Sandham, was an interior decorator. His mother was Elizabeth Tate Sandham. Both parents came to Canada from England. After he completed his education in Montreal, Henry Sandham went to work for William Notman, a photographer. He began painting landscapes.

On May 23, 1865, Sandham married Agnes Fraser, the daughter of John Fraser, a Canadian journalist. Two of their six children lived to maturity. Sandham's painting, *Beacon Light, St. John Harbor*, was selected by Princess Louise in 1870 for the National Gallery in Ottawa. Sandham was one of the first artists appointed to establish the Royal Canadian Academy of Arts.

In 1880, Sandham went to England and France, then returned to work in Boston as a book illustrator. He illustrated *Lenore* by Edgar Allan Poe, *King Noanett: A Story of Old Virginia and the Massachusetts Bay* by F.J. Stimson and Helen Hunt Jackson's *Ramona*. In 1902, he went to California to illustrate Jackson's book *Glimpses of California and the Missions*. In 1909, he provided the illustrations for Montcrieff's *Adventures in America*. He illustrated various publications, such as the *Century* and *Harper's New Monthly Magazine*. A volume titled *Pictures of Canadian History*, with many of Sandham's drawings, was published 10 years after his death.

Sandham's painting of the *Founding of Maryland* was exhibited at the World's Columbian Exposition in Chicago in 1893. At the Boston Art Club in 1890, he exhibited *The March of Time*, a 12- by 20-foot painting showing veterans of the Grand Army marching across the Boston Common during a reunion. This and other works are now in the National Gallery of Art in Washington. These historical paintings followed his *Dawn of Liberty* depicting the Battle of Lexington. It now hangs in the Town Hall at Lexington.

Sandham left Boston for London in 1901, where he remained. He was buried at the large privately owned Kensal Green Cemetery in London.

Sandham's painting *Dawn of Liberty* is reproduced on the stamp issued on April 19, 1975, commemorating the bicentenary of the Battle at Lexington.

208

William Saroyan

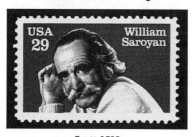

Scott 2538
Born: August 31, 1908, Fresno, California
Died: May 18, 1981, Fresno, California

William Saroyan was the son of Amenak Saroyan, his father, and Tekoohi Saroyan, his mother. Saroyan's parents were immigrants from Armenia, but William was born in California. Saroyan's works were original, cheerful, humorous and somewhat autobiographical. His short stories and plays portrayed courageous characters who overcame everyday adversities. His light-hearted tales encouraged the downhearted people of the great Depression and lifted their demoralized spirits. *Short Story* magazine published a collection of Saroyan's writings in 1934 under the title *The Daring Young Man on the Flying Trapeze*. During the next six years, Saroyan produced more than 500 stories. He wrote a collection of stories titled *Inhale and Exhale.*

Saroyan spent about five years in an orphanage after his father died. His education never went beyond grammar school in Fresno. He worked at odd jobs, ran messages for Western Union, and helped in his uncle's vineyard. At 17, he left to see "some of the rest of the world."

As a teenager, Saroyan knew he was a writer. He followed three rules: "Pay no attention to other people's rules, forget anybody who every wrote anything and learn to typewrite." His many writings include fictional memories, such as *My Name is Aram, The Human Comedy* and *The Adventures of Wesley Jackson.*

On April 13, 1939, his first dramatic work, the one-act play *My Heart's in the Highlands,* was performed. It was followed the same year by the five-act play *The Time of Your Life.* Saroyan jotted down this chef d'oeuvre in six days. He won the Pulitzer Prize for this play, but he refused the award because he did not believe commercialism should reward the arts. Brooks Atkinson, journalist and critic, described the play as "a prose poem in ragtime." In 1969, Clive Barnes selected it as one of the 50 best plays of the American theater.

Saroyan's postwar writings were more melancholy memoirs. Before he died, he said, "Everybody has got to die, but I have always believed an exception would be made in my case." In 1963, he wrote *Not Dying*, and in 1969, he wrote *Don't Go, but if You Must, Say Hello to Everybody*.

Saroyan was honored on a 29¢ commemorative in the Literary Arts series. The stamp was a joint issue with the Soviet Union.

Alexander Scammell

Scott 644
Born: March 27, 1747, Mendon (now Milford), Massachusetts
Died: October 6, 1781, Williamsburg, Virginia

Alexander Scammell's parents came to Menden, Massachusetts, about 1737 from Portsmouth, England. His father, Samuel Leslie Scammell, was a practicing physician who died when Alexander was 6 years old. His mother was Jane Libbey Scammell. Alexander and his brother were placed under the guardianship of the Reverend Amariah Frost. Alexander graduated from Harvard College in 1769. He taught school at Kingston, Massachusetts, and at nearby Plymouth. By 1776, he was reading law in the office of John Sullivan at Durham, New Hampshire. He was engaged to Abigail Bishop of Medford, Massachusetts. The Revolution thwarted any wedding ceremony at that time.

When the war broke out, Scammell was a brigade major with Sullivan's brigade. He participated in the siege of Boston and in the expedition to Canada the next year. He was Sullivan's aide-de-camp during the Long Island campaign. Fortunately Washington arrived just in time to rescue him and his men from a blundering maneuver.

In October 1776, he was assigned as brigade major in General Charles Lee's division and elevated to colonel of the 3rd Continental Battalion. He was with General Arthur St. Clair at Ticonderoga. When John Burgoyne advanced toward New York from Canada and encountered American forces, two battles took place, both at Freeman's Farm near Saratoga. Burgoyne was surrounded and surrendered his 5,800 men to General Horatio Gates. In the battle, Scammell was wounded but attended the surrender.

He succeeded Timothy Pickering as adjutant general of the Continental Army. It fell to him to arrest his former commander, General Lee, for almost turning the Battle of Monmouth into a fiasco in 1780. He also directed the hanging of Major John Andre, the Colonialists' vindiction for Nathan Hale.

Scammell took command of the 1st New Hampshire Regiment and led a party of continental light horse until September 30, 1781, when he was captured at Yorktown while on a reconnoitering mission. He died 15 days later at Williamsburg of wounds he received after his capture.

On the 1927 Surrender of Burgoyne stamp, Scammell is the third person from the left standing in full view wearing a hat.

Philip John Schuyler

Scott 644
Born: November 11, 1733, Albany, New York
Died: November 18, 1804, Albany, New York

Philip John Schuyler was Johannes and Cornelia Van Cortlandt Schuyler's eldest son. His father died in 1741 when Schuyler was about 8. At age 15, he went to New Rochelle, New York, to study under the Reverend Peter Stouppe, who taught him French and mathematics. When he came of age, rather than claim full inheritance by primogeniture, he shared with his sister and brothers.

He was commissioned by Governor James De Lancey to command a company in General William Johns' expedition against Crown Point. Schuyler participated in the Battle at Lake George on September 8, 1755. He married Catherine Van Rensselaer of Claverack, New York. In the spring of 1756, he was under Colonel John Bradstreet. The following year he resigned, only to return to the army in 1758 with the rank of major under Lord Howe. Schuyler took part in Abercrombie's ill-fated expedition against Ticonderoga and was with Colonel Bradsteet when Fort Frontenac on Lake Ontario was captured.

The final settlement of his father's estate, which included a third of his grandfather's land, resulted in his owning thousands of acres of land along the Mohawk Valley and the Hudson as well as land in Saratoga. He developed Saratoga for lumbering and milling and owned four ships to ply the Hudson.

Schuyler accepted membership in the provincial delegation. On June 19, 1775, Washington appointed him major general in command of the Northern Department. He had difficulties with the Burgoyne campaign, so General Gates was given command in the Northern Department. Congress preferred charges of incompetence against Schuyler, but he was acquitted with honor by a court martial in 1778. In early 1779, he resigned.

He entered the state Senate in 1780. He was involved in the ratification of the Constitution by the Poughkeepsie Convention. He was one of the first two to represent New York in the U.S. Senate but was defeated for re-election in 1791 by Aaron Burr. He defeated Burr in 1798, but ill health prevented him from taking his seat in the Senate. His wife died in 1803. Burr killed his son-in-law, Alexander Hamilton, in a duel on July 11, 1804.

On the 1927 Surrender of Burgoyne stamp, Schuyler is the first person from the right.

David Randolph Scott

Scott 1435
Born: June 6, 1932, San Antonio, Texas

In 1954, David Scott completed training at the U.S. Military Academy, West Point, and received a bachelor of science degree. At the Massachusetts Institute of Technology, he received his master of science in aeronautics and astronautics and an engineer of aeronautics and astronautics degree.

In 1963, he was selected to be an astronaut. He was pilot of the *Gemini 8* flight, along with Neil Armstrong. The flight was aborted. Scott was the command module pilot of the *Apollo 9* Earth-orbiting mission that tested the Lunar Module. He was the backup commander of *Apollo 12*, and commander of *Apollo 15*, becoming the seventh man to walk on the moon. With James Benson Irwin, he was the first to ride on the moon in a vehicle, the Lunar Rover.

The *Apollo 15* mission was launched from Cape Kennedy, Florida, July 26, 1971. The lunar module, *Falcon*, touched down on the moon four days later. Scott and Irwin landed just 400 feet northeast of their target, while Alfred M. Worden, commander of the *Endeavour*, circled above. The next morning they spent six and a half hours outside the *Falcon* deploying scientific equipment.   In the "moon buggy," they drove toward the Apennines and Hadley Rill. On August 1, Scott and Irwin took an eight-mile run in the Lunar Rover to gather crystalline rocks. In the afternoon, they rejoined Worden in the *Endeavour* and returned to Earth. They splashed down August 7. The flight time was 295 hours 12 minutes, approximately 12 days and eight hours. It was the fourth manned lunar landing and the first to use the Lunar Rover. On this mission, the first live pictures of a lunar module lift-off was transmitted.

Scott and his crewmates Irwin and Worden admitted carrying 400 unauthorized stamped covers to the moon, which they planned to sell after their return. For this, they were removed from astronaut status.

In July 1972, Scott became special assistant for mission operations for the Apollo-Soyuz Test Project and, in April 1975, was appointed director of NASA Dryden Flight Research Center, Edwards, California. On October 30, 1977, he established his own company, Scott-Preyss Associates, now Scott Science and Technology Inc., Lancaster, California.

Scott is depicted riding over the moon surface in the Lunar Rover on the 1971 Space Achievement stamp.

Roger Sherman

Scott 1687a
Born: April 19, 1721 (old style), Newton, Massachusetts
Died: July 23, 1793, New Haven, Connecticut

When Roger Sherman was 2 years of age, his family moved from Newton to Stoughton. He learned farming chores and shoemaking from his father. He also learned to be "honest as an angel," so John Adams said of him. Thomas Jefferson said Sherman was "a man who never said a foolish thing in his life."

After a few years of elementary school, Sherman was on his own for an education. He read much on theology, mathematics and law, subjects that formulated his lifestyle. In 1743, at the age of 22, he went to New Milford in western Connecticut to make his life. He opened a cobbler shop. In 1745, he was appointed county surveyor. He published almanacs and ran a general mercantile store. He was admitted to the bar in 1754 at the age of 33.

His political acumen grew through his experience in serving in several local offices and as justice of the peace, member of the county court and representative in the legislature. He moved to New Haven in 1761. He was a benefactor and treasurer of Yale College from 1765 to 1776. In 1784, he was elected the first mayor of New Haven.

At the 1787 Philadelphia Convention, he presented the Connecticut Compromise, which recommended two houses in Congress, one with equal representation from each state and one proportional to populaton. During the Revolution, he was a leader in Congress. He published, in 1784, with Richard Law, a revised tome on Connecticut law.

Sherman was the only person to sign each of the four documents: the Continental Association, the Declaration of Independence, the Articles of Confederation and the Federal Constitution. Fittingly, he served his last four years in the House of Representatives and in the Senate.

He is shown second from the left on the first stamp of the second American Bicentennial souvenir sheet, issued in 1976.

John French Sloan

Scott 1433
Born: August 2, 1871, Lock Haven, Pennsylvania
Died: September 7, 1951, Hanover, New Hampshire

John Sloan was a realist painter. He painted real-life situations. In the 1930s, he was not accepted by many of the so-called social realists because he refused to incorporate what he called "socialist propaganda" into his art. He was one of the original members of "The Eight" students of Robert Henri, painters who were also dubbed the "Ashcan school." They painted scenes of everyday city life along the waterfront, the Lower East Side, The Bowery and in West Greenwich Village. These same painters organized the epoch-making Armory Show in 1913, bringing European trends to America.

Sloan attended evening classes at the Pennsylvania Academy under Robert Henri. He enrolled at the Academy from 1892 to 1894, at which time he also worked as an artist-reporter for the *Philadelphia Inquirer*. He was employed in a similar capacity for the *Philadelphia Press*.

He produced art posters in the art nouveau style during the 1890s. In 1896, he began painting seriously in oil. His first recognized work was *East Entrance, City Hall, Philadelphia*, 1901, now in the Columbus Gallery. He created drawings and etchings to illustrate books, especially for Paul de Kock's novels.

He settled in New York City in 1904 and began creating etchings and paintings of New York City life in voyeuristic views of backyards, restaurants, street corners, and parks. He searched for his subject matter on the city streets.

He joined the Socialist Party in 1909, providing the artwork for *The Call* and *The Coming Nation*. He became the editor of *The Masses* from 1912 to 1916. However, he did not use his art too politically.

As time passed, he leaned more to landscapes and interior scenes. His techniques and his renditions changed with influences from Vincent Van Gogh and Hardesty Maratta. His *The City from Greenwich Village* shows a spectacle of the city. In 1939, he completed the mural *The First Mail Arrives at Bronxville, 1846*, for the Bronxville, New York, Post Office. Among his other fine paintings are notably *Haymarket* and *The Wake of the Ferry*.

Sloan was a teacher at the Art Students League from 1914 to 1938. He was one of the organizers of the Society of Independent Artists.

Sloan's *The Wake of the Ferry* is shown on a 1971 stamp.

Richard Dobbs Spaight

Scott 798
Born: March 25, 1758, New Bern, North Carolina
Died: September 6, 1802, New Bern, North Carolina

Richard Dobbs Spaight's father, Richard Spaight, was born in Ireland and emigrated to America. His mother was Margaret Dobbs. When Spaight was 8 years old, his parents died. He was sent to Ireland for schooling and advanced through the University of Glasgow. He returned to America in 1778. In 1779, he was in the House of Commons for the borough of New Bern.

He was present at the Battle of Camden, serving as an aide to General Richard Caswell, who also was governor of the state from 1776 to 1780. Spaight left the military service to serve again in the House of Commons, representing New Bern or Craven County from 1781 to 1787 and again in 1792. He served on several committees. He was chosen speaker on January 1, 1787.

He had been defeated for the Continental Congress, but when a vacancy occurred, he was selected to fill the seat. This led to his being elected to the Congress in 1784 and 1785. He served on several committees.

In 1787, he was an advocate of a stronger federal government. He was chosen as a delegate to the federal Constitutional Convention. He voted for the Constitution. With his fellow North Carolina peers, William Blount and Hugh Williamson, he penned his name to the famous document. He failed in his bid for governor in 1787, but was a member of the state convention in 1788. In 1789, he was the Anti-Federalist candidate for federal senator but was unsuccessful. It was this year that North Carolina finally ratified the Constitution on November 21.

Spaight's health failed, and he traveled about the country in search of a cure. When his health improved, he ran for governor in 1792 and was elected. He served three terms, 1792 to 1795. In the final year of his term, he married Mary Leach of Holmesburg, Pennsylvania. They had three children.

Spaight served as a member of Congress from December 10, 1800, to March 3, 1801. He did not run for re-election. He was a staunch Republican. In the election of the president by the House, he voted for Thomas Jefferson. He became involved in a heated correspondence with John Stanly, a prominent Federalist leader. A duel resulted, and Spaight was killed.

He is depicted on the 1937 Constitution Sesquicentennial stamp.

Myles Standish

Scott 549
Born: 1584, probably Lancashire, England
Died: October 3, 1656, Duxbury, Plymouth County, Massachusetts

Myles Standish was a soldier of fortune, serving in the Low Countries. In 1620, he was hired by the Pilgrims sailing on the *Mayflower* to America to act as their military adviser and guardian. The *Mayflower* anchored on November 21 off Cape Cod, and on December 26, the first Pilgrims stepped on land across the bay at what was to become their winter camp, later called Plymouth.

Many became ill from the poor food and the cold weather. Standish and spiritual leader William Brewster escaped illness. Both worked to help the sick. Standish's wife, Rose, died. Until her death, Standish considered himself an employee of the colony. After this experience, he was considered a member of the colony. He was one of the 41 who signed the Mayflower Compact.

Standish learned the local Indian language and was able to negotiate with them. He designed and superintended the building of a fort that gave the Pilgrims protection, and he instructed the men in the ways of defending themselves if necessary. The colony was secure for the next 50 years.

In 1624, Standish was named one of the five assistants to the governor. In 1628, he was instrumental in disbanding the licentious Thomas Morton's home at Merry Mount. He had Morton sent back to England because he sold guns to the Indians and forestalled the Pilgrims trading on the Kennebec. Morton returned to Plymouth in 1643, and again Standish ordered him to leave.

Standish's second wife, Barbara, came over on the *Anne* in 1623. They married in 1624. Of their six children, four sons lived to adulthood.

In 1625, the Pilgrims were without rights to land and property. Isaac Allerton and Edward Winslow failed to make the necessary arrangements with the Merchant Adventurer or the Council for New England. Standish returned to England to obtain essential supplies. He returned in April 1626.

He was one of the bondsmen to assume the debt of the colony and was attorney of the Council for New England. He served as treasurer. He and Alden founded Duxbury in 1631, where they lived for the remainder of their lives.

Standish is one of the Pilgrims on the 1920 2¢ Pilgrim Tercentenary stamp.

Francis Edgar Stanley

Scott 2132
Born: June 1, 1849, Kingfield, Maine
Died: July 31, 1918, Boston, Massachusetts

Francis E. Stanley's father, Soloman, was a teacher and farmer. His mother was Apphia French. Francis Stanley and his identical twin brother, Freelan, attended school in Kingfield. In 1871, Francis graduated from the Farmington State Normal and Training School. He taught school for several years in Maine. He also made crayon portraitures and sold them.

On January 1, 1870, he married Augusta May Walker. They had three children. In 1874, he gave up teaching and moved his family to Lewiston, Maine. He began using photography and became widely known in New England for his fine crayon portraits and photographs. He experimented with dry plate photography. He went into partnership with his twin brother and founded the Stanley Dry Plate Company in Lewiston. They established a new plant in Newton, Massachusetts, in 1890. Five years later they sold their company to the Eastman Kodak Company of Rochester, New York.

Francis experimented with automobiles propelled by steam engines and created a model that operated successfully in 1897. It required a light-weight, efficient, high-pressure steam boiler. He designed a light-weight, reversing, two-cylinder engine, called the Stanley Steamer. In 1899, the Stanley brothers drove their "Flying Teapot" to the top of Mount Washington, 6,288 feet high, in two hours and 10 minutes. Five years later they drove it in 28 minutes.

The brothers organized a company and began to manufacture 100 Steamers. They sold the business to John Brisben Walker of New York, who organized the Mobile Company of America. He formed the Locomobile Company of America to produce the steam-propelled automobile.

In 1902, the Stanley brothers bought back the patent from Locomobile and started the Stanley Motor Carriage Company. Francis developed a unit steam engine for individual steamers to run on interurban railway tracks.

Francis' collection of *Theories Worth Having* was privately published a year after his death. Ironically, he died in 1918 as a result of an automobile accident. Freelan lived in Boston. He died on October 2, 1940.

The Stanley Steamer is depicted on the 1985 12¢ Transportation coil.

217

Richard Stockton

Scott 1693
Born: October 1, 1730, Princeton, New Jersey
Died: February 28, 1781, Princeton, New Jersey

Richard Stockton's father, John Stockton, was the presiding judge of the Court of Common Pleas in Somerset County, New Jersey. His wealth permitted him to generously support the College of New Jersey located then in Newark, and he was mostly responsible for the removal of the college to Princeton.

Richard studied at the Academy under the direction of the Reverend Samuel Finley in Nottingham, Maryland, before entering the College of New Jersey. He graduated in 1748. He read law in the office of David Ogden of Newark and advanced in the legal ranks from being licensed in 1754 as an attorney, to counselor in 1758. In 1764, he was raised to barrister of the highest rank, answering to the doctor of the civil law as a sergeant-at-law.

He married Annis Boudino. They had two sons and four daughters. His eldest son, also Richard, was a prominent lawyer and judge. His eldest daughter, Julia, married Dr. Benjamin Rush.

In 1766, as a trustee of the College of New Jersey, the board commissioned Stockton to travel to London to persuade John Witherspoon of Paisley to accept the position as president of the College of New Jersey. Witherspoon accepted.

Stockton returned home in 1767. In 1774, he was commissioned one of the justices of the Supreme Court . During this time, he improved and completed "Morven," his home in Princeton.

He was elected to the Continental Congress on June 22, 1776, in time to sign the Declaration of Independence. Before he could return to Princeton, the British had invaded New Jersey. He was captured, thrown in jail at Perth Amboy and transferred to New York. When he was released, his health was failing, his estate was overrun, and his fortune depleted.

On the third stamp of the 1976 Declaration of Independence set, of the four men seated, Richard Stockton is the first on the left.

Thomas Stone

Scott 1691
Born: 1743, Poynton Manor, Charles County, Maryland
Died: October 5, 1787, Alexandria, Virginia

Thomas Stone was the great-great-grandson of William Stone (1603-60), English colonial administrator who emigrated to Virginia about 1628 and served as sheriff. He was also governor of Maryland. Thomas was born in 1743, the eldest son of David and Elizabeth Jenifer Stone. He received his classic education from a Scottish school master, then went to Annapolis to read law under the tutilage of Thomas Johnson. He was admitted to the bar in 1764 and set up law practice in Frederick, Maryland.

In 1768, he married Margaret Brown. In 1771, the couple moved to Fort Tobacco. Helped by a £1,000 dowry, the Stones built Habre-de-Venture (Harbor of Happiness), one of the most beautiful examples of Colonial architecture in the South.

In 1774, Stone was the lawyer who opposed Thomas Johnson, Samuel Chase and William Paca in their testing the legality of the poll tax for the support of the clergy. These same persons were later his peers in Congress.

Stone took his place in the Continental Congress on May 13, 1775, and served until October 1778. He was a member of the committee that framed the Articles of Confederation. He voted for the Declaration of Independence. Though his sympathies were with the Colonists for the break with England, he was more moderate in his feelings than his peers. He signed the Declaration. He made few speeches, was quiet in his actions and wrote little; thus, he is the least known of the Maryland signers. He was elected state senator from Charles County in 1776 and served until his death. He was elected to the Congress of the Confederation in 1783 and took his seat in 1784, but declined re-election.

He was elected to the Constitutional Convention in Philadelphia but declined. He died in October 1787. Three children survived him.

On the first stamp of the 1976 Declaration of Independence set, of the five men standing, Stone is the third from the left.

William Strickland

Architecture USA 15c

Scott 1782
Born: November 1788, Navesink, New Jersey
Died: April 6, 1854, Nashville, Tennessee

William Strickland moved his family from New Jersey to Philadelphia when William was age 2. The elder Strickland worked as a carpenter on the building of the Bank of Pennsylvania in 1801. He followed the detailed plans designed and drawn by well-known architect Benjamin Henry Latrobe. Young William played at the building site. In 1803, at the age of 14, he joined Latrobe as an apprentice. After two years, he left Latrobe to work in New York City.

In 1808, Strickland returned to Philadelphia and designed the Masonic Hall. He created engravings for books and magazines, designed theatrical scenery, and surveyed. He married Rachel McCollough Trenschard in 1812.

During the War of 1812, he built redoubts around Philadelphia. He won an architectural competition for his design of the Second Bank of the United States, modeled after the Parthenon. Latrobe came in second and accused Strickland of stealing his plans. History still debates the controversy.

Strickland designed churches, houses and theaters in the city and the Naval Asylum (now the U.S. Naval Home). The Naval Asylum was designed on the order of the Temple on the Ilissos in Athens. In 1828, Strickland restored Independence Hall and added its present steeple. He also designed the U.S. Mint, completed in 1833. The Merchants' Exchange has survived since 1834.

Strickland also supervised the building of major canals. He surveyed for railroads. He designed the U.S. Mint, New Orleans. The Mint Museum of Art, 1836, in Charlotte, North Carolina, is Greek revival style. It was destroyed by fire in 1844 then rebuilt in 1936 to the exact same plan. Strickland designed the Atheneum in Providence, Rhode Island, completed in 1836.

In 1845, he moved his wife and six children to Nashville, where he designed the First Presbyterian Church and St. Mary's Church. He designed the Tennessee State Capitol in Nashville. It is Greek revival with the tower modeled after the Choragic Monument of Lysikrates in Athens.

Strickland became ill in 1851, and his son Francis continued his work. When Strickland died, he was buried in the vault of the Tennessee Capitol.

A stamp in the 1979 American Architecture set shows the Philadelphia Exchange Building designed by Strickland.

Harry Clayton Stutz

Stutz Bearcat 1933
11 USA

Scott 2131
Born: September 12, 1876, Ansonia, Darke County, Ohio
Died: June 25, 1930, Indianapolis

Harry Clayton Stutz was born on the farm of his parents, Henry J. and Elizabeth Snyder Stutz, near Ansonia in Darke County, Ohio. He attended public school and apprenticed to the mechanist trade. At age 21, he opened his own machine shop in Dayton, Ohio, about 1897.

Stutz was one of the first persons in Dayton to own an automobile. He repaired and manufactured farm pumping engines. Since he was familiar with engines, he learned the workings of an automobile. In 1903, he became manager of the Linsey-Russell Axle Company in Indianapolis. He also worked at the G.&J. Tire Company and the Schebler Carburetor Company. From 1906 to 1910, he worked for Marion Motor Company as engineer and factory manager. He designed a pleasure car that he said had an "underslung" design.

In 1910, Stutz teamed up with Henry Campbell and opened the Stutz Auto Parts Company. In 1911, they organized another company, the Ideal Motor Car Company. The company manufactured a car designed by Stutz. His car was entered in the first of the Indianapolis 500 races. It finished eleventh.

Two years later, the Auto Parts Company and the Ideal Motor Car Company merged into the Stutz Motor Car Company. Stutz sold the company and joined with Campbell to organize the H.C.S. Motor Car Company of Indianapolis. The H.C.S. (for Harry Clayton Stutz) manufactured luxury cars and taxicabs. From 1913 to 1919, the Stutz car became well-known. For the first two years, it won most of the auto races around the country.

Stutz turned to airplane engines. He designed a four-cylinder engine that he was promoting to the airplane manufacturers at the time of his death.

Stutz also was a great sportsman. He was an expert trapshooter. He had one of the finest collections of sporting guns in the United States.

He had married Clara M. Dietz of Dayton in 1898, with whom he had a daughter, Emma Belle (Horn). This marriage ended in divorce. In 1924, he married Blanch Clark of Indianapolis. After 1924, Stutz lived in Orlando, Florida. He died during an appendectomy.

The Stutz Bearcat is shown on the 1985 11¢ Transportation coil.

Louis Henry Sullivan

Scott 1931
Born: September 3, 1856, Boston, Massachusetts
Died: April 14, 1924, Chicago, Illinois

Louis Henry Sullivan was the son of the proprietor of a dancing academy in Boston. He attended the local elementary and high schools and attended the Massachusetts Institute of Technology (MIT) from 1872 to 1873. He studied at the Ecole des Beaux-Arts in Paris. He worked in Philadelphia for the firm of Furness and Hewitt until the Panic of 1873.

He joined his family in Chicago and worked for W. Le Baron Jenny, where he met Dankmar Adler from Lengsfeld, Germany, who came to Chicago in 1861. In 1881, Sullivan teamed up with Adler. They designed and completed the Auditorium Theater in Chicago in 1890. It featured receding elevated rows of seats and nearly perfect acoustics. It brought them national recognition.

Function was Sullivan's forte. The years with Adler were his most productive. The Wainwright Building in St. Louis (the first real skyscraper) and the Guaranty Building in Buffalo were tall steel-framed buildings in which the use of the basic materials created the designs that dominated the style. Sullivan's structural theories were put to use in the Transportation Building at the World's Columbian Exposition (1893) and the Gage Building in Chicago.

Following this period, academic classicism dominated building designs. Sullivan's principles were too advanced for the builders of the time, and his commissions waned.

The Depression of 1893 was hard on Sullivan, as was the breaking up of his partnership with Adler. From 1899 to 1904, he built the Carson, Pirie, Scott department store in Chicago, displaying its clean-cut, purely functional beauty. It was 50 years ahead of its time. Sullivan built a few Midwestern banks.

One of his apprentices was Frank Lloyd Wright, who believed in, and expanded on, Sullivan's principles. Sullivan's working progress was recorded in the book, *Autobiography of an Idea* by Frank Lloyd Wright, published in 1924, the year Sullivan died in poverty.

The National Farmer's Bank in Owatonna, Minnesota, by Sullivan was chosen for the fourth stamp of the 1981 American Architecture set.

John Augustus Sutter

Scott 954
Born: February 15, 1803, Kandern, Baden, Germany
Died: June 18, 1880, Washington, D.C.

Johann August Suter was born in Germany of Swiss parents and grew up in Switzerland. He was an ambitious person, generous to a fault and adventurous. This personality combination resulted in a shotgun marriage, five children and a pile of debts. Suter left Switzerland and arrived in America in 1834. He changed his name to John Augustus Sutter and joined a German community in Missouri. Fleeing from debt again, he headed west to Santa Fe, then to John McLoughlin's Fort Vancouver in Oregon. He found transportation to Hawaii and Alaska, and by 1839, he was in California.

On his trip overland, he created figmental fabrications of his background and reputation. He obtained Mexican citizenship, borrowed money and acquired large tracts of land in the Sacramento Valley, where he created an impressive establishment called New Helvetia. Sutter, a small and bald man with a trim mustache and polite manners, used Indians for unskilled labor, but also housed skilled artisans in his compound. He prospered. He ate the best food and drank the best wine, dispensing hospitality to fit his grandiose position. He had an army of Indians uniformed in red, blue and green, his own artillery and coined his own money. He was made a captain in the Mexican army.

Sutter favored statehood for California. He was friendly to Americans, helped settlers as they arrived from 1841 on, and was helpful to John Fremont, though Fremont held him in suspect. From 1841 to 1845, many different groups of immigrants ran through his fort and left debts, or stole his property.

Then came the Mexican War. The conquest of California was a small part of the campaigns. The Treaty of Guadalupe Hidalgo ceded the land west of the Rockies to the United States in February 1848, including all of California. The title to Sutter's land came in question. James Wilson Marshall, a carpenter working on a sawmill on Sutter's property, discovered gold. Prospectors ran over Sutter's land, and by 1852, he was bankrupt. In 1864, the government awarded him a pension of $250 per month.

In 1873, he moved to Lititz, Pennsylvania. While in Washington, D.C., seeking relief from Congress, he died.

Sutter's Mill is featured on a stamp issued January 24, 1948.

Geraert Terborch

Letters
mingle souls
Donne

Terborch

10c US

Scott 1534
Born: 1617, Zwolle, Netherlands
Died: December 8, 1681, Deventer, Netherlands

Geraert Terborch (or Gerard Ter Borch) learned to paint from his father. His father was a painter for the first four years of Terborch's life, then he took a position in the municipal treasury. His father had spent several years in Rome and had returned with drawings by Italian artists.

When Terborch was 8 years old, he rendered a drawing of a horse and rider. He traveled to Amsterdam in 1632, when he was 15. He made several trips to the Netherlands and elsewhere in Europe, investigating works of art. In 1634, he began to seriously study art, working under Pieter de Molijn in Haarlem. In 1635, he was a free master of the Guild of St. Luke. In July, he went to London. According to some art historians, he traveled extensively around Europe. He went to Spain and may have been under the tutorship of Valazquez.

His mother was from Antwerp, Belgium, and after stopping in Paris, he visited his mother's home. He moved to Amsterdam, where he worked for the next five years. From 1645 to 1648, he was in Munster, Germany, during the meeting of European delegates ratifying the treaty that made the United Terborch Provinces independent. Terborch made miniature portraits of these delegates on copper and wood. Two portraits of the Netherlands delegates still exist. He also created portraits of the Spanish and French ambassadors. More important, however, are his renditions of the ceremony of the swearing of the oath ratifying the treaty. He included a likeness of himself among the group.

Terborch returned to Amsterdam, then went to The Hague and Kampen. He married in Deventer and apparently made that his home from 1654 until the time of his death. He took an honorary office in the city government and painted group portraits of the regents. His portraits are small, dignified and elegant.

Terborch's painting *Lady Writing Letter* was chosen for the fifth stamp in the Universal Postal Union series of June 6, 1974.

Charles Thomson

Scott 1687d
Born: November 29, 1729, County Derry, Ireland
Died: August 16, 1824, "Harriton" near Philadelphia, Pennsylvania

Charles Thomson is best remembered for his long term as secretary of the Continental Congress. He was also the man chosen to notify George Washington that he had been elected president of the United States. Thomson's life began dismally. His mother died in Ireland, and his father, John Thomson, left with Charles for America. Within sight of land, his father died aboard ship, leaving Charles one of six orphans among the passengers to set foot on American shores at New Castle, Delaware. He was 10 years old.

He entered Dr. Francis Alison's academy at New London, Chester County, Pennsylvania. Upon finishing school, he conducted a private school. In 1750, at the age of 21, through his acquaintance with Benjamin Franklin, he received an appointment as tutor at the Philadelphia Academy. In 1757, he was the schoolmaster of the Latin school that became the William Penn Charter School. He taught until 1760, then began a successful venture in the mercantile trade.

In 1757, at the Treaty of Easton, he was the scribe for the Delaware Indians. To honor his integrity, he was adopted into their tribe and named "Man Who Tells the Truth." In 1759, he published, in London, a treatise regarding the alienation of the Delaware and Shawnee Indians from British interests.

Thomson advocated independence and was a Pennsylvania Son of Liberty. Joseph Galloway blocked him from being a delegate to the Continental Congress. Through John Adams, who called him the "Sam Adams of Philadelphia," he was appointed secretary. Thomson sat at the secretarial table of the Congress for 15 years. He had hoped for an office under George Washington's presidency, but it was not to come. He resigned as the Continental Congress' secretary and retired to "Harriton" to write, making translations of the Septuagint and the New Testament and other theological tomes. He lived to age 95.

Thomson is shown standing by John Hancock, who is shown seated, in the fourth 18¢ stamp in the second 1976 American Bicentennial souvenir sheet.

Giovanni Battista Tiepolo

Christmas USA 20c

Tiepolo: National Gallery of Art

Scott 2026
Born: March 5, 1696, Venice, Italy
Died: March 27, 1770, Madrid, Spain

Giovanni Battista Tiepolo was the son of a ship-owner and merchant. He married Maria Cecilia Guardi. He and his wife had nine children, two of whom, Giovanni Domenico and Lorenzo Baldissera, became accomplished painters.

Tiepolo developed a bold and fluent style. His early works in 1715 were *The Sacrifice of Abraham*, in the Church of St. Maria dei Dereletti, and *Crossing of the Red Sea*, in the Church of St. Rocco, both in Venice. His *Repudiation of Hagar*, now in Milan, was his first signed and dated work. Commissions followed from Doge Giovanni II Cornaro.

About 1720, Tiepolo went to Udine to fresco the Palazzo Arcivescovile for Archbishop Dionisio Dolfin. He also painted frescoes in the Chapel of the Sacrament in the cathedral and created various decorations in the castle.

In 1731, he was in Milan, where he frescoed the ceiling in the Palazzo Archinto. In Bergamo, he frescoed the vault of the Capella Colleoni with allegorical figures of Justice, Wisdom, Faith and Charity. In 1737, he was again in Milan to fresco the Chapel of St. Vittore in the Church of St. Amrogio and the ceiling of the sacristy. He created the frescoes of Palazzo Clerici, where he painted the *Course of the Sun on Olympus*. In the 1740s, he executed numerous large-scale secular decorations for Venetian palaces. In the Palazzo Labia, he executed the story of Anthony and Cleopatra. In Wurzburg, he was engaged by Prince Philipp von Greiffenclau to decorate the sumptuous Residenz.

He returned to Italy in 1753 and worked steadily at Florence, at Vicenza and at Venice. In 1759, he returned to Urdine, where his sons joined him, then to Verona to execute his great *Triumph of Hercules*. In 1761, King Charles III of Spain asked him to decorate the new Royal Palace in Madrid. The king commissioned him to fresco the apse of the Church of St. Ildefonso, Aranjuez. Tiepolo died with his brush in his hand.

Tiepolo's *Madonna and Child* is shown on the 1982 Christmas stamp.

226

Robert Troup

Surrender at Saratoga 1777 by Trumbull
US Bicentennial 13 cents

Scott 1728
Born: 1757, ?New York
Died: Janury 14, 1832, New York, New York

Robert Troup's father, also named Robert, was the captain of the privateer *Sturdy Beggar*. His mother was Elinor Bisset. The couple had been married 20 years when Robert was born. According to records in the State of New Jersey, his father died in 1768 and left a will that provided means for young Robert to attain an education. He graduated from King's College (now Columbia University), New York, in 1774. He continued his studies of law in the office of Thomas Smith of Haverstraw, New York, and later with John Jay.

At the outbreak of the Revolution, he was commissioned a lieutenant and assigned to the Continental Army in Long Island. He was made aide-de-camp to Brigadier General Timothy Woodhull. He and three other officers were captured by the British. They were taken aboard the *Jersey*. On December 9, 1776, he was freed at the Provost Prison, New York City, in a prisoner-of-war exchange, and was assigned to the Army stationed in New Jersey.

On October 4, 1777, he was advanced to lieutenant colonel and was attached to General Horatio Gates as a staff officer. He took part in the Battle of Stillwater and was present at the surrender of Burgoyne on October 17, 1777.

He was appointed secretary of the newly created Board of War. In 1779, this board was abandoned, and Troup was transferred as secretary of the Board of the Treasury. He resigned from the Army and returned to study law with William Paterson and Aaron Burr. Troup was elected to the New York State Assembly and was judge of the U.S. District Court of New York in 1796. He was a staunch advocate for New York to adopt the Constitution.

Troup became agent for Sir William Pulteny and, for 30 years, guarded the land transactions, which sold slowly at first and left debts. He worked and lived both in Geneva and New York City as Pulteny's land was bought and settled.

Troup helped found Geneva College (now Hobart and William Smith Colleges) in Geneva and was a backer of the Erie Canal.

On the painting *Surrender of Burgoyne* by John Trumbull on the stamp issued October 7, 1977, Robert Troup is last in line on the far right.

227

John Trumbull

Scott 1361
Born: June 6, 1756, Lebanon, Connecticut
Died: November 10, 1843, New York, New York

John Trumbull was the son of Governor Jonathan Trumbull of Connecticut. A talented drawer in his youth, John Trumbull assisted his father in drawing maps of Connecticut's Western land claims and did some painting. He graduated from Harvard at the age of 17 and taught school until the outbreak of the Revolutionary War. From 1775 until 1777, he served in the Connecticut regiment. He later was an aide to General Washington, then adjutant to General Horatio Gates. He was promoted to colonel before he was 21.

He served as a volunteer in the Rhode Island campaign of 1778. He studied art in Boston. In 1780, he sailed to England to study with Benjamin West. He was seized in London on a trumped up charge of treason and held prisoner. Edmund Burke intervened and arranged his release. Trumbull went to Amsterdam, where he completed a full-length portrait of George Washington.

In 1882, he returned to West's studio. Thomas Jefferson encouraged him to capture scenes of the Revolution for posterity. His *Declaration of Independence*, with 48 portraits, took more than eight years to complete.

In 1793, John Jay invited him to serve as his secretary in England. In 1804, he married Sara Hope Harvey. In 1813, he returned to painting. He was commissioned to do four large canvasses of historical scenes for the rotunda of the U.S. Capitol. It took him seven years to accomplish his assignment. The canvasses include *The Declaration of Independence*, *The Surrender of General Burgoyne at Saratoga*, *The Surrender of Lord Cornwallis at Yorktown* and *The Resignation of General Washington at Annapolis*.

From 1817 to 1836, he was the president of the National Academy of Fine Arts. He gave his unsold paintings to the Trumbull Art Gallery at Yale University. In 1841, he wrote his autobiography.

Trumbull's *The Battle of Bunker Hill* is reproduced on a 1968 stamp.

Jonathan Trumbull

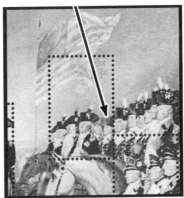

Scott 1686d
Born: March 26, 1740, Lebanon, Connecticut
Died: August 7, 1809, Lebanon, Connecticut

Jonathan Trumbull's parents were Jonathan and Faith Robinson Trumbull of Lebanon, Connecticut. The elder Trumbull was the last Colonial governor of Connecticut from 1769 to 1776 and the first governor of the state. Jonathan Jr.'s brother Joseph was born in 1737. A younger brother, John, the artist, was born 16 years later. Another Joseph Trumbull was born in 1782 and was governor of Connecticut in 1849 and 1850. Another John Trumbull, born in Westbury, Connecticut, was a poet, essayist and judge. Thus, two Jonathans, two Josephs and two Johns have confused history students. Yet another John H. Trumbull served as governor of Connecticut from 1925 to 1931.

Jonathan Trumbull Jr. graduated from Harvard College at the age of 19. He was second in the class in 1759. Three years later he was awarded a master's degree. In 1769, he married Eunice Backus of Norwich, Connecticut. He was elected selectman of Lebanon. He served variously in the state legislature.

On May 28, 1775, Trumbull was chosen paymaster of the New York Department of Military Forces. On July 23, 1778, his brother Joseph died, and five days later Jonathan resigned his post as paymaster in order to settle his brother's affairs. His brother had served as commissary general of the Army.

Trumbull was the first to be elected by Congress as comptroller of the treasury in 1778. He resigned in April 1779. On June 8, 1781, he was appointed secretary to General George Washington. He was elected to the First, Second and Third Congresses. In 1794, he succeeded Stephen Mix Mitchell in the Senate. He resigned in 1795 to serve his state as deputy governor.

Upon the death of Oliver Wolcott in December 1797, he succeeded as governor and served in this post until his death from congestive heart failure in 1809. He had one son and four daughters.

Trumbull is the first equestrian on the right on the fourth stamp of the 1986 Surrender of Lord Cornwallis at Yorktown Bicentennial souvenir sheet.

John Vanderlyn

Scott 118
Born: October 15, 1775, Kingston, New York
Died: September 23, 1852, Kingston, New York

John Vanderlyn's parents, Nicholas and Sarah (Tappen) Vanderlyn, lived in Kingston, Ulster County, where John was born and raised. He attended the Kingston Academy until he was 16. He did odd jobs for a wagon painter and blacksmith, where he first met Aaron Burr. In 1792, his brother Nicholas introduced him to Thomas Barrow, a printseller in New York who hired him. Vanderlyn studied drawing under Archibald Robertson in New York. He copied the portraits of Gilbert Stuart and painted portraits in New York and in Kingston. One Stuart portrait was that of Aaron Burr. The portrait was so well copied that Burr sponsored Vanderlyn to train under Stuart.

After nine months with Stuart, Vanderlyn returned to paint an original portrait of Burr and Burr's daughter, Theodosia. For this, Burr financed Vanderlyn's stay in Paris from 1796 to 1801, where he studied under Antoine Paul Vincent. Vanderlyn returned in 1801 and tried his hand at painting the Niagara Falls. It was engraved and published in London in 1804.

In Paris in 1803 to 1805 and in Rome from 1805 to 1807, he became a good friend of Washington Allston. While in Rome in 1806, he painted *Marius Amid the Ruins of Carthage.* In 1808, it won for him a gold medal at the Paris Salon. He spent another seven years in Paris from 1808 to 1815 and did very well for himself. He traveled in Europe when time permitted. He made copies of the masters in the Louvre. In 1812, he painted his *Ariadne*, a nude figure.

The House of Representatives commissioned Vanderlyn to make a full-length copy of Stuart's Washington in 1832. In 1837, he was commissioned, along with three other artists, to paint historical paintings for the rotunda of the Capitol. He went to Paris to paint *The Landing of Columbus*. He hired a French artist to assist him. Some say the hired artist did most of the work.

Vanderlyn's final years were met with failures. He returned to Kingston in 1852, three weeks before his 77th birthday. He rented a hotel room and was found dead in bed the next morning. He was given a grand funeral by his hometown and buried in Wiltwych Cemetery, Kingston. He never married.

His painting *The Landing of Columbus* is shown on the 15¢ 1869 stamp.

Giovanni de Verrazano

Scott 1258
Born: circa 1485, Greve, near Florence
Died: circa 1529, Darien Island (Panama), Central America

In 1524, King Francis I of France sent Giovanni da Verrazano of Florence westward to seek the coveted passage to the East. Though Verrazano failed to find the passage, he was the first European in recorded history to enter the beautiful harbor of what is today New York.

He probably landed first off the coast of North Carolina, about February. He went north to Newfoundland, passing by or investigating the Hudson River, Manhattan Island and Narragansett Bay.

Verrazano's cruise along this coastline of North America from North Carolina to Newfoundland was a region the Dutch mapmakers henceforth popularized as New France to vent their own derision on Emperor Charles V's comprehensive claims. This gave Francis I the right to claim a portion of the new land in America.

Verrazano returned to France and arrived at Dieppe on July 8, 1524, and recorded the first real description in history of this coastal area of North America. In 1534, Verrazano's success led Jacques Cartier of St. Malo to a series of voyages on which he explored the Gulf and River of St. Lawrence southwest to what is still called Lachine (La Chine, "the China") Rapids. His explorations strengthened French claims to include the sites of Quebec and Montreal and the neighboring northern country.

Verrazano set out on another voyage in 1528, crossing the Atlantic on his way to Central America, the land where Balboa had seen the Pacific Ocean, now Panama. It is possible he intended to go to Brazil, still in search of a passage to the East. Verrazano's life ended somewhere along this voyage. He was either killed and eaten by the Indians on Darien Island (Panama) or hanged as a pirate.

The Verrazano-Narrows Bridge across New York Bay, begun in 1959 and completed in 1964, was named in his honor. It is shown on a 1964 stamp.

George Walton

Scott 1692
Born: 1741, near Farmington, Virginia
Died: February 2, 1804, College Hill, Georgia

George Walton was the son of Robert and Sally Houghes Walton. He apprenticed to a carpenter. He went to Savannah to study law and was admitted to the bar in 1774. He was on the Committee of Correspondence and the Committee of Safety. In 1775, he married Dorothy Camber. He was also a member of the group that organized Georgia's Provisional Congress. He helped draw up the Articles of Association.

Walton was a delegate to the Continental Congress in 1776 and 1777. He signed the Declaration of Independence. He also signed the Articles of Confederation. He served in Congress again in 1780 and 1781.

In 1777, he was appointed colonel of the 1st Regiment of the Georgia Militia. When the British captured Savannah, Walton was taken prisoner. He was in the prisoner exchange of 1779. In November, he was elected governor of Georgia. Walton served only until January 1780.

While he was at the Continental Congress, he was a member of the Commission on Western Lands and treasurer of the Board of Indian Affairs. He was a member of the Executive Committee in Charge of Federal Affairs in Philadelphia. He negotiated a treaty with Six Nations, at Easton, Pennsylvania, in 1777. In 1781, he was appointed commissioner of Augusta, Georgia. In 1783, he negotiated a treaty with the Cherokee Indians in Tennessee.

Walton was chief justice of Georgia from 1783 to 1789. He was elected again as governor from 1789 to 1790 and again chief justice in 1793. In 1788, he was a member of the Georgia Constitutional Convention, which ratified the U.S. Constitution on January 2, and was a presidential elector in 1789.

He served as judge of the Superior Court variously from 1790 to 1804 and served in the U.S. Senate from 1795 to February 20, 1796.

On the second stamp of the 1976 Declaration of Independence set, Walton is the first man seated on the far left.

232

Earl Warren

Scott 2184A
Born: March 19, 1891, Los Angeles
Died: July 9, 1974, Washington, D.C.

Earl Warren earned a doctorate in jurisprudence two years after his bachelor of laws degree in 1912 from the University of California in Berkeley. He was admitted to the California bar in 1914. He was deputy city attorney of Oakland. He served a stint of duty in the Army during World War I.

From 1920 to 1925, he was deputy district attorney, and from 1925 to 1939, he served as district attorney of Alameda County. He was attorney general of California from 1939 to 1943. He was elected governor of California in 1942, 1946 and 1950. President Eisenhower selected Warren as the 14th chief justice of the United States in 1953. He was confirmed by the Senate March 1, 1954.

In 1948, however, Warren had failed to win the title of vice president on the Republican ticket headed by Thomas E. Dewey. He lost the Republican nomination for president in 1952.

As governor of California, Warren favored compulsory flag salute in schools and outlawing the communist party. He was instrumental in the Japanese internment camp disgrace. He had all the earmarks of a conservative, but in the Supreme Court, he took a liberal position. Eisenhower was unhappy with this liberal position. Eisenhower was reported to have said that the appointment of Warren to the court was "the biggest damned-fool mistake I ever made." This remark came after Brown versus Board of Education, the decision that racial segregation in education violated the 14th Amendment. This was on May 17, 1954. Two years later, Congress signed the Southern Manifesto, denouncing the decision and calling for reversal.

During the Kennedy and Johnson administrations, Warren headed a strong liberal majority. From his court came monumental decisions regarding racial discrimination, criminal justice and civil liberties. President Johnson assigned him to investigate the assassination of President Kennedy. Warren offered his resignation to Johnson in 1968, but carried on another year. His career ended while working with the Federal Judiciary Center.

Warren is honored on a stamp issued in March 1992.

Joseph Warren

Bunker Hill 1775 by Trumbull

US Bicentennial 10c

Scott 1564
Born; June 11, 1741, Roxbury, Massachusetts
Died: June 17, 1775, Breed's Hill, Charlestown, Massachusetts

Joseph Warren was the eldest son of Joseph and Mary Stevens Warren and the elder brother of John Warren (1753-1815). When Joseph was 14, his father died. It was 1755, the year Joseph entered Harvard College. Upon graduation in 1759, he taught school as the master of the Roxbury Grammar School. He studied medicine as a student of Dr. James Lloyd. He began practice in Boston in 1764, the year he married Elizabeth Hooton. He was an excellent practitioner. He inoculated John Adams for smallpox, and the two became friends.

Warren espoused the Whig cause and became active in politics. He also became closely associated with Samuel Adams and made a number of speeches at Faneuil Hall. He wrote for the *Boston Gazette*. He was a member of the North End Caucus and other clubs consisting of professional men. After the *Liberty* affair, when John Hancock's sloop was seized, Warren involved himself in meetings supporting the cause with Hancock, Samuel Adams and James Otis.

After the Boston Massacre in 1772, he went with a committee to insist that Governor Hutchinson remove the occupying troops. He was a member of the Committee of Safety. In 1772, he helped draw up a State of Rights of the Colonists. In 1774, he headed the Boston delegation to the county convention and numerous other public duties and activities. He availed himself for most of the important local committees and made another oration on the Massacre.

When the crisis came to a head, he abandoned his practice and became a soldier. He was chosen president pro tempore of the provincial congress. On June 14, 1775, the provincial congress elected him a major general.

On the night of June 16, 1775, while the British were taking over Bunker Hill, Warren sent Paul Revere and William Dawes to warn the countryside. On June 17, Warren took command at Breed's Hill. In the heavy fighting, he was shot by a British soldier and died in the field.

Warren is the central figure lying wounded in the portion of John Trumbull's painting *Battle of Bunker Hill* on the stamp issued June 17, 1975.

234

William Whipple

Scott 1691
Born: January 14, 1730, Kittery, Maine
Died: November 10, 1785, Portsmouth, New Hampshire

William Whipple was the eldest of five children of William and Mary Cutt Whipple. While he was a boy, Whipple took to sea duty, as was usual for boys growing up on a seaport. The town of Kittery is in the far southern tip of the state of Maine. On nearby Badger Island, the *Ranger*, John Paul Jones' ship, was launched in 1777 at the time when Whipple was serving in the Continental Congress and while he was with his militia at Freeman's Farm (Saratoga) and in Rhode Island. In the early 1750s, Whipple became a master of a ship, sailing many ocean voyages and transporting and trading slaves.

Whipple gave up the sea in 1760 and went into partnership with his younger brother Joseph in the mercantile business at Portsmouth. Whipple was an ardent patriot. He joined the provincial congresses and was a member of the provincial council and the State Committee of Safety. He was closely associated with John Langdon of Portsmouth, another seafarer who became a wealthy shipowner and supervised the building of ships for the Continental Navy. This included the building of the *Ranger*.

Whipple negotiated the surrender of Burgoyne. Langdon was also present, although neither are included in John Trumbull's painting memorializing the event. As a member of the Continental Congress in 1776, Whipple signed the Declaration of Independence along with New Hampshire's Josiah Bartlett and Matthew Thornton. Thornton also was not included in Trumbull's painting.

Whipple returned to serve his state in the legislature and as associate justice of the Superior Court. He was married to Catharine Moffatt of Portsmouth. They had no children. He died while on circuit.

Of the men seated behind the men standing, Whipple is the second from the left on the first stamp of the four 1976 Declaration of Independence stamps.

Anne Matilda McNeill Whistler

Scott 737
Born: September 27, 1804, Wilmington, North Carolina
Died: January 31, 1881, London, England

Anne Matilda McNeill was born in Wilmington, South Carolina. On November 3, 1831, she married Major George Washington Whistler. The couple was living in Lowell, Massachusetts, when their eldest son, James Abbott McNeill Whistler, was born. The family went to St. Petersburg, Russia, where her husband supervised the building of a railroad from St. Petersburg to Moscow. While in St. Petersburg she encouraged young Whistler to study at the St. Petersburg Academy of Fine Arts.

In 1849, Major Whistler died, and the Whistlers returned to the United States. Young Whistler's mother encouraged him to attend West Point. He studied at Pomfret, Connecticut, and in 1851 received his appointment to the U.S. Military Academy. He failed chemistry in his junior year and left the academy. He left for Paris in 1855 and never returned to America.

In 1863, Anne Whistler went to England to live with her son. In a few years, he painted the famous picture *Arrangement in Grey and Black*, which later he called *Portrait of My Mother*. It is now in the Louvre, Paris. Of the portrait of his mother, Whistler had this to say: "Take the picture of my mother, exhibited at the Royal Academy as an *Arrangement in Grey and Black*. Now that is what it is. To me it is interesting as a picture of my mother: but what can or ought the public to care about the identity of the portrait?"

The public called it *Whistler's Mother*. Of the portrait, Anne Whistler had this to say in a letter to her sister Kate Palmer: "I was not as well then as I am now, but never distress Jemie by complaints, so I stood bravely, two or three days, whenever he was in the mood for studying me his pictures are studies, & I so interested stood as a statue! but realized it to be too great an effort, so my dear patient Artist who is gently patient as he is never wearying in his perseverance — concluded to paint me sitting at my ease." At the end of the letter, she wrote what Jemie said: "Oh Mother it is mastered, it is beautiful!" She concluded the letter: "It was a Mother's unceasing prayer while being the painter's model gave the expression which makes the attractive charm."

Whistler's Mother was chosen for the Mothers of America stamp issued to commemorate Mother's Day, May 2, 1934.

236

Edward Higgins White II

Scott 1331a
Born: November 14, 1930, San Antonio, Texas
Died: January 27, 1967, Kennedy Space Center, Cape Kennedy, Florida

Edward Higgins White II was a lieutenant colonel, a graduate of the U.S. Military Academy in 1952, who transferred to the Air Force. In 1955, he flew F-100s and F-86s with the 36th Fighter Day Wing in Bitburg, Germany, with his West Point track team buddy Edwin "Buzz" Aldrin. White later graduated from the University of Michigan with a master of science degree in aeronautical engineering. He was selected for astronaut training in September 1962. He was the first astronaut from West Point.

White was selected for the flight of *Gemini IV*. He was to fly as pilot with James McDivitt as mission commander. The launch was on June 3, 1965, and the press contingents had gathered at the Cape and in Houston at the newly inaugurated control center. A space walk (Extra Vehicular Activity or EVA) was scheduled for the mission.

White had trained extensively for an EVA. (The cosmonaut Alexei A. Leonov had already accomplished this feat in *Voskhod II* on March 18, 1965.) After a slight delay, when the launch pad gantry stuck, the lift off was flawless. Five minutes later, *Gemini IV* was in orbit. White went through stressful preparation for the EVA while attaching his umbilical system and the emergency oxygen checkpack. While over the Indian Ocean, he opened the hatch, squirted compressed gas from his zip gun and maneuvered himself to the end of his tether. He was in space for 20 minutes testing the effects. He was not disoriented nor did he experience space sickness. One of the photographs showed White floating freely in space, his thruster gun in his right hand, the sun reflecting brightly from his protective visor, and the U.S. flag sewn on his left shoulder documenting him as an American astronaut. The flight ended June 7 with 97 hours, 48 minutes flight time.

On January 27, 1967, the launch team of *Apollo I* mounted the spacecraft atop an operational Saturn IB rocket. At 1 p.m., the astronauts were placed in their seats — Gus Grissom on the left, White in the middle and Roger Chaffee on the right. A fire broke out in the cockpit, and the three astronauts perished.

White is seen making an EVA in the protective spacesuit tethered to the *Gemini IV* capsule on the 1967 Accomplishments in Space stamp.

Stanford White

Stanford White 1853-1906 NYU Library New York

Architecture USA 18c

Scott 1928
Born: November 9, 1853, New York, New York
Died: June 25, 1906, New York, New York

Stanford White was the son of Richard Grant White (1822-85), a well-known Shakespearean scholar, philologist and essayist who contributed many influential articles for New York newspapers and magazines.

Young White's education was erratic, but he showed talent as an artist. A family friend, artist John La Farge, discouraged White from becoming a painter. White joined the firm of architects Gambrill and Richardson. Henry Hobson Richardson, also a family friend, took White under his guidance and involved him in the drafting of Richardson's now famous Boston's Trinity Church. White went to Paris to live with the family of Augustus Saint-Gaudens. He designed the pedestal for Saint-Gauden's memorial statue of Admiral David C. Farragut unveiled at Madison Square in New York City in 1881.

In 1880, White formed a partnership with architects McKim and Mead. White combined many styles until developing the enormous shingled structures such as the Casino at Newport, Rhode Island (1881). He designed and supervised the construction of many luxurious homes in New York City, Newport and the Berkshires. Among his architectural renderings are the Villard Houses, the Century and Metropolitan clubs, the Tiffany and Gorham buildings, the New York Herald Building, the Presbyterian Church at Madison Square Garden (torn down in 1919) and the old Madison Square Garden, where he had an apartment in the tower.

White also designed the buildings of New York University and the University of Virginia. He designed furniture, jewelry, picture frames, stained-glass windows, pedestals for statues, memorial monuments and grave markers. He used his artistic ability to design book and magazine covers as well.

White was attending a performance at the Madison Square Garden Roof when the deranged Harry K. Thaw, a wealthy playboy, jealous of White's former relationship with Thaw's wife, the former chorus girl Helen Nesbit, shot and instantly killed him.

The New York University Library building designed by White was chosen for the first stamp of the American Architecture series issued August 28, 1981.

238

James Wilkinson

Surrender at Saratoga 1777 by Trumbull
US Bicentennial 13 cents

Scott 1728
Born: 1757, Calvert County, Maryland
Died: December 28, 1825, Mexico City, Mexico

James Wilkinson was well schooled by private tutors and early became interested in medicine. He went to Philadelphia to study, but he turned instead to a military career. In 1776, at the age of 19, he was commissioned a captain in the Revolutionary Army. He served in the siege of Boston and then went to Montreal under Benedict Arnold's command. In December 1776, he was made aide-de-damp to General Horatio Gates. He served at Trenton and Princeton under General George Washington and was advanced to lieutenant colonel in 1777 as deputy adjutant general for the northern department.

Wilkinson was present at the surrender of General John Burgoyne and was sent as the messenger to report the victory at Saratoga. Because of his dawdling, it took him 18 days to report. Nevertheless, he was awarded a sword, and Congress brevetted him brigadier general.

In January 1778, he became secretary of the Board of War. He was a hard drinker and could not resist intrigue. He fell in with the Irish soldier of fortune Brigadier General Thomas Conway in a cabal to replace Washington with Gates as commander in chief. For this he was forced to resign his honors.

He served as clothier general, but his accounts became so tangled he was relieved of his duties on March 27, 1781. He married Anne Biddle and took up farming. His greed and his desire for recognition and position spun a career of entanglements, successes and failures.

He bungled business affairs. Wilkinson held various political positions. With profiteering in mind, he exceeded his authority. He faced several court martials and was acquitted repeatedly, then reassigned. He bungled his assignment in Canada and was recalled to Washington, where his career ended. His wife died. He married again in 1810 and, with his wife and daughters, lived on a plantation south of New Orleans. Ever restless, he went to Mexico to obtain a land grant in Texas but died before his acquisition was settled.

Of the two small figures between and behind Burgoyne and Gates on the 1977 Surrender of Burgoyne stamp, Wilkinson is on the right.

Archibald M. Willard

Scott 1631a
Born: August 22/26, 1836, Bedford, Ohio
Died: October 11, 1918, Cleveland, Ohio

Archibald Willard grew up around the Cleveland area until the Civil War. He served as a soldier and flagbearer. He then worked as a painter of carriages. At age 37, he went to New York City to study art. He concentrated on battle scenes that were inspired by his Civil War experiences.

Willard painted at least four versions of a drummer boy, an old man drummer and a fife player rallying up enthusiasm and leading soldiers in a march. In his picture, the flag, which is authentically illustrated with its 13 stars, is prominently displayed between the two adults to the right of center of the scene. Oddly enough, since Willard himself was a color bearer, the bearer of the flag is not visible. He used the son of railway pioneer and builder John H. Devereux as the model for the drummer boy.

This painting, which became familiar to young and old alike, stirred up patriotism. It was originally titled *Yankee Doodle*. But *Yankee Doodle* also was the title of a song composed about 1750 by Dr. Richard Shuckburg, a physician of the British Army at Albany, New York. Dr. Shuckburg intended for the song to poke fun at the Yankee troops. This song first appeared in *A Selection of Scotch, English, Irish, and Foreign Airs* by James Aird. In the early days of the Revolutionary War, the song was used to poke fun at the Colonial soldiers. Colonel Hugh Percy marched his troops to Concord and Lexington singing this tune, but when he was routed by the minutemen, the minutemen chased his troops back to Boston drumming and singing their version of the ditty.

The name of the painting was changed to *The Spirit of '76*. It was painted for the 1876 American Revolution centennial. It was purchased by Devereux, the drummer boy's father, and presented to the town of Marblehead, Massachusetts, where it is displayed in Abbott Hall at Washington Square along with the original deed of £16 that bought the land from the Indians back in 1684.

The Spirit of '76 appears on a strip of three stamps issued in 1976.

William Williams

Scott 1693
Born: April 8, 1731, Lebanon, Connecticut
Died: August 2, 1811, Lebanon, Connecticut

William Williams' father, Solomon Williams, was the pastor of the first Congregational Church. His mother was Mary Porter Williams. Young Williams graduated from Harvard in 1751 and returned home to continue his theological studies with his father. His father's cousin, Colonel Ephraim Williams, serving with the New York forces at Lake George in 1755, took young Williams to serve on his staff. The British won the battle, but Ephraim Williams was injured and died. After the battle, Williams returned to Lebanon.

On February 14, 1771, Valentine's Day, he married Mary Trumbull, the daughter of Jonathan Trumbull (1710-85), the state chief justice of the Supreme Court who was to become the first governor of the state.

Williams was an ardent backer of the cause, writing for his father who was governor during the Revolution and supporting the cause by financing the Ticonderoga troops that captured the fort. He gave up his home to the French officers when they were in Lebanon. He was a colonel in the 12th Regiment but resigned to attend the Continental Congress. He signed the Declaration of Independence. He assisted in framing the Articles of Confederation.

During his lifetime, he served long years in numerous positions. He was selectman of the city of Lebanon, town clerk, member of the lower house of the state, member of the governor's council and on special committees. He was involved in Indian affairs, boundary adjustments and represented Connecticut's common interest in New England. He voted for the adoption of the Constitution for Connecticut at Hartford in 1788. He was judge of the Windham County Court and judge of probate for the Windham District. He had three children.

On the third stamp of the four stamps representing the 1976 Declaration of Independence set, two men are standing behind the three men seated. Williams is the man on the left.

Hugh Williamson

Scott 798
Born: December 5, 1735, West Nottingham, Pennsylvania
Died: May 22, 1819, New York, New York

Hugh Williamson's father, a clothier, came to Chester County, Pennsylvania, from Dublin, Ireland, in 1730. He married Mary Davidson, who had been brought to America from Ireland as an infant and had been captured by Blackbeard the pirate. Hugh studied for the ministry at New London Cross Roads, Chester County, and nearby Newark, Delaware. He excelled in mathematics and was in the first class to graduate from the College of Philadelphia.

The Presbyterian doctrines disgusted him, so he turned to the study of medicine while serving as professor of mathematics at the College of Philadelphia. He studied at Edinburgh, London and Utrecht, where he received his doctor of medicine degree. He returned to Philadelphia to practice medicine.

Medical practice was too harsh for his delicate constitution, so he turned to business. He was appointed to study the transits of Venus and Mercury. He published a paper on comets. In 1773, he went on a mission to the West Indies for an academy at Newark and then to Europe. While in Boston Harbor, he witnessed the Boston Tea Party. He took the news to England and told the Privy Council that revolt in America was imminent. He obtained the Hutchison-Oliver letters that came from Massachusetts and delivered them to Benjamin Franklin. They were published and created a sensation.

Williamson and Franklin collaborated on experiments with electricity. In December 1776, Williamson learned of the Declaration of Independence, and with some dispatches, he sailed for America. His ship was captured off the Delaware capes, but he escaped. He went to Charleston, South Carolina, to start a mercantile business but settled in Edenton, North Carolina, instead. Governor Caswell appointed him surgeon of the state troops.

In 1782, he was a member of the House of Commons and the Continental Congress. He went to the Annapolis Convention in 1786 but was a day late. Governor Caswell appointed him to succeed Willie Jones in the delegation to the Federal Convention in 1787. He signed the U.S. Constitution.

In January 1789, he married Maria Apthorpe. In 1793, he moved to New York and devoted the next 25 years to literary and scientific pursuits.

Williamson is depicted on the 1937 Constitution Sesquicentennial stamp.

Thomas Willing

Scott 1692
Born: December 19, 1731, Philadelphia, Pennsylvania
Died: January 17, 1821, Philadelphia, Pennsylvania

Thomas Willing was the eldest child of 11 children born to Charles and Anne Shippen Willing. Charles Willing was a prosperous merchant in Philadelphia who had emigrated from England. Thomas was sent to England in 1740, at age 9, where his paternal grandparents looked after him. He went to school at Bath and Wells in Somersetshire. When he was 17, he studied at Watt's Academy in London and read English law at the Inner Temple.

He returned to Philadelphia and became a partner with his father. Charles Willing was mayor of Philadelphia. He died of yellow fever. Thomas teamed up with Robert Morris, forming the prosperous Willing, Morris & Company.

In 1763, he was mayor of Philadelphia and the next year was elected to the provincial assembly and served until 1767, when he became justice of the Supreme Court of the province. He was an ardent champion of the rights of the Colonies, but resisted the break from Great Britain.

He served as president of the first Provincial Congress of Pennsylvania in 1774. He was elected to the Second Continental Congress. When Richard Henry Lee of Virginia on June 7 proposed his resolution for independence, Willing voted against it. His English ties were not compatible with the impending conflict, and he did not sign the Declaration of Independence.

He was not re-elected to the Pennsylvania delegation to the Congress, and he lost his seat as justice of the Provincial Supreme Court. When the British occupied Philadelphia, Willing refused to take the oath of allegiance to the king. He worked to keep the mercantile business alive during the war.

In 1781, he was president of the Bank of North America. George Washington selected him to head the Bank of the United States. He was its president from 1791 to 1797. In 1807, he suffered a paralytic stroke. He retired.

On the second stamp of the series of four 1976 Declaration of Independence stamps, of the men seated, Willing is second from the left.

243

Wendell Lewis Willkie

Scott 2193
Born: February 18, 1892, Elwood, Indiana
Died: October 8, 1944, New York, New York

Wendell Willkie was the son of Herman Francis and Henrietta Trisch Willkie. His father practiced law in Elwood, Indiana. Wendell went to school in this agricultural town, northeast of Indianapolis. He completed his bachelor of arts and bachelor of laws degrees from Indiana University at Bloomington. He was admitted to the Indiana bar. He studied at Oberlin College in 1916 and returned to practice law with his father in the Willkie and Willkie law firm. On January 14, 1918, he married Edith Wilk. They had one son, Philip Herman.

Willkie had enlisted in the Army on April 6, 1917, the day war was declared. He served as first lieutenant in the 325th Field Artillery in the Allied Expeditionary Forces overseas and was advanced to captain.

In 1919, he was admitted to the Ohio bar and joined the firm of Mather, Nesbitt and Willkie in Akron. He was a partner in the firm of Weadock and Willkie in New York City. He was admitted to the New York bar in 1930. In 1933, he was selected president of the Commonwealth and Southern Corporation, a utilities holding company that encompassed 11 eastern states. His law firm was known as Willkie, Owens, Otis, Farr and Galligher. He rescued the electric company from failure in the face of goverment competititon from the huge federal Tennessee Valley Authority. By doing so, he became a recognized critic of Franklin D. Roosevelt's New Deal and economic policies.

In 1940, he was selected Republican presidential nominee to oppose Roosevelt. Willkie lost the election by five million votes. After the election, he supported Roosevelt's defense policies but was critical of other issues. He advocated postwar international cooperation, made a trip around the world as the president's personal envoy and wrote *One World*.

His actions alienated him from the Republican stronghold. His cooperation cost him his position as front runner in the Republican Party. He was defeated in the Wisconsin primaries and dropped out of the race. In August 1944, he suffered a fatal heart attack and died in October.

Willkie is portrayed on a Great Americans stamp issued in 1992.

James Wilson

JULY 4,1776

Scott 1692
Born: September 14, 1742, Carskerdy, County Fife, Scotland
Died: August 21, 1798, Edenton, North Carolina

James Wilson was the son of William and Aleson Landale Wilson. He attended the University of St. Andrews, near his home, from 1757 to 1759. He then attended the University of Glasgow and the University of Edinburgh until 1763. He studied accounting, then left for America, arriving in New York in mid-October 1765, when the Stamp Act Congress was meeting.

Through letters of introduction to Richard Peters, the secretary and trustee of the College of Philadelphia, Wilson was given the position of Latin instructor. He was awarded a master of arts degree. But law seemed more promising than teaching. After two years of study, he was admitted to the bar in November 1767. In 1768, he went to Reading, Pennsylvania, to practice law but soon moved to Carlisle, Pennsylvania, where he enjoyed a large practice.

He married Rachel Bird on November 5, 1771. In 1774, he headed the Committee of Correspondence at Carlisle and was elected to the first provincial congress at Philadelphia. He was a delegate to the First Continental Congress.

On May 3, 1775, he was elected colonel of the 4th batallion of Cumberland County Associators. Three days later he was elected to the Second Continental Congress. He signed the Declaration of Independence. He remained in the Continental Congress until 1777. He served in 1783 and again from 1785 to 1786. He was a member of the group who bypassed the Articles of Confederation and composed a workable Constitution. He signed the Constitution. He became the first professor of law at the University of Pennsylvania in 1789 and that same year was appointed associate justice to the U.S. Supreme Court.

Wilson's wife died in 1786 and left him with six children. He married Hannah Gray in 1793. This marriage failed. He was in debt and went to Edenton, North Carolina, where he suffered mental derangement and died.

On the the second stamp of the 1976 Declaration of Independence set, of the men seated, Wilson is third from the right.

245

Edward Winslow

Scott 550
Born: October 18, 1595, Droitwich, Worcestershire, England
Died: May 8, 1655, between Hispaniola and Jamaica, West Indies, at sea

Edward Winslow was one of the wealthier and more educated members of the Pilgrims who sailed to America in 1620. He joined the Separatist congregation of John Robinson and William Brewster at Leiden, Holland, in 1617.

When the Pilgrims formed the colony at Plymouth, it was Winslow's diplomatic dealings with Yellow Father or Chief Massasoit that resulted in a treaty of peace that lasted throughout Massasoit's life. Massasoit died in 1661.

The Winslows suffered severe illness during the first hard winter in Plymouth. His wife died. William White, another shipmate, also died, leaving his wife Susanna and their child, Peregrine, the first child born in the colony. In May 1621, Winslow and Mrs. White were married. This was the first marriage ceremony in the colony.

Winslow and William Bradford wrote about the early experiences of the colonists. This was included in works by George Morton known as *Mourt's Relation* or *A Relation or Journall of the beginning and proceedings of the English Plantation setled at Plimoth in New England* (1622).

Winslow returned to England in the winter of 1623-24 and 1624-25 to bolster English support for aid to the colony. He wrote and published *Good Newes from New England* or *A true Relation of things very remarkable at the Plantation of Plimoth* in 1624. In 1629, he was selected as the colony's official agent and, as such, made many trips to England. In 1635, he was detained by Archbishop William Laud for violating ecclesiastical laws and spent four months in jail. He was governor of the colony in 1633, 1636 and 1644.

Winslow became so involved in the English Civil War that he never returned to America. He undertook various positions with the Commonweath government. In 1654, he went with Admiral William Penn and General Robert Venables in an attempt to seize the West Indies. He was struck down by a fever and died aboard ship. He left a son, Josiah Winslow, born in Plymouth in 1629, who became its governor in 1673 and the following year established the first public school in Plymouth.

Edward Winslow is depicted on the 1920 Pilgrim Tercentenary 5¢ stamp.

John Witherspoon

Scott 1687c
Born: February 5, 1723, Gifford, Haddingtonshire, Scotland
Died: November 15, 1794, Tusculum, near Princeton, New Jersey

John Witherspoon was a prominent Presbyterian minister from Scotland, who was called to America to become one of the College of New Jersey's (now Princeton) early executives. He served New Jersey during the Revolutionary War and was the only clergyman to sign the Declaration of Independence.

Witherspoon was the son of the Reverend James and Ann Walker Witherspoon of Yester Parish. His early education was at the ancient grammar school at Haddington. At 13, he entered the University of Edinburgh. Seven years later he received his divinity degree. In 1745, he was ordained. In 1748, he married Elizabeth Montgomery. Five of their 10 children lived to adulthood.

In 1764, the University of St. Andrews conferred upon him the degree of doctor of divinity. He served the ministry well, writing prolifically and speaking outwardly on controversial religious subjects. He took the conservative side and acted as moderator at the Synod of Glasgow and Ayr. He fought a good fight until 1768, when the College of New Jersey sought him for the presidency of their fledgling institution. He served as president until his death.

In New Jersey, in 1775, he was selected as a member of the Committee of Correspondence. He was a member of the New Jersey Provincial Congress and the Continental Congress from 1776 to 1782. His urging on July 2, 1776, hastened the signing of the Declaration of Independence on July 4. He was a member of the Board of War and the Secret Committee on the Conduct of War.

Through the difficult years from 1785 to 1789, he was engaged in the plan of organizing the Presbyterian Church along national lines. His wife died, and in 1791, he married the young widow Ann Dill, with whom he had two daughters. Witherspoon was blind and ill the last two years of his life. He died at Tusculum, his farm home near Princeton at age 71.

He is shown third from the left on the third stamp of the second American Bicentennial souvenir sheet issued May 29, 1976.

Oliver Wolcott

Scott 1693
Born: November 20, 1726, Windsor, Connecticut
Died: December 1, 1797, Litchfield, Connecticut

Oliver Wolcott's father was Roger Wolcott, colonial governor from 1750 to 1754. His mother was Sarah Drake Wolcott. Oliver was the youngest son of 15 children. He attended Yale, graduating in 1747. In 1745, he was commissioned by Governor George Clinton as captain of a company that fared poorly on a French Canadian expedition. After the peace treaty of 1748, he returned home. He studied medicine but gave it up. His father owned land in Litchfield County, and when the county was being organized in 1751, young Wolcott went to Litchfield to become its sheriff for the next 20 years. On January 21, 1755, he married Laura Collins, with whom he had five children.

Wolcott held various local offices. He was judge of the Court of Probate for Litchfield and judge of the county courts in Litchfield. In 1771, he was a major in the militia. He was advanced to colonel in 1774 and went to Boston to confer with General Gage. He was commissioner of Indian affairs in the Northern Department meeting with Six Nations at Albany.

He was elected to the Continental Congress in October 1775 and attended regularly until 1783. He supported the Declaration of Independence and belatedly signed it in October. He was a brigadier general. In 1777, he joined Gates against Burgoyne. As a major general in 1779, he defended the Connecticut seacoast. He was involved with the Treaty of Fort Stanwix in 1784 to make peace with Six Nations. He was chosen lieutenant governor in 1787. In 1789, he concluded a treaty with the Wyandottes.

On the death of Samuel Huntington, he became governor of Connecticut. As a presidential elector, he voted for Adams and Pinckney in 1797. He died in December 1797. One son, Oliver, was governor of Connecticut from 1817 to 1827. Thus three generations of Wolcotts were Connecticut governors.

On the third stamp of the four 1976 Declaration of Independence stamps, two men are standing behind the three men seated. Wolcott is on the right.

George Wythe

Scott 1691
Born: 1726, Elizabeth City County (now Hampton), Virginia
Died: June 8, 1806, Richmond, Virginia

The legal act of inheriting property played an important role in the life and death of George Wythe. He was the son of a wealthy family in Virginia. When he was 3 years old, his father died. In the will, the entire family estate was inherited by his brother. He briefly attended the grammar school of the College of William and Mary. His studies were focused almost entirely on law.

When Wythe was 20, he was admitted to the bar. He married Ann Lewis, but she died during their first year of marriage. He moved to Williamsburg, where he practiced law as a legislative clerk, then as the attorney general and member of the House of Burgesses. In 1755, he married Elizabeth Taliaferro. The same year he inherited the family estate from his brother. Within five years, he was enjoying a flourishing law practice and the tutorship of law students in his office, one being Thomas Jefferson.

Wythe opposed the proposed Stamp Act in 1765. At first, he advocated autonomy for the Colonies within the British Empire but then supported the revolution for independence. He was a delegate to the Second Continental Congress and signed the Declaration of Independence.

He returned to Williamsburg in 1776, becoming a judge and legal educator. With Jefferson, George Mason and Edmund Pendleton, he drew up the law code for the state of Virginia. He was elected one of the three justices of the High Court of Chancery in 1778. He participated in the Constitutional Convention of 1787 and advocated Virginia's ratification of the Constitution.

He was the first professor of the newly organized Law School of William and Mary College from 1779 to 1790. He died at age 80, after being poisoned by a grand-nephew seeking inheritance. Before he died, he disinherited the youth. After his death, his slaves were freed.

On the first stamp of the four 1976 Declaration of Independence stamps, of the men seated behind the men standing, Wythe is the first on the far left.

St. Francis Xavier

Scott 1443
Born: April 7, 1506, Xavier Castle, Navarre, Spain
Died: December 3, 1552, Shang-ch'uan Tao Island (near Canton), China

Francisco de Yasu y Xavier was the youngest son of Juan de Yasu, an official of Navarre, and Maria Aznarez de Sada, Xavier y Azpilcueta. When Xavier was 9, his father died, and his elder brothers were considered by Spain as traitors to France. Xavier and his mother were left in poverty.

Xavier was destined to be a missionary. In 1525, he entered the University of Paris. His roommate at the College de St. Barbe was Peter Favre of Savoy. By 1530, Xavier began teaching classes on Aristotle at the College de Dormains-Beauvais and studying theology. Ignatius Loyola arrived in Paris in 1528, and during the last two years of Favre's and Xavier's magisterium, Loyola was their mentor. In 1534, Francis and six others vowed with Loyola to form the Society of Jesus. Two years later they met in Venice. They traveled to Rome to visit Pope Paul II, who authorized their ordination.

Francis Xavier was ordained at Venice on June 24, 1537. In September 1540, Pope Paul III approved the Society of Jesus. John II of Portugal recruited two missionaries from Loyola for work in the eastern Portuguese colonies. Xavier was sent to Goa, India, on April 7, 1541. However, he became ill and spent the winter in Mozambique. He didn't arrive in Goa until May 6, 1542. This was his headquarters. From Goa, he went to the southern area to work among the Paravas of the Fishery Coast. This consumed two years of his time.

In 1545, he set out for Malacca by way of Madras and Ceylon, arriving in September. He returned to Malacca in May 1547. In 1549, with three Japanese and two Jesuits, Francis set out for Japan, arriving in Kagoshima on August 15, 1549. In Japan, he converted about 2,000 people.

He sailed to the island of Shang-ch'uan Tao near Canton, China. A Chinese trader promised to smuggle him into Canton but failed to appear. Xavier was stranded. On November 21, 1552, he was struck with a serious fever and, on December 3, he died. His body was returned to Goa and placed in the Church of Bom Jesus. He was canonized in 1622. In 1929, Pope Pius XI declared St. Francis Xavier to be the patron saint of missions. His feast day is December 3.

San Xavier del Bac Mission in Tucson was named for St. Francis. It is shown on the fourth stamp of the 1971 Historic Preservation issue.

250

Frederick Coffay Yohn

Herkimer at Oriskany 1777 by Yohn
US Bicentennial 13 cents

Scott 1722
Born: February 8, 1875, Indianapolis, Indiana
Died: June 5, 1933, Norwalk, Connecticut

Frederick Yohn was the son of Albert Brown and Adelaide Ferguson Yohn. His father was a partner in the Yohn Brothers booksellers of Indianapolis. Yohn's parents were scholarly and artistic, and taught him to draw. While in high school, he drew portraits at the Republican state convention that were published by an Indianapolis newspaper in lieu of photographs.

He studied at the Indianapolis Art School. He spent three years at the Art Students' League in New York City, under Henry Siddons Mowbray. He opened his own art studio on New York's 23rd Street. He enjoyed painting and drawing pictures depicting action. He was inspired by the works of Adolphe Menzel, Daniel Vierge, Edwin Abbey, Howard Pyle and Alphonse de Neuville.

In January 1908, he married Gertrude Klamroth, a musician, and moved to Westport, Connecticut. In 1910, he moved to the Silvermine Guild of Artists, four miles northwest of Norwalk on the Silvermine River. The first year of his professional career, he received a commission to illustrate James Barnes' *For King or Country*. In 1898, he illustrated, in part, Henry Cabot Lodge's article in *Scribner's Magazine*, titled The Story of the Revolution. For *Scribner's Magazine*, he went to England and completed 17 illustrations for Theodore Roosevelt's article Oliver Cromwell. He illustrated such books as *The Little Shepherd of Kingdom Come*, *The Trail of the Lonesome Pine* and others by John Fox Jr., as well as books by Mary Johnston, D.D. Wiggins, F.H. Barnett, Frederick Palmer, Jack London and others. He painted Spanish-American War scenes for *Collier's Weekly* and official war pictures for *Scribner's Magazine*, showing all branches of the service, though he never witnessed a battle.

In 1930, the *Boston Herald* published his five paintings of the Massachusetts Bay Colony. More than 100 of his works are in the Library of Congress.

Yohn was an adherent to detail and authenticity. His drawings and paintings provide picture references for historians. His painting *Herkimer at Oriskany* appears on the 1977 13¢ American Bicentennial stamp.

Count Ferdinand von Zeppelin

Scott C13
Born: July 8, 1838, Konstanz, Baden, Germany
Died: March 8, 1917, Charlottenburg (Berlin), Germany

Ferdinand von Zeppelin was the son of a court official of the old German state, the constitutional monarchy of Wurttemburg. He began his advanced education at the Ludwigsburg Military Academy, then proceeded to the University of Tubingen. In 1859, he was given a military commission. Four years later, he was in the United States applying his military expertise with the Army of the Potomac in the midst of the Civil War.

After the war, he joined a party of adventurers to the headwaters of the Mississippi. While in Minnesota, he experienced an ascent in a lighter-than-air balloon, his introduction to a field for which his name would one day be famous.

In 1866, Zeppelin was back in Europe and engaged in the Seven Weeks' War, fighting for Wurttemburg against the Prussians. This was a prelude for the Franco-Prussian War of 1870-71. Zeppelin was a cavalry officer. He remained in the army until 1891, when he retired with the rank of general.

Free to ply his curiosity of balloons and lighter-than-air craft, he spent most of his money experimenting with dirigible balloons. Nearly broke, he received financial help from the imperial treasury and funds raised through public subscription. By 1900, he had developed a dirigible, the LZ-1, that flew for 20 minutes. It had a metal framework that contained a series of gasbags separated by wire bracings. Zeppelin had problems with the elements. Wind wrecked his crafts, sending them crashing. Escaping hydrogen gas caused fires.

By 1910, a commercial ship was developed that was used for sightseeing. It was named the *Delag*. By 1914, Zeppelin had built 30 lighter-than-air ships. During World War I, Germany produced 72 more such aircraft.

But frequent disasters did not stop the development of the ships. The most successful was the *Graf Zeppelin*, 776 feet long and with a total of 3.9 million cubic feet volume. It made a trip around the world in 1928 and flew many notable voyages without a single mishap. It was retired in 1939.

Other ships were not so fortunate, and their disastrous terminations squelched the advancement of the likes of the *Graf Zeppelin*. Zeppelin's dream of huge lighter-than-air luxury liners filling the skyways was ripe when he died in 1917, but the airplane and the jet supersonic airliner has replaced his dream.

Zeppelin's name and airship appears on three 1930 airmail stamps, and the *Graf Zeppelin* airship is depicted on the 1933 Century of Progress airmail issue.

252

Topical Index

Stutz, Harry Clayton

Aviation, Astronautics:
Aldrin, Edwin Eugene "Buzz," Jr.
Armstrong, Neil Alden
Irwin, James Benson
Lindbergh, Charles Augustus
Piper, William Thomas
Quimby, Harriet
Scott, David Randolph
White, Edward Higgins II
Zeppelin, Count Ferdinand von

Blacks:
DuBois, William E.B.
Matzeliger, Jan Ernest

Children:
Columbus, Diego (son)
Baby Jesus

Educators:
Humphrey, Hubert Horatio
Karman, Theodore von
Moore, Clement Clark
Thomson, Charles
Williamson, Hugh
Wilson, James

Engineers:
DeForest, Lee
Karman, Theodore von
Marconi, Guglielmo

Entertainers:
Abbott, William A. "Bud"
Benny, Jack
Bergen, Edgar
Brice, Fanny
Costello, Lou
Hardy, Oliver Nowell
Jacobs, Lou
Laurel, Arthur Stanley Jefferson
Ringling, John

Explorers:
Aldrin, Edwin Eugene "Buzz," Jr.
Armstrong, Neil Alden
Cabrillo, Juna Rodriguez
Columbus, Bartholomew
Columbus, Diego (brother)
Escobedo, Rodrego de
Hudson, Henry
Irwin, James Benson
Ojeda, Alonso de
Pinzon, Martin Alonso
Pinzon, Vincente Yanez
Sanchez, Rodrego
Scott, David Randolph
Verrazano, Giovanni de
White, Edward Higgins II

Government and Diplomacy:
Adams, Samuel
Alden, John
Armstrong, John
Bartlett, Josiah
Bassett, Richard
Bedford, Gunning
Blair, John
Blount, William
Brearly, David
Broom, Jacob
Butler, Pierce
Carroll, Charles
Carroll, Daniel
Carver, John
Chase, Samuel
Chavez, Dennis
Clark, Abraham
Clinton, George
Clymer, George
Columbus, Bartholomew
Columbus, Diego (brother)
Columbus, Diego (son)
Dayton, Jonathan
Ellery, William
Floyd, William
Gadsden, James

Gerry, Elbridge
Gilman, Nicholas
Gorham, Nathaniel
Hancock, John
Harrison, Benjamin
Hart, John
Hewes, Joseph
Hooper, William
Hopkins, Stephen
Hopkinson, Francis
Humphrey, Hubert Horatio
Huntington, Samuel
Ingersoll, Jared
Jackson, William
Jenifer, Daniel of St. Thomas
Johnson, William Samuel
King, Rufus
Langdon, John
Lee, Richard Henry
Lewis, Francis
Livingston, Philip
Lynch, Thomas, Jr.
McHenry, James
McKean, Thomas
Middleton, Arthur
Mifflin, Thomas
Minuit, Peter
Morris, Gouverneur
Morris, Lewis
Nelson, Thomas
O'Neill, William Owen "Buckey"
Otis, Samuel Allyne
Paca, William
Paine, Robert Treat
Paterson, William
Pinckney, Charles
Pinckney, Charles Cotesworth
Rush, Benjamin
Rutledge, Edward
Rutledge, John
St. Clair, Arthur
Schuyler, Philip John
Sherman, Roger
Spaight, Richard Dobbs

Standish, Miles
Stockton, Richard
Stone, Thomas
Thomson, Charles
Troup, Robert
Trumbull, Jonathan
Walton, George
Warren, Earl
Whipple, William
Williamson, Hugh
Willing, Thomas
Wilson, James
Witherspoon, John
Wolcott, Oliver
Wythe, George

Human Rights:
DuBois, William E.B.
Clinton, George

Indians:
Powhatan

Inventing, Science and Technology:
DeForest, Lee
Fust, Johann
Karman, Theodore von
Marconi, Guglielmo
Otis, Elisha Graves
Piper, William Thomas
Stanley, Francis Edgar
Stutz, Harry Clayton
Zeppelin, Count Ferdinand von

Law and Order:
Bedford, Gunning
Blair, John
Brooks, John
Chase, Samuel
Chavez, Dennis
Clark, Abraham
Cobb, David
Ellery, William

Grosvenor, Thomas
Heyward, Thomas
Hooper, William
Huntington, Samuel
Ingersoll, Jared
King, Rufus
McKean, Thomas
Paca, William
Paine, Robert Treat
Paterson, William
Pinckney, Charles
Pinckney, Charles Cotesworth
Read, George
Rutledge, Edward
Rutledge, John
Sherman, Roger
Stockton, Richard
Troup, Robert
Warren, Earl
Whipple, William
Willkie, Wendell Lewis
Wilson, James
Wolcott, Oliver
Wythe, George

Military, Hunting and Arms:

Aldrin, Edwin Eugene "Buzz," Jr.
Armstrong, John
Armstrong, Neil Alden
Bouquet, Henry
Brooks, John
Cobb, David
Dayton, Jonathan
Dearborn, Henry
Eastman, Seth
Forbes, John
Gadsden, James
Grosvenor, Thomas
Heyward, Thomas
Iwo Jima Marines
Jackson, William
Laurens, John
Lewis, Morgan
Lincoln, Benjamin

Lynch, Thomas Jr.
Mifflin, Thomas
Morgan, Daniel
Nelson, Thomas
O'Neill, William Owen "Buckey"
Parker, John
Phillips, William
Pitcairn, John
Prescott, William
Read, George
Riedesel, Friedrich Adolph von
Scammell, Alexander
Schuyler, Philip John
Scott, David Randolph
Troup, Robert
Trumbull, John
Trumbull, Jonathan
Warren, Joseph
Wilkinson, James

Musicians, Composers:

Porter, Cole

Photography:

Brady, Matthew B.

Physicians:

Bartlett, Josiah
Brooks, John
Rush, Benjamin
Warren, Joseph
Williamson, Hugh

Pilgrims and Pioneers:

Alden, John
Allerton, Isaac
Blount, William
Bradford, William
Brewster, William
Carver, John
Minuit, Peter
Standish, Miles
Sutter, John Augustus
Wilkinson, James

Bibliography
A listing with suggested further reading

Abigail Adams: *Those Who Love,* Irving Stone; *Abigail Adams,* Janet P. Whitney; *Abigail Adams, An American Woman,* Charles W. Akers; *The First Ladies: Intimate Biographical Portraits of the President's Wives from Martha Washington to Pat Nixon,* Sol Bargman; *Abigail Adams, A Biography,* Phyllis Lee Levin (Ballantine Books, 1988); *The Adams Chronicles,* Jack Shepherd (Little, Brown & Co., Boston, 1975); *Adams, An American Dynasty,* Francis Russell (American Heritage, 1976); *Presidential Wives: An Anecdotal History,* Paul F. Boller, Jr. (Oxford 1988)

John Adams: *John Adams* (2 vols.), Page Smith; *Honest John Adams,* Gilbret Chinard; *The Complete Book of U.S. Presidents,* William A. De Gregorio; *The Presidents: A Reference History,* Charles W. Akers, Henry F. Graff, Ed.; *The Adams Chronicles,* Jack Shepherd; *Adams, An American Dynasty,* Francis Russell; *Debrett's Presidents of the United States of America,* David Williamson

John Quincy Adams: *John Quincy Adams, "Old Man Eloquent,"* Bennet C. Clark; *John Quincy Adams, Biography,* Marie B. Hecht; *The Complete Book of U.S. Presidents,* William A. De Gregorio; *The Presidents: A Reference History,* Edward Pessers, Henry F. Graff, Ed.; *The Adams Chronicles,* Jack Shepherd; *Adams, An American Dynasty,* Francis Russell; *Debrett's Presidents of the United States of America,* David Williamson; *Profiles in Courage, "He'd Rather be Right,"* John F. Kennedy (Harper and Brothers, 1955)

Samuel Adams: *Sam Adams, Pioneer in Propaganda,* John C. Miller (Boston, 1936)

Jane Addams: *Jane Addams,* James W. Linn; *Forty Years at Hull House,* Jane Addams; *Beloved Lady (Jane Addams),* J.C. Farrell

Louisa May Alcott: *Louisa May Alcott: Her Life, Letters, and Journals,* Ednah D. Cheney

Edwin Eugene Aldrin Jr.: *Men from Earth,* "Buzz" Aldrin (Bantum Book, NY, July 1989); *Return to Earth,* Edwin Eugene Aldrin Jr.

Horatio Alger: *Alger, a Biography Without a Hero,* Herbert R. Mayes; *Horatio Alger,* Ralph Gardner

Ethan Allen: *Ethan Allen,* Steward H. Holbrook; *Ethan Allen,* John Pell

Susan B. Anthony: *Susan B. Anthony: Rebel, Crusader, Humanitarian,* Alma Lutz; *The Life and Work of Susan B. Anthony* (2 vols.), H. Husted

Edwin Howard Armstrong: *Man of High Fidelity: Edwin Howard Armstrong,* Lawrence Lessing

Neil Alden Armstrong: *Man's Reach for the Stars,* Roy A. Gallant

Henry Harley Arnold: *Harley "Hap" Arnold: Dictionary of American Military Biography* (3-vols.), Ed. Roger J. Spilter; *Hap: General of the Air Force Henry Arnold,* Thomas Coffey; *Global Mission,* H.H. Arnold

Chester Alan Arthur: *Chester A. Arthur: A Quarter Century of Machine Politics,* George F. Howe; *The Complete Book of U.S. Presidents,* William A. De Gregorio; *The Presidents: A Reference History,* Bernard A. Weisberger, Henry F. Graff, Ed.; *Presidents of the United States of America,* David Williamson

John James Audubon: *John James Audubon,* John Burroughs; *John James Audubon,* Alice Ford; *John James Audubon,* Margaret & John Kieran (Random House, NY, 1954); *Mr. Audubon's Lucy,* Lucy Kennedy (Crown, NY, 1957); *John James Audubon,* M. Keam Cleary (Crescent)

Stephen Fuller Austin: *The Life of Stephen F. Austin,* Founder of Texas, 1793-1836, Eugen C. Barker

Vasco Nunez De Balboa: *Life and Letters of Vasco Nunez de Balboa,* Charles L.G. Anderson

Abraham Baldwin: *Abraham Baldwin,* Henry C. White

Benjamin Banneker: *A Pictorial History of Black Americans,* Langston Hughes, Milton Meltzer, and C. Eric Lincoln; *Dictionary of American Negro Biography.* Rayford W. Logan & Michael R. Winston, Eds. (Norton, 1982)

Francois de Barbe-Marbois: *Louisiana in French Diplomacy,* E. Wilson Lyon

258

Bibliography

John Barry: *Gallant John Barry*, William Bell Clark; *The History of Commodore John Barry*, M.J. Griffin

Ethel Barrymore: *Memoirs*, Ethel Barrymore; *The Oxford Companion to American Theatre*, Gerald Bordman; *Actors and Actresses* Vol. 3, James Vinson, Ed.; *The House of Barrymore*, Margot Peters (Knopf, NY, 1990)

John Barrymore: *Confessions of an Actor*, John Barrymore; *Good Night Sweet Prince*, Gene Fowler; *Actors and Actresses*, Vol. 3, James Vinson, Ed.; *The House of Barrymore*, Margot Peters

Lionel Barrymore: *We Barrymores*, Lionel Barrymore; *Actors and Actresses*, Vol. 3, James Vinson, Ed.; *The House of Barrymore*, Margot Peters

Frederic Auguste Bartholdi: *How They Built the Statue of Liberty*, Mary J. Shipiro; *The Statue of Liberty: Birth to Rebirth*, Sue Burchard

Clara Harlowe Barton: *The Life of Clara Barton, Founder of the American Red Cross* (2 vols.), William E. Barton

Alexander Graham Bell: *Alexander Graham Bell, The Man Who Contracted Space*, Catherine Dunlap Mackenzie

Thomas Hart Benton: *An Artist in America*, Thomas Hart Benton

Mary McLeod Bethune: *Mary McLeod Bethune*, Catherine Owens Peare; *A Pictorial History of Black Americans*, Langston Hughes, Milton Meltzer, and C. Eric Lincoln; *Mary McLeod Bethune: A Biography*, Rackham Holt

George Caleb Bingham: *George Caleb Bingham: River Portraitist* (Norman, Oklahoma, 1959)

Hugo LaFayette Black: *Mr. Justice Black*, J.P. Frank

Elizabeth Blackwell: *Pioneer Work on Opening the Medical Profession to Women*; *Autobiographical Sketches*, Dr. Elizabeth Blackwell; *History of Medicine in the United States*, Francis R. Packard

Montgomery Blair: "Montgomery Blair," in *Maryland in National Politics*, Jesse Frederick; "The Public Career of Montgomery Blair, Particularly with Reference to His Services as Postmaster General of the United States," in *Record of the Columbia Historical Society*, XIII

Simon Bolivar: *Simon Bolivar*, Guillermo Sherwell; *Bolivar*, H.R. Lemley; *The Passionate Warrior*, T.R. Ybarra; *Man of Glory, Simon Bolivar*, Thomas Rourke (William Morrow and Company, Inc., 1939)

Daniel Boone: *Daniel Boone*, Reuben Gold Thwaites; *Daniel Boone, Wilderness Scout*, S.E. White; *Master of the Wilderness, Daniel Boone*, William R. Shelton; *Great Lives, Great Deeds*, "Wilderness Trail Blazer," Donald Culross Peattie, (Reader's Digest, 1964)

William Jennings Bryan: *Memoirs of The First Battle*, W.J. Bryan; *Political Evangelist 1860-1908*, Paolo E. Coletta; *Bryan, The Great Commoner*, John C. Long

James Buchanan: *The Life of James Buchanan* (2 vols.) George T. Curtis; *The Complete Book of U.S. Presidents*, William A. De Gregoreo; *The Presidents: A Reference History*, Elbert B. Smith, Henry F. Graff, Ed.

Pearl Sydenstricker Buck: *My Several Years*, Pearl S. Buck

Ralph Johns Bunche: *A Pictorial History of Black Americans*, Langston Hughes, Milton Meltzer, and C. Eric Lincoln; *Ralph Bunche, Champion of Peace*, Jean Gay Cornell; *Ralph Bunche, UN Peacemaker*, Peggy Mann; *Ralph Bunch, Fighter for Peace*, J.A. Kuglemas

Luther Burbank: *Partner of Nature*, Luther Burbank; *Luther Burbank, His Life and Work*, H.S. Williams

John Burgoyne: *Gentleman Johnny Burgoyne*, F.J. Hudleston; *Fathers of the Revolution*, Philip Guedala

Richard Evelyn Byrd: *Alone*, Richard E. Byrd

Antoine Laumet de la Mothe Cadillac: *The History of Detroit and Michigan*, Silas Farmer; *The Story of Detroit*, George B. Catlin

Dorothy Rothchild Parker Campbell: *The Portable Dorothy Parker Introduction*, Brendan Gill (The Vicking Press, NY, 1973)

Andrew Carnegie: *Andrew Carnegie*, Alvin F. Harlow; *Incredible Carnegie*, John K. Winkler; *Autobiography of Andrew Carnegie*, Andrew Carnegie; *Andrew Carnegie*, Joseph

More Who's Who on U.S. Stamps

Frazier Wall (University of Pittsburgh Press, 1970)

Rachael Louise Carson: *Silent Spring*, Rachael L. Carson; *Sea and Earth: The Life of Rachael Carson*, P. Sterling

Philip Carteret: *The Founding of American Civilization; The Middle Colonies*, T.J. Wertenbaker

Enrico Caruso: *Enrico Caruso, His Life and Death*, Dorothy Caruso; *Caruso, His Life in Pictures*, Francis Robinson; *Caruso*, Howard Greenfield; "Enrico Caruso," *Musicians Since 1900, Performing in Concert and Opera*, David Ewen, Ed.

George Washington Carver: *George Washington Carver: An American Biography*, Rackham Holt; *A Pictorial History of Black Americans*, Langston Hughes, Milton Meltzer, and C. Eric Lincoln; *George Washington Carver, Scientist and Symbol*, Linda O. McMurry

Mary Cassatt: *Miss Mary Cassatt, Impressionist From Pennsylvania*, Frederick A. Sweet; *Mary Cassatt*, Forbes Watson; *National Gallery of Art*, John Walker, (Harry N. Abrams Inc., NY, 1984)

Willa Sibert Cather: *Willa Cather Living*, Edith Lewis; *Spokesmen: Modern Writers and American Life*, T.I. Whipple (J.C. Squire, Ed.); *Willa Cather, The Emerging Voice*, Sharon O'Brien (Fawcett Columbine, NY, 1987)

Cary Lane Chapman Catt: *Cary Chapman Catt, A Biography*, Mary Gray Peck

Octave Chanute: *Aviation, An Historical Survey*, C. Gibbs-Smith

John Chapman: *Johnny Appleseed, Man and Myth*, Robert Price

Charles II: *Charles II, King of England, Scotland and Ireland*, Ronald Hutton

Winston Churchill: *Winston Churchill: An Informal Study of Greatness*, Robert L. Taylor (Doubleday and Company, 1952)

George Rogers Clark: *George Rogers Clark, His Life and Public Service*, Temple Bodley; *The Life of George Rogers Clark*, James A. James

Grenville Clark: *World Peace Through Law*, Grenville Clark and L.B. Sohn

William Clark: *Original Journals of the Lewis and Clark Expedition*, (8 vols.), *Meriwether Lewis and William Clark*, Reuben Gold Thwaites, Ed.; *Trails of the Pathfinders*, George Bird Grinnell

Henry Clay: *Life of Henry Clay*, Carl Schurz; *Henry Clay, Spokesman for the New West*, Bernard Mayo; *Henry Clay: Statesman for the Union*, Robert V. Remini (W.W. Norton & Co., NY, 1991)

Samuel Langhorne Clemens (Mark Twain): *The Autobiography of Mark Twain*, Charles Neider, Ed.; *Mark Twain: A Biography* (2 vols.), Albert B. Paine; *A Short Life of Mark Twain*, Albert Bigelow Paine; *Mark Twain's America*, Bernard De Voto; *Mark Twain*, Edgar Lee Masters; *Mark Twain and His World*, Justin Kaplan, (New York, Harmony Books, 1974)

Roberto Clemente: *The Pictorial History of Baseball*, John S. Bowman and Joel Zoss

Stephen Grover Cleveland: *Grover Cleveland: A Study in Courage*, Allen Nevins; *Grover Cleveland: The Man and the Statesman*, Robert McNutt McElroy; *The Complete Book of U.S. Presidents*, William A. De Gregorio; *The Presidents: A Reference History*, John A. Garraty, Henry F. Graff, Ed.; *Debrett's Presidents of the United States of America*, David Williamson

Shobal Vail Clevenger: "Shobal Clevenger; An Ohio Stonecutter in Search of Fame," *Art Quarterly*, Spring, 1966

William F. Cody: *The Life of Buffalo Bill*, William F. Cody (Indian Head Books, Marboro Books Corp., NY, 1991)

George Michael Cohan: *George M. Cohan, Prince of the American Theater*, Ward Morehouse

Christopher Columbus: *Admiral of the Ocean Sea*, (shorter version, *Christopher Columbus, Mariner*), Samuel Eliot Morison; *Christopher Columbus, The Dream and the Obsession, A Biography*, Gianni Granzotto (translation by Stephen Sartarelli); *The Journal of Christopher Columbus*, Cecil Jane, translator; *The Mysterious History of Columbus*, John Boble Wilord (Aldred A. Knopf, NY, 1991); *The Voyages of Columbus*, L. Camusso

Henry T.P. Comstock: *The Story of the Mine*, C.H. Shinn; *The Big Bonanza*, C.B. Glasscock

James Cook: *Captain Cook, Explorer and Navigator*, Y.G. Rowe; *Captain Cook's Voyages*, E.S. Hodgson; *Voyage of Discovery, Captain Cook and the Exploration of the Pacific*, Lynne

Bibliography

Witney (California, 1989); *Great Lives, Great Deeds, "Discoverer Supreme."* (Reader's Digest, 1964)

John Calvin Coolidge; *The Autobiography of Calvin Coolidge,* J.C. Coolidge; *Calvin Coolidge: The Man Who Is President,* William Allen White; *The Complete Book of U.S. Presidents,* William A. De Gregorio; *The Presidents: A Reference History,* Donald R. McCoy, Henry F. Graff, Ed.

James Fenimore Cooper: *James Fenimore Cooper: An Introduction and Interpretation,* Warren S. Walker; *American Men of Letters Series,* T.R. Lounsbury, Ed. by James Fenimore Cooper (his grandson); *Letters and Journals of James Fenimore Cooper,* James Franklin Beard, Ed.; *The Whig Myth of James Fenimore Cooper,* Dorothy Waples

Nicolaus Copernicus: *Nicolaus Copernicus* (Berlin 1883-84), (Vol. 1, 2 parts), Dr. Leopold Prowe; *Copernicus, the Founder of Modern Astronomy,* Bernard I. Cohen

John Singleton Copley: *John Singleton Copley* (2 vols.), Jules David Prown; *John Singleton Copley: American Portraits,* Barbara Neville Parker and Anne Bolling Wheeler

Francisco Vasquez De Coronado: *Coronado, Knight of the Pueblos and Plains,* Herbert E. Bolton; *Coronado's Seven Cities,* George P. Hammond

Crazy Horse: *Crazy Horse, the Strange Man of the Oglalas,* Mari Sandoz; "Crazy Horse" in *American Indian Warrior Chiefs,* Jason Hook; *Crazy Horse, Sacred Warrior of the Sioux,* Jason Hook; *Who was Who in Native American History; Indians and Non-Indians From First Contacts Through 1900,* Carl Waldman (Facts on File, 1990)

David Crockett: *David Crockett: The Man and the Legend,* J.A. Schackford; *Uncommon Americans,* D.C. Seitz; *Crockett: A Bio-Bibliography,* R.B. Hauck

Glenn Hammon Curtiss: *Aviation, An Historical Survey,* C.H. Gibbs-Smith

Harvey Williams Cushing: *History of Medicine in the United States,* Francis R. Packard

Manasseh Cutler: *The Life, Journals, and Correspondence of Manasseh Cutler,* W.P. and Julia P. Cutler

Dante Alighieri: *Dante and His World,* Thomas C. Chubb; *Dante Alighieri* (forward by C.S. Singleton), Paget Toynbee; *Dante,* Thomas G. Bergin

Virginia Dare: *The First Americans, 1607-1690,* T.J. Wertenbaker; *The Colonial Period of American History* (4 vols.), C.M. Andrews

Jefferson Davis: *The Life of Jefferson Davis,* William E. Dodd; *Jefferson Davis* (3 vols.), Hudson Strode; *Jefferson Davis, The Unreal and the Real,* Robert M. McElroy; *Jefferson Davis,* Clement Eaton (Free Press, 1979); *Jefferson Davis, The Man and His Hour, A Bibliography,* William C. Davis

Stephen Decatur: *Life of Stephen Decatur,* A.S. Mackenzie; *First Americans in North Africa,* L.B. Wright and J.H. Macleod

Lee De Forest: *Television, Today and Tomorrow,* Lee De Forest; *Father of Radio,* Lee De Forest

George Dewey: *Autobiography of George Dewey,* George Dewey; *The Life and Letters of Admiral Dewey,* C.M. Dewey, (Ed.)

John Dewey: *Biography of John Dewey,* M.H. Thomas and H.W. Schneider; *John Dewey: Master Educator,* William W. Brickman and Stanley Lehrer, Eds.

Emily Elizabeth Dickinson: *Emily Dickinson: An Interpretative Biography,* Thomas H. Johnson; *The Life and Letters of Emily Dickinson,* Martha D. Bianchi; *The Years and Hours of Emily Dickinson,* Jay Leyda; *Emily Dickinson,* Cynthia G. Wolf (New York, Addisson-Wesley, 1988)

Everett McKinley Dirksen: *Gallant Men, Everett Dirksen* (Grammy Award 1968 on Capitol Records)

Walter Elias Disney: *Directors/Filmmakers,* Vol. 2, Christopher Lyon, Ed.; *Walt Disney's America,* Christopher Finch; *Walt Disney and Other Assorted Characters,* Jack Kinney

Dorothea Lynde Dix: *Life of Dorothea Lynde Dix,* Francis Tiffany; *Dorothea Dix, Forgotten Samaritan,* Helen F. Marshall

John Donne: *The Progress of the Soul: The Interior Career of John Donne,* (New York, 1968); *John Donne Poems,* Sir Herbert Grierson, Ed. (The Franklin Library, Franklin Center, Pennsylvania, 1978)

More Who's Who on U.S. Stamps

Stephen Arnold Douglas: *Stephen A. Douglas: A Study in American Politics*, Allen Johnson; *The Eve of Conflict: Stephen A. Douglas and the Needless War*, G.F. Milton; *Stephen A. Douglas*, Allen Johnson; *The American Statesman Series*, Arthur M. Schlesinger, Jr., Ed. (Chelsea House 1983)

Frederick Douglass: *Frederick Douglass*, Benjamin Quarles; *Life and Writing, Frederick Douglass*, P.S. Foner, Ed. (4 vols.); *Black Writers and the American Civil War; Black Involvement and Participation in the War Between the States*, Richard A. Long, Ed.; *Dictionary of American Negro Biography*, Rayford W. Logan & Michael R. Winston, Eds. (Norton 1982); *Frederick Douglass*, William S. McFeely (W.W. Norton Co., NY, 1991)

Charles Richard Drew: *History of Medicine in the United States*, Francis R. Packard; *Dictionary of American Negro Biography*, Rayford W. Logan and Michael R. Winston, Eds. (Norton, 1982)

John Foster Dulles: *The Eisenhower Years: Affairs of State*, R. Rovere; *Politics and Policy*, J.L. Sundquist; *The Devil and John Foster Dulles*, T. Hoopes; *Dulles, a Biography of Eleanor, Allen and John Foster Dulles and Their Family Network*, Leonard Mosley (Dial, 1978)

Paul Lawrence Dunbar: *Paul Lawrence Dunbar: Poet of His People*, William Brawley; *A Pictorial History of Black Americans*, Langston Hughes, Milton Meltzer, and C. Eric Lincoln; *Dictionary of American Negro Biography*, Rayford W. Logan and Michael R. Winston, Eds.

Jean Baptiste Pointe Du Sable: *A History of Chicago*, Louise Pierce

Amelia Earhart: *The Fun of It*, Amelia Earhart; *Aviation: An Historical Survey*, C.H. Gibbs-Smith; *Last Flight*, Amelia Earhart (Orion, 1988); *The Sound of Wings: The Life of Amelia Earhart*, Mary Lovell (St. Martins Press, NY, 1989); *Amelia Earhart: A Biography*, Doris L. Rich, (Laurel, 1989)

George Eastman: *Photography, A Short Critical History*, B. Newhall

Thomas Alva Edison: *Edison, The Man and His Work*, George S. Bryan; *Edison; His Life, His Work, His Genius*, W.A. Simonds; *Great Lives, Great Deeds, "The Electric Thomas Edison,"* Charles Edison (Reader's Digest, 1964)

Albert Einstein: *The Science and the Life of Albert Einstein*, Abraham Pais; *Einstein*, Ronald W. Clark; *Great Lives, Great Deeds, "He Charted the Cosmos,"* Joseph Phillips (Reader's Digest, 1964); *Einstein: His Life and Times*, Philipp Frank; *Albert Einstein*, Leopold Infeld; *Albert Einstein: A Photographic Biography*, K. Sugimoto

Dwight D. Eisenhower: *Ike, His Life and Times*, Pers Brendon (Harper and Row 1986); *Ike, A Pictorial Biography*, William F. Longgood (Time-Life Books, NY, 1969); *Crusade in Europe*, D.D. Eisenhower; *Eisenhower: A Centennial Life*, Michael R. Beschloss (Harper Collins, NY, 1990); *The Complete Book of U.S. Presidents*, William A. De Gregorio; *The Presidents: A Reference History*, Fred S. Greenstein, Henry F. Graff, Ed.; *Debrett's Presidents of the United States of America*, David Williamson

Charles William Eliot: *The Life of Charles W. Eliot*, E.H. Cotton; *Charles W. Eliot, The Man and His Beliefs*, W.A. Neilson

Thomas Stearns Eliot: *The Achievement of T.S. Eliot*, F.O. Matthiessen; *T.S. Eliot*, Philip R. Headings; *T.S. Eliot: The Man and His Work*, Allen Tate, Ed.; *T.S. Eliot, a Life*, Peter Ackroyd; *T.S. Eliot*, Bernard Bergonzi

Edward Kennedy "Duke" Ellington: *The World of Duke Ellington*, Stanley Dance; *A Pictorial History of Black Americans*, Langston Hughes, Milton Meltzer, and C. Eric Lincoln

Ralph Waldo Emerson: *The Life of Ralph Waldo Emerson*, Ralph R. Rusk; *Ralph Waldo Emerson*, George E. Woodberry; *Ralph Waldo Emerson*, Oscar W. Firkins

John Ericsson: *Yankee from Sweden*, Ruth Morris White; *A Life of Ericsson*, William Conant Church

Leif Erikson: *Voyages to Vinland*, E. Haugen; *The Voyages of the Norsemen to America*, W. Hovgaard; *Norse Discoveries and Exploration of America*, Edward Reman

Douglas Fairbanks: *The Great Movie Stars*, David Shipman; *The Film Encyclopedia*, Ephraim Katz; *Actors and Actresses*, Vol. 3, James Vinson, Ed.

Philo Taylor Farnsworth: *Who Was Who with World Notables*, Vol. 5 (1969-1973), Marquis Who's Who

David Glasgow Farragut: *David Glasgow Farragut* (2 vols.), Charles L. Lewis; *Admiral*

262

Bibliography

Farragut, Alfred Thayer Mahan (Reprint Haskell House, 1968)

William Faulkner: *William Faulkner*, H.M. Campbell and R.E. Foster; *William Faulkner: A Criticale Study*, Irving Howe; *William Faulkner, The Man and the Artist, A Biography*, Stephen B. Oates (New York, Harper and Row, 1987); *William Faulkner*, Fredrick R. Karl

Ferdinand of Aragon: *Ferdinand and Isabella*, Felipe Fernandez-Armesto (Dorset Press, NY, 1975)

W.C. Fields: *W.C. Fields: His Follies and Fortune*, Robert Lewis Taylor; *The Great Movie Stars*, David Shipman; *The Film Encyclopedia*, Ephaim Katz; *Actors and Actresses*, Vol. 3, James Vinson, Ed.

Millard Fillmore: *Millard Fillmore, Biography of a President*, Robert J. Rayback; *The Complete Book of U.S. Presidents*, William A. De Gregorio; *The Presidents: A Reference History*, Norman A. Graebner, Henry F. Graff, Ed.; *Debrett's Presidents of the United States of America*, David Williamson

Edward Joseph Flanagan: *The Romance of the Homeless Boy*, Edward Joseph Flanagan; "Miracle of the Heart," (television movie); "Father Flanagan and Boys Town," *America Magazine* (November 8, 1986), Clifton Stevens; *Dictionary of American Catholic Biography*, John J. Delaney (Doubleday & Co., Garden City, NY, 1984)

Henry Ford: *The Legend of Henry Ford*, Keith T. Sward; *Henry Ford: A Great Life in Brief*, Roger Burlingame; *The Complete History of the Ford Motor Company*, Richard M. Langworth; *The Fords: An American Epic*, Peter Collier and David Horowitz (New York, Summit Books, 1987); *"Tin Lizzie," from U.S.A.*, John Dos Passos (New York, Harcourt, Brace & Company, Inc., 1937); *"King of the Road,"* Joe McCarthy (Holiday, 1957)

Stephen Foster: *Popular American Composers*, David Ewen

Francis of Assisi: *St. Francis of Assisi*, Omer Engelbert (tr. E.M. Cooper); *St. Francis of Assisi*, Johannes Jorgensen; *St. Francis of Assisi*, G.K. Chesteron; *Great Lives, Great Deeds, "Everybody's Saint,"* Donald Culross Peattie (Reader's Digest, 1964)

Benjamin Franklin: *The Autobiography of Benjamin Franklin*, Benjamin Franklin (John Bigelow, Ed); *The Private Franklin*, Claude-Anne Lopez and Eugene W. Herbert; *Benjamin Franklin*, Carl C. Van Doren; *Benjamin Franklin, Englishman and American*, Verner W. Crane; *Benjamin Franklin: Inventor, Statesman, and Patriot*, R. Conrad Stein; *Benjamin Franklin, His Life as He Wrote it*, Esmond Wright, Ed.

John Charles Fremont: *Memoirs of My Life*, John Charles Fremont; *Fremont: Pathmaker of the West*, Allan Nevins; *John Charles Fremont: An Explanation of His Career*, Cardinal L. Goodwin; *John Charles Fremont: Character as Destiny*, Andrew Rolle (1991)

Daniel Chester French: *Memories of a Sculptor's Wife*, Mary French; *Daniel Chester French, Sculptor*, Adeline Adams

Robert Frost: *Robert Frost: The Early Years, 1874-1915* and *Robert Frost: The Years of Triumph, 1915-1938*, Lawrence Thompson

Robert Fulton: *Robert Fulton*, Henry W. Dickinson; *Steamboats Come True*, James Thomas Flexner; *Robert Fulton, A Biography*, Cynthia Owen Philip (Franklin Watts 1985)

Abraham Alfonse Albert Gallatin: *The Life of Albert Gallatin*, Henry Adams; *Albert Gallatin*, Raymond Walters, Jr.

Thomas Hopkins Gallaudet: *Life of Thomas Hopkins Gallaudet*, E.M. Gallaudet

Bernardo de Galvez: *Bernardo de Galvez in Louisiana*, John W. Caughey

Mohondas K. Gandhi: *Gandhi, A Memoir*, William L. Shirer; *Mahatma Gandhi: A Bibliography*, Bal Ram Nanda; *Gandhi, His Life and Message for the World*, Louis Fischer; *Great Lives, Great Deeds, "A Visit with Gandhi,"* Louis Fisher (Reader's Digest, 1964)

James A. Garfield: *James A. Garfield, Party Chieftain*, Robert Granville Caldwell; *The Complete Book of U.S. Presidents*, William A. De Gregorio; *The President: A Reference History*, Bernard A. Weisberger, Henry F. Graff, Ed.; *Debrett's Presidents of the United States of America*, David Williamson

Giuseppe Garibaldi: *Garibaldi*, Denis Mack Smith; *Garibaldi and the Making of Italy*, George M. Trevelyan; *Garibaldi and His Enemies*, Christopher Hibbert

Horatio Gates: *Horatio Gates: Defender of American Liberties*, Samuel W. Patterson

Henry Lou Gehrig: *The New York Yankees: An Illustrated History*, Donald Honig (Crown);

263

More Who's Who on U.S. Stamps

The Greatest First Basemen of All Time, Donald Honig (Crown); *Record Profiles of Baseball's Hall of Famers*, John A. Mercurio (Harper)

Walter F. George: *Congressional Conservatism and the New Deal*, J.T. Patterson

George Gershwin: *George Gershwin: His Journey to Greatness*, David Ewen; *Jazz and the White Americans*, N. Leonard; *George Gershwin's Song-book*, George Gershwin (Herman Wasserman, Ed.)

Amadeo Peter Giannini: *Giannini's Dream*, C. Singer

Lillian Evelyn Moller Gilbreth: *Living With Our Children*, Lillian Gilbreth; *Cheaper By the Dozen*, Frank B. Gilbreth, Jr. and Ermantine Carey

Robert Hutchins Goddard: *Rocket-Development: Liquid-Fuel Rocket Research, 1929-1941*, R.H. Goddard, Esther Goddard and G. Edward Pendray, Eds.

George Washington Goethals: *Goethals, Genius of the Panama Canal*, J.B. and Farnam Bishop; *And the Mountain Will Move*, M.P. DuVal, Jr.

Samuel Gompers: *Seventy Years of Life and Labor*, Samuel Gompers; *Samuel Gompers, Champion of the Toiling Masses*, R.H. Harvey

Ulysses Simpson Grant: *Grant, A Biography*, William S. McFeely; *The Personal Memoirs of U.S. Grant* (2 vols.), U.S. Grant; *The Complete Book of U.S. Presidents*, William A. De Gregorio; *The Presidents: A Reference History*, John Y. Simon, Henry F. Graff, Ed.; *Bruce Catton, U.S. Grant and the American Military Tradition*, Oscar Handlin, Ed. (Little, Brown & Co. 1954); *The Generals: Ulysses S. Grant and Robert E. Lee*, Nancy Scott Anderson and Dwight Anderson (Vintage 1987); *Great American Generals, Ulysses S. Grant*, Vol. 1, (Gallery Books, 1990); *Debrett's Presidents of the United States of America*, David Williamson

Francois J.P. De Grasse: *Triumph of Freedom, 1775-1783*, J.C. Miller; *France in the American Revolution*, J.B. Perkins

Horace Greeley: *Horace Greeley: Nineteenth Century Crusader*, Glyndon G. Van Deusen; *Horace Greeley: Printer, Editor, Crusader*, Henry L. Stoddard

Adolphus Washington Greely: *Reminiscences of Adventure and Service*, A.W. Greely

Nathanael Greene: *Nathanael Greene*, T. Thayer; *The Turning Point of the Revolution*, H. Nickerson

David Wark Griffith: *D.W. Griffith: American Film Master*, Iris Barry; *The Film till Now*, Paul Rotha and Richard Griffith; *Directors/Filmmakers* Vol. 2, Christopher Lyon, Ed.

Thomas Grosvenor: "The Grosvenor Family" in *A Brief History of The Family of Nathan Allen and Mary Putnam, His Wife, Late of Fort Plain, Montgomery County, New York and of the Families of Rev. Aaron Putnam of Pomfret, Conn., the Bukeley, Prescot, Hall, Grosvenor, and Other Families which the Allen Family were Connected by Blood or Marriage*, A.L. Allen (Poughkeepsie, NY, January 10, 1895)

Johannes Gutenberg: *The Origin of Printing in Europe*, Pierce Butler; *A Short History of the Printed Word*, Warren Chappell

Nathan Hale: *Nathan Hale, The Ideal Patriot*, William Ordway Partridge; *Nathan Hale, 1776*, H.P. Johnson

Alexander Hamilton: *The Life of Alexander Hamilton* (2 vols.), John T. Morse Jr.; *Alexander Hamilton, Henry Cabot Lodge, The American Statesman Series*, Arthur M. Schlesinger, Ed.; *Alexander Hamilton*, Henry James Ford

Dag H.A.C. Hammarskjold: *Markings, Dag Hammarskjold*, translated from the Swedish by Leif Sjoberg and W.H. Auden (Alfred A. Knopf, 1964); *The United Nations*, Leland M. Goodrich; *Dag Hammarskjold, The Statesman and His Faith*, Henry P. Van Dusen (Harper & Row, 1967); *Hammarskjold, A Pictorial Biography*, (New York, The Viking Press, 1952); *Dag Hammarskjold: Custodian of the Bushfire Peace*, Joseph P. Lash (Garden City, New York: Doubleday & Co., 1961); *Dag Hammarskjold: A Spiritual Portrait*, Sven Stolpe (New York; Charles Schribner's Sons, 1966)

William Christopher Handy: *Father of the Blues*, W.C. Handy; *American Music*, Gilbert Chase; *The Jazz Tradition*, William Martin; *A Pictorial History of Black Americans*, Langston Hughes, Milton Meltzer and C. Eric Lincoln; *Dictionary of American Negro Biography*, Rayford W. Logan and Michael R. Winston, Eds. (Norton 1982)

John Hanson: *The Strange Story of John Hanson*, H.J. Stoeckel; *The Articles of Confedera-*

Bibliography

tion, Merrill Jensen; *The Birth of the Republic, 1763-1789*, Edmund S. Morgan

Warren Gamaliel Harding: *The Shadow of Blooming Grove: Warren G. Harding in His Times*, Francis Russell; *The Complete Book of U.S. Presidents*, William A. De Gregorio; *The Presidents: A Reference History*, Robert K. Murray, Henry F. Graff, Ed.

Oliver Nowell Hardy: *The Films Till Now*, Paul Rotha and Richard Griffith; *A History of the Movies*, Benjamin Hampton; *The Great Movie Stars*, David Shipman; *The Film Encyclopedia*, Ephraim Katz; *Actors and Actresses*, Vol. 3, James Vinson, Ed.; *Laurel and Hardy* (Chartwell)

William Michael Harnett: *Smithsonian*, "Will the Real William Harnett please stand up," March 1992, Vol. 22, No. 12, page 52

Joel Chandler Harris: *Joel Chandler Harris, Editor and Essayist*, Julia Collier Harris, Ed.; *Joel Chandler Harris: Folklorist*, Brewer Brooks Stella

Benjamin Harrison: *Trilogy: Benjamin Harrison: (1) Hoosier President, (2) Hoosier Statesman, (3) Hoosier Warrior*, Harry J. Sievers S.J.; *The Complete Book of U.S. Presidents*, William A. De Gregorio; *The Presidents: A Reference History*, Louis W. Koenig. Henry F. Graff, Ed.

William Henry Harrison: *Old Tippecanoe: William Henry Harrison and His Times*, Freeman Cleaves; *William Henry Harrison*, Dorothy B. Goebel; *William Henry Harrison: His Life and Times*, James A. Green; *The Complete Book of U.S. Presidents*, William A. De Gregorio; *The Presidents: A Reference History*, Richard P. McCormick, Henry F. Graff, Ed.; *Debrett's Presidents of the United States of America*, David Williamson

Bret Harte: *Mark Twain and Bret Harte*, Margaret Duckett; *Bret Harte: Argonaut and Exile*, Geroge R. Stewart, Jr.

David Hartley: *David Hartley, M.P.: With Bibliography*, G. H. Guttridge (California 1926)

John Harvard: *Out of Smalle Beginnings: An Economic History of Harvard College; the Puritan Period, 1636-1712*, Margery S. Foster; *The Founding of Harvard College*, Samuel Eliot Morison

Nathaniel Hawthorne: *Nathaniel Hawthorne*, Randall Stewart; *Nathaniel Hawthorne*, Mark Van Doren

Rutherford B. Hayes: *Rutherford B. Hayes and his America*, H. Barnard; *Rutherford B. Hayes*, H.J. Eckenrode; *Life of Rutherford B. Hayes* (2 vols.), C.R. Williams; *The Complete Book of U.S. Presidents*, William A. De Gregorio; *The Presidents: A Reference History*, Keith Ian Polakoff, Henry F. Graff, Ed.; *Debrett's Presidents of the United States of America*, David Williamson

George Peter Alexander Healy: *Reminiscence of a Portrait Painter*, George P.S. Healy

Ernest Hemingway: *Papa Hemingway*, A.E. Hotchner (Random House 1966); *Hemingway: And His World*, A.E. Hotchner; *Ernest Hemingway: A Reconsideration*, Philip Young (University Park, Pa. 1966); *Ernest Hemingway: A Life Story*, Carlos Baker (New York 1969)

Patrick Henry: *Patrick Henry*, (3 vols.), William W. Henry; *Patrick Henry: Patriot in the Making*, Robert Douthat Meade; *Great Lives, Great Deeds, "Voice of Liberty,"* Donald and Louise Peattie (Reader's Digest, 1964)

Matthew Alexander Henson: *A Negro at the North Pole*, Matthew A. Henson (New York 1912); *The North Pole*, Robert E. Peary (New York, 1910)

Victor Herbert: *The Story of America's Musical Theater*, David Ewen

Nicholas Herkimer: *Attack on Quebec*, Harrison K. Bird; *Dedication of the Oriskany Monument*, Oneida Historical Society; "Nicholas Herkimer," *Proceedings of the New York State Historical Association* (1904)

James Hoban: "James Hoban, the Architect and Builder of the White House," *American Catholic Historical Researches*, (January, 1907), M.J. Griffin

Hollow Horn Bear: *Who Was Who in Native American History; Indians and Non-Indians From First Contacts Through 1900*, Carl Waldman (Facts on File 1990)

Oliver Wendell Holmes Jr.: *Mr. Justice Holmes and the Supreme Court*, Felix Frankfurter; *The Holmes Reader*, Julius J. Marke, Ed.; *Honorable Justice, The Life of Oliver Wendell Holmes*, Sheldon M. Novick (Little, Brown & Co., 1989); *Justice From Beacon Hill, The Life and Times of Oliver Wendell Holmes*, Liva Baker; *Yankee From Olympus, Justice Holmes and His Family*, Catherine Drinker Bowen (Little, Brown and Company, Boston, 1944); "The Great Dissenter,"

More Who's Who on U.S. Stamps

Beverly Smith, *The American Magazine*, (The Crowell Pub. Co., 1933)

Winslow Homer: *The Life and Works of Winslow Homer*, Gordon Henricks (Harry N. Abrams, Inc., NY, 1979); *Winslow Homer*, K.F. Jennings

Herbert C. Hoover: *Memoirs*, (3 vols.), Herbert Hoover; *Our Unknown Ex-President*, Eugene Lyons (Doubleday and Company, 1948); *The Complete Book of U.S. Presidents*, William A. De Gregorio; *The Presidents: A Reference History*, David Burner, Henry F. Graff, Ed.; *Debrett's Presidents of the United States of America*, David Williamson

Mark Hopkins: *Early Letters of Mark Hopkins*, Anonymous; *Mark Hopkins*, No. 4, Vol. 1, Monographs of the Industrial Education Association, F. Carter and L.W. Spring

Edward Hopper: *Edward Hopper*, R. Gunter Renner; *Edward Hopper*, S. Marker.

Samuel Houston: *Sam Houston, Colossus in Buckskin*, G. Greel; *The Raven: The Life of Sam Houston*, M. James; *Profiles in Courage*, "Sam Houston's Magnificent Last Stand," John F. Kennedy (Harper and Brothers, 1955)

Elias Howe: *Sincere's History of the Sewing Machine*, William Ewers and H.W. Baylor

Julia Ward Howe: *Julia Ward Howe*, Laura E. Richards and Maud Howe Elliott; *Reminiscences*, Julia Ward Howe

Henry Hudson: *Magnificent Adventures of Henry Hudson*, Philip Vail (New York, 1965); *Great Lives, Great Deeds, "The Westward Voyager,"* Llewelyn Pewys (Reader's Digest, 1964)

Charles Evans Hughes: *Charles Evans Hughes*, M.J. Pusey; *Charles Evans Hughes and the Supreme Court*, S. Hendel

Cordell Hull: *Memoirs* (2 vols.), Cordell Hull; *Cordell Hull* (2 vols.), J.W. Pratt

Hubert H. Humphrey: *The Cause in Mankind*, Hubert H. Humphrey (Frederick A. Praeger, Publisher, New York, 1964)

Washington Irving: *The Life of Washington Irving*, (2 vols.), Stanley T. Williams; *The World of Washington Irving*, Van Wyck Brooks; "The Author's Account of Himself," *Selections from The Sketch-Book*, Washington Irving, (The American Book Co. 1901)

Queen Isabella I: *Admiral of the Ocean Sea* (2 vols.), Samuel E. Morison; "Ferdinand V (The Catholic) 1452-1516 and Isabella I 1451-1504" in *100 Greek Kings, Queens and Rulers of the World*, Frank Usher, John Canning, Ed. (Taplinger 1968); *Ferdinand & Isabella*, Filipe Fernandez-Armesto

Iwo Jima: *Iwo Jima: Monument, Memories and the American Hero*, Karal Ann Marling and John Wetenhall (Harvard University Press, 1991)

Andrew Jackson: *The Life of Andrew Jackson*, John Spenser Bassett; *Life of Andrew Jackson* (3 vols.), James Parton; *Andrew Jackson and the Course of American Empire, 1767-1821*, Robert Remini (Harper 1977); *The Complete Book of U.S. Presidents*, William A. De Gregorio

Thomas Jonathan Jackson: *Mighty Stonewall*, Frank Emerson Vandiver; *Lee's Lieutenants, a Study in Command*, (3 vols.), Douglas Southall Freeman; *Stonewall Jackson and the American Civil War* (2 vols.), George F.R. Henderson; *Lee and His Generals*, Captain William P. Snow; *They Called Him Stonewall: A Life of Lieutenant General T.J. Jackson, C.S.A.*, Burke Davis (Fairfax); *The Great American Generals*, Vol. 2, Thomas J. "Stonewall" Jackson (Gallery Books 1990)

John Jay: *John Jay*, Frank Monaghan; *John Jay, the Nation, and the Court*, Richard B. Morris; *John Jay, Defender of Liberty*, F. Monaghan

John Robinson Jeffers: *Robinson Jeffers*, L.C. Powell; *Robinson Jeffers*, Frederic I Carpenter

Thomas Jefferson: *Jefferson the Virginian*, D. Malone; *Thomas Jefferson, A Biography*, Nathan Schachner; *Thomas Jefferson and the New Nation*, Merrill D. Peterson; *Thomas Jefferson, Man of Science*, Silvio A. Bedini (Macmillan, 1989); *Jefferson*, Saul D. Padover; *Thomas Jefferson, an Intimate History*, Fawn M. Brodie (Bantum 1975); *The Complete Book of U.S. Presidents*, William A. De Gregorio; *The Presidents: A Reference History*, Merrill D. Peterson, Henry F. Graff, Ed.; *Debrett's Presidents of the United States of America*, David Williamson

Jesus of Nazareth: *The Illustrated Life of Jesus Christ*, Joseph Rhymer

Andrew Johnson: *Profiles in Courage*, John F. Kennedy; *The Age of Hate: Andrew Johnson and the Radicals*, George F. Milton; *Andrew Johnson and Reconstruction*, E.L. McKitrick; *Andrew Johnson*, Hans L. Trefousese; *The Complete Book of U.S. Presidents*, William A. De Gregorio; *The*

Bibliography

Presidents: A Reference History, Albert Castel, Henry F. Graff, Ed.; *Debrett's Presidents of the United States of America*, David Williamson

Lyndon Baines Johnson: *JFK and LBJ, The Influence of Personality upon Politics*, Tom Wicker; *Sam Johnson's Boy*, Alfred Steinberg; *The Years of Lyndon Johnson, The Path to Power*, Robert A. Caro; *Lyndon Johnson and the American Dream*, Doris Keans Goodwin; *The Complete Book of U.S. Presidents*, William A. De Gregorio; *The Presidents: A Reference History*, Henry F. Graff, Henry F. Graff, Ed.; *Debrett's Presidents of the United States of America*, David Williamson

Louis Jolliet: *Essays Relating to the Jolliet-Marquette Expedition, 1673*, Francis B. Steck; The Life and Voyages of Louis Jolliet, Jean Delanglez

Casey Jones: *Fireside Book of Folk Songs*, Margaret Bradford Boni

John Paul Jones: *John Paul Jones: A Sailor's Biography*, S.E. Morison; *John Paul Jones*, Lincoln Lorenz; *John Paul Jones, Fighting Sailor*, Armstrong Sperry (Random House 1953)

Robert Tyre Jones Jr.: *Golf is My Game*, Robert T. Jones

Scott Joplin: *A Pictorial History of Black Americans*, Langston Hughes, Milton Meltzer, and C. Eric Lincoln; *Dictionary of American Negro Biography*, Rayford W. Logan & Michael R. Winston, Eds.

Chief Joseph: *The Saga of Chief Joseph*, Helen Addison Howard; *Old Chief Joseph and Young Chief Joseph of the Wallowa Nez Perce Indians*, Grace Bartlett, (1967, Joseph, Oregon); *"I Will Fight No More Forever" Chief Joseph of the Nez Perce War*, Merrill D. Beal (Ballantine 1988); *Chief Joseph: Guardian of the Nez Perce*, Jason Hook

Joseph of Nazareth: *Joseph, Dictionary of Saints*, John J. Delaney (Doubleday & Co., Garden City NY 1980)

Kamehameha I: *The Hawaiian Kingdom*, (3 vols.), Ralph S. Kuykendall; *Hawaii: An Informal History*, Gerrit P. Judd

Elisha Kent Kane: *Adrift in the Arctic Ice Pack*, E.K. Kane; *The Second Grinnell Expedition for Sir John Franklin, 1853, '54, '55*, E.K. Kane

Stephen Watts Kearny: *Commerce of the Prairies: or, The Journal of the Sante Fe Trail*, Josiah Gregg; *The Santa Fe Trail*, R.L. Duffus; *Laws for the Government of New Mexico*, S.W. Kearny

Helen Adams Keller: *The Story of My Life*, Helen Keller; *Midstream — My Later Life*, Helen Keller; *Helen Keller, Sketch for a Portrait*, Van Wyck Brooks (E.P. Dutton & Co., NY 1956); *Journey Into Light*, Ishbel Ross (Appleton-Century-Crofts, 1951)

John Fitzgerald Kennedy: *With Kennedy*, Pierre Salinger; *Kennedy*, Theodore C. Sorensen; *The Making of the President, 1960*, Theodore H. White; *The Life and Words of John F. Kennedy*, James Playsted Wood, et al; *John F. Kennedy, Man of the Sea*, Tazewell Shepard Jr., Captain U.S.N. *"John F. Kennedy, Man of the Sea*, Tazewell Shepard Jr., Captain U.S.N. *"John F. Kennedy (1917-1963)" 100 Great Kings, Queens and Rulers of the World*, Jan Fellows-Gordon, John Canning, Ed.; *The Complete Book of U.S. Presidents*, William A. De Gregorio; *The Presidents: A Reference History*, Carl M. Brauer, Henry F. Graff, Ed.; *Debrett's Presidents of the United States of America*, David Williamson

Robert Francis Kennedy: *Heir Apparent: Robert Kennedy and the Struggle for Power*, William V. Shannon; *The Fitzgeralds and the Kennedys: An American Saga*, Doris Kearns Goodwin; *Robert F. Kennedy, The Myth and the Man*, Victor Lasky (Trident Press 1968); *Robert Kennedy in His Won Words*, Robert Kennedy, (New York, Benton Books, 1988)

Jerome David Kern: *Composers in America*, C.R. Reis; *Our Contemporary Composers*, J. T. Howard and A. Mendel

Francis Scott Key: *Francis Scott Key, Author of the Star Spangled Banner*, Francis Scott Key Smith

Martin Luther King Jr.: *Martin Luther King, Jr., In the Mountain Top*, William Roger Witherspoon; *Martin Luther King, Jr., A Peaceful Warrior*, Ed Clayton; *Martin Luther King: A Critical Biography*, David L. Lewis; *The Martin Luther King Story, A Study in Apostasy, Agitation, and Anarchy*, Dr. James D. Bales (Christian Crusade 1967); *The Life and Words of Martin Luther King, Jr.*, Ira Peck (Scholastic 1968); *Let the Trumpet Sound: The Life of Martin Luther King, Jr.*, Stephen B. Oates (Mentor, NY, 1982)

More Who's Who on U.S. Stamps

Henry Knox: *Henry Knox, A Soldier of the Revolution*, Noah Brooks; "General Henry Knox," *Illinois State Historical Society Journal*, (Vol. 18)

Thaddeus Kosciuszko: *Kosciuszko in the American Revolution*, Miecislaus Haiman; *T. Kosciuszko and the Partition of Poland*, Franciszek Rychlicki

Lajos Kossuth: *Ludwig Kossuth*, A. Somogyi; *Memories of My Exile*, L. Kossuth

Marquis de Lafayette: (1) *Lafayette Comes to America*; (2) *Lafayette Joins the American Army*; (3) *Lafayette and the Close of the American Revolution*, Louis Gottschalk; *Lafayette* (2 vols.), Brand Whitlock

Fiorello Henry La Guardia: *The Man La Guardia*, L.W. Limpus and B.W. Leyson; *Making of an Insurgent*, F.H. La Guardia; *La Guardia in Congress*, H. Zinn

Sidney Lanier: *Sidney Lanier, a Biographical and Critical Study*, Aubrey Harison Starke; *The Centennial Edition of Sidney Lanier*, Charles R. Anderson, Ed.

John Langdon: *John Langdon of New Hampshire*, Lawrence Shaw Mayo (Concord, N.H., 1937)

Benjamin Henry Latrobe: *Benjamin Henry Latrobe*, Talbot Hamlin; "Architects of the American Capitol," James Q. Howard in *The International Review*, Vol. i

Frank Charles Laubach: *Forty Years with the Silent Billion*, Frank C. Laubach

A. Stanley J. Laurel: *The Films Til Now*, Paul Rotha and Richard Griffith; *A History of the Movies*, Benjamin Hampton; *The Great Movie Stars*, David Shipman; *The Film Encyclopedia*, Ephraim Katz; *Actors and Actresses*, Vol. 3, James Vinson, Ed.; *Laurel and Hardy*, (Chartwell)

Jason Lee: *History of Methodist Missions, Part I: Early American Methodism*, Wade C. Barclay; *Winning Oregon*, M.C. Jacobs

Robert E. Lee: *Robert E. Lee: A Biography*, (4 vols.), Douglas Southall Freeman; *Lee*, D. S. Freeman (Scribners 1986); *Robert E. Lee*, in *Great American Generals* (Gallery Books 1990); *Robert E. Lee*, Earl Schenck Miers; *The Lees of Virginia*, B.J. Hendrick; *The Lees of Virginia: Seven Generations of an American Family*, Paul C. Nagel (Oxford 1990); *General Lee: His Campaigns in Virginia 1861-1865, With Personal Reminiscences*, Walter H. Taylor; *Gray Fox: Robert E. Lee and the Civil War*, Burke Davis (Fairfax)

Vivien Leigh: *Vivien; The Life of Vivien Leigh*, Alexander Walker, (New York, Wiedenfeld & Nicolson, 1987); *Vivien Leigh, A Biography* by Hugo Vickers.

Meriwether Lewis: *Meriwether Lewis and William Clark, Original Journals of the Lewis and Clark Expedition*, Rueben Gold Thwaites, Ed.; *The Journals of Lewis and Clark*, Bernard DeVoto, Ed.; *Meriwether Lewis*, Richard H. Dillon

H. Sinclair Lewis: *The Art of Sinclair Lewis*, David J. Dooley; *Sinclair Lewis: An American Life*, Mark Schorer

Abraham Lincoln: *Abraham Lincoln, The Prairie Years*, (2 vols.), and *Abraham Lincoln, The War Years*, (4 vols.), Carl Sandburg; *The Complete Book of U.S. Presidents*, William A. De Gregorio; *The Presidents: A Reference History*, Gabor S. Boritt, Henry F. Graff, Ed.; *With Malice Toward None: The Life of Abraham Lincoln*, Stephen B. Oates; *Lincoln, the Man*, Edgar Lee Masters; *Abraham Lincoln, The Boy and the Man*, James Morgan; *Abraham Lincoln: A Biography*, Benjamin P. Thomas; *Life of Lincoln*, Charles Carleton Coffin; *Lincoln, A Novel*, Gore Vidal

Thomas "Tad" Lincoln: *Mary Lincoln, Wife and Widow*, Paul M. Angle; *Mary Lincoln: Biography of a Marriage*, Ruth P. Randall

Charles Augustus Lindbergh: *We, Charles A. Lindbergh*; *The Spirit of St. Louis*, Charles A. Lindbergh; *The Last Hero: Charles A. Lindbergh*, Walter S. Ross; *Lindbergh; A Biography*, Leonard Mosley (Garden City, NY, Doubleday & Company, 1976); *Great Lives, Great Deeds*, "A Thrill that Swept the World," Francis and Katharine Drake (Reader's Digest, 1964)

Walter Lippmann: *Walter Lippmann and the Philosophy of International Politics*, Anwar H. Syed; *Walter Lippmann: a Study in Personal Journalism*, David E. Weingast

Robert R. Livingston: *Chancellor Robert R. Livingston and His Family*, J.L. Delafield

Belva Ann Bennett Lockwood: *A Women of the Century*, Frances E. Willard and Mary A. Livermore

Jack London: *Jack London and His Times: An Unconventional Biography*, Joan London; *Jack London*, Charles Walcutt

Crawford Williamson Long: *Dr. Crawford W. Long*, J. Jackson; *Crawford Williamson*

Bibliography

Long, F.L. Taylor
  Henry Wadsworth Longfellow: *Longfellow: His Life and Work,* Newton Arvin; *Henry Wadsworth Longfellow: Portrait of an American Humanist,* Edward C. Wagenknecht
  Louis XVI: *Louis XVI,* Bernard Fay (translated by Patrick O'Brian); *French Policy and the American Alliance of 1778,* E.S. Corwin
  Juliette Low: *Juliette Low and the Girl Scouts,* Anne Hyde Choate and Helen Ferris
  James Russell Lowell: *The Lowells and Their Seven Worlds,* Ferris Greenslet; *James Russell Lowell: His Life and Word,* Ferris Greenslet; *Victorian Knight-Errant: A Study of the Early Literary Career of James Russell Lowell,* Leon Howard
  Martin Luther: *Luther and His Times,* Ernest G. Schwiebert; *Luther,* Fraz Lau (tr. by Robert Fisher)
  Mary Lyon: *Life of Mary Lyon,* Beth B. Gilchrist
  Clara Maass: *William Crawford Gorgas: His Life and Work,* Marie D. Gorgas and Burton J. Hendrick; *Walter Reed and Yellow Fever,* H.A. Kelley
  Douglas MacArthur: *American Caesar, Douglas MacArthur, 1880-1964,* William Manchester; *Our Jungle Road to Tokyo,* R.L. Eichelberger; *Who Was Who in World War II,* John Keegan, Ed. (Dorset 1991); *MacArthur,* S.L. Myer; *Douglas MacArthur, The Far Eastern General,* Michael Schaller; *The MacArthur I Know,* General George C. Kenney (Duell, Sloan and Pearce, 1951)
  Mary McCauley "Molly Pitcher": *General Charles Lee, Traitor or Patriot,* J.R. Alden
  John McCormack: *Musicians Since 1900, Performers in Concert and Opera,* David Edwin, Ed.; *The Great Irish Tenor,* G.T. Ledbetter; *John McCormack: His Own Life Story,* J. McCormack and P. Key
  Cyrus Hall McCormick: *Cyrus Hall McCormick,* (2 vols.), William T. Hutchinson
  Thomas Macdonough: *History of the U.S. Navy,* D.W. Knox; *Sea Power in Its Relations to the War of 1812,* A.T. Mahan
  Edward Alexander MacDowell: *Edward MacDowell,* Lawrence Goilman; *Our American Music,* John Tasker Howard
  Ephraim McDowell: *History of Medicine,* Fielding H. Garrison; *Ephraim McDowell, Father of Ovariotomy and Founder of Abdominal Surgery,* August Schachner; *History of Medicine in the United States,* Francis R. Packard
  William McKinley: *The Life of William McKinley,* Charles S. Olcott; *The Complete Book of U.S. Presidents,* William A. De Gregorio; *The Presidents: A Reference History,* Paul W. Glad, Henry F. Graff, Ed.; *Debrett's Presidents of the United States of America,* David Williamson
  John McLoughlin: *Dr. John McLoughlin, The Father of Oregon,* Frederick V. Holman; *Winning Oregon,* M.C. Jacobs
  James O'Brien McMahan: *Atoms and Peace,* R. Lapp; *American Scientists and Nuclear Weapons Policy,* R. Gilpin; *The Domestic Control of Atomic Energy,* R.A. Dahl and R.S. Brown
  Dolley Madison: *Memoirs and Letters of Dolley Madison,* Dolley Madison, Lucia B. Cutts, Ed.; *The First Ladies: Intimate Biographical Portraits of the Presidents' Wives, From Martha Washingon to Pat Nixon,* Isabel Ross; *Presidential Wives: An Anecdotal History,* Paul F. Boller, Jr. (Oxford 1988)
  James Madison: *James Madison Builder: A New Estimate of a Memorable Career,* Abbot E. Smith; *The Life of James Madison,* Gaillard Hunt; *The Complete Book of U.S. Presidents,* William A. De Gregorio; *The Presidents: A Reference History,* Ralph Ketcham, Henry F. Graff, Ed.; *Debrett's Presidents of the United States of America,* David Williamson
  Ramon Magsaysay: *The Magsaysay Story,* Carlos P. Romulo and Marvin M. Gray
  Horace Mann: *Horace Mann and the Common School Revival in the United States,* Burke A. Hinsdale
  Carl Mannerheim: *Field-Marshal Mannerheim,* Tancred Borenius; *The Memoirs of Marshal Mannerheim,* C. Mannerheim (tr. by Eric Lewenhaupt)
  Jacques Marquette: *The Life and Voyages of Louis Jolliet,* Jean Delanglez; *The Jolliet-Marquette Expedition,* Francis B. Steck
  George C. Marshall: *George C. Marshall,* Forrest C. Pogue; *The Marshall Story,* R. Payne; *Who Was Who in World War II,* John Keegan, Ed.

More Who's Who on U.S. Stamps

John Marshall: *Life of John Marshall*, (4 vols.), Albert J. Beveridge; *John Marshall*, James B. Thayer, et. al.; *John Marshall*, Albert J. Beveridge; *The American Statesman Series*, Arthur M. Schlesinger, Jr. Ed. (2 vols.); *Great Lives, Great Deeds*, "Inspired Justice," Donald Culross Peattie (Reader's Digest, 1964); *In the Bible*, Alberta Rae (Sune) Richards (The Geographical Publishing Company, Inc., Gastonia, NC 1962).

Thomas G. Masaryk: *T.G. Masaryk*, Eduard Benes; *Defender of Democracy: Masaryk of Czechoslovakia*, E. Ludwig

George Mason: *George Mason, Constitutionalist*, Helen D. Hill

Edgar Lee Masters: *Across Spoon River*, E.L. Masters

Charles Horace Mayo: *The Doctor's Mayo*, Helen Clapesattle

William James Mayo: *The Mayo Legacy*, Gunther W. Nagel; *The Mayo Clinic*, Lucy Wilder

Philip Mazzei: *Recherches Historiques et Politiques sur les Etats-Unis de L'Amerique septentrionale*, P. Mazzei; *Friend of Jefferson: His Life and Letters*, R.C. Garlick Jr.; *Jefferson's "Zealous Whit"*, (1975), Sr. Margherita Marchione, MPF; *My Life and Wanderings*, (1980), Sr. Margherita Marchione, MPF; *Selected Writings and Correspondence*, 3 volumes (English edition 1983 - Italian edition 1984), Sr. Margherita Marchione, MPF; *The Constitutional Society of 1784*, (1984), Sr. Margherita Marchione, MPF

George Meany: *George Meany and His Times*, Archie Robinson (Simon & Schuster, NY, 1981)

Andrew W. Mellon: *Andrew W. Mellon*, Philip H. Love; *Mellon's Millions*, Harvey O'Connor

Herman Melville: *Melville's Early Life and Redburn*, William H. Gilman; *Herman Melville: A Biography*, Leon Howard; *Redburn, His First Voyage*, Herman Melville

Michelangelo: *Great Lives, Great Deeds*, "The Epic of Michelangelo," Donald Culross Peattie (Reader's Digest, 1964); *The World of Michelangelo 1475-1564*, Robert Coughlin, (Time-Life Books, NY, 1966); *Michelangelo*, Frederick Harett (Harry N. Abrams, NY, 1984); *Michelangelo*, Jeffery Daniel; *Michelangelo*, B. Lamarche-Vadel (Konecky & Konecky)

Edna St. Vincent Millay: *Edna St. Vincent Millay and Her Times*, E. Atkins; *Millay in the Village*, A. Cheney

Robert A. Millikan: *Autobiography*, R.A. Millikan

Margaret Mitchell: *Road to Tara: The Life of Margaret Mitchell*, A. Edwards; *Gone With The Wind*, Margaret Mitchell

James Monroe: *James Monroe*, William P. Cresson; *The Complete Book of U.S. Presidents*, William A. De Gregorio; *The Presidents: A Reference History*, Harry Ammon, Henry F. Graff, Ed.

John Bassett Moore: *Realism in American Foreign Policy: The Diplomacy of John Bassett Moore*, Richard Megaree (Northwestern University, 1963)

Robert Morris: *Robert Morris, Patriot and Financier*, Ellis P. Oberholtzer; *Forgotten Patriot: Robert Morris*, Eleanor May Young

Samuel F.B. Morse: *The American Leonardo: The Life of S.F.B. Morse*, Carleton Mabee

Grandma Moses: *Grandma Moses: The Artist Behind the Myth*, Jane Kallir; *My Life's History*, Anna Mary Robertson Moses

Lucretia Coffin Mott: *James and Lucretia Mott, Life and Letters*, Anna D. Hallowell

John Muir: *Alaska Days with John Muir*, S.H. Young; *Life and Letters of John Muir*, W.F. Bad; *The Story of My Boyhood and Youth*, John Muir (Sierra Club 1989)

Ethelbert W. Nevin: Ethelbert Nevin, J.T. Howard

Jean Nicolet: *Wisconsin, Its History and Its People*, M.M. Quaife; *Wisconsin, Its Story and Biography*, A.O. Barton

Chester W. Nimitz: *Nimitz*, E.B. Potter

George W. Norris: *George W. Norris*, R. Lowitt; *The Tennessee Valley Authority*, C.H. Pritchett; *TVA and the Grass Roots*, P. Selznick

Adolph Simon Ochs: *An Honorable Titan, a Biographical Study of Adolph S. Ochs*, Gerald W. Johnson; *The Story of the New York Times, 1851-1951*, Meyer Berger

James Edward Oglethorpe: *James Edward Oglethorpe, Imperial Idealist*, Amos A. Ettinger

Eugene Gladstone O'Neill: *O'Neill*, Arthur Gelb and Barbara Gelb; *Eugene O'Neill*,

Bibliography

Frederic Carpenter
    Jesse Owens: *Blackthink, My Life as Black Man and White Man,* Jesse Owens with Paul Neimark (William Morrow, 1970); *Jesse Owens, An American Life,* William J. Baker (New York, Free Press, 1986)
    Ignacy Jan Paderewski: *Paderewski,* Charlotte Kellogg; *Paderewski: Pianist and Patriot,* Antoni Gronowicz (tr. by J. McEwen)
    Thomas Paine: *Paine,* D.F. Hawke; *Political Writings,* Moncure Daniel Conway, Ed.; *Thomas Paine,* A.J. Ayer; *Great Lives, Great Deeds,* "Crusader for Common Sense," Max Eastman (Reader's Digest, 1964)
    George N. Papanicolaou: "Lax Laboratories," *The Wall Street Journal,* (Vol. 127, No. 88, Western Edition, Monday, November 2, 1988, page 1)
    Dorothy Parker: See Dorothy Rothchild Parker Campbell
    Francis Parkman: *The Journals of Francis Parkman,* Mason Wade; *Life of Francis Parkman,* G.H. Farnham; *Francis Parkman, Heroic Historian,* Mason Wade
    Alden Partridge: *Dictionary of American Military Biography,* Roger J. Spilter
    George S. Patton Jr.: *Patton: The Man Behind the Legend (1885-1945),* Martin Blumenson; *The Patton Papers, 1885-1940,* Martin Blumenson (Hoghton Mifflin 1972); *Portrait of Patton,* Garry H. Semmes; *The Last Days of Patton,* Ladislas Farago (New York, Berkley Books, 1982); *Who's Who in World War II,* John Keegan, Ed. (Dorset 1991)
    Charles Willson Peale: *Charles Willson Peale,* (2 vols.), Charles Coleman Sellers; *Charles Willson Peale and His World,* Edgar P. Richardson, Brook Hindle, and Lillian B. Miller (New York, 1982)
    Robert Edwin Peary: *Peary,* William H. Hobbs; *Secrets of Polar Travel,* Robert E. Peary; *Great Lives, Great Deeds,* "Peary of the Pole," Jo Chamberlin (Reader's Digest, 1964)
    William Penn: *William Penn, 1644-1718,* William W. Comfort; *William Penn,* W.I. Hull; *William Penn,* C.O. Peare; *William Penn, A Biography,* Sidney G. Fisher; *William Penn and the Founding of Pennsylvania, 1680-1684, A Documentary History,* Jean R. Soderland, Ed. (Pennsylvania 1883); *Great Lives, Great Deeds,* "Pioneer of Freedom," Donald Culross Peattie (Reader's Digest, 1964)
    Frances Perkins: *Labor and the New Deal,* M. Derber and E. Young, Eds.; *People at Work,* Frances Perkins
    Matthew C. Perry: *The Great Commodore,* Edward M. Barrows; *Indestructable Commodore Matthew Perry,* Arthur Ormont; *Old Bruin,* S.E. Morison; *Matthew C. Perry,* W.E. Griffis
    Oliver Hazard Perry: *Oliver Hazard Perry,* Charles J. Dutton; *Building of Perry's Fleet in Lake Erie, 1812-1813,* Max Rosenberg
    John Joseph Pershing: *John J. Pershing,* Richard O'Conner
    John Frederick Peto: *The Art of John F. Peto and the Idea of Still-Life Painting in America,* (National Gallery of Art, Exhibition Catalogue, Washington D.C., 1983); *Smithsonian,* "Will the Real William Harnett please stand up," March 1992, Volume 22, Number 12, page 52
    Franklin Pierce: *Franklin Pierce,* Allan Nevins; *Franklin Pierce: Young Hickory of the Granite Hills,* R.F. Nichols; *The Complete Book of U.S. Presidents,* William A. De Gregorio; *The Presidents: A Reference History,* William W. Freehling, Henry F. Graff, Ed.; *Debrett's Presidents of the United States of America,* David Williamson
    Pocahontas: *The Three Worlds of Captain John Smith,* Philip L. Barbour; *Seventeenth Century America: Essays in Colonial History,* J.M. Smith, Ed.; *Jamestown 1544-1699,* Carl Bridenbaugh; *Pocahontas and Her World,* Philip L. Barbour; *Who Was Who in Native American History; Indians and Non-Indians From First Contacts Through 1900,* Carl Waldman (Facts on File 1990)
    Edgar Allan Poe: *Edgar Allan Poe: The Man Behind the Legend,* Edward C. Wagenknecht; *The Complete Works of Edgar Allan Poe* (Biography Contemporary Notices), James A. Harrison, Ed.; *Edgar Allan Poe: His Life and Legacy,* Jeffrey Meyer (Scribners, 1992)
    James Knox Polk: *James K. Polk* (2 vols.), Charles Coleman Sellers; *The Complete Book of U.S. Presidents,* William A. De Gregorio; *The Presidents: A Reference History,* David M. Pletcher, Henry F. Graff, Ed.; *Debrett's Presidents of the United States of America,* David Williamson

More Who's Who on U.S. Stamps

Juan Ponce de Leon: *Ponce de Leon*, F.A. Ober; *A History of the United States*, Vol. 1, Edward Channing; *The Coming of the White Man*, H.I. Priestley

Cole Porter: *Cole Porter, a Biography*, Charles Schwartz (Dial Press, NY, 1977); *The World of Music, A Treasury for Listener and Viewer*, K.B. Sandved, Ed., (The Waverley Book Company Ltd., London, 1957); *Cole: A Biographical Essay* by Brendan Gill, Robert Kimball, Ed. (Holt, Rinehart & Winston, NY, 1971)

David Dixon Porter: *The Life of David Dixon Porter*, R.S. West Jr.

Wiley Post: *Aviation, An Historical Survey*, C.H. Gibbs-Smith

John Wesley Powell: *Biographical Memoir of John Wesley Powell* (National Academy of Sciences, Biographical Memoirs, Vol. 8), William M. Davis; *Canyon Voyage: Second Powell Expedition*, F.S. Dellenbaugh

Joseph Priestley: *Life of Joseph Priestley*, A. Holt; "The Never Views of Priestley and Lavoisier," *Annals of Science*, 1941

Casimir Pulaski: *Dictionary of American Military Biography*, Roger J. Spilter

Joseph Pulitzer: *Pulitzer*, William A. Swanberg; *Joseph Pulitzer: Front Page Pioneer*, Iris Noble; *Joseph Pulitzer*, D. Seitz

Rufus Putnam: *Putnam's 1886 Journal: The Memoirs of Rufus Putman and Certain Official Papers and Correspondence*, (Marietta, Ohio, College Library), Rowela Buell, Ed.

Ernest Taylor Pyle: *Ernie Pyle in England, Here is Your War*; and *Brave Men*, E.T. Pyle; *Ernies's War, The Best of Ernie Pyle's World War II Dispatches*, David Nichols, Ed. and Biographer; *The Story of Ernie Pyle*, Lee Miller

Red Cloud: *The American Heritage Book of Indians*, Alvin M. Josephy, Ed. and William Brandon; *Sioux Indian Leaders* (Chapter 6), Mildred Fielder; *Who Was Who in Native American History; Indians and Non-Indians From First Contacts Through 1900*, Carl Waldman (Facts on File 1990); *Red Cloud and the Sioux Problem*, James C. Olson; *Bury My Heart at Wounded Knee*, Dee Brown

Walter Reed: *Microbe Hunters*, Paul De Kruif; *Walter Reed and Yellow Fever*, H.A. Kelly

Frederic Remington: *Frederic Remington, Artist of the Old West*, Harold McCracken; *Frederic Remington's Own West*, Harold McCracken, Ed.; *Frederic Remington*, James K. Ballinger (Harry N. Abrams, NY, 1989); *Frederic Remington: The Masterworks*, Michael Edward Shapiro and Peter H. Hawssrick, et al. (Abradale Press, Harry N. Abrams, NY, 1991); *Frederic Remington*, S. Craze (Crescent)

Ernst Reuter: *City On Leave: A History of Berlin 1945-1962*, Philip Windsor

Bernard Revel: *The New Standard Jewish Encyclopedia*, Geoffrey Wigoder, Ed.

Paul Revere: *Paul Revere and the World He Lived In*, Esther Forbes; *Paul Revere*, Emerson G. Taylor

James Whitcomb Riley: *The Youth of James Whitcomb Riley and the Maturity of James Whitcomb Riley*, Marcus Dickey; "James Witcomb Riley," *Century Magazine* (October 1927), Edgar Lee Masters

John Ringling: *The Ringlings*, Alvin F. Harlow (New York, 1951); *Circus King*, Henry Ringling North (New York, 1960); *Those Amazing Ringlings and Their Circus*, Gene Plowden (Caldwell, Ohio 1967)

Norman Rockwell: *My Adventures as an Illustrator*, Norman Rockwell; *The Rockwell Portrait, An Intimate Biography*, Donald Walton (Sheed Andrews and McMeel, Inc., Kansas City, 1978)

Jack Roosevelt Robinson: *I Never Had It Made*, Jack R. Robinson (1972); *Wait Till Next Year*, Carl Thomas Rowan; *Jackie Robinson*, Maury Allen; *Baseball's Great Experiment: Jackie Robinson and His Legacy*, Jules Tygiel (Oxford, Oxford University Press, 1983); *Record Profiles of Baseballs Hall of Famers*, John A. Mercurio (Harper)

Comte de Rochambeau: *Rochambeau*, Jean E. Weelen; *Rochambeau, Father and Son*, Jean E. Weelen (tr. by Lawrence Lee)

Knute K. Rockne: *Autobiography of Knute Rockne*, Knute Rockne (1931); *American Football: Its History and Development*, Alexander M. Weyland; *Rockne: The Coach, The Man, The Legend*, Jerry Brondfield

James Charles Rodgers: *My Husband Jimmy Rodgers*, Carrie Rodgers; *The Country Music*

Bibliography

Book, Michael Mason, Ed.; *Million Selling Records*, Joseph Murrell

William P.A. "Will" Rogers: *Will Rogers, His Life and Times* (An American Heritage Biography), Richard M. Ketchum; *The Great Movie Stars*, David Shipman; *The Film Encyclopedia*, Ephraim Katz; *Actors and Actresses*, Vol. 3, James Vinson, Ed.; *Autobiography of Will Rogers*, Donald Day, Ed.; *Great Lives, Great Deeds*, "The Uncommon Will Rogers," Eddie Cantor (Reader's Digest, 1964)

Anna Eleanor Roosevelt: *This I Remember and This Is My Story*, E. Roosevelt; *Eleanor Roosevelt*, T.K. Hareven; *Eleanor and Franklin*, J. Lash; *The First Ladies: Intimate Portraits of the President's Wives from Martha Washington to Pat Nixon*, Sol Bargman; *Presidential Wives; An Anecdotal History*, Paul F. Boller, Jr. (Oxford 1988)

Franklin Delano Roosevelt: *Franklin D. Roosevelt*, (4 vols.), Frank B. Freidel; *The Roosevelt I Knew*, Frances Perkins; *F.D.R., A Biography*, Ted Morgan; *Franklin D. Roosevelt: A Rendezvous with Destiny*, Frank Friedel (Little, Brown 1989); *Franklin D. Roosevelt: His Life and Times, An Encyclopedic View*, Otis L. Graham, Jr. & Meghan Robinson Wander, Eds. (DaCapo 1990); *The Roosevelt Myth*, John T. Flynn (The Devin-Adair Company, NY 1956); *The Complete Book of U.S. Presidents*, William A. De Gregorio; *The Presidents: A Reference History*, David M. Kennedy, Henry F. Graff, Ed.; *Debrett's Presidents of the United States of America*, David Williamson

Theodore Roosevelt: *The Rise of Theodore Roosevelt*, Edmund Morris; *Theodore Roosevelt*, Henry F. Pringle; *Theodore Roosevelt: An Autobiography*, T. Roosevelt; *The Complete Book of U.S. Presidents*, William A. De Gregorio; *The Presidents: A Reference History*, Richard M. Abrams, Henry F. Graff, Ed.; *Debrett's Presidents of the United States of America*, David Williamson

Elizabeth Griscom "Betsy" Ross: *The Evolution of the American Flag*, L. Balderston; *Origin and History of the American Flag*, G.H. Preble

George Ross: *Rossiana*, H.P. Read

Charles Marion Russell: *Charles Russell*, S. Craze (Crescent)

George Herman "Babe" Ruth: *My Dad, The Babe*, Dorothy Ruth Pirone. *The Pictorial History of Baseball*, John S. Bowman and Joel Zoss; *Babe Ruth*, Martin Weldon; *The Babe and I*, Bill Slocum; *The Babe as I Knew Him*, Waite Hoyt; *The New York Yankees: An Illustrated History*, Donald Honig (Crown); *Record Profiles of Baseball's Hall of Famers*, John A. Mercurio (Harper); *Great Lives, Great Deeds*, "The Sultan of Swat," Jack Sher, (Reader's Digest, 1964) and (Sport, 1946)

John Rutledge: *Mr. Rutledge of South Carolina*, Richard Barry (1942)

Sacagawea: *Lewis and Clark, Partners in Discovery*, John Bakeless; *The Course of Empire*, Bernard De Voto

Augustus Saint-Gaudens: *Augustus Saint-Gaudens*, B. Hollingsworth; *The History of American Sculpture*, Lorado Taft

Haym Salomon: *Finances of the United States from 1775-1789*, C.J. Bullock

William Thomas Sampson: *The Santiago Campaign*, Joseph Wheeler; *Rear Admirals Schley, Sampson and Cervera*, James Parker;

Jose de San Martin: *San Martin, the Liberator*, John C. Metford; *San Martin, Knight of the Andes*, Ricardo Rojas

Carl Sandburg: *Carl Sandburg: A Bibliography*, North Callahan; *The America of Carl Sandburg*, Hazel Durnell; *Carl Sandburg*, Richard Crowder; *Great Lives, Great Deeds*, "Prophet in Poetry," Ralph McGill (Reader's Digest, 1964); *Carl Sandburg, A Biography*, Penelope Niven (Charles Scribner's Sons, NY, 1991)

Santa Claus: *Knickerbocker's History of New York*, Washington Irving

Winthrop Sargent: *Mississippi Through Four Centuries*, Richard A. and Nannie P. McLemore

William Saroyan: *Saroyan, A Biography*, Lawrence Lee & Barry Gifford (Harper & Row, NY, 1984)

Winfield Scott Schley: *Forty-Five Years Under the Flag*, Winfield Scott Schley; *The Campaign of Santiago de Cuba* (3 vols.), Herbert H. Sargent; *Rear Admirals Schley, Sampson and Cervera*, James Parker

More Who's Who on U.S. Stamps

Carl Schurz: *Carl Schurz, Militant Liberal*, Joseph Schafer; *The Americanization of Carl Schurz*, Chester V. Easum

Blanche Stuart Scott: *Aviation, An Historical Survey*, C.H. Gibbs-Smith

Winfield Scott: *Winfield Scott, the Soldier and the Man*, Charles W. Elliott; *Old Fuss and Feathers: The Life and Exploits of Winfield Scott*, Arthur Douglas Howden Smith

Sequoya: "The Life and Work of Sequoya," *Chronicles of Oklahoma* (June 1930), J.B. Davis; *Who Was Who in Native American History: Indians and Non-Indians From First Contacts Through 1900*, Carl Waldman (Facts on File 1990)

Junipero Serra: *Junipero Serra: The Man and His Work*, A.H. Fitch; *The Founding of Spanish California*, C.E. Chapman

John Sevier: *John Sevier as a Commonwealth Builder*, James R. Gilmore; *History of the Lost State of Franklin*, S.C. Williams

William Henry Seward: *William Henry Seward*, Glyndon G. Van Deusen; *The Alaska Purchase*, J.M. Callahan

William Shakespeare: *Shakespeare: A Biographical Handbook*, Gerald E. Bentley; *Shakespeare's Life and Times: A Pictorial Record*, Roland M. Frye; *Shakespeare: His World and His Work*, Max M. Reese; *William Shakespeare: A Compact Documentary Life*; the Rev. Ed. S. Schoenbaum; *Shakespeare*, Martin Fido

Philip Henry Sheridan: *Sheridan*, Joseph Hergesheimer; *Sheridan the Inevitable*, Richard O'Connor

Roger Sherman: *Roger Sherman, Signer and Statesman*, Roger Sherman Boardman (1938)

William T. Sherman: *Sherman, Fighting Prophet*, Lloyd Lewis; *William Tecumseh Sherman*, James M. Merrill; *The General Who Marched To Hell: Sherman and The Southern Campaign*, Earl Schenck Miers (Dorset 1990); *William T. Sherman*, Vol. 4 of *Great American Generals* (Gallery Books, 1990)

Igor Sikorsky: *Igor Sikorsky, His Three Careers in Aviation*, Frank J. Delear; *History of Aviation*, John W.R. Taylor and Kenneth Munson, Ed. (pages 216-219)

Sitting Bull: *Sitting Bull, Champion of the Sioux*, Stanley Vestal; "Surrender of Sitting Bull" *South Dakota Historical Collection*, E.H. Allison; *Great Indian Chiefs*, Albert Britt; *"The True Story of the Death of Sitting Bull" Proceedings and Collections*, Vol. 2, Nebraska State Historical Society, E.G. Fechet; *Bury My Heart at Wounded Knee*, Dee Brown

Alfred E. Smith: *Al Smith and His America*, Oscar Handlin; *Al Smith: Hero of the Cities*, Matthew and Hannah Josephson

John Smith: *Captain John Smith: His Life and Legend*, Bradford Smith; *Captain John Smith*, Everett H. Emerson; *The Three Worlds of Captain John Smith*, Philip Barbour; *Jamestown 1544-1699*, Carl Bridenbaugh; *The Works of Captain John Smith*, (3 vols.) Philip Barbour, Ed.

William Saroyan: *Saroyan: A Biography*, Lawrence Lee & Barry Gifford

John Philip Sousa: *The March King and his Band: The Story of John Philip Sousa*, Kenneth W. Berger; *Men of Music*, Herbert Weinstock; *Marching Along*, J.P. Sousa

Elmer Ambrose Sperry: *Elmer Sperry, Inventor and Engineer*, Thomas P. Hughes; *Great Moments in Aviation*, Michael J.H. Taylor

Lawrence B. Sperry: *Aviation, An Historical Survey*, C.H. Gibbs-Smith

Francis Edgar Stanley: *Theories Worth Having*, Francis E. Stanley; *Motoring in America, The Early Years*, Frank Oppel, Ed.

Edwin McMasters Stanton: *The Life and Public Service of Edwin M. Stanton*, 2 vols., George C. Gorham (Boston 1899); *Edwin McMasters Stanton, Lincoln's Great War Secretary* (New York, 1905); *Stanton, The Life and Times of Lincoln's Secretary of War*, Benjamin P. Thomas and Harold D. Hyman (Knopf, 1962)

Elizabeth Cady Stanton: *Eighty Years and More*, Elizabeth Cady Stanton; *Elizabeth Cady Stanton as Revealed in Her Letters, Diary and Reminiscences*, T. Stanton and H.S. Blatch

Vilhjalmur Stefansson: *Unsolved Mysteries of the Arctic*, V. Stefansson; *My Life with the Eskimo*, V. Stefansson

John Steinbeck: *John Steinbeck*, Warren G. French; *The Wide World of John Steinbeck*, Peter Lisca; *Steinbeck: A Life in Letters*, Elaine Steinbeck and Robert Wallsten (Penquin Books, 1976)

Bibliography

Charles P. Steinmetz: *Loki: The Life of Charles Proteus Steinmetz,* J.N. Leonard; *Charles Proteus Steinmetz,* J.W. Hammond; *The Electrical Genius of Liberty Hall,* Floyd Miller (McGraw-Hill Book Co., 1962)

Baron Von Steuben: *General Von Steuben,* J.M. Palmer

Adlai Ewing Stevenson: *Adlai Stevenson,* Lillian Ross; *Adlai Stevenson: Patrician Among Politicians,* Bert Cochran; *Adlai Stevenson: A Study in Values,* Herbert J. Muller; *Adlai Stevenson, His Life and Legacy, A Biography,* Porter McKeever (New York, William Morow & Co., 1989)

Harlan Fiske Stone: *Harlan Fiske Stone,* A.T. Mason

Lucy Blackwell Stone: *The History of Woman Suffrage,* Susan B. Anthony, Elizabeth Cady Stanton, and Mathilda Gage

Igor F. Stravinsky: *Chronicles of My Life, I. Stravinsky;* Stravinsky, A. Tansman; "Igor Stravinsky," *Horizon,* Vol. 1, No. 1

Gilbert Charles Stuart: *Gilbert Stuart,* James Thomas Flexner; *Gilbert Stuart,* Charles Mount

Harry Clayton Stutz: *Motoring in America, The Early Years,* Ed. by Frank Oppel

Peter Stuyvesant: *Peter Stuyvesant: An Historical Documentation,* Martha Eerdmans, Ed.; *A Landmark History of New York,* Albert A. Ulmann

Anne Mansfield Sullivan: *Anne Sullivan Macy: The Story Behind Helen Keller,* Nella Braddy; *Teacher: Anne Sullivan Macy; a Tribute by the Foster-Child of Her Mind,* Helen Adams Keller

John Sullivan: *Dictionary of American Military Biography,* Roger J. Spilter

Sun Yat-sen: *Sun Yat-sen: His Life and Its Meaning,* Lyon Sharman; "Sun Yat-Sen (1866-1925)," Ian Fellows-Gordon, *100 Great Kings, Queens and Rulers of the World,* John Canning, Ed. (Taplinger 1967); *The Man Who Changed China: The Story of Sun Yat-Sen,* Pearl S. Buck (Random House, NYC, 1953)

Robert A. Taft: *A Foreign Policy for Americans,* Robert A. Taft; *A Man of Courage,* Robert A. Taft, Caroline T. Harnsberger; *The Tafts, An American Family,* Isabel Ross

William Howard Taft: *American Family: The Tafts,* Isabel Ross; *The Life and Times of William Howard Taft* (2 vols.), Henry F. Pringle; *The Complete Book of U.S. Presidents,* William A. De Gregorio; *The Presidents: A Reference History,* Paolo E. Coletta, Henry F. Graff, Ed.; *Debrett's Presidents of the United States of America,* David Williamson

Henry Ossawa Tanner: *A Pictorial History of Black Americans,* Langston Hughes, Milton Meltzer, and C. Eric Lincoln; *Dictionary of American Negro Biography,* Rayford W. Logan and Michael R. Winston, Ed. (Norton 1982)

Zachary Taylor: *Zachary Taylor,* Holman Hamilton; *Zachary Taylor* (Southern Biography Series), Bernard Dyer; *The Complete Book of U.S. Presidents,* William A. De Gregorio; *The Presidents: A Reference History,* Norman A. Graebner, Henry F. Graff, Ed.; *Debrett's Presidents of the United States of America,* David Williamson

Nikola Tesla: *Tesla, Man Out Of Time,* Margaret Cheney; "Nikola Tesla," *Science,* Vol. 127, Kenneth M. Swezey; *Lightning in His Hand — The Life Story of Nikola Tesla,* Inez Hunt and Wanetta W. Draper; *The Inventions, Researches and Writing of Nicola Tesla,* Nikola Tesla

Sylvanus Thayer: *Dictionary of American Military Biography,* Roger J. Spilter

Henry David Thoreau: *The Magic Circles of Walden,* Charles R. Anderson; *Walden,* William David Thoreau; *Thoreau,* J.W. Krutch; *The Heart of Thoreau's Journals,* O. Shepard, Ed.; *Henry Thoreau: A Life of the Mind,* Robert D. Richardson Jr. (California, 1986); "Thoreau at Walden," from *The Flowering of New England,* Van Wyck Brooks, (New York, E. P. Dutton & Company, Inc., 1936)

James F. Thorpe: *American Football: Its History and Development,* Alexander M. Weyand

Arturo Toscanini: *Arturo Toscanini: An Intimate Portrait,* Samuel Chotzinoff (Alfred A. Knopf, New York, 1956)

Harry S. Truman: *Truman,* Ray Jenkins; *Mr. President: The First Publication from the Personal Diaries, Private Letters, Papers and Revealing Interviews of Harry S. Truman, Thirty-second President of the United States of America,* William Hillman, Ed.; *Memoirs* (2 vols.), H.S. Truman; *Plain Speaking; An Oral Biography of Harry S. Truman,* Merle Miller (Berkley 1974); *Where the Buck Stops,* Margaret Truman, Ed. (New York, Warner Books, 1989); *Debrett's*

More Who's Who on U.S. Stamps

Presidents of the United States of America, David Williamson; *Truman,* David McCullough (New York, Simon & Shuster, 1929)

John Trumbull: *John Trumbull,* Irma B. Jaffe (1975)

Sojourner Truth: *The Narrative of Sojourner Truth,* Olive Gilbert and William Lloyd Garrison; *A Pictorial History of Black Americans,* Langston Hughes, Milton Meltzer, and C. Eric Lincoln; *Dictionary of American Negro Biography,* Rayford W. Logan and Michael R. Winston, Eds. (Norton 1982)

Harriet Tubman: *Harriet, the Moses of Her People,* Sarah H. Blackford; *Harriet Tubman,* Earl Conrad; *A Clouded Star,* Anne Parish; *A Pictorial History of Black Americans,* Langston Hughes, Milton Meltzer, and C. Eric Lincoln; *Dictionary of American Negro Biography,* Rayford W. Logan and Michael R. Winston, Eds. (Norton 1982)

Mark Twain: See Samuel Clemens

John Tyler: *John Tyler, Champion of the Old South,* O.P. Chitwood; *The Complete Book of U.S. Presidents,* William A. De Gregorio; *The Presidents: A Reference History,* Richard M. McCormick, Henry F. Graff, Ed.; *Debrett's Presidents of the United States of America,* David Williamson

Martin Van Buren: *The Autobiography of Martin Van Buren,* John C. Fitzpatrick, Ed.: *Martin Van Buren and the Making of the Democratic Party,* R.V. Remini; *The Complete Book of U.S. Presidents,* William A. De Gregorio; *The Presidents: A Reference History,* James C. Curtis, Henry F. Graff, Ed.; *Debrett's Presidents of the United States of America,* David Williamson

Alfred V. Verville: *Aviation, An Historical Survey,* C.H. Gibbs-Smith

John Wayne: *The John Wayne Story,* George Carpozi, Jr., (Arlington House, NY, 1979)

Mary Edwards Walker: *History of Medicine in the United States,* Francis R. Packard

Earl Warren: *Super Chief: Earl Warren and His Supreme Court, A Judicial Biography,* Bernard Schwartz (New York University Press, NY, 1983)

Booker T. Washington: *Booker T. Washington, Educator and Interracial Interpreter,* Basil J. Mathews; *Up From Slavery: An Autobiography,* Booker T. Washington; *Dictionary of American Negro Biography,* Rayford W. Logan and Michael R. Winston, Eds. (Norton 1982); *Great Lives, Great Deeds,* "Apostle of Goodwill," O.K. Armstrong (Reader's Digest, 1964)

George Washington: *George Washington, a Biography,* John R. Alden; *George Washington* (4 vols.), James Thomas Flexner (Little, Brown 1965-1972); *Washington, the Indispensable Man,* James Thomas Flexner (Little, Brown 1974); *George Washington, The Making of an American Symbol,* Barry Schwartz; *George Washington,* John Marshall (Chelse 1983); *Washington,* Douglas Southall Freeman (Scribners 1985)

Martha Custus Washington: *Martha Washington,* Anne Hollingworth Wharton; *The Family Life of George Washington,* Charles Moore; *The First Ladies: Intimate Portraits of the President's Wives from Martha Washington to Pat Nixon,* Sol Bargman; *Presidential Wives; An Anecdotal History,* Paul F. Boller, Jr. (Oxford 1988)

Anthony Wayne: *Anthony Wayne, Trouble Shooter of the American Revolution,* Harry E. Wildes; *Mad Anthony Wayne,* Thomas A. Boyd

Daniel Webster: *Daniel Webster,* Claude Moore Fuess; *Daniel Webster,* Frederick A. Ogg

Noah Webster: *Letters of Noah Webster,* Harry R. Warfel, Ed.; *Noah Webster: Schoolmaster to America,* Harry R. Warfel

Ida Wells: *Dictionary of American Negro Biography,* Raford W. Logan and Michael R. Winston, Eds. (Norton 1982)

Benjamin West: *America's Old Masters,* James Thomas Flexner

Joseph West: *A History of South Carolina, 1865-1960,* Ernest M. Lander; *South Carolina: A Short History, 1520-1948,* David D. Wallace

Edith Wharton: *An Autobiography,* Edith Wharton; *A Backward Glance* (Scribner's 1964); *Portrait of Edith Wharton,* Percy Lubbock; *Edith Wharton: A Study of Her Fiction,* Nevius Blake; *Henry James & Edith Wharton Letter 1900-1915,* Lyall H. Powers, Ed. (Scribner's 1990)

Joseph Wharton: *The Wharton School — Its First Fifty Years,* E.R. Johnson; *General of the Wharton Family,* A.H. Wharton

James Abbott McNeill Whistler: *Whistler,* James W. Lane; *Whistler,* James Laver; *The Man Whistler,* Hesketh Pearson; *I, James McNeill Whistler, An "Autobiography,"* Lawrence

Bibliography

Williams (Simon & Shuster 1972); *Whistler, A Biography*, Stanley Weintraub (NY, Dutton, 1974)

Edwin Higgins White II: *Man's Reach for the Stars*, Roy A. Gallant; *Men From Earth*, Buzz Aldrin & Malcolm McConnell (Bantam Books, NY, 1989)

Paul Dudley White: *History of Medicine in the United States*, Francis R. Packard

William Allen White: *The Autobiography of William Allen White*, W.A. White; *The Man From Kansas*, David Hinshaw; *William Allen White's America*, Walter Johnson; "William Allen White," *Modern Short Biographies and Autobiographies*, Marston Balch (Harcourt Brace 1941)

Walter Whitman: *Walt Whitman, An American: A Study in Biography*, Henry S. Canby; *Walt Whitman, Builder for America*, Babette Deutsch; *Walt Whitman*, Edgar Lee Masters; *Walt Whitman, The Making of the Poet*, Paul Zweig (Basic Books, Inc., NY, 1984); *Great Lives, Great Deeds*, "Poet of Our Land," Max Eastman (Reader's Digest, 1964)

Eli Whitney: *The World of Eli Whitney*, Jeanette Mirsky and Allan Nevins; *Eli Whitney and the Birth of American Technology*, Constance M. Green

John Greenleaf Whittier: *Whittier, Bard of Freedom*, Whitman Bennett; *John Greenleaf Whittier, Friend of Man*, John A. Polland

Harvey Washington Wiley: *An Autobiography*, H.W. Wiley

Charles Wilkes: *Magnificent Voyagers: The U.S. Exploring Expedition, 1838-1842*, Herman J. Viola and Carolyn Margolis, Eds., (Smithsonian 1985)

Frances Elizabeth Caroline Willard: *Glimpses of Fifty Years*, Frances Willard; *Frances Willard: From Prayers to Politics*, Mary Earhart

Roger Williams: *Master Roger Williams*, Elizabeth Winslow; *Roger Williams: His Contribution to American Thought*, Perry Miller; The Irrepressible Democrat: Roger Williams, Samuel H. Brockunier (1940)

Woodrow Wilson: *Woodrow Wilson: The Man, His Times and His Task*, William Allen White; *"Woodrow Wilson" from Masks in a Pagent*, William Allen White, (New York, The Macmillan Company, 1928); *Woodrow Wilson* (2 vols.), Arthur Walworth; *Edith and Woodrow*, Tom Schachtman; *Woodrow Wilson, A Medical and Psychological Biography*, Edwin A. Weinstein; *The Presidency of Woodrow Wilson; Prelude to a World Crisis*, Leon H. Canfield (Fairleigh Dickinson 1966); *The Complete Book of U.S. Presidents*, William A. De Gregorio; *The Presidents: A Reference History*, Arthur S. Link, Henry F. Graff, Ed.; *Debrett's Presidents of the United States*, David Williamson

Carter Godwin Woodson: *A Pictorial History of Black Americans*, Langston Hughes, Milton Meltzer and C. Eric Lincoln; *Walking Proud*, M.S. Scally; *Mis-Education of the Negro*, C.G. Woodson; *Dictionary of American Negro Biography*, Rayford W. Logan and Michael R. Winston, Eds. (Norton 1982)

Frank Lloyd Wright: *An Autobiography*, F.L. Wright; *In the Nature of Materials, 1887-1947, The Buildings of Frank Lloyd Wright*, Henry R. Hitchcock; *Many Masks, a Life of Frank Lloyd Wright*, Brendan Gill (New York, Ballentine Books, 1988); *Frank Lloyd Wright*, Maria Constantino

Orville Wright: *The Wright Brothers*, Fred C. Kelly; *How We Invented the Airplane*, Orville Wright (Fred C. Kelly, Ed.); *Wilbur and Orville, A Biography of the Wright Brothers*, Fred Howard

Wilbur Wright: *Miracle at Kitty Hawk*, Wilbur and Orville Wright (Fred C. Kelly, Ed.); *Wilbur and Orville, A Biography of the Wright Brothers*, Fred Howard

Francis Xavier: *Francis Xavier, Dictionary of Saints*, John J. Delaney (Doubleday & Co., Garden City, NY, 1980)

John Watts Young: *Manned Spacecraft*, Kenneth Gatland; *Man's Conquest of Space*, William R. Shelton; *Astronauts and Cosmonauts Biographical and Statistical Data*, Congressional Research Service Library of Congress

Whitney Moore Young Jr.: *A Pictorial History of Black Americans*, Langston Hughes, Milton Meltzer and C. Eric Lincoln; *Whitney M. Young, Jr.: The Story of a Pragmatic Humanist*, Richard Bruner; *To Be Equal, and Beyond Racism; Building an Open Society*, W.M. Young Jr.; *Dictionary of American Negro Biography*, Rayford W. Logan and Michael R. Winston, Eds. (Norton 1982)

Mildred "Babe" Didrikson Zaharias: *The Life I've Led*, Mildred Didrikson Zaharias

About the Author

Dr. Richard Louis Thomas is a retired ophthalmologist who lives in Scottsdale, Arizona. He has been a stamp collector since the early 1930s, when he searched incoming parcels in the back room of his father's jewelry store for his favorite stamp, the 14¢ American Indian definitive of 1923. He prefers to call this the Hollow Horn Bear stamp.

Thomas' initial fascination with this one stamp led to a more general interest in people depicted on stamps, and their stories. This in turn led to the preparation of a workbook from which his Who's Who on U.S. Stamps columns in *Linn's Stamp News* were drawn.

In 1991, Linn's published 413 of Thomas' capsule biographies in a book titled *Who's Who on U.S. Stamps*. *More Who's Who on U.S. Stamps* continues where the best-selling *Who's Who on U.S. Stamps* left off. Taken together, *Who's Who* and *More Who's Who* contain biographies of virtually every individual depicted or honored on a U.S. stamp between 1847 and 1992.

Thomas was born April 28, 1918, in Fairbury, Nebraska. He graduated from Hebron High School in 1935 and Hebron Junior College in 1937. He received a bachelor of arts degree from the University of Nebraska in 1937 and a bachelor of science in medicine from the University of Nebraska in Omaha in 1943. He received his doctor of medicine from the University of Nebraska in Omaha in 1943 and interned at St. Joseph College, Omaha.

Thomas was in the 97th Division, 386th Regiment in World War II. He served as regimental surgeon in the 3rd Army with General George Patton. Following the war, he served in Japan with Douglas MacArthur. He was discharged in 1946.

Thomas served his residency in ophthalmology at Barnes Hospital in St. Louis and practiced ophthalmology in Lincoln, Nebraska, from 1950 to 1979, when he retired to Scottsdale.

He is a Diplomat of the American Board of Ophthalmology, 1954; Fellow of the American Academy of Ophthalmology, 1955; Fellow of the American College of Surgeons, 1957, and Diplomat, International Congress of Ophthalmology, 1960.

He is a member of the American Philatelic Society, American Philatelic Society Writers' Unit No. 30, American Topical Association, Perfins Club, Butterfly and Moth Stamp Club of Great Britain, Arizona Precancel Club and Westminster Village Stamp Club in Scottsdale.

His writing experiences include columnist for *Linn's Stamp News* and *Canadian Connection.* He also contributes articles to the *American Philatelist,* journal of the American Philatelic Society; *Topical Time,* journal of the American Topical Association; and *Swallowtail,* journal of the Butterfly and Moth Stamp Club.